MW01702582

The Book of Truth

www.thewarningsecondcoming.com

The Book of Truth

Maria Divine Mercy

Coma Books

Coma Books

Published by Coma Books
Dublin
Ireland

www.comabooks.com

First published 2012
1 3 5 7 9 10 8 6 4 2

A CIP catalogue record for this book is available from
the British Library

ISBN 978-1-909448-00-1

Production by **author***ization!*
E: martin-west@btconnect.com

Printed in Poland

Dedicated to
Mother of God, Mother of Salvation

CONTENTS

Part 2

Part 3

Part 5

Part 6

The Seal of the Living God

Book of Revelation 7.2

"After this I saw four angels standing at the four corners of the earth holding back the four winds of the earth so that no wind could blow on land or sea or against any tree. Then I saw another angel come up from the East, holding the seal of the living God. He cried out in a loud voice to the four angels who were given power to damage the land and the sea, "Do not damage the land or the sea or the trees until we put the seal on the foreheads of the servants of our God.

The Seal featured on the cover of this book was created as a result of a divine message received by Maria Divine Mercy from God the Father at 12.20am on 20th February 2012 in which He told her he was giving the world the "Seal of the Living God" to protect everyone from the antichrist.

Extract from this message

My daughter tell My children that I do not relish the thoughts of punishing My children for I love them.

They are mine, my cherished creation. To see how the evil one has corrupted their souls is a constant torment to Me, their beloved Father. I desire to take all of you loving children who know and understand My love for you, into My beautiful New Paradise on earth.

I promise you that the persecution will be swift and that you will be protected.

For I now bequeath the Seal of My Love and Protection.

With this you will **escape the notice of those who will cause hardship** in your countries.

My Seal is My promise of Salvation. My power will surge through you with this seal and no harm will come to you.

This is a miracle children, and only those who bow before Me, their Lord and Creator of all things, as little children with love in their hearts for Me, can be blessed with this divine gift.

Rise now and accept My Seal, the Seal of the Living God.

Recite this Crusade Prayer (33) to acknowledge My Seal and accept it with love, joy and gratitude.

O My God, My loving Father
I accept with love and gratitude
Your Divine Seal of Protection

Your Divinity encompasses my body and soul for eternity
I bow in humble thanksgiving and offer you my deep love and loyalty
To you my Beloved Father

I beg you to protect me and my loved ones with this special Seal
And I pledge my life to your service forever and ever
I love you Dear Father
I console you in these times Dear Father

I offer you the Body, Blood, Soul and Divinity of your dearly beloved Son
In atonement for the sins of the world and for the salvation of all your children.

Amen.

Your loving Father in Heaven

God of the Most High

To download this Seal free of charge log onto **www.thewarningsecondcoming.com**

INTRODUCTION

"The Book of Truth – prepare for The Second Coming"

It was 3am on November 9th 2010 when Maria woke up suddenly. No sooner had she looked at the time, glowing in red from the digital clock beside her bed, did she became aware that her body felt different. She felt weightless and experienced a sizzling sensation in her stomach which seemed to travel all the way to her feet touching every nerve and every muscle.

Then switching on the bedside lamp a series of powerful emotions, both physical and spiritual, surged like an electrical current throughout her entire body. Confused and overwhelmed she sat up. She was immediately drawn to a picture of Jesus on the locker beside her bed.

The face in the image began to change. It became lifelike. To her amazement the image of Jesus smiled at her and His lips began to move as if He was speaking. His face was animated, with various expressions of tenderness, concern and compassion infused throughout the image. Although she could not hear His voice she knew, instinctively, that He wanted to communicate with her.

She knew immediately, that this was a divine presence. Paradoxically, she felt a soothing calmness which was at odds with the somewhat surreal atmosphere in the room. Trembling, as the tears poured down her face, she became like a small child before him. And then she had this powerful urge to write down what she knew Jesus was telling her.

At the back of her mind came the realisation that a door had just opened. A switch had been turned on and that there was no going back.

Grabbing an old envelope and plucking a pen beside her bed the words began to form in her mind.

She wrote down what she heard as it was dictated to her in a gentle but authoritative manner. Each word was formed, clearly, precisely and without pause as her pen touched the paper.

The first words she wrote were "Your Will is my command". Without understanding why she wrote this she knew, in her heart, that it was a natural and spontaneous response. Somehow she knew that she was supposed to write this first. And then came the first message given to her by Jesus Christ.

The message, dictated to her, contained 745 words and it took her exactly 7 minutes to write the message down word for word from beginning to end.

The following morning, in the cold light of day, she was overcome with a sense of unreality. With a sinking feeling she knew that what had happened during the night was very real. And so she read the message. Trembling with shock and disbelief the tears flowed as the truth began to sink in.

An intelligent woman, Maria, a mother of four children, led a busy and fulfilled life. Used to dealing with the many challenges of day to day business, she would have been the first to dismiss such claims. Yet, she knew in her heart that not only was she not imagining the message but that she would never have the capacity to produce a script like this.

Nervously she picked up the picture of Jesus again and looked at it. Waiting. Challenging the picture to move again. And it did. This time she cried, pleaded with Jesus to give her a sign as to whether the whole thing was in her imagination.

It was 11am. The picture changed like before, and the face of Jesus came to life again. He was dressed in white with a gold trim around his neck. His face was long and thin. He had reddish brown wavy hair to his shoulder, piercing blue eyes and was surrounded by a dazzling penetrating light.

This light, Maria says, is very strong and drains you of energy. He looked at her tenderly, with concern, compassion and a deep abiding love. Then He smiled.

Her body experienced the same sizzling, weightless feeling again. She wrote down the next message, a private one. Much shorter than the night before. This time Jesus told her not to be frightened. That, yes, He was communicating with her. He urged her not to run away and to be strong. He reassured her that she was not imagining it.

And so the messages began although Maria, in the beginning, had no idea what they were about or what they meant. She was very frightened at the public reaction to such messages and was relieved when Jesus told her he wanted her to remain hidden for many reasons.

As the truth slowly dawned on her that the messages, were in fact authentic, although she privately hoped that they wouldn't be, she assumed that she was another visionary, another seer.

This was not the case. Jesus eventually told her who she was. He told her she was the end time prophet (a term she had never heard of before) and that she had not been chosen. She had been sent as the 7th Messenger to communicate, on behalf of Jesus, the seals contained in the Book of Revelation to prepare the world for His Second Coming.

Since then she has received a message almost daily from Jesus Christ. Some of the messages are given to her by the Virgin Mary, the Mother of God who has given Maria a new title by which she wishes to be known, the Mother of Salvation.

The first message she received from God the Father was in June 2011. Just before she received this message she was given a message by the Holy Spirit who announced that God the Father wished to communicate with her.

She trembled throughout the taking down of this message, not because she was frightened but because of His power and the pure love He has for the whole of humanity. He explained to her why He created the world in the first place. It was so He could have a family.

Maria is a Roman Catholic but says, that up to the time she received the messages, she was a lukewarm practitioner. She believed in God but she was not devout in the traditional sense. However in the months leading up to the first message she had experienced a spiritual renewal and had witnessed private apparitions of the Virgin Mary although she kept this to herself.

As a result of the apparitions she began to pray more and recite the Holy Rosary. It was while reciting the Rosary before a statue of Our Lady on the 8th November 2010 that Our Lady gave her a message, which she wrote down, but had no idea what it meant.

Maria has been told that the Second Coming of Christ is imminent and that she is the last messenger, the last prophet. She has been told she is the 7th Messenger, the 7th angel, who will announce to the world the contents of the Seals in the Book of Revelation as they are opened by the Lamb of God, Jesus Christ.

The messages given to her, comprise the Book of Truth, foretold in the Book of Daniel for the end times.

They are being given to the world to help spread conversion so that all of God's children can be saved from the antichrist who is due to appear in the world shortly.

God she says wants to save everyone, including hardened sinners. All those saved will enter into a New Paradise on Earth where we will have a mind, body and soul. They will live in splendour, love, peace, harmony and will want for nothing. This is the inheritance which God has promised all of his children.

It will surpass anything we could ever imagine, she says but only those who turn to God and ask for forgiveness can enter.

They will have eternal life.

If they reject God they will be thrown into the fires of Hell with the antichrist, the false prophet and all those who follow Satan.

And we don't have much time.

ABOUT THE BOOK OF TRUTH

The Book of Truth is mentioned in Daniel 10:21. This is where a mysterious Book of Truth is referred to. Gabriel explains to Daniel that everything that has been revealed to him about the future and the end times is to be found in the Book of Truth. Daniel is told to seal it up as it is to be left to another time called "The Time Of The End."

Part 1.

First Volume

Messages 1-49

Monday, November 08, 2010 to Saturday, February 19th, 2011

First Message from the Virgin Mary
Monday, November 08, 2010 15:30 hours

(Announcing the future prophecies still to be received by private visionary who had no idea as to what she was being asked to do at this point.)

My child you have a responsible job to do and you must not let anyone stop you. The Truth has to get out. You havc been chosen to do this Work. My child, stay strong. Look to God above for guidance to do my Work.

You have all the saints working with you. The figures[1] (see end of Message) you saw are all there to help you spread my Infinite Messages for all the world to hear. You are being guided. You won't find it easy but you love to persevere. What is happening has all been foretold. You are an instrument in communicating the Word of God to all of His children.

Never forget, God loves all His children including those sinners who have offended Him. Beg for Mercy for each and every one of you. The Holy Family will reunite.

(Pause.... at that point I was surprised so I asked Our Lady "Have I got this part right? She smiled gently and continued...)

Pick up your pen, that's right and spread the Truth before it is too late.

These Messages are of Divine Origin and must be respected. I trust you to make sure that they are delivered effectively to a disbelieving world.

It is most important that you stay strong for my beloved Son. I know you suffer for Him, with Him and through Him. Rejoice because this is good. You are blessed, my child, to have been chosen for this Work. Stay strong.

---

1 *The figures referred to are the images of various saints who appeared to the visionary during the private apparition but she had no idea as to who they were until later other than those identified above e.g. Pope John Paul II, Saint Faustina and Saint Joseph and two other figures, which are unidentified.

Pray for guidance every day. You will get stronger as time goes by. Do not fear I am with you and your family every day. You are being filled with the Holy Spirit so that you can unveil the Truth about my Father's plan on earth.

My Child cast your doubts aside. You are not imagining this divine Message. Scriptures foretold are about to unfold.

Pray for all God's children. My dearly beloved Son hurts so much every day. He is tormented by the sins of man. His suffering has reached unprecedented levels not experienced since His death on the Cross.

You have the energy and spirit required with God's blessing, to carry out your Mission. Your purification is complete. You are ready for the battle that awaits you.

Go now, my child. Put on your armour. Stand with your head held high and help fight the Evil One. Do not despair from time to time if you feel isolated. You have all the angels and saints - including Pope John Paul II, Saint Faustina and Saint Joseph guiding you every step of the way.

Thank you my child for the faith you have shown. You are a fighter and very much loved by God the Father and my dearly beloved Son. You are one with Jesus and your hand is being guided by the Holy Spirit.

Go now, my child, to do the Work using all the tools available to you at this most important time in the history of mankind.

God Bless you my child

Your Loving Mother in Christ,

Mary Queen of the Earth

First Message received from Our Saviour Jesus Christ
Tuesday, November 09, 2010 03:00 hours

Behold the time is near for you to tell the world that Justice will befall all those who reject Me. My Mercy knows no bounds to all those who follow the Truth of My suffering on the Cross.

Joy to those of My followers who reject the temptations they are faced with every day. Others who turned their backs on My Teachings are blind to the promises made by Me when I died for their sins on the Cross.

I am in deep pain and feel desolate with the abandonment that I suffer from My beloved sinners for whom I gave up My earthly Life.

The earth is in darkness at this time. They, My followers, suffer greatly with Me when they witness a world of sinners who have not only turned their back on God My Eternal Father but on Me Who suffered a Great Sacrifice to save them from the realms of eternal damnation.

I am distressed and cry bitter tears of disappointment and sorrow at the way I have been rejected for the second time. I urge My followers to gather together at this time of sorrow in the world. They must leave aside their indifference to pray and join with Me to help those whose souls have been stolen by the Evil One.

There is still time for sinners to repent. There is no easy way. It has to be from the heart. Believers do not be afraid to raise your voices in unison to declare the love that I have for all.

Christians, Muslims, Hindus, Jews and for all those faiths deduced by the fallible mind of mankind - I call on you all, one last time, to open your eyes to the True Word of God, the God that sent you the Word through the prophets. The Truth was written and documented in the Holy Word of the Scriptures, which no man can amend, change or attempt to twist to his own interpretation. There is only one God. So put down your weapons, open your eyes and follow Me to Eternal Life.

I love you all so much that I gave up My Life for you. Have you forgotten this? Through My Divine Mercy I implore all of you to turn back to Me one last time. Through My Mercy I come back to earth to try and help you to look into your hearts and seek the Truth. Do not allow the Deceiver to destroy you. Seek the Truth. Love - Pure Love - is the path to My Father's Kingdom.

Please remember My Divine Mercy. I love each and every single one of you. Pray for forgiveness now. Hold out your hands and let Me guide you to My Father's Kingdom. I am returning to earth as foretold. That time is drawing so quickly that many will not be prepared. So many will be shocked and taken unawares that they will not believe it is happening. There is not much time now for My prophets to help prepare mankind for this Great Event.

Believers I call on you all to heed My Warning. Spread the Truth. Urge people to ask for My Mercy. I will strive to save every single soul who repents right up to their very last breath.

I cannot, and will not, interfere with their free will. I beseech you to listen and heed My Word. I love all of you. I ask you to pray for conversion before the End Times, which are almost upon us. I have no wish to frighten My followers but I beseech all of you now to save souls. You must remind everyone of the urgency to rid their minds of worldly pursuits. Instead seek out the virtues of simple humility, devoid of ego and idolatry.

The ordinary people will have to lead the way in spreading the Truth about My Second Coming.

Because of the rapidly evolving spiritual darkness, spread by atheism and the surge of Satanic worship in the sad and ungrateful world of today, it is the simple souls, the true believers, who will have to take on this task.

Pray now for the salvation of mankind as the world now heads into the Great Tribulation as foretold in Sacred Scripture. It will be up to mankind's own free will whether or not they are prepared to seek redemption for their sins. The must never be afraid. My Love is ever Merciful.

Your Saviour Jesus Christ

Mankind faces final cleansing

Thursday, November 11, 2010   00:20 hours

Yes My beloved daughter it is I. You and I will work side by side in preparing the world for the times facing mankind as the earth faces the final cleansing.

It is important that this cleansing takes place for without it there can no Eternal Life for My children. There will be difficulties facing all My children, especially, My followers for this is part of the battle that must be fought to win souls.

Relax. Let your heart feel My Love, My daughter. Accept it is a Gift from Me. You may be surprised but I am your family. You are at home with Me in My Kingdom. You now have a job to do. Hold My Hand and I will take your mind to guide you to bring My children back to My Sacred Heart. Rest now My child.

Your Loving Christ Jesus

Your Loving Saviour

Second Message from the Virgin Mary

Thursday, November 11, 2010 12:20 hours

You, my strong child of God, are very special. I will always work with you for you have seen both sides of life here on earth. You, my child have to comprehend what God's Work is all about. Bless you my loved one and thank you.

Yes, my sweet child, you have been given the Graces for your Work. The moment the Holy Spirit entered your soul you were ready to work.

My unconditional love for you will make you stronger as the days pass. Please don't worry, as it is a negative emotion and will only hold you back. Pray to me your eternal Mother every day. I will never leave you or let you down with your Work.

You my sweet child have been given a very special Gift and now you must use it in the way you only know how too. Yes my child I understand that this is very frightening for you at this time. Always be assured I am with you every step on your journey. Peace be yours.

In your heart, I shall dwell, always. Bless you my child and thank you for responding.

Mother of Peace and Hope

Sins are breaking My Sacred Heart

Friday, November 12, 2010 03:00 hours

Write this My daughter. The hours are ticking. Do not ignore My request to publish My Warning to mankind. There is a need now to repent. My children must hear My Warning now. My daughter, communicate with Christian Groups first to impart My pleas.

Stay strong. I have chosen you for this Work so that My pleas for redemption will be heard quickly. Write the Book and communicate My Messages using modern communications such as the Internet and the media. While My request is urgent I will hold your hand so that you can understand the Message.

You are stronger than you think. Pray to Me more daily My Divine Mercy. Fear not. Why are you so frightened? Eternal Life, when Heaven and Earth merge, as one is to be welcomed. It is what man has strived for since time began. Don't be fooled by the attractions that earth has to offer. They pale into significance when compared with the splendour of My Father's Kingdom. You will be sent support as soon as your plan begins to unfold.

These last few days have been overwhelming for you yet you have accepted, in your heart, what I am asking of you. It is difficult and perhaps a little frightening for you to take all of this in but it is important that you trust in Me.

Hold Me in your heart and lean on Me. Surrender any doubts you have and your task will be easier. You must remind people of My promise and refer to My Written Word. Fall back on Scripture to make sense. Never ever be afraid to remind people how their sins are breaking My Sacred Heart and piercing the Soul of My Eternal Father.

We, My Mother and all the saints, will hold your hand and give you strength. You will be sent practical guidance and doors will be opened to help you in your Work.

Beware of those who create obstacles to delay you in your communications. Pray for them and move on. I know you are tired but My request has to be responded to quickly.

It is time for rest now My child. You are responding well and with faith and courage. Never give up.

Your Beloved Saviour Jesus Christ

This Book will change lives & save souls

Friday, November 12, 2010 15:00 hours

Go ahead do what needs to be done in order for people to see and hear My Divine Messages

I trust you dear daughter to use whatever means you feel will ensure that people read the Messages. You need all your energy to write the Book. This Book[2*] will change lives, save souls and has been foretold. Yes, the Book is what was prophesied. You are the writer. I am the Author.

Do not be surprised or overwhelmed for this is a very sacred task and you have been chosen to do this Work with Me. It will take you three months. I want you to publish it around the world. It must be large, powerful and sought out by millions just like the Holy Bible.

My daughter, you can publish this 'in conversation with the secret prophet'. It is okay to do this. Why do you fear My child? You are being guided from Heaven. You must stay strong. Trust in Me. Surrender. I will hold your hand at every step of the way. I will speak with you later.

Your Loving Saviour Jesus Christ

The Warning of Hell and the Promise of Paradise

Saturday, November 13, 2010 03:00 hours

My beloved daughter you have come through a terrible persecution, which I permitted to free your soul from the torments of Hell. You are now free and your spirit will enable you to spread My Word so that mankind can be released from the suffering that awaits them should

2 ** The book Jesus refers to is the first volume of Messages presented to the world in February 2011.*

they be so foolish as to succumb to the Evil One.

You, My daughter, were sent right from the start. I am making you stronger all the time in but a few days. What do you think you will be like in a week, a year or two? A fighter, brave to the last, you will work with Me to clear the souls of My dearly beloved children for whom I hold a deep and utterly loving compassion. The love courses through My Veins like a river. My compassion never dwindles despite the fact that they turn the other way.

I will save them from the Torments of Hell

Tell them, My daughter, that I will save them from the torments of Hell. I need them to turn to Me in their joyless confused state. There is only one way to love and peace. That will be in My New Paradise when Heaven and Earth will become one. Don't they know this? Have they never heard of My promise of old? The promise of Eternal Life, where they - all mankind who turn to Me - will be lifted body, soul and mind into the New Earth and Heaven when they combine once again as the Paradise for so long promised to My Father's children.

Believe I beseech you. Think. If you have never been exposed to Holy Scripture then ask yourself this simple question. If you feel love in your hearts where do you think this comes from? Is it love that makes you feel gentle, humble, yearning and free of all ego? If so then this is the love that I promise all My children who turn back to Me.

How worldly ambitions leave you empty

It is hard, I know, dear children to believe in a different world to the one in which you live. Remember that this world was Created by God, the Eternal Father, then it was soiled by the works of The Deceiver. He, Satan, is extremely cunning. You, My children, must surely know that the worldly ambitions, which you find insatiable do not fulfil you? You feel an emptiness, which you cannot explain or understand. Isn't this so? And then you strive for more and more. But, yet, you are still not satisfied when you feel you should be. Why is that? Have you looked into your hearts and asked why? Why? The answer is very simple.

God created mankind. Mankind was tempted by Satan. Satan exists in this beautiful world that My Eternal Father created out of Pure Love. Sadly he, Satan, will exist until My Second Coming. He will then be exposed for the sheer lies and deception, which he has manifested in My children. By then it will be too late for many of My children including those who are unsure or hesitant in believing in the Divine Superior Creation of My Father's Kingdom.

Do not reject Me

Listen! I, Jesus Christ, the Saviour sent to give you all a second chance to enter My Father's Kingdom hear now My promise. Listen to My Voice, sent by Divine Grace through My visionaries and prophets in today's world and understand that all My children are equal in My Father's eyes.

Those who follow Him are blessed but suffer torture for the souls who do not believe and who refuse to listen. God made the world. It did not appear from nowhere. Man did not, nor could not invent such a Miracle which science will never be able to explain. The Divine Supernatural can never be truly understood until all children of God surrender in mind, body and soul to the Pure Love that I offer.

Please, I beseech all of you do not reject your Creator. Please do not listen to the deceit of the lies you have been told by The Deceiver, through divisions of the Free Masons, the Illuminati, the false prophets and the bizarre and totally evil cults that have evolved through the naivety of man.

Satan is real

Mankind is weak. Even the most holy of followers fall prey to the constant temptations of the Evil One. The problem is that they, those who seek pleasure, do not believe he is real. Others do know he is real and that he does exist. They are the ones who cause Me the most heartbreak.

Wounds opening once again and festering

I am suffering to such an extent that the Wounds inflicted upon Me at My terrible Crucifixion, to which I succumbed, are opening once again and festering, leaving Me in the utmost painful agony of Body, Soul and Divinity. Yet I will never give up loving all of you.

I call on you from the Heavens and on behalf of My Eternal Father Who created each and every onc of you out of Pure Love to stand firm. Reject Satan. Believe that he exists. Accept that he does. Open your eyes. Can't you see the havoc he causes in your lives? Are you blind?

A Message to the rich

To the rich I say stop. Think and ask God for just one moment, is your role in living God's commandments pleasing to you? Does it feel right? Have you denied Me at the expense of worldly excesses? These same excesses and pleasures will leave you empty of heart. You will know, in your own heart, that it does not feel right. Yet you will still thirst for more of the empty, and yet exciting promises that you are given by the Deceiver in return for your soul.

A Message to those who follow the Illuminati

I implore all of you, especially My children who have been sucked into the Illuminati and other such evil entities. Once there you are doomed to eternal damnation. Don't you understand that what you have been promised in return for your soul is a lie? A deceitful and frightening lie. You will never receive the gifts promised by this sinister messenger from the depths of Hell. As your Saviour on the Cross, I gave up My Life to save you please do not let Me lose you now. I love you My children. I weep as I implore you one last time not to reject Me in favour of the Deceiver.

I will forgive all who confess

I cannot interfere with your free will because that is one of the Gifts given to you when you were born in the Light of God. I will be coming, as Scriptures foretold very shortly - sooner than anyone can comprehend. The world will plunge into darkness and despair. Yet I will forgive all and every single one of My children who, when their sins are revealed to them, no matter how offensive they are, instantly at the moment of Confession.

They will enter body and soul into Paradise when Heaven and Earth will become one, where all of you will live for eternity with your Family forever and ever.

Promises that Paradise has to offer.
No illness, bodily corruption, no sin - just love. That is the promise of My Paradise. No one will want for anything. Every one will live in harmony, joy and love.

The reality of Hell
Do not reject this life for the life you have been promised by Satan! You are being lied to. If you follow this path where God, or I, Jesus Christ Your Saviour, is not a part then you are on the path to eternal damnation. You will scream with terror when you realise the error. By then you will plead for Mercy, you will tear at your face, pull out your hair, but, because you have free will, a Gift from My Father, it cannot be taken away from you. When you choose this false path you will suffer damnation and burn in Hell forever. It is very real.

The greatest damnation when you know you will never see the Face of God
The biggest damnation is finally realizing that there is a God. That I, your Saviour Jesus Christ, actually exists and there will be no way, at that stage, to save yourselves. Your family may look at you from the other side. When that happens and you realise the awful truth it will be too late. Remember these Words.

The greatest damnation is when you know that you will never see the Face of God. That will be the greatest torment and one that will stay with you forever in the fires of Hell where pain is constant and unrelenting. You will, instead of enjoying the Paradise promised to you, through the lies of The Deceiver, end up in the terrifying corridors of Hell. It is very real and represents suffering for eternity.

Please, all of you who do not believe I am communicating with mankind, I ask that you pray to My Sacred Heart. Pray My Divine Mercy at 3 o'clock each day. I will respond to your request with Love, which you will feel instantly. Hold My Hand children. Don't let go. I love you all so much that I gave up My Life for each and every one of you so that you could be saved.

This time I come to Judge. Much as I love you I cannot interfere with the Gift of free will, which was bestowed on you by My beloved Father. I hope, that through My modern day visionaries and prophets that you will finally listen. The Truth is the way remember to eternal salvation and a new beginning when Paradise returns to Earth.

The lies of Satan
The lies, no matter how seductive, are just that. Lies, designed to steal the beloved souls, which cannot be released by My Father, the Creator and Maker of Earth.

Your Divine Saviour

Jesus Christ

Sign of the End Times but Glory will Return to Earth
Sunday, November 14, 2010 23:00 hours

My dear daughter, do not feel guilty for the doubts you have felt today. This is natural. Your understanding of spiritual matters is not as strong as it should be but that is okay.

I will guide you and you will understand, in time, the purpose of your Mission. I need you to keep strong in your Work and your obedience to

Me. This is a difficult task and one, which will be emotionally draining for you.

I am sending you a spiritual director to help you cope with the enormity of the task that must be completed. Such is the task that without this Work more souls will be lost to The Evil One. My daughter, you have committed to this task before I sent for you to do this Work.

I am guiding your spiritual director. He will know the Truth when you speak. By now you will have gleaned just some of the sins of mankind in the last two days in a way not possible for you up to now. Did you see the difference? Did you feel strange when you looked at My children? You saw them in a different light did you not? That is the Power of the Holy Spirit, which I have blessed you with.

The love you felt in your heart for My children and the priest you saw at Mass today is also the Gift I give you with the Power of the Holy Spirit. You will see, feel and hear the sins of mankind now to such an extent that you will feel the pain that I do. You will also see the Love I have for My children through your eyes, which mirror My Heart.

Do not be afraid of these Gifts, My child. Do not feel you cannot handle this task because the strength you will be given through My Graces will make you so strong. You will never look back. Nor will you want to.

You feel weak now. This is the feeling of My Divine Power surging through your body. The heat is the Love I have for you. Do not cry My child. So far you have been extraordinarily strong and so accepting although it is but a few days now since I first spoke with you. No, My child, you are not imagining this. You keep questioning yourself and those close to you.

Those who sell their souls to Satan

Now, write this. The world is heaving with the weight of darkness and the evil plotting of the Evil One who continues to entice and seduce My beloved children. They have been ensnared to such an extent that many of them squirm like animals even in the face of mankind. How many poor souls fed by lust, greed and vanity, appear to those with faith in such a poor sorry state? They, in their vanity, believe that they have real power. The power they have been promised by Satan. Many of these children have chosen to sell their souls and proudly boast of the fact.

More of My children are attracted to the glamour and riches of his promises for all the world to see. No, they are not ashamed to boast of the fact that they belong to him. What promises he has made, are not just lies, they have been given to them out of pure hatred. Satan hates humanity.

He lies to My children and tells them he can give them anything, but sadly it is a lie. Those who follow him and his empty promises will not and cannot be saved.

Pray, pray, pray for My children. My daughter I know you are tired but heed this. For the believers who are lukewarm and who are not aligned directly with The Evil One in the extreme - they too have to be wary. They, including My followers and some of My sacred servants, Bishops and Cardinals sneer at the faith of My children. Their spirituality has been lost behind the greed in certain quarters where gold and riches mask the Divine Gifts they were given as disciples of God.

The Church has lost its way and is plunging into darkness. This, My child has been foretold and it is a sign of the End Times. This is when the last pope will emerge and the world will be lost under the misguided direction of the False Prophet.

Revelations as to how My Second Coming will be preceded will be given to you My child so that your words might be listened in order that souls will be prepared before The Great Warning. Do not fret. Life will continue. Glory will return to Earth. My children will be redeemed from the clutches of the Evil One who will be destroyed. It is important that he does not, through his deceit, take My children with him into the depths of Hell.

My Word has to be strong. My children must listen. It is out of Pure Love that I am giving them this Warning, because I come as Judge and not Saviour. It is through the prayers of My Beloved Mother and My followers throughout the world that the time for Judgement has been delayed in the past. This time it will not be.

No one will know the date of the Second Coming

You will not be told of the date nor will My children. It cannot be revealed. This is why it is important that all My children are prepared. For those who will not prepare, they cannot say that they have not been given the Truth. When the Warning happens they will realise the Truth. Yes, if they confess and admit their sins they will receive My Blessing. If they don't they will be cast into Hell. My Mercy will have expired by then.

Go now, My child. Prepare the Word for the world to hear. Tell My children, the believers, not to fear. Tell them to pray for the non-believers. Then tell the non-believers to turn back to Me. Do everything possible to urge them to open their hearts.

Your Saviour Jesus Christ Who comes to Judge the living and the dead.

The Second Coming

Monday, November 15, 2010 03:00 hours

Thank you My daughter for persevering in My Truth and understanding that My communication with you is very real. You will feel My Spirit in your body when I come to reveal to you My Divine Message necessary for mankind to understand in these times. I bring a Message of Pure Love and Passion to My Father's children. These Messages are to explain to all God's followers first the need to fall to their knees now and understand the Truth of the Book of John.

The time has come for My Second Coming, the Signs of which are already being revealed to those who know the prophecies foretold so long ago. Look, what do you see now? The signs are visible now. Man does not realise the terrible descent to which he is being exposed. The wicked lie, fronted and accepted by unsuspecting governments, hides unnoticed in the guise of salvation.

Hear Me now My children. The antichrist is ready to spring. Stay on guard, open your eyes and heart to the Truth or you will perish. Fear not My beloved followers for you will lead My flock into the Holy Adoration of My Eternal Father. The Food of Life will be plentiful to those believers during the dark days ahead. Stay together. Love each other. Give each other the strength so that you can unite all races, creeds and believers everywhere towards My Father's Kingdom.

It will be your job to demonstrate the Love of God, the goodness, the love, the hope and the Truth of Eternal Life, which awaits all of mankind. It will be by praying together, dropping your exterior wall of pride and shyness that you will become the powerful force. Together you will be strong. Your faith in Me, your Divine Saviour, will help convert the non-believers. These people, many of whom, through no fault of their own, are ignorant of My Love. They may feel love for each other but do not understand where this comes from. Guide them, My children of God, towards the Light.

I am the Bread and I am the Light. My Light will keep you all safe. But I urge you to be generous in heart and soul and think of those poor souls who need guidance. You must do this through example and show these souls how to become closer to Me. They must be coaxed gently, but firmly, along the path. It is important to wake them up from their slumber of ignorance before it is too late.

My children do you not understand the Teachings in My Father's Book? The Book that reveals the Sign for My coming back to earth must be studied and accepted as the Truth. God, My Eternal Father, through the prophets does not lie. He does not contradict. You are now being shown the heavenly signs foretold and you must prepare now. You and your families will be lifted with Me in the blink of an eye.

Please, please pray for guidance. Believers get ready now to fight in My Name and stand up against the antichrist. People will smile at you when you remind them of the prophecies contained in the Book of John. You will be accused and scolded with wry amusement for your views and concerns. Ignore this for you have a duty to Me. Now. Pray, pray and coax the non-believers to accept the Teachings. Do not be frightened, for many of you frightened for the future and your families I have this to say. As the time comes you and your families will be lifted with Me, in the blink of an eye, to the Heavens. Then you will receive the Gift of Eternal Life when Heaven and Earth become one. This is what is meant as the New Paradise. It will be a time of great glory, love and perfection for all My followers

Stay strong. You must endure a short period of torment, but your faith will keep you strong. Remember I love all of you. Love Me in return and help Me save as many souls as possible. You are My powerful army and the time is now to prepare for battle. I will lead you all to My Father's Kingdom.

Your Loving Saviour

Jesus Christ

Global Power, The antichrist and Mark of the Beast
Monday, November 15, 2010 11:00 hours

You are now realizing the Truth and accepting My Message for what it is. Write this My daughter. The speed at which the prophesies are unfolding is becoming evident for all to see. Watch the changes that will become apparent with My Church as one of the first signs. This is when The Deceiver will lead My disciples astray.

The second sign will be seen in the way many of you will no longer be in control of your own country. This includes all material control and the military. My children, their leaders and all those with responsibility for caring for their people, will lose all control. They will be like a boat with no rudder. This boat they steer will be aimless and they will be lost.

My children you must pray hard now to loosen the grip these evil groups of people will exert over you. They are not of God's Kingdom and through the cunning deceit of their exterior you will not realise that this is a powerful force that is careful not to reveal itself.

You, My children, will be none the wiser. You will think that you are living in tough times but this façade is designed to make you think this. Rise up My children now.

Mark of the Beast

Do not accept the Mark. If more of you do not accept then you are stronger in numbers. This Mark - the Mark of the Beast will be your downfall. It is not what it seems. By agreeing you will be removed further and further away.

Beware of the Plan, driven by the Deceiver, to remove all signs of My Eternal Father and the Teaching of Scriptures from your life. You will see this in schools, colleges, hospitals, and in the constitution of your countries. The biggest abomination, which causes Me deep pain, is the abolition of the Teachings of Scripture from those who practice their Adoration of Me, their Divine Saviour. Very soon you will see that My Word, and the Teaching of the Truth will be abolished and punishable.

You My dearly beloved children will suffer greatly in My Name. These evil forces are responsible for this. They are led by Satan. You will find them everywhere and especially in those leaders in authority whom you depend upon to survive. Children do not be frightened for yourselves, rather be frightened for those poor misguided souls. So infested are they with the Deceiver that they find it difficult to pull away such is the grip he holds. These people are not to be trusted. Be careful how you communicate with them. They will hold you in such a vice-grip because they will control everything. You will find it difficult to fight them, as they will control even your bank, your property, your taxes and the food you need to survive.

But this will not last long for their days are numbered. Should they abide by their slavery to evil they will plunge into an abyss of such terror that to describe their fate would be too terrifying and so frightening that man would drop like a stone - dead - were he to glimpse just one minute of the torment they will endure.

The Battle is about to begin and unfold, as the Hand of My Eternal Father will fall swiftly in punishment for their sins, which is about to be witnessed on this earth, the sins which I died for. No man is a child of God who bears witness to or colludes in this sinister, but orderly, army of destruction. This evil army filled with the demons from the pits of Hell perform acts of such evil magnitude that innocent people could not possibly fathom.

I have no wish to frighten My children but the truth will be exposed for what it is in time. Rise up now My children. Fight the forces of evil before they destroy you. Be wary of Global Rule in any shape, size, form or code. Look at your leaders carefully and those who control your daily access to money, which will feed you and keep you alive. You need to stock pile food now.

You have not received this Message in a way that reflects My Teachings but hear Me now. These prophecies have been foretold. My children must listen carefully. The spirit of darkness is growing and you, My followers, must stay strong. Keep your belief in Me alive through prayer. All of My followers must say the prayer, The Divine Mercy, each day. It will strengthen souls and will help them find favour at the moment of death.

My children please do not let My Message frighten you. My followers have a duty to Me now. Let Me say this. Remember you will be filled with the Holy Spirit as soon as you accept My Word. Do not fear because you have been chosen. You, My army of followers, will lead to the defeat of the Evil One. To do this you must pray.

I come with a Message of Pure Love. Do you not realise that you will experiencc Paradise when Heaven and Earth join as one? There is nothing to fear for you, My followers, will be lifted body, soul and mind into the realms of the Divine Hierarchy. You will see your loved ones. Those loved ones who have found favour with My Eternal Father.

Do as I say. Pray, talk to Me, love Me, trust in Me. In return I will give you strength. Pray for protection through the recital of the Most Holy Rosary given to you with blessings from My beloved Mother. This prayer must be said to help protect you from the Evil One on the one hand. On the other hand you must ask for protection for those people with whom you come into contact so that they cannot contaminate you or diffuse the faith you hold in your heart for Me.

Pray for My visionaries and prophets so that they are protected. Pray for My beloved sacred servants, those holy devout servants sent by Me to guide you. They, just like My followers, suffer torment by the Evil One. He will never stop trying to blind you from the Truth and will use every devious tactic to convince you that your faith is false. Hear Me. He, the Deceiver, will use logic and reasoning, couched in a soft gentle manner to convince you he brings hope into your lives. He will, through the antichrist, strive to make you believe he is the Chosen One.

The antichrist.
Many of My followers will fall prey to this despicable deceit. Be on your guard. He will be seen as the messenger of love, peace and harmony in the world. People will fall to their knees and adore him. He will show you his power and you will believe it is of a Divine source. But it's not. He will instruct you in a manner that will seem odd at times. True believers will know he is not of the Light. His boastful, pompous demeanour will be

hidden behind pure evil. He will strut and show what will appear to be true compassion and love for all. Behind this façade he is full of hatred for you, My beloved children. He laughs behind closed doors.

My children, he will confuse you terribly. He will appear powerful, confident, humorous, caring, loving and will be seen as a saviour. His handsome face will appeal to all but he will soon change. He will wreck havoc in the world and will murder many. His acts of terror will be clear for all to see. He will destroy your independence and he will be instrumental in bringing about the Mark - the Mark of the Beast. You, My children, will have to be strong. Do not accept the Mark because if you do you will come under his evil hypnotic influence.

Many will die for their faith in Me. No do not fear because if you suffer for Me, in Me, with Me you are chosen. Pray, pray not to submit to his reign of terror. Stand up fight for Me.

Do not let the antichrist for all his convincing charm win over your souls. Let Me hold you in My Arms, cradle you with My Divine Grace now to give you the strength to fight for the Truth. My Love for you will never die. You should never choose this route or you too will be lost to Me. It will be hard but help will be given to My children in many, many ways to ease your suffering. Go now and pray My Divine Mercy and prepare for the final battle.

Jesus Christ King of My People

Saviour & Just Judge

Warning to Clergy
Tuesday, November 16, 2010 09.55 hours

My daughter you were rejected yesterday as people tried to put doubts in your mind. You suffered for this. Do not despair My Word will be heard. You will face obstacles that will make you feel disillusioned with the Work.

My daughter I am guiding you. You must remember this and never forget My promise. I did, as you requested, and allowed you to sleep peacefully last night. You are stronger now. Can't you feel this?

Be careful who you communicate with. My followers, or those you think are My followers, are not always as they seem. You must do what your heart tells you.

The world may seem as it always has but there is change and it is happening now. This change is leading mankind into a darkness that will envelop them and which clouds their love for Me.

Why must My children keep questioning the Truth? They do not follow My Teachings, yet they were given this gift from My Apostles who, through love for Me and by the Power of the Holy Spirit, gave the world a very special Gift. The Gift of Truth was taught and spread to all My children throughout the world. Many children followed this guidance through the ages.

Others, while knowing the Truth, decided to twist it to suit their own means, desires, lust and quest for power. My followers then could not distinguish between the Truth of the Word of God and the falsehoods spread by those who were misguided. This is how the Deceiver works. He causes confusion, despair and a sense of hopelessness and has been doing this since My death on the Cross. But hear Me now. He will not win My daughter. The forces of Heavenly guidance will instil in the children their belief once more through the Teachings of My prophets.

Ask My children to be alert to the changes they see in the world. Ask them to open their hearts, their eyes and minds to witness the lies spread by Satan. From him springs a web of promises designed to make My children feel attracted to external wonders. The wonders and false glory are empty.

They are not reflective of love nor do they offer any real comfort once the emptiness of them are revealed.

The forces of evil are getting stronger now My child; they are planned by Satan through his army of wicked followers. These followers, through greed and love of self, follow in docile adoration and will be led into his flash paradise. His promised paradise is nothing but black darkness and by the time My children realise this the time for redemption will have passed.

Prayer for Salvation

All of My children must, even if it be for the love of their own families, wake up to this evil if they want to save each other. My Love will keep them guided if they turn to Me now. They must never be afraid to turn and say:

"O my Lord lead me to Your Kingdom and protect me from the darkness that has engulfed my soul. Hear me now O Sacred Heart and through Your Goodness let your Light of Love and Protection shine through."

Those of My children who say this prayer will be heard. Their pleas for salvation, for they and those whom they love, will be answered. I have, through My visionaries guided by My Blessed Mother, painstakingly tried to send warnings to the world. Many, many times My visionaries, though rejected in the beginning, were finally accepted. This time they will not be afforded the dignity of time for their Messages to be heard by enough of My people.

Beware of false prophets

Be Wary of False Prophets. But I must warn My children to be wary of false prophets. Many genuine visionaries have been misled. Visionaries who are genuine will be given the graces that will emit My Truth in such a way that they will be accompanied by supernatural occurrences and miracles that cannot and won't be denied.

My Heart breaks when I see the way in which many of them have been denied by My most sacred disciples. These same disciples, whom I have sent to teach My children, are failing in their task. They must turn now to Me for guidance and pray for the graces required to lead My people.

My sacred servants are very special and those who have received the Sacraments must hear My plea. Your duty now is to Me. Renew your vows now. Believe and follow My Sacred Message. Be strong for you are now all being called to bear witness to the Truth in the Book of Revelation and accept that the time has come. Prepare now for this Great Event. Do not deny Me or turn your back. Preach with strength and conviction. Do not water down My Teachings and tell My followers that everything will be okay. This is not the message for which you were called. Your duty to Me, your Divine Saviour, is to inform your flock of the Truth.

My children must not be told that all of them will be saved. This is an untruth. Because it is only those who seek out My forgiveness and surrender to Me and My Teachings who will be saved.

Why do you not follow the Teachings of Scripture? Why do you use excuses? Why do you misguide and convince My children that God will forgive all? My Eternal Father will only forgive those who believe in Me and who repent.

Did My death on the Cross not tell you anything? I died to save mankind from the folly of Satan. Yet you, through misguided tolerances, teach My children a lie. You have fallen victim to the pressure of mankind to camouflage the Holy Doctrine for which you were called to preach.

Have you no shame? So caught up in the worldly attractions that the earth has to offer are you that you follow false dogma dictated to you by the popular tolerance that Satan has spread among My children. These poor misguided children need direction. They also must understand the difference between human interpretation and that Divine Promise made by Me.

Why would My children not believe in Divine Intervention? Why do you play this down when it is presented to you? My priests hear My plea. Pray that My Message of Truth will be heard.

Message to Bishops

To My Bishops I say this. Put down your robes, turn your back on the riches, which you have given credence to. Seek out the humility that is required of you. Obey My Word now or face the consequences. Your duty is to Me and My Eternal Father. How blind you have become. Signs are now being given through visionaries, in the sky, and you have failed to heed them. Instead you sit in your castles and sneer. For this your sins will not be forgiven.

The sins of My sacred disciples, those who chose My path, offend Me greatly. Open your eyes, your hearts and go back to the Teachings in My Sacred Book.

Message to Cardinals

To My Cardinals I say this. To what lofty heights have you risen that you have forgotten the Sacraments or the Truth of My Teachings to lead My flock. Come down now and follow My Guidance. Do not be distracted by the falsehoods, which have gripped mankind. Don't you, too, deny Me.

I ask you all to pray for My beloved brave Pope, the last True Pope. You My disciples are being led astray by the Deceiver. He has made himself known in the corridors of My Church and his evil ways now present themselves. To those of you who have eyes keep watching, in front of you and behind you. He will snatch your soul if you give in to his deceit.

Please pray now for all of you. Beg for My Guidance. Beg forgiveness and let Me lead you again.

To those of you who will question this instruction, listen now. Why would I not communicate with you in this way? I taught you all through the Apostles who, with the Guidance of the Holy Spirit, gave the world My

Messages, which have lived on since. Now the time is near. All your life you prayed for guidance. At this time now, I urge you to hear My plea.

Your Divine Saviour

Jesus Christ

Cast all doubts aside

Tuesday, November 16, 2010 23.00 hours

Write this My daughter. The doubts creeping into your mind are to be expected. Yes, you are being tempted to turn your head but he, the Deceiver, will never win you from Me. My beloved daughter you are stronger than you think because very few chosen souls would be able to deal with this Great Sacred request in the way that you have. It takes courage to deal with the way in which I communicate with you. You did not run away cowering in fear. You knew right from the first that this was a Divine Communication from the highest and most Holy Hierarchy.

You are going to experience extra enlightenment shortly, which will cast all your doubts away. When this happens your mind will open up more to receive these special graces, which must be bestowed to fill you with the courage and determination needed to help bring about this prophecy.

Yes, My daughter, much to your astonishment you are the chosen one to fulfil the prophecies contained in the Book of John to prepare mankind for the cleansing, which is to unfold shortly. Once the fear, hesitation and uncertainty leaves you, My beloved daughter, you will rise and complete this very special task that I ask of you. Now do as I say. You are to recite My Divine Mercy at 3 o'clock each day to help save souls. You must continue to recite the Rosary given to the world by My most precious Mother who is to work with Me to prepare for

My Second Coming on this earth.

Many souls are lost to Me now with more and more being snatched from Me daily by The Evil One. They cannot be taken from Me. Please help Me save their poor souls. Cast all doubts aside. Just remember your task. Help open their eyes to enable them to redeem themselves in the eyes of My Eternal Father. If you can just keep thinking of the final outcome you will understand why this is important and why it is a calling made from the Pure Love I hold for all My children in My Heart.

Think of it like this. The love of a devoted parent knows no bounds. If one child strays and walks the path of doom the heartbreak and distress caused and felt by the parent is like a sword piercing the heart. Any parent who loves their children will endeavour to fight for them to the end. They never give up. Ever. So it is with Me. I will do everything in My Divine Power, without interfering with man's free will to turn their hearts back to My Sacred Heart. You, My daughter, will help Me do this.

I don't need to remind you of the need for obedience and complete abandonment to Me. This is the calling for which you have been chosen. Take up your sword now. You have to fight side by side with your Divine Saviour in one last attempt to bring about the salvation of all My children before the Day of Judgement.

Go now in peace and love to receive My Body today.

Your Loving Saviour

Jesus Christ

Message to Agnostics & Atheists
Thursday, November 18, 2010 21.00 hours

To those who claim not to believe in Me I have this to say. Ask yourself this question: Can you remember a time that you did? Think back to when you were a child when you did believe in God. It does not matter what religion your parents followed. Did you believe? What changed? Was it influence by others? Did they tell you that there was a rational answer to your being in existence?

It has, since the beginning of time, been difficult for My children to accept any other existence outside of this one. Yet look around the world and see the wonders of the Creation by My Eternal Father. The sun, the moon, the sea, the rivers, the plants, the animals and all the wonders of Creation and answer this. Where did all this come from? Do you really believe it emerged from something other than a Superior Being? Be warned when you hear the lies spread by so-called fortune-tellers that exist in the New Age Movement. They are being led into what they believe to be the truth and the excitement of the life promised to them in a new era. This era, to which they have been led to believe, is a new paradise. A form of man controlled, but glorious centre of the universe. It is a false doctrine. Many people of God, including those who believe, mistakenly confuse their belief in this doctrine with that of the Light.

They are being guided by the demons. Some know that they are. Others don't. Pray that they see the Truth before they continue on their futile path to emptiness.

To the atheists I say this. I love you no matter how you offend Me. To the atheists, who are being led and influenced by other beliefs, stop and think. In their quest to follow manmade reasoning they are simply believing in another faith. The belief that man is in control. He is not. Yet these same people, My precious children, for whom I will fight, are being encouraged to follow Satan, the Deceiver, and enemy of mankind. Ask the Atheist who goes to extraordinary lengths to pressurise God's children why he does this?

Is it not enough to simply deny Me? Why do these people lie? Many of these atheist groups have an agenda to entice and seduce My children into a false doctrine. Make no mistake their belief is another form of religion, a religion that exalts the power of intelligence, reason and pride. They emulate the very traits of Satan. They, in their blindness, follow another faith - the adulation of the Dark where no love exists.

So passionate are these atheists, so proud of their religion that they do not understand that what they stand for is a religion - the religion of the Deceiver who laughs at their stupidity.

Atheists hear Me one last time. Turn back to the Scriptures now. Look at the Book of John and consider the Truth as it begins to unfold now. Does it not seem real to you now as your bear witness to events, as they are laid bare, layer-by-layer each day before you.

Can't you see that My Word, My Prophecy foretold so long ago may be the Truth? Open your eyes and talk to Me once as follows:

"God if You are the Truth reveal to me the sign of Your Love. Open my heart to receive guidance. If You exist let me feel Your Love so I can see the Truth. Pray for me now"

As I call on you, one last time I say this. Love is not made by man. You cannot see it but you can feel it. Love comes from the Eternal Father. It is a Gift to mankind. It does not come from the darkness. The darkness that you feel is devoid of love. Without true love you cannot feel. You cannot see the Light. You cannot see any future. I am the Light. I am the future. I bring you glory and life ever after. Turn now and ask for My help. Do that and I will answer you and envelop you in My Arms.

My tears of joy will save you, as you become My beloved child again. Come now and join Me in Paradise.

Your Loving Saviour

Jesus Christ

Rise of Satanic Groups and World Control

Saturday, November 20, 2010 07.20 hours

My daughter, tell My children the serpent is about to spring. They must not allow themselves to fall into his evil trap from which there is no return.

He, the serpent has many guises. His followers, brainwashed with the promises of power and glory by each other are plotting now to inflict a range of events around the world, which will cause untold grief, pain and horror everywhere.

My children will be none the wiser. Those children, who have been shown the Truth and who are guided by Me, are brave souls. They are trying desperately to warn the world of these terrible groups, splintered in all directions, all with one goal in mind. Littered in every country, present in every level of authority they plot in secret.

There are those innocent members, part of the evil society who do not realise the reality of the Truth. Instead they go about, do their good deeds without understanding the acts of evil their elders are perpetrating in secret. Make no mistake these seniors are devout followers of Satan and engage in rituals of adoration, which were other people to witness them, they would retch with horror at the obscene acts of Satanic worship and allegiance to the Evil One's promises that are at the core of their organizations.

For those of you who find the words of My brave souls amusing, hear Me now. Failure to understand the Truth and to listen to those brave voices will destroy your life, your faith and your livelihood. For so long these people have been plotting for control. Their works are evident in many, many countries but are designed to happen in such a way that those children who go about their day to day business do not realise what is happening.

Serpent will spring now!

When I say the serpent is about to spring I mean now. He, and his wicked evil army of proud and hungry beasts are marching with speed and determination in every walk of life. They run your life in ways that you are not aware of. Because they are being guided by the Deceiver, they are cunning, charming, smart of tongue, greedy, ruthless and have only one goal in mind. They, through the banks, modern communications, the military, religious organizations and government will want to rule you all. Watch out and listen now.

Not Conspiracy theories

My Warning and those of My beloved children will be dismissed as conspiracy theories. Sadly they are not. This situation, My daughter, has not come about suddenly. This group, and I am referring to just one group now, have been plotting, scheming and recruiting from the upper echelons in society for centuries. They have murdered those who have exposed them in the past. They have murdered leaders, including renowned and talented figureheads down through the centuries. They are brothers in blood and devour the flesh of mankind.

Satanic Relics

They pay homage to the obscene relics and signs that the serpent desires. This, make no mistake, is a powerful and frightening group. So powerful are they that it will be hard to escape from their clutches once your livelihoods, food and money are reliant on them.

My children many, many people in power, in governments, banks, food industries and aid agencies do not know what is happening nor will they until the end of the Great Tribulation, which is about to take place. Then they will see the Beast emerge who will bring about swift change so that all of you will have to fight like never before to hide from his evil regime.

Once the Beast and his followers control your money they will control all except one thing. They cannot and must never try to steal your souls. Yet this is exactly what they will try to do.

For those of you who question this Message of Truth, sent to you because of the desire I have to help you, guide you and reveal the Truth hear Me now. If you do not believe this Message I urge you to see the Light. I plead with you to watch and be on your guard for the signs of these evil power hungry beasts, who salivate at the plan and the false glory they will yield.

Make no mistake controlling your ability to earn money and your access to it will not be enough. No, they will want much, much more from you. They will want to control what you eat, drink and where you live. To do that you need now to take the following action to protect yourself.

Find Shelters

Please find shelter as groups of believers. I will send you the Light to help you survive. Begin to grow your own food. Save what food you can and put it away. Begin to plan now as if awaiting a storm. Know that darkness will descend to such an extent, that to survive, you must be prepared.

Listen to the prophets. Don't make the same mistakes when My people would not listen to My prophet Noah. They turned their backs on him. Refuse to listen. They went about their day-to-day lives as they ate and laughed in total oblivion to the horrible fate that awaited them.

Rise now. Turn to My Eternal Father God, the Most High for guidance. Prepare your families for the forthcoming seeping darkness about which you cannot fathom now. Pray, Pray, Pray for the courage not to accept the Mark of the vicious beast. He, through his evil army, will try to inflict what at first will be an evil identity stamp. This will be given to you and presented as essential in order for you to draw down money, buy food, travel, live in your homes and trade. This is the ultimate control. You will and your genuine political leaders will be powerless.

I urge the media, those not infected with this evil group, to look and see what is happening. Expose all who support the Serpent and his army but thread carefully.

My children, be fearful of the group and know that they really are there and that the claims made by those brave strong people who are trying to expose them are true.

For those of you who may think how a message from Divine sources could sprout such sensational 'nonsense'. Think again. Go back and read the Scriptures. The Words contained in My Father's Book of Truth are correct. They tell of events from ancient times. They yield the Truth in order to guide you to God. The Words of My prophets then and now represent the full Truth of life to come.

The warnings contained in the Book of John, although many people today find them hard to decipher, are based on events, which will now enfold.

The Book of Revelation accurately foretells a series of events, which will be triggered by Satan as the End Times approach. He knows the Truth that his days are numbered. But he tells My poor children, who adore him, that paradise, of a different but more enticing one than the one promised by God awaits them. Therefore, in his final battle with My Eternal Father, he will do anything to steal the souls and as many as possible before the wrath of My Father descends.

He, Satan, is in a hurry. Run the other way. Fend for your families and pray like you have not done for a very long time. Prayer will protect you all. Renew your faith now and when the three days of darkness descends on the earth, they, My followers will light their homes with ease. The terrible darkness of which no man can fathom is blacker than night.

To the non-believers and those who sing the praises of the Beast they will realise the Truth at that point. Because they will not escape the blackness as it descends.

Stand up My children now and fight. Plan for survival in both body and soul as the evil deeds of these people unfold before your eyes.

Your Loving Saviour

Jesus Christ

Conversion

Sunday, November 21, 2010 01.30 hours

Today, My daughter, I bring a Message of hope and peace to all of My children who may feel that these Messages have represented fear. Know that for even those of you who find it difficult to believe in Me, My Eternal Father and the Holy Spirit do not worry. Many of you, My dear children, want to believe but because of your reasoning and logic, where you evaluate all things based on rational thinking, you will find it hard to believe in the supernatural.

Fear not. By praying, even just once a day and asking My Sacred Heart to pour out My Love on you, you will very soon feel differently. Many of you - those who are vague in your beliefs - envy others with a deep faith. You must understand that I love all of you. Like a parent each of you holds a deep and special place in My Heart. You must never feel you are not worthy of My Love.

Did I not love you to such an extent that I willingly gave up My life for you in the hope that you would be given a second chance to come back to Me?

Children, you will always be pushed aside by others for expressing a belief in your Divine Creator. When this happens remember that this is something that man must suffer on this earth for their love for Me. Never let this belief in Me, your Divine Saviour, fade or be hidden from those who will look at you with pity.

Yes, many of My children, influenced by human reasoning and logic, deliberately placed in their closed souls will question your beliefs. To insult you further they will be embarrassed by your faith and while they will not publicly admit it, they feel a curious jealousy. This jealousy springs from the certainty that dawns on them, that inside their souls there is emptiness. No matter how hard they look inwards they cannot understand why this is the case. Meanwhile, you the believer will undergo humiliation through the embarrassed eyes of onlookers with a weak faith or none at all.

Never be afraid or embarrassed to own up to the love you have in your hearts for My Eternal Father. Be open about your faith. Wear your love proudly for Me for all to see. By doing so you are leading by example.

Never try too hard to impose, through logical reasoning, your beliefs to non-believers in an aggressive manner. Instead show your brothers and sisters, love and support, even though you know they need guidance. When they see the forthright manner in which you voice your love for Me openly and with joy in your heart, they will begin to wonder.

By leading others, through the example of love, respect and good deeds, they will be drawn towards the light. Many won't understand why at first. But in time and especially by the power of your prayers, they will walk towards Me.

I urge you all to pray for the conversion of all souls. This includes those people known to you personally whom you feel are in need of prayers for difficulties they encounter in this life. Pray too for the conversion of those poor children lost to Me through the darkness, which blinds them to the Truth. Pray especially with compassion and love for those who follow, actively, the path of the Deceiver. They, more than anyone else, need your prayers.

Make known, to all you come in contact with, details as to how each of them can be redeemed, even at the moment of death, by reciting the chaplet of the Divine Mercy.

Please, please give this to everyone who will listen. Urge them, if you dare to read it and remember because if you do and they do recite it in their last few breaths they can and will be saved by Me.

Never be ashamed of the Crosses you wear

Never feel insulted when non-believers laugh or poke fun at you when you pray. Never be ashamed of the Crosses you wear for protection. Do not hide these symbols of the love you hold for Me, your Divine Saviour, My Eternal Father or the Holy Spirit. By proudly wearing these badges of holy honour you will lead others towards Me. Despite outward scorn you may experience from these people, inwardly, they envy you for your faith. Many of these observers feel a hollow emptiness inside due to their lack of faith. Prayer, My children, can help Me win over their souls. Say this prayer for them.

"My Dear Lord, I hold out my arms to ask You to take my beloved brother/sister into Your tender arms. Bless them with Your Sacred Blood and give them the grace needed to allow them to receive the Spirit of Your Love to lead them into eternal salvation."

When you, My believers, are openly challenged by others about your faith first say this:

"I am a follower of Christ Who suffered death at the hands of non-believers. Because of that, as a follower of Christ, I will always suffer indignity because of my love for Him from others. That is the cross I bear and am proud of this fact. He, my Saviour, died not just for my sins but for yours."

When they proudly boast of the fact they are agnostic or atheists tell them this. Ask them if they will feel different when their life on this earth draws to a close. Then give them this advice. On your deathbed remember this prayer of the Divine Mercy even if you are still unsure. Open your hearts and ask My Eternal Father to forgive them. Remember My promise. As Judge, as well as your Saviour, I will forgive - right up to each of My children's last breath on this earth. Tell them to pray hard so that they can open their hearts just once.

Prayer leads all My children closer to My Kingdom on earth when Heaven and Earth will merge as one. The power of prayer will only be truly understood when My children open their hearts and call out. Ask, and if it is God's Will, your prayers will be answered.

Never deny your children the Sacrament of Baptism

Lastly, pray for the little children, your sons and daughters and the youth in the world. Each of them, deserve to be shown the Truth. They were not shown the Truth of God's Love or given guidance by their parents due to the spiritual darkness, which has existed on earth over the last two decades. Even if your own faith is weak do not shirk your duty, as parents, to give them access to the Sacraments especially Baptism. Never take it upon yourself to deny this most important Sacrament to your own child. Many parents who proudly stand firm as they shout about their views of disbelief are damaging their children's souls. Give your children the gift of the Sacraments. In time, they will either thank you for this or deny Me. That will be up to them. Deny Me if you must but do not steal the souls of My children. You may be their parents on earth but they are the children of My Eternal Father, the Creator and Maker of all things. Do not try to take them into the darkness with you. Remember again that despite your own beliefs I love you all.

Your Divine Saviour and Judge

Jesus Christ, Son of the Eternal Father

Call to all Churches & Creeds to unite against Evil

Sunday, November 21, 2010 15.00 hours

To My churches around the world hear My call. All you children and followers belong to Me. So many of you are following the teachings of your church and God the Creator of Mankind. That is good. Many of you interpret the Teachings of My Eternal Father in different ways. This has come about through the interpretations of the prophets since time began.

Many prophets interpreted the Teachings of God in the way that the Message was received by them. Some of My prophet's words have been tampered with. All of My prophets were given the Truth. Not all of My prophets managed to ensure that their followers stayed on one path to Eternal Life.

All paths lead to God, the Creator of mankind. The followers of God interpret the Teachings in different ways that lead to confusion. Once confusion sets in you can be sure that the only way is to simplify your beliefs. Simply believe in and honour your Creator.

I call on all the churches, religions and faiths around the world to pray for mankind and those of no faith - now. Love of God does not have anything to do with the destruction of life. No man has the right, in My Name, or My Eternal Father's, to take a life in His Name. Instead, come together and unite in your love for your Creator in the face of evil as it swiftly arises all around you.

My children let Me remind you of God's laws. The Ten Commandments sent to you by My Eternal Father, through His most holy and devout prophet Moses. These rules were designed to instruct God's children as to the ways in which they must pay homage to Him to guide them towards the Truth. So many people today have forgotten this. Those who have not, rarely consider what they really mean. Those who do not understand the Ten Commandments chose to interpret them in a way that is far removed from the Truth. To those I say please read

The Ten Commandments and listen or risk facing the Wrath of God. Their meaning must not be diluted behind false love, false compassion or by justifying sin in the face of what you have been told.

The first Commandment tells you to Adore only one Creator, My Eternal Father, and to avoid idolatry. Yet that first Commandment has been thrown asunder in favour of false gods. By false gods I do not necessarily mean only people in high places or those who exalt themselves at the highest so that you, My children, fall down in ecstasy at their feet. Yes this is an offence and deeply insulting in the eyes of God. The idolatry I now refer to is mankind's love of power and money, which can drive My children into empty despair. This despair leads to the breaking of the other rule, the sin of self-obsession. The desire to look after your own road in life at the expense of your soul will be your downfall. Love of self, is not love. It is vanity. Yet that is a popular doctrine today. You are, under the guise of false compassion, exalting yourself and denying God. Your lack of humility will bring about your destruction. When you place yourself ahead of others they, and other people, will suffer for it. This Commandment must not, ever, be broken. Human reasoning, which is used to justify sin, is an absurdity.

Obsession with Celebrity

For the young people who have lacked guidance for so long they are now being sucked into the abyss of idolatry in ways that are clear for all to see. The very idols My young children worship are, for the most part, not of the Light. Many have sold their souls to The Devil, a fact they proudly boast of.

Their hypnotic appeal, through their music and words convince My children that this is the true path to follow. Their appealing immorality encourages their followers to emulate them. When they do they, My children, block the Light as they too are sucked into eternal darkness. The obsession with celebrity in the world of today means that My children feel anxious all the time as they strive to reach the same heights as those who follow the Deceiver claim to enjoy.

Come now all My children, of all churches and creeds. Join together and fight for the right to retain belief in God the Eternal Father, the right to love one another, the right to Pure Love, the Love of God, the Eternal Father, Creator of Heaven and Earth.

Your Loving Saviour and Just Judge

Jesus Christ

The Great Warning, A Gift out of Mercy
Monday, November 22, 2010 02.00 hours

My beloved daughter I am so pleased at the way you follow My Words with complete faith and obedience. My Love for you is strong. So too is your love for Me. You now feel Me very close to your heart. You are one with Me now My daughter. I and My Eternal Father, as well as the Holy Spirit - the Blessed Trinity, rejoice with your response to this very important calling. We, and all the angels and saints walk with you every day to protect you in this most Sacred Work.

Take heart and continue to hold My Hand. Allow Me to guide you in your words to give mankind a chance to finally understand the Truth before the Great Warning. This Great Warning, out of Mercy and Love as a last Gift to My children, will happen soon. Every single one of My children will be shown their lives, their sins, their wrong doings and every single insult they were responsible for against their brothers and sisters, all during a mystical experience. Not one man, woman or child on this earth will be excluded.

Some will be deeply shocked and saddened by the sins in their lives and will immediately turn to Me, their Just Judge and redeem themselves. They will, out of love and sorrow, ask for Mercy.

Others will be so sickened and shocked by the way in which their sins will be revealed that they will drop dead before they have a chance to ask for forgiveness.

And then there will be those who follow the Deceiver. They, in their terror, when they see the wicked sins in their past life flash in front of them will flee. They will try to hide but there is nowhere to go. Ducking and diving they will either accept what they see and ask for forgiveness there and then. Or they will turn away and squirm in shame and horror but will not ask for Mercy.

Then there is the final sinner. When his sins are shown to him all he will do is argue and deny that he committed these grievous offences against God's Commandments. He will simply deny the truth and turn his back into the darkness of Eternal Hell.

No one will be turned away from My Mercy

Why won't My children understand this? If they are genuinely repentant and desire to come and live with Me on the New Earth, where Heaven and Earth become one, why don't they ask for forgiveness? No one will be turned away from My Just Mercy if they show remorse. Yet, so caught up in their pursuit of selfish goals, they fail to grasp the consequences.

Wake up now all of you. Accept the changes you are about to witness, through the evil actions of mankind. The signs that have been foretold and which will pre-empt My return to earth.

Let Me guide you to Paradise

Through this prophet and the Book of Truth I plead with you once more out of My precious love for you all, turn to Me now before time runs out. Let Me hold you in My Arms. Let My Love flow through you in mind, body and soul. Open your hearts and let Me guide you to My Paradise on Earth where you will enjoy Eternal Life. Why would you wish to choose the other doomed path to nowhere when the Truth has been revealed?
My Heart heaves with worry and sadness when I think of My children

who just refuse to accept the Truth of My promise. I say, one more time, turn to Me now and talk to Me. Ask Me to come back into your heart. I will make Myself fit within your soul. I give you this promise, even for those most hardened of souls. Just one word is all you need to say. Ask Me to show you My Presence by saying:

"Jesus I feel lost. Open my heart to accept Your love and show me the Truth so that I may be saved."

My Words of Warning are not a threat. This event has been known since My death on the Cross. Why do you think it cannot happen? The Truth lies in the Scripture for all to understand. I will act as your Saviour right up to the last minute before I come, as Just Judge so that I can finally lead My children to My family of great love, joy and happiness where will all live in harmony for eternity.

Satan and his followers will be plunged into darkness forever. My family will witness the joy and Divine Heavens, which no man, were they to glimpse just a taste of what it promises, would turn their back on this pure happiness in My Father's Kingdom.

Pray, pray for forgiveness and enter My Father's Kingdom in glory where you, and your loved ones, will be welcomed into the Light of Pure Love.

I will fight to win you all back

I died for all of you and I will fight to win you all back to Me, despite the darkness of evil in the world up to the very last moment.

Please let Me show you how much I love you once more. Take My Hand now, place your head on My Shoulder and your gentle soul will be set aflame with a love you have forgotten.

Your Love Saviour

Jesus Christ

Warning of Nuclear War
Tuesday, November 23, 2010 03.00 hours

My daughter, you are suffering because of the Work you are doing on My behalf. The darkness you feel is coming from the Deceiver who strikes every hour through others, people you know, through his darkness to attack you. Despite your feelings of despair you are, in fact, being protected. He, the Deceiver I have told you will not harm your soul. You must continue to pray the Most Holy Rosary for constant protection from torment. By praying this powerful adoration to My Blessed Mother you will see a difference.

The Work, which you strive to continue to complete, on My behalf is not easy but you must stay strong My daughter. For it is the Work that, when revealed to the world, will bring peace and contentment to My children.

They, My children, when they understand the Truth will know they are not being thrown asunder and forgotten by their Creator. The comfort they will experience through the knowledge I will give them through this Book will draw them closer to Me.

Plan for the War ahead

Fear not, My daughter you are safe though you do feel powerless and fear uncertainty. The world including your own country is about to experience more pain as a result of global control, which will render people powerless so this is why it is important to prepare now.

I have told you before that you must tell My children to start to plan now before the fearsome global war commences. The war, which I speak about, is being orchestrated by the Red Dragon now. The Dragon, the new world enemy, is scheming now and will destroy cities in the West. The time is close. Pray, pray for conversion as this evil cannot be stopped, as there is not enough prayer to prevent it. Pray for those souls, who through this nuclear war will die.

Three Years before the Plot Unfolds

Pray for those souls now. As a global power takes over gently with a false compassion they will, My daughter, aim to control your freedom to live, eat and pray. That is why My people must strive to become self-sufficient. Grow your food. Find shelters in time where you can meet to give homage to your Divine Saviour. Just keep strong. Don't tell too many people why you are doing this. It will take only three years for the signs of this plot to unfold before your eyes. By then your plans will yield a form of support, which you may have questioned and thought, from time to time, as being strange. Grow your own food now. Buy the seeds that will not be available for sale in the future now. This will feed your family as the global famine takes place.

Go now and prepare.

Your Loving Saviour

Jesus Christ

Stairway to spiritual perfection

Wednesday, November 24, 2010 02.30 hours

Write this My beloved daughter. Faith has a way of deserting My most devout followers when they least expect it. This is important as it tests their faith so that they will come back into My Heart, all the more strong for the experience. Fear not, this is a trial, which I allow My children to endure so that they will become stronger.

It is not easy to retain your faith in Me, My children, as there are so many obstacles, which block your devotion. You will, from time to time, feel a complete emptiness in your soul. This can leave you in an agitated state because you feel alone without a crutch.

For My faithful followers you must understand this. I, despite the loneliness you may experience, am never far away. All of these episodes have one goal, to strengthen your faith in such a way so as to ensure that you move a few steps towards Me each time. This is what is called the stairway to spiritual perfection that is Heaven. It is a long stairway and can take a very long time to reach the upper steps. Each step can represent a new revelation into what lessons you must experience before you can attain the graces you need to elevate your souls to the spiritual perfection needed to enter My Father's Paradise.

As each step is mounted a new awareness of which I expect of you is realised. Hard at times, unfair, it may seem, at other times. But for each step you climb the more astute you become in understanding the Truth of My Teachings.

Some climb these steps quickly while others take their time. Some of My devout followers may lose courage and back one step, two steps or three at a time. This is natural. Others who move too quickly gain a confidence that convinces them they understand all spiritual matters. But this is the Deceiver's way of making you believe and accept this false confidence. All gifts bestowed on you can only come from Me. They are given to you, My faithful followers, out of My boundless Love for you. You must never assume that because your faith is strong that this is all your doing. Yes, your faith may be strong because of your tenderness of heart. Yet this is also a Gift from Me. You must, in order to reach the top step, be humble in your love for Me. Show virtue at all times.

Show confidence in your faith by all means as this is pleasing to Me. But never fall into the trap of believing you know the full mysteries of the Divine Realm. As humans born with original sin, only time will reveal these mysteries to you, My children.

Strive always to accept everything even the trials I may send you, as a Gift from Me. All My Gifts are bestowed to make you strong in your love for Me.

I am so very proud of all My children who believe in Me and show Me honour and respect. So that I can lift you up to the full Glory of My Father's Paradise you need to aspire to the glory of perfect union in Me.

To do this, My children, takes a little time and requires patience before you yield to the total abandonment of your soul to Me. Once that happens you become part of My Mystical Body for eternity.

Surrender, My children, to My absolute Pure Love and you will never have to look back or fear for you will be safe in My Arms.
Keep strong My faithful children even in the face of obstacles for I will never desert My beloved devoted followers. Ever.

Your Loving Saviour

Jesus Christ

Global Plan to deplete world population and overthrow world leaders

Friday, November 26, 2010 03.00 hours

My beloved daughter you will be sent guidance from a spiritual director soon. But remember many of My followers are called by Me but not all accept. I cannot, as you know, interfere with free will, a Gift to mankind. No matter it is important now to continue with this urgent Work so that My children will listen and be saved.

The Signs

Make no mistake change is afoot and shortly there will be so many signs that there will be few people on this earth who will fail to notice them. The signs I speak about as those, which are being given through My visionaries through the apparitions of My beloved Blessed Mother in Europe. Many people who open their minds and unlock their trapped souls will understand that this communication comes from the Heavens. When My children see the miraculous signs, which will be visible through the sun they will then know the Truth.

Ignore the scorn, ridicule and hatred that will be shown when people read the contents of this manuscript. The same thing happened to My Apostles who with the Gift of the Holy Spirit produced their Work. You too, My daughter, have been given this Gift. Never reject it or doubt it. It is real and you now know this. Your doubts have, at last, begun to fade.

I will, as I have told you, send you help. Evidence of this promise is now beginning to unfold. I will also give you information of future events, which you must reveal to all including the disbelievers. What does it matter if they won't believe at first, because as events roll out, they will have no choice but to acknowledge the Truth?

Plan to orchestrate a war

There is a vicious plan underway by world powers to orchestrate a war - the intention being to reduce the world's population. Pray, pray now to help deflect the level of damage these evil people want to cause on earth. Their allegiance to the Deceiver means that, through the satanic powers they receive under his influence, they are determined to carry out this task at all costs.

Plans to overthrow Pope Benedict Plans are also underway to take over churches and various faiths including the Vatican. My Pope, My beloved Benedict is surrounded by those plotting his downfall. Other world leaders, unaware of the underlying powers hidden within their own ranks, are also going to be targeted with a view to toppling them.

My children wake up and fight. This is a very real war unlike any war witnessed on the earth. It is a war on you, each and every one of My children. You are the target. The problem is that you cannot see the enemy. Cowards at heart they don't have the courage to reveal themselves.

Secret Meetings
Self-obsessed they meet in secret within your own community and are scattered in every walk of life. You will find them not only in the corridors of your government but in your justice systems, the police force, business communities, education systems and the military.

Never let these people dictate to you how to pray. Watch how they will try to manage your life and start preparing now for what lies ahead.

Warning on Global Vaccinations
First of all pray in groups. Pray for these people who are ardent supporters of Satan. Prayer will help to avert some of these disasters. Watch out for the atrocities they will try to inflict through vaccination. Trust no sudden global initiative to vaccinate, which may seem compassionate in its intention. Be on your guard. Country by country these are colluding to control as many people as possible.

Fear not because I will protect My followers who pray to Me. Pray too for those brave souls among you who have decided to spread the Truth. Many of these people are being laughed at but they are speaking for the most part the truth.

Stock Pile food
Do not rely on food suppliers. Prepare now for the future. Start collecting food and planting your own. Stock up as if a war is coming. Those who do will be all right. Prayer and devotion will strengthen your souls and save you from these people's evil ways. Never let them control your mind or beliefs through their insistence on introducing laws designed to destroy families. They will strive to separate families by encouraging separation including the promotion of divorce, sexual and religious freedom.

Murder of World Leaders
They will promote hatred between nations, murder world leaders through assassination and capture people's liberty by forcing them to rely on their dictatorship.

The wrath of God will shortly be seen as He will not tolerate their wickedness for much longer unless these people who have chosen to follow their satanically inspired organizations turn their backs on this evil atrocity. Pray for them.

Be careful what people in your countries you vote for. Watch how they are presented to you by the words they speak. Listen to those who are trying to warn you. I urge you to pray for those who don't so that they may be converted in order that they, too, can be saved.

These events, which I speak of, are going to begin to happen shortly. Stick tightly together, keep your own food supplies ready, seek to grow your own vegetables and other survival items. This is a war against you but it won't seem like it. Just be on your guard.

Churches will be banned

Those of you who pluck up the courage to go back to your church never be fearful of praying or showing your faith openly. For those of you who take My Church for granted then don't. For it is only when this very Gift, which represents your faith openly, is taken away from you that the Truth will finally dawn on you. And this will make you angry.

My daughter, tell My people, not to panic. They My followers will be saved and will be lifted with Me into the clouds to await My New Paradise on earth. They will enjoy My New Paradise and will reunite with their departed families in this New Eternal Life. They must stay strong, pray and show love for one another. Pray, pray, pray especially for those lost, deceived souls who have no idea what their actions will mean for their future in the next life.

Those with lukewarm souls

For My other children, those with lukewarm souls, pray also. They must turn back to Me and soon. Children, for the love of one another, do not hesitate to warn these people of the Truth. Show them, through example, the importance of prayer so they too will not be lost.

Stay strong. Never surrender to the army of the Deceiver. Ever. Stand up for what you believe in. Protect your family now. Turn back to Me. Pray My Divine Mercy every single day. For Christians everywhere pray the Rosary. Let My Mother bring you back to Me through her intercession.

My children I cry for you all and need My followers now to gather in force with Me against this evil. Prayer is the answer.
Your beloved Saviour Jesus Christ

Book of Revelation

Friday, November 26, 2010 12.00 hours

My dearly beloved daughter today is a day when My Heart is broken by the unrest and deep unhappiness in the world. I watch in distress as the world rises in anger against each other. Much of the sadness springs from the knowledge that these prophecies will unfold yet much of mankind will be none the wiser.

Pray for Russia to be consecrated to My Blessed Mother
They still refuse to acknowledge that these events were foretold in the Book of John. So, so many will now suffer because of lack of faith. Pray now that Russia will finally relent and allow itself to be finally consecrated in My Blessed Mother's Name. Pray, pray, pray for this to happen because it will be through prayer that this great achievement will be possible. If this happens then millions will be saved. For the danger is that the communist forces will rise with the serpent and join together leaving you, My children, powerless.

Look now at the velocity as the nations rise to fight. The speed of global events will cause much consternation as these unfold in their intensity. My followers you must listen. Prayer groups will be essential in spreading conversion and to diffuse these disastrous events. Even those of you, complacent in your lives where you take everything for granted, you will no longer be able to ignore these events. You must listen to Me now and accept that those events predicted in the Book of Revelation are coming to pass.

Hold your hands in prayer now. Even if you hold just a spark of affection in your heart for Me ask Me to hold you so that I can ignite and strengthen your faith in Me.

I will fight for each one of you

I will fight right to the bitter end to bring you all closer to My Heart, whether you are a child, a teenager, a young adult, middle aged or old - in My eyes you are all the same. You are My precious beloved family - each and every single one of you. No one is excluded, even those of you who do not accept that I exist. Even those of you who do but hate Me - I still love you. My Love is passionate beyond your knowing and I will do everything in My power to bring you back into My fold. I will not give up your soul to Satan that easily.

Please turn to Me

Please turn to Me - no matter how many doubts you hold - and let Me fill your heart with My Divine Love. Just one taste of that Love will help you prepare for Eternal Life in Paradise with Me, My Eternal Father and your brothers and sisters. This is your inheritance, your rightful inheritance.

Don't squander this chance of salvation. When your life on earth comes to an end you will have two choices in the after life. Heaven in Paradise or the depths of Hell with Satan who will take you with him through the sins he tempts you to commit on earth. Open your eyes now. Remember death on earth can take place on any day, at any time and when you least expect it.

Through this Message I beg you to see the Truth before the Day of Judgement. Always remember I love you. No matter how grievously you have sinned. When you turn to Me and ask Me for forgiveness from the bottom of your heart you will be pardoned. Even during you last breath.

Your Beloved Saviour Jesus Christ

Call on Believers to convert lost souls

Friday, November 26, 2010 15.00 hours

My dearly beloved daughter, the Blessed Trinity unites with you as one to drive forward the Divine Truth to every soul in the world as a matter of urgency.

You, My daughter, now feel the pain and suffering in your heart in union with Me for mankind. Their lost faith brings you a deep sadness and sense of fear for their future.

My beloved loyal and devout followers are now, at this time, uniting around the world through the bond of powerful Divine Love to fight to save souls from damnation.

These, My children of the Light, come from all nations. They will recognise each other instantly irrespective of their race, colour or creed. I am guiding them so that this army of love will help strengthen the faith of mankind at this point in history.

Never before have I made My Presence so evident within the hearts of believers. They feel the suffering I endure as I witness the heart wrenching badness that emits from man even among those who you would deem to be kind and thoughtful. Love of self is destroying My children.

Selfishness and lack of consideration for those around you and for the vulnerable leaves a stain of shame that is hard to erase. The cruelty that man shows to his neighbour, all with one motive in mind – self-satisfaction, has reached an all time high. The obsession with their own needs is a sin in the eyes of My Eternal Father.

So many false excuses, made in the name of self worth, are completely unacceptable and against My Teachings. Love one another. Treat others, as you would expect to be treated yourself. Think of others needs before your own. Stand up for the human rights of your brothers and sisters when they face the injustice of others. Never ever justify punishing one person in order to gain material advantage. Show love and compassion even for your enemies. This is not an easy task because of the materialist insecurities My children feel. The symptoms of the selfish obsession with wealth, beauty and so called success that many people believe to be natural attributes of the human make up cause terrible confusion.

The idea where people are brainwashed into putting their own needs first in the name of self worth has been implanted in the human psyche for a long time but this philosophy has been reinforced by the powers of modern communication. When My children hear these messages almost daily through TV, the media, the cinema, music and the Internet they accept these messages as being important.

Despite the false promise these beliefs, which are appealing in that they offer self-gratification, which is hard to reject, represent, My children accept the lie, the lie that has been planted by the Deceiver - Satan.

The disquiet they feel soon afterwards, having taken advantage of someone else, is hard for them to understand. They, My children, having won the coveted prize are not happy. They then seek out more and more of the same; so insatiable is their appetite. But it is useless. They can't fully satisfy themselves. They are devoid of real joy, a natural contentment, and don't understand the emptiness they feel inside.

When you place yourself first before others that is selfish. When you take unfair advantage over those who are weaker and more vulnerable than you that is sinful. When you damage that person's ability to live in dignity and then deprive them of the right to feed their families adequately that deeply offends Me. I suffer with these souls. Do onto your neighbour a wrong and you do this to Me. When you hurt your neighbour through words of spite you are guilty of inflicting pain in My Heart.

When man punishes another through violence I endure the pain of My Passion on the Cross. I relive it. I feel their pain as you inflict bodily harm on them. When you are a murderer you are guilty of the final indignity of nailing Me to the Cross.

Children know this. Sin will lead you to Hell. This is frightening for those believers who see Me as a Merciful Judge. My promise of unlimited Mercy, which I will give to each and every one of you who repents, is still guaranteed. But how can I save those who will not see the error in their mixed up lives?

Preaching the Truth of My Teachings is important. It is because of the appeal of so many distractions, which abound that many of My children will find it extremely difficult to recognise the Word of God. Many will not have knowledge of God's Teachings through the prophets or through Holy Scripture. Many simply don't want to know. For others they will refuse to listen even if the Word is spread through My prophets and visionaries of today with clear signs for all to see. This is why it will be up to the believers to pray for the others. Special prayers are needed now. By praying to The Divine Mercy, the powerful prayer, given to My beloved Sister Faustina, much conversion will take place.

When that happens I request that all My children rejoin in prayer groups to continue to pray for and give guidance to these prodigal children of Mine - your brothers and sisters.

In My Name and the Blessed Trinity I urge My beloved children to join forces in union with My Heart and help Me save their souls. I love them all so much that I weep sad and bitter tears of terror for them. I don't want to lose them.

Help Me, My followers in the Light, to reunite these lost souls with My family so that they too will experience the True Paradise for which they strive so desperately.

Hold out your hand to theirs. Talk to them. Listen to them. Show them compassion even when they throw it back in your face in scorn. Show patience. Above all make them feel My Love for them through you.

They will find it hard to dismiss you then even if they mock you. Through your prayers you can, and will, save their souls.

I salute you My precious followers. You bring tears to My eyes with the love and devotion you show to Me, My Blessed Mother, Queen of the Heavens and the Blessed Trinity.

We, and all the angels and saints in Heaven rejoice in your response to this calling now. So go do your Work in the Name of My Eternal Father. Bring back My flock.

Your devoted Saviour

Jesus Christ.

Persecution of Genuine Visionaries
Monday, November 29, 2010 12.48 hours

My daughter, write this to warn the world of the persecution being inflicted on My chosen souls sent to the world to impart the Truth in order to save souls in advance of My Second Coming.

You will notice that My chosen visionaries, seers and prophets are the ones who will be rejected outright over and above the false prophets. These beautiful souls of mine, chosen for their simple devotion, will suffer in union with Me, the rejection that I suffered at the hands of mankind.

Those who suffer in Me, with Me and because of Me are the genuine prophets. They are the souls who will be tormented, treated with contempt and condemned outright on My behalf. They will also be rejected by My own Church, though not by all My sacred servants. Devout followers, who follow My Teachings closely, will also be tempted to reject them until, in time, the Truth will slowly dawn on them.

Since the beginning of time when I chose to send prophets into the world, out of My Divine Mercy, to remind you all of My Teachings, very few were believed at first. Many were scorned and viewed to be suffering from a vivid imagination, depression or simply condemned as being deluded. Most of these prophets were, themselves, overwhelmed when they experienced their first Divine encounter. Many of them doubted these mystical experiences for some time before they accepted the authenticity of them. They were slow to reveal their experiences to any. It took them time to accept.

All of My chosen souls, while accepting their calling, were reluctant to reveal the Messages or instructions from Me even to those sacred servants of mine including nuns, priests, Bishops and Cardinals. They felt in awe of these people and knew in their hearts, that the questions imposed on them would be very difficult to deal with. Many who were called did not reveal their Messages and used prayer and personal suffering to carry out their duty to Me.

Others who did reveal the Messages, as instructed by My Blessed Mother and I, were not believed. It was only through the Divine manifestations, which became evident in time that they were believed.

I urge all My followers to listen to your heart. Look at the Messages imparted by My precious visionaries and seers. These Messages are being given to you out of Pure Love to help guide you and save souls. That is the objective. If you decide that they are not of Divine origin pray for guidance. If you decide that they are then pray, pray, pray for My visionaries that they will be listened to.

Now let Me warn you of the signs to watch out for when My genuine visionaries are persecuted in My Name. Followers of the Deceiver, seeing their Light, will target them not lightly but with a viciousness that will take your breath away. Not only will they torment them through ridicule but they will go to tremendous lengths to discredit them, and all in My Name. The pain that My disciples suffer is nothing to the pain that it causes Me. My suffering has reached such a level in recent times that I am reliving, all over again, the terrible torture I endured when I died for your sins, all sins, for all mankind. Including those who torment Me and My visionaries. Including those murderers, those people who publicly deny Me and boast about it and for the terrible evil in the world at present.

Please listen to My visionaries. You will feel it in your hearts when you hear the Truth. Please do not fall into the trap of those who persecuted the visionaries of My Blessed Mother including Saint Bernadette or My little children at Fatima. They were treated with the utmost disrespect, especially by My sacred servants. They are the ones who hurt the most when My Divine manifestations are given to mankind out of Love. My Heart suffers more when they do not believe in the supernatural Divine nor recognise it when it is presented to them.

Please pray for My visionaries and especially My visionaries whose Messages cannot be denied for the love they show and the warnings they contain, for they are My true visionaries. You will recognise them by the insults, slander, torment and abuse they receive at the hands of My children.

If you look at the abuse they receive and then look at the lies that are spread about them in such a demeaning way you will then have to ask yourself. If this person has been tormented so far and not believed why does the abuse continue so harshly? Then you will have your answer. Pray to the Holy Spirit for guidance in discerning My true prophets, visionaries and seers from the rest who are deceiving you.

Your beloved Saviour

Jesus Christ

Quest for Wealth

Tuesday, November 30, 2010 12.00 hours

My beloved daughter concentrate and listen to what I have to say. You are now in the throes of a transition from the time you received the first Message to the present ones. Please understand that these Messages are coming from Me and please stop your doubts now. This will enable you to concentrate on the Work for which you have been called.

In relation to matters, which are occurring in the world it is now becoming clearer by the day what the evil World Order are trying to inflict on the world. The United Nations, one of the many fronts for this New World Order, are trying to stamp out all My Teachings and will use every lethal weapon at their disposal to do this.

Fear not because My believers will fight hard and will not deny Me especially in those countries which are consecrated to Me and who have a devout and unshakable faith. They will not stand back and allow this. But for many because of the costs involved in ensuring that their children are guided in the Light, they will be powerless.

As explained to you before, the Wrath of My Eternal Father is about to be shown on the earth as man inches nearer and nearer in their attempts to disown Me.

The world looks the same. People seem the same. The world of television with its rose tinted appeal seems the same. People bury their heads in the sand. They think that the world will continue as it is. Sadly they are mistaken. My duty to My children is to save you. Not to allow you continue to be sucked into an empty vacuum of promises, empty dreams and false ambitions. These are the pleasures to which you gave allegiance for many, many years. These are the promises that those of you, through no fault of your own, were convinced was the path to follow for self-worth. Self-gain. Self-Reward. You were told to look after number one whatever the cost, the number one being you. You with your ambitions, lust for wealth for yourself and your children, desire to become better than your brothers and sisters, and a constant relentless quest for self acclaim were fooled.

These ambitions were fed to My children, through the appeal and gloss of these ambitions by the Deceiver. Many of My children will laugh at this Message and say that this is not true. Unfortunately the Deceiver exists and most of My children do not accept that he does.

He is cunning in that he hides behind things, people, acts and appealing incentives. His glamorous allure means that today if you ask a person, which they would accept - money or a chance to reunite with their lost families - and they will opt for money. Ask another if they would betray their brother or sister for material gain. And the answer will be yes. Ask a young child if they would trade their simple life for a life of wonder and excitement and the answer will be yes.

Why then do My children find it hard to understand that once the grand prize has been awarded to them do they then feel they need more and more? A wealthy man who gains once will constantly continue to attain more. The reason for this is that Satan's gifts leave a raw empty feeling inside you that you do not understand. So you continue in your quest to seek out more and it is usually at the expense of the welfare of your neighbour. No man gains huge wealth without the people he met on the way suffering to some degree. No person who gains fame will get there unless someone else has had to do without. A man that does not share his wealth is doomed. A person who has nothing tends to share more than those who have been blessed with material comforts.

My Teachings cannot be watered down

Why do My children ignore these Teachings, taught by My Apostles since the New Scriptures were produced? Why do they not heed the doctrine they contain? Do they believe that they were written by My disciples so that people would not listen? These Teachings have not changed since I left this earth. They are there for a reason. You can change their interpretation, water it down, add new meaning or delete some parts but one thing will remain. And that is the Truth. The Truth will always stay the same. It cannot and will not be changed to suit mankind. Heed this now. Sit up and listen. You cannot expect to follow this route and enter My Father's Kingdom. Many of you justify the wealth and glory you gain and attribute this to luck. What you may not realise is that many of you sold your souls to the Evil One in the process.

Some of My children do know that they have committed this grave sin and think nothing of it. Others genuinely believe that they are simply doing the best for themselves and their families but they must understand that financial security is acceptable. Quest for luxury and wealth is not.

The reality is that vast amounts of wealth are gained through sin. Wealth that may be gained without sin will lead to sin.

Despite the Teachings of My Father's Church throughout the world people still do not accept My Teachings. Wealthy people who strive for material gain have one God. Poor people who strive for wealth have one God. They are both the same. Money. Money is useless if it is acquired dishonestly and where those less fortunate do not benefit from the experience.

Money, material wealth and all good things gained by those people who consider themselves fortunate must be shared among those who need it. Money given away to charity is meaningless if it is done in order to seek glory or attention.

Be assured that with the evil that is being planned now in the world when the desire to leave you with empty pockets becomes a reality only then will you realise how little value money holds. When they, the evil entity, take over your money and render you powerless to touch it without agreeing to their terms then you will finally realise that you will need an alternative route to happiness.

Your money will be worthless. You will need then to survive the way of the jungle. Those with survival instincts will find it easier than those who never had to work on their bended knees before. Seeds to grow your own food will mean more to you than a million dollars. A simple fruit will mean more to you than a flashy car. Because when you are stripped bare you will call out to your Maker your Creator. It is only then, and only then, will you realise that all that matters is the love in your heart. Because without love you cannot grow, nor can you enter My Father's Kingdom.

Think now. Be careful in your quest for wealth. Stop now before it is too late. Share and divide and follow My Path. This is a tough lesson for My children who feel a sense of insecurity.

Your beloved Saviour

Jesus Christ

The Warning to Mankind
Tuesday, December 07, 2010 03.15 hours

Yes My beloved daughter I am back. Write this. You, My daughter, having turned your back on Me by denying the Truth will now help Me lead My people back to the Light, the Light of the Truth.

No man will be denied the chance by Me to see the Truth of God. They will be shown Mercy by the Gift of proof to be given to them that I exist. They will be given this Gift when, during The Warning, they will finally know the Truth. Sadly not all will turn, even at that stage, towards Me or My Father's Eternal Kingdom.

My daughter I have not communicated with you for a number of days. This was deliberate. The time afforded you was to allow you digest carefully the content of My Messages.

You will know by now that these Messages come from Me and they all deal with very important issues. I think you can now discern the Truth of My Teachings between that of your imagination. My daughter you can see now the hurt and distress I feel when you witness almost daily the frustration that I, and My Eternal Father feel at the attitudes of this sad, empty and disbelieving world.

Not only do the disbelievers cause you pain, but through the gifts and graces that I have given you, you also see the confusion that exists even in the minds of My followers. They too are not easily convinced by the Truth when it is given to them as a Gift of Love from Me through My prophets.

What a long winding road this is for My children when striving towards the Truth and the promises that I have given them. Looking at My children every day, in person, on the street, on TV, in the media and amongst your neighbour you see them through My eyes now. What do you see? Total oblivion to the spiritual world and a lack of real purpose in their lives, a sense of hopelessness, despite the attractions of worldly pursuits.

My children do not realise it now but they are going through a cleansing. This purification, where they are experiencing an acute sense of emptiness due to lack of material goods has been allowed by Me. Yet is has all been caused by the greed of mankind. By allowing people the right to their own free will, then they, the evil perpetrators of the collapse of the banking system worldwide will continue with their cunning deceit.

I have allowed My people, the innocent victims, to undergo this cleansing. It is very important that they do because the hardships that they endure will help cleanse their souls.

Very soon as material goods become less and harder to attain they will see life in a deeper way. Simplicity will help open their eyes to the Truth, the Truth of what is really important. Without this purification, when My children are permitted to suffer for the sake of their souls, they cannot and will not become closer to My Heart.

Stripped bare of the material goods for which they held such an idolatry obsession in the past they will turn back to the Truth. With clarity they will see the love in each other's souls. So too will they very quickly see the evil in all its ugly glory in those who follow the lure of self-obsession and greed. They will now view these people, who are given credence in the media as being those one should look up to and admire, in the same way in which I view them. That is with utter despair and sadness.

Go now My daughter and understand your task with clear eyes. You now know the Truth. You no longer doubt. Spread the Truth of salvation as soon as possible to afford people the chance of redemption before the Great Warning.

Your beloved Saviour

Jesus Christ

The Next Life
Saturday, December 11, 2010 09.15 hours

My dearly beloved daughter you are ready now to move forward and continue with the task of completing My Holy Book of Truth. You, My daughter, have been undergoing the cleansing required to give you the strength with this Work.

My children, so caught up in this world of two parts, do not realize that soon all will be one. The two parts involve sorrow and joy. Sorrow exists in the world in a way that causes deep confusion and despair. It is a sorrow unlike any other since the foundation of earth.

The sorrow that is felt today is based on loss, which has come about because material things have been taken away. There is also the longing for peace in mind, body and soul. This will only come about through humility, acceptance and love of My Eternal Father. Then there is the joy.

I smile with love when My children laugh, smile and enjoy themselves. This is a Gift from Me. Laughter and joy is an important Gift to mankind once it is pure and not at the expense of each other.

My children of little faith it is hard, I know, to stop and say I am turning back to God. So many of you are unaware as to Who the Eternal Father is. Few understand that He watches over them every single day of their lives - each and every one of them. He smiles, laughs and feels a great sense of joy when His children are happy He does not, however, look with favour on those whose joy, or assumption of joy, is achieved without love in their hearts.

I, Your Saviour, Jesus Christ, love you all, My children, too. Yet I am one with My Eternal Father. I smile on you all and hope that you will come back to Me.

Come on to Me My children as one and move towards Me with open hearts.

For many of My children the Messages, which refer to My Second Coming on earth strikes fear in their hearts. There is no need to fear. This will be a moment of absolute joy, glory and pure happiness. Because for all of you who turn your hearts back to Me I will hold you in My Arms and will cry tears of joy.

Believers please, please pray now for those who do not believe or who have lost their way. The farmer who rounds up his flock will always strive to seek out relentlessly the ones who are lost. The sweetness of victory he feels when they come back with his fold is similar to that feeling I get when My lost children return to Me.

Children, even during moments of joy and laughter on this earth please remember one thing. This is but a glimmer of the pure happiness and joy that will exist on the New Earth when the lost Paradise emerges. When this happens, the chosen people, those who live good lives, believe in their Creator, will join with the resurrected dead. Those people, friends and family who have passed from the life, will join with Me in this new glorious eternity. Remember children, it is important not to take this earth for granted. Nor to assume everything in it is under your control, because it is not. As you continue to be consumed by its promises, disappointments, joys and wonders, remember it is only a temporary place. A passing stage, before entering My Father's Kingdom - the New Heaven and Earth which becomes one.

One final call, My children, pray to Me in your own words. Ask Me to guide you. Ask Me to show you love and the Truth in a way that will make sense. Don't keep your head buried in the sand or you will not enjoy the glory of the New Earth.

Empty Path to nothingness

Children who sneer and deny Me will tell you there is no life after this one. Let Me assure you they are not only denying themselves access to Paradise, instead they are choosing an empty path to nothingness. In some cases, they are following the deceit of the Deceiver - the Evil One - who moves so silently and with a deadly prowess, that they, not believing he exists, follow blindly holding his hand through the gates of Hell.

My suffering in Garden of Gethsemane

When My believers see these people strut arrogantly and boasting of their atheism they feel a terrible suffering. They, who have taken up My Cross, feel the agony I suffered during My time in the Garden of Gethsemane. This is where I knew that, even though I willingly made the ultimate Sacrifice when I accepted death as a means to give My children a chance to win a place in My Father's Kingdom, I knew deep down it would not make a difference to some of My children. This was the worst agony and the one that made Me sweat Blood. The terror I felt for those lost souls still exists in Me today.

Those of you who ask - if you are God, or you are Jesus Christ, then surely you can do anything? My answer is, of course, except for one thing. I cannot interfere with your free will given to mankind. It will be up to My children to make this their final choice of their own free will.

Your Loving Christ

Your Saviour Jesus Christ

Call to stop Murder/Abortion

Thursday, December 16, 2010 13.10 hours

Write this My daughter. Death dealt out to innocent victims is one of the greatest sins which man can inflict on his brother. It is the most grievous sin of the flesh and causes Me deep pain. The lack of regard that mankind today has for human life is becoming increasingly evident in the world.

Life is a precious Gift from God. No man has the right to take the life of another. No man has the right to take the life of a child still to take his first breath at the time of birth. This crime is heinous and unforgivable. All souls come from My Eternal Father and are created at the moment of conception. Little children, innocent souls, are being murdered by the very people sent to nurture them - their own mothers, who are responsible for their being denied the right to be born.

Why do My children stand back and do nothing? In the name of freedom these little angels from My Father's Kingdom are being taken off this earth before the time assigned to them, as children of God, has taken place. Do these women not understand that the lives they place so little value on are those of God? These children are suffering. They endure agonizing pain during their murder, and it is justified by governments, the medical profession and these women's families. Have they no remorse in their souls?

Do they not realise that their heinous act is no different to that act when man murders man?

In fact it is an even greater sin, as these children are helpless. These women must ask for mercy if they are guilty. Or ask for guidance from Me if they are considering an abortion. Either way they will be judged by their sin. Sins of the flesh are the most offensive in My Father's eyes. No amount of justification for murdering another fellow being is acceptable by Me or My Eternal Father.

Wake up now My children and understand that the taking of life will lead the perpetrators into the eternal fires of hell. There will not return from this abyss full of demons. Those same demons, who through the work of The Deceiver - Satan - convinces the murderer that what he or she is doing is right! He will cunningly convince mothers, for example, that they are making the 'right decision'. Using every trick associated with human reasoning he will make the person justify the act even though it is wrong. He will use the lie that the murderers have rights of their own. That they must look after their own interests first. In the name of human rights the lie is manifested so that the rights of a mother and her freedom to live life as she chooses is to be admired. The lie then convinces her that it is right and correct to murder her child.

Please understand that the escalation of genocide in the world has been foretold. It is one of the many signs spoken of in relation to the End Times.

Stop all of you now. Listen. Murder is a very serious offence. Do it and you will not be saved. There is no going back. Repent those of you who have committed this terrible sin. Ask for forgiveness now. I, through My Mercy, will hear your prayer. You can, and will be saved, if you are truly sorry for your grievous sin. I will listen. I will forgive. But time is not on your side.

Believers pray hard for these lost and wandering children of mine who have been misled by The Deceiver and his minions in positions of power. They need your prayers now. You must, all of you, defend the right to human life, which cannot be tampered with by human hands in any circumstances.

Pray to Me every day. Offer any sufferings you may have for the innocent victims.

Your Beloved Saviour

Jesus Christ

The Book of Truth

Saturday, December 18, 2010 09.40 hours

Well now you know that what I promise comes to fruition. I have sent you a spiritual director, the person I chose right at the beginning of your journey. It takes time for the chosen few to take up the Cup for My Work. My daughter you need a spiritual director so that My Messages are fully understood by a servant of mine. That way the Word will spread and people will realise the Truth. This will be a path full of bumps and short laneways, which appear suddenly to throw you into a different direction but have no fear. You are now being guided and will feel a greater confidence with your Work.

Now write this. The Book of Truth is being presented to mankind to help them redeem themselves in My Heart. They are being given a choice to proclaim My Glory before I come back as a merciful Saviour and Just Judge. I never want to inflict punishment on My children but, in certain circumstances, those who partner the Deceiver in full knowledge and who place him and his evil minions in such high regard, to the point of paying homage to him before an altar, cannot be saved. They know who they are. They will find it very hard to turn back to Me. Pray for them.

Who Satan Attacks

The Deceiver has very little time left on earth to wreck havoc and so he has intensified his activities everywhere. He targets mainly My sacred servants in My Father's Church, the young and the beautiful as well as the highly intelligent.

Those who continue to boast that they do not believe in Me or My Eternal Father will be given just one more chance to open their hearts.

It pains Me to watch them. It is like looking at a car full of people, My precious children, driving during a thick fog towards a cliff. They have taken a wrong turn and now, while believing they are heading back to the comfort of their own homes, are about to plunge into deep darkness without any hope.

Prophecies foretold will now be revealed

To get My children to listen will not, My beloved daughter, be easy. You must persevere despite the obstacles. Patience is important. These Messages are very precious and full of love as well as warnings. They, My children, must stop and understand that the prophecies foretold so long ago will now be revealed. These events are about to take place on this earth and the time is very, very short.

I will never reveal date of My Second Coming

I will never reveal to you the date of My Second Coming My beloved daughter because that is not for your knowing. But before I come I am communicating with the entire world now so that I can show My children My Just Mercy.

My Mother working on My behalf

My beloved Mother, working on My behalf, is spreading Messages through the chosen visionaries. Other chosen prophets are suffering privately, by choice, to save souls. I allow them to suffer My pain as a gesture of such enormous generosity by these most devout believers. They are responsible for the salvation of many. But they suffer not only the sufferings endured by Me on the Cross, but feel the pain I suffer today. In addition, they suffer ridicule, abuse and mockery from time to time. Yet through their humility they endure in silence or, in some cases, for all to see. Others, My sacred servants who opt for a life of solitude do Me a great service. Their special sacrifice of self-denial again helps to save souls

Gifts from God taken for granted Communicating the truth in a modern world, where technology has been taken to such dizzy heights, is difficult. My Voice is like a faint cry in the wilderness shoved to one side in favour of titillation.

My children fail to understand all the wonders that are brought about for the good of man through technology is a Gift from the Eternal Father. All the wonders of drug development for the good of mankind is also a Gift. Yet these gifts are taken for granted because My children think that this is all man's doing but it's not.

Gift of Intelligence

The Gift of intelligence, just like the Gift of song, is a Gift from the Divine Realm, and it is precisely because these are gifts from God, that they are targeted by Satan the Evil One. It is through his influence that technology is tampered with to destroy and cause destruction in the world. How he laughs when he sees wars erupt and when technology is used to spy or kill. How he laughs again when the technology of medicines is used not just to kill but to justify the killing. All these frightening crimes against humanity, enabled by technology, are being hidden behind the façade of so called tolerance.

Tolerance as a mask for evil

Tolerance can be the most perfect mask for evil. It is clear for anyone who is alert, through My Teachings, to immediately spot when these crimes against mankind unfold before your eyes. In the name of tolerance people are murdered, denied their freedom and, above all, the right to fight for moral justice. O yes children be aware, alert and on your guard when you hear the word "tolerance" as it is one of Satan's favourite games of deceit.

People fail to stand up for Christianity
My children, despite the world of modern communications, fail to stand up and admit their Christianity. This is mainly because of the fact that they, most Christians, live in the western world. They are scared that they will be laughed at and bullied. They are absolutely correct. They will. But heed this. My children always suffer some kind of ridicule when they take up My Cross. They can then be sure that they are doing My Work.

He who suffers on My behalf will receive great blessings and many graces. But the Christians who do fight for the right to proclaim My Name in public will suffer the most. He or she must stay strong. You are My hope on this earth. Without My devout followers, My children cannot be taken over that final threshold to My Father's Kingdom.

I love all of My followers. I am in their hearts and they know this. Heed My Word now through this prophet. Do not ignore these Messages. They will help, through word of mouth, save millions of souls throughout the world before My Second Coming.

Go now in peace and love.

Your devoted Saviour

Jesus Christ.

The Great Tribulation
Monday, December 20, 2010 10.00 hours

Heed this My daughter. Mankind is being warned, through these Messages, of the axe that will befall those who continue to reject the Eternal Father. The time is drawing close for the Advent of the Great

Tribulation. This event will commence from the end of 2012 and must not be confused with the time or the date for My Second Coming on Earth. For this, My children, is not being foretold in these Messages. Anyone who attempts to give My children a date for My Second Coming is a liar and not a true prophet. I am, however, revealing years of specific events leading up to My Second Coming, through this prophet.

God won't allow a plan to deplete world population to happen

The Great Tribulation, as foretold so long ago, will now unfold before the eyes of a disbelieving world. This is when the Sword of Justice will strike everywhere. My Eternal Father is not prepared to stand back and allow the evil plan, being plotted right now behind closed doors and designed to deplete the world's population, to be realised.

This evil group, devout followers of Satan, have attempted in the past to inflict genocide on My Father's children. They failed. They are trying again. They will fail again but not before they cause terrible destruction.

Believers should not fear

My Eternal Father, in His Mercy, will have to intervene to stop them even though it pains Him to unleash the global disasters that lie ahead. Believers do not fear for yourselves or your families. You are being protected. But please, please pray the Holy Rosary and My Divine Mercy at all times to help ease and avert some of these disasters.

Start planning now. These people, as they attempt to control your money, your health, your food and even your faith must be fought. Stand up and protect yourselves and your families using prayer. Call on all those saints you revere to aid you as intercessors of My Eternal Father.

Global disasters to strike

As these global disasters commence with dramatic changes in weather patterns - which have already begun in a mild form - they will be seen as the result of global warming. Yes, mankind has damaged the earth in a very ugly manner but these disasters will have nothing to do with climate change.

My Eternal Father could, if He decided, sit back and do nothing. Then these evil power hungry and deluded groups of powerful decision makers would win. By sucking My innocent children into their snare of hypnotic allegiance to Satan, the Evil One, they would steal souls. That will not be allowed.

Calling all religions to join together

It is time now for My Father's children and followers, as well as those who believe in the Superior Being that is God, the Creator and Maker of all things, to join forces as one. Irrespective of which path you follow God, or whether you believe in Me, His only beloved Son, stand together as one. Fight the group that represents the Evil One. He is your enemy if you believe in God, the Eternal Father. He is trying to stop you from entering Paradise by lying to his followers that he, too, will take them to an equally beautiful divine paradise. Those poor deluded and trustworthy followers cannot see through the deceit because they are blinded by the lure of materialist glory.

Prophecies in Book of John now come to Light

Pray, pray, pray, all of you every single day. Very soon all will understand the Truth of Holy Scripture. All will understand, finally, that the Teachings contained in My Father's Book are accurate. They don't lie. Prophesies foretold in the past came to light. Prophecies contained in the Book of John will now come to light. These Messages given to this prophet are to prepare My children to enter My Father's Kingdom.

Go now spread My Truth. Save each other from the clutches of the Deceiver before it is too late.

Your Loving Saviour Jesus Christ.

Third Message from the Virgin Mary
Monday, December 20, 2010 10.00 hours

Listen to me my child. You must stay strong for my beloved Son Jesus the Christ. He is too important and special for you to turn away with doubts in your mind. Yes it is easy to become confused in this Work but you will have to trust in Him completely. He needs you to surrender and give Him your absolute trust.

My child it has not been easy for you with this Work. But as I have said before you love to persevere. You will succeed in the completion of your Work. I urge you to get back into a routine of daily prayer. For it is through my Most Holy Rosary that you will be protected. His Work is very Sacred my child, so out of respect please obey my Son by trusting in Him completely. Push aside your doubts my child for you have been given special graces by the Holy Spirit. The Truth now lies in your heart, soul and mind. This is why you have found it easier to write the Messages, which my beloved dear Son gives you.

He loves you my child and has chosen you for one of the most important tasks ever this century. Your Work is being compared to that requested of Sister Faustina. You are undergoing similar sufferings that she endured. Do not fear these sufferings, which include the lack of ability to pray and the daily doubts which are normal. They will pass. All the saints, including St Faustina walk with you my child and guide you every day.

The Work you are undertaking on behalf of me and my beloved Son has been foretold. It is one of the most important ways in which you can save souls. Do not falter or hesitate. Always, always call on your Beloved Mother for assistance. I am there for you. Please pray daily to my Son by reciting His Divine Mercy Chaplet. That way you will be closer to Him and you will feel Him move in your heart.

Take courage and move ahead now. Look with love towards the precious path that leads to the Blessed Trinity. All are with you. You will suffer but consider this a grace for without suffering you cannot remain close to my Son's Heart.

That's all for now. Turn and open your heart now towards my beloved Son, Jesus the Most High.

Love and Peace

Our Lady of the Roses

My Pain and Suffering today
Wednesday, December 22, 2010 02.40 hours

My daughter I have been suffering terribly for the sins of mankind and the cruel rejection of My Existence, which is so common now in the world that the number of believers who turn their back on Me has risen to extraordinary proportions.

The pain suffering and agony is ever more pronounced as the world celebrates Christmas. I know in My Heart that, while this is the most important Christian Feast, My Teachings are not being proclaimed in the way they should.

My beloved daughter you must persevere in your own sufferings both of the mind and the soul. They will bring you closer to My Sacred Heart, only then, when you endure these trials of suffering, when you become in union with Me.

My daughter, pray, pray, pray that other souls will relieve the agony I endure. O if only I could save souls quickly and embrace them in My Loving Arms My Heart would mend. But many souls will not turn back to Me. You must work hard to convince them of the Truth, My daughter. Never ever give up.

You have been full of doubts but I know that deep within your heart you realise that these Messages of Mercy, for the salvation of souls, are truly coming from Me and My Eternal Father.

Persevere, accept suffering, be humble, patient and act with dignity when challenged in My Name.

Go now with renewed vigour love and strength to win back the souls of My beloved children.

Your Loving Saviour

Jesus Christ

Why I Became Man

Friday, December 24, 2010 20.15 hours

My beloved daughter, thank you for responding to My call. It is with joy that I communicate with you at this special celebration of My birth. The love that fills My Heart by the faith and devotion shown by all My children is very precious.

This is the time for My children, everywhere to reflect on My life on earth. It is a time for them to consider the implications that My birth represents for all of mankind. It is because of My birth that man will seek salvation. It is through the Love of My Eternal Father for all His children that He made the ultimate Sacrifice. That He had to watch a baby born, see him grow as a child, through to adulthood shows clearly His Love and determination to save all His children. He loves all His children so much, that He asked Me to live life as a human being yet knowing that I would be humiliated and ridiculed. He allowed this to happen.

My birth is a Sign to all that God, the Eternal Father, loved His children so much that He made a huge Sacrifice. By allowing Me to come to earth to live amongst you all, He showed His compassion and desire to save you by permitting My death. If He had not sent Me, man could not be saved. Yet those who rejected Me are still unsure as to the Truth of the promises made by God, the Eternal Father. There is much confusion still. All that matters now is for mankind to understand the promises and reality of the New Heaven and Earth, which has been designated to all God's children. This is the greatest Gift of all and is the Gift you were all meant to share with Him until Satan destroyed it all by tempting Eve.

People today see the Teachings in the Old and New Testaments, in many ways, as old fables. Many still do not understand that the Teachings contained in these Scriptures were and still are authentic. Because in many instances references are made to events, which took place in the spiritual realm, people find it hard to believe that these could have happened. They have come to this conclusion because they are evaluating the contents through logical thinking based on what happens on earth. But they are wrong.

My coming on the earth was orchestrated, as a last chance to wake up the world so all would realise that God is all forgiving. My role was to show you, through My Teachings and death on the Cross, the Pathway to Heaven.

Remember then at Christmas that My birth was to help you begin to re-evaluate your belief in the Heavens to which you are all entitled to be part of. By remembering My Life you can now join with Me in My Father's Kingdom if you open your hearts and ask Me to embrace you once more.

Your Divine Saviour and Just Judge

Jesus Christ

False Teachers & Prophets

Saturday, December 25, 2010 10.20 hours

I am the beginning and the end. It was through Me that My Eternal beloved Father created the world and it will be through Me that it will end. I am the Light and the Saviour Who will bring all those who believe in Me into the promised Paradise. Those who, despite all My Teachings and the efforts of My prophets, still refuse to accept Me will not enter My Father's Kingdom.

Those of you who have been given the Gift of the Truth through the Scriptures must open your eyes now and accept My Teachings and the prophecies given to My prophets. The time is finally approaching when I will return to Earth to reclaim My beloved followers. Through My modern prophets, I will sadly though still be rejected. You all must listen and read the Messages from Me, which are being given to you out of Mercy and understand the significance of them.

My Teachings have never changed You must remember that My Teachings are the same as they have always been. Those who come in My Name must be watched carefully. If they proclaim My Word then they are of the Light. When you find My Teachings to be changed in any way that seems strange to you walk away. Do not listen. These unfortunate people have been tempted by the Evil One to distort My Teachings deliberately to lead you astray and confuse you.

Any doctrine that has not originated from Holy Scripture and which claims to proclaim the Truth is a lie. This is a sin against Me and is a grievous attack on Me and My Eternal Father.

False Messiah

These false teachers will begin to make themselves known all over the world shortly. You will find them everywhere shouting at the top of their voices. Seeking attention. Some will impress My children to such an extent that even My genuine followers will believe they have special divine powers. One, in particular, will exalt himself to such lofty heights that people will mistakenly believe him to be the Messiah.

It is going to take a lot of courage, single mindedness and strength for My children to stick by Me and allow Me to guide them through this dangerous jungle full of demons. The demons now being unleashed by Satan as the last days begin to unfold will come disguised as My followers and prophets. They are now colluding to target My genuine visionaries, seers and prophets. They will try to seduce them with false doctrine. They will twist the Truth to suit their immoral ways, which from an external perceptive, will be hard to discern. My devout followers, sacred servants and prophets will know immediately who these evil people are. They will find their declarations to be painful and disturbing but what will cause terror in their hearts is the fact that so many Christians will fall for their charming personalities. So convincing will they be that many will draw the very sacred servants who have designated their lives to Me and My Eternal Father into their evil snare.

Call on Christians to stand up

Those devout followers of Mine blessed with the graces of the Holy Spirit I call on you now. Take up your weapon of faith and stay strong. Challenge them. Teach people the Truth by reminding them constantly of the Truth, which is contained in My Father's Book - the Book of Truth. These Teachings will last forever.

It may be difficult for you, My children, to stand up and be counted but hear Me now. If you do this you will help souls. Your brothers and sisters in the world are your family. I will bring you all with Me into the Paradise, which I have promised all My children. Please, please help Me not to leave any of you behind. It will break My Heart if I can't save all My beloved children. It will be through prayer, sacrifice and perseverance on the part of My followers everywhere that My Will, will be granted.

Take up the Cup of Salvation now in My Name. Follow Me. Let Me guide you all. Let Me embrace you in My Heart as we unite together to save mankind from the Deceiver.

Remember this. I love every one of My children to such an extent that victory, without bringing all of them into Eternal Life, will be bittersweet and will break My Heart.

Pray, pray, pray now all of you and remember the Words - I am the Alpha and the Omega.

Your Beloved Saviour

Jesus Christ, King of the Earth and Just Judge for all of mankind.

Celebrating Christmas
Saturday, December 25, 2010 12.30 hours

My beloved daughter why do you hesitate? Don't you know that you are being guided daily? You know in your heart surely that all you need to do is sit down, open your heart and you will, shortly, hear My Message. Trust in Me. Surrender. Believe that when you pass Me over your fears, worries, concerns and questions that I will take them away from you and respond accordingly. You must now put the time aside to take heed of these most urgent Messages for all of mankind. Do not hesitate to forge ahead with this most Sacred Work.

Now heed this My beloved daughter. As Christians all over the world turn to pay homage to My birth in Bethlehem, many will simply pay respect without real love in their hearts. Many will though become close to My Heart. Others will simply nod, smile and speak briefly about the significance of this most important time in celebrating the biggest Gift ever bestowed on My Father's Children since the beginning. Yet when My children, My devout followers, celebrate Christmas they are distracted by the pomp and ceremony associated with worldly goods.

How many Christians explain to their children the significance of My birth? How many remind themselves of the humility shown by My beloved Mother and her most holy spouse Saint Joseph? How many understand that I became man to save the human race from the path to Hell? It was this simple Message that became distorted through the centuries and was camouflaged by ostentation. Nevertheless it has been acknowledged by devout Christians as a time to reflect on their allegiance to Me their Saviour. Please, I urge you children to use this Feast to pray for all those in the world who need to wake up to the fact that they have an inheritance. This is where a special place has been reserved for each of them in My Father's Kingdom should they chose to accept it.

Time for Great Warning Decided

So caught up, are My children, with news every minute of the day that, while it may affect their lives, it is of no consequence in the Eternal Life. Children it is time for you all to examine your conscience now before the Great Warning, which precedes My Second Coming. Use prayer in your own simple words to ask for Divine guidance.

The time for the Great Warning is now decided. Be alert. Stay on your guard.

Your Divine Saviour and Just Judge

Jesus Christ

Warning to Believers not to reject genuine Prophets

Tuesday, December 28, 2010 11.00 hours

My beloved daughter you are now being given the final Messages for mankind to digest before the End Times in order to save their souls.

There are now a vast number of angels being scattered all over the world as foretold to prepare the earth for My arrival. Many of these angels are in human form and, like you My beloved daughter, they chose this role. Their evolvement at birth was timed to dovetail with the final Warning and the End Times. Likewise, the demons released from the depths of Hell are being unleashed. They, when they present themselves on this earth, do so through temptation and lies. They attract My children who are open to their influence. They infect those souls who are already in the dark. They enter their spirit by lying to them and convincing them that their belief in Me and My Eternal Father is nonsense.

These people do not have any outward appearance that you would associate with what you consider to be evil. They will appear, instead, to be knowledgeable, smart and inspiring. They will also be very convincing when preaching what My good children consider to be the truth. Sadly, though, there will be no love in their hearts and you need to be on your guard against their Teachings.

Now I want to call on My believers. You, My children, through prayer and faith have received the gifts I promise all those who follow Me. You are given different gifts and each Gift is designed to impart My Word in different guises.

Assessing Visionaries
For those to whom I give the Gift of knowledge to help you identify those who come in My Name and those who come in Satan's name, please be very careful. It is only right that you be on your guard against false prophets. However, never ever judge those who say they come in My Name without clearly assessing their messages first. You must never judge those messages sent by Me through 'outward appearances'. Because a man says he comes in My Name do not assume that your assessment of him is infallible. Watch out for those prophets who suffer ridicule or who cause outrage when they claim that they are receiving Divine Messages from Me or My Blessed Mother.

Do not succumb to the temptation of casting immediate judgment on them before you listen carefully to the messages themselves. These messages will not simply relate to My Teachings they will relate to My Word and will be full of love. They will instruct you how to live your life in My Name in order to achieve salvation.

Never be alarmed when My genuine prophets claim to receive messages about future events to which they are privy. Don't attempt to commit the sin of prejudice by judging these messages by the class of people these prophets represent. Some will lack education. Some will be the opposite and will be articulate. Many will not fit in with your understanding as to what constitutes a holy' person.

But there are ways you can be assured of their authenticity. Those who are communicating with My beloved Mother will, in most instances, predict the apparitions she foretells to the hour and the date. Many incidents will be witnessed by those attending such apparitions. In the case of where My Messages are imparted to mankind they will be given to the world without the prophet attempting to seek glory.

Casting Judgement on People

Finally My believers, despite their allegiance to Me, will still pour scorn on those who foretell future events and cast aspersions on those blessed with healing powers from the Holy Spirit. Stop and wake up from your peaceful slumber. These prophets will upset your routine because they do not sit comfortably with your holy group. They will not fit in with the way you expect. Heed this. If you judge these people based on hearsay and third party gossip or innuendo you are guilty of sin. Sin against My prophets deeply offends Me. When you reject My genuine seers and prophets you are turning your back on Me.

Yet this is exactly what is happening in the world today as more visionaries go public. It is not easy for My believers. Just remember that Messages from My prophets must be read before you judge and this includes even those that may come from the false prophets. Ask for guidance when you are considering these Messages. Authentic Messages will be full of love. Yet they will be firm in their authority. Messages that go against everything you have learned about My Teachings and those of My Apostles, no matter how subtle, will be easily evaluated.

Don't remain silent about your faith

Go now My children and open your hearts to My prophets. They are there to give you the assurances that the time has come for Me to prepare you all to speak up on My behalf. Remember glory is given to My prophets who speak up despite the humiliation and scorn they have to endure. Punishment will, however, be meted out to those who say they follow Me but who remain silent about their faith but who will, on the other hand, be quick to speak out against My genuine visionaries. You know in your hearts that those you have condemned are speaking of events to come, which you find very difficult to accept. You may ask why is My Saviour Jesus Christ working through such individuals? After all they are not holy followers according to my standards. Well My question to you is this. Why do you believe that only the chosen few who devote their lives to prayer have the authority to dismiss those who speak outside of your circles? Did you not learn anything? Do you not understand that those who spend their lives dedicated to prayer can also fall victim to the Deceiver?

My genuine prophets will be hated

Remember I, too, was ridiculed, mocked, rejected and looked down upon by the elders and priests when I was on Earth. If I was hated then you can be assured that My genuine prophets will be the most hated just as they will be revered in other places.

Shame on you all. My prophets will not spring from your groups yet you must honour them. They will be the most unlikely prophets because of the lives they have led. Some will come from poor backgrounds. Some will come from wealthier backgrounds. Some will come with little education while others will be born with the Gift of literacy. These are My chosen prophets. Listen to their voices before you condemn them.

Pray for them. Pray that My Word, given to these prophets, is not rejected. Don't you too reject My Word. The unbelievers will always try to discredit these brave souls who speak My Word aloud but that is to be expected. It is when My believers, and especially those in prayer groups, convents and other ministries outwardly reject My genuine seers that My Heart breaks in two. Listen to My Words. They will never deviate from the Truth, no more than you, My beloved followers, can sway the Truth to suit your interpretation.

Open your eyes. Wake up. The signs have commenced for all to see. You, My believers, don't have much time. Listen. Pray. Unite and proclaim My Word in unity to save souls before time runs out.

Your beloved Christ

Jesus the Saviour and Just Judge.

Media and Other Censorships to come
Saturday, January 01, 2011 02.00 hours

My beloved daughter the time has come for yet another year when My beloved children will learn more from Me about how to adapt their lives so that when I come as Judge mankind will be ready.

My beautiful children, all of whom I hold close to My Sacred Heart, you must listen to Me now. I will never forsake you when you recognise Me and the Truth of the New Paradise - the promise I gave you all before I died on the Cross for your sins. The time is drawing close now My beloved children. Never fear. If you love Me and believe in Me what is there to fear? For love is not fearful. Love is joy, happiness and for all of you who believe in the Eternal Life. In Heaven there is nothing to fear. I love you all.

Mother of God's role in Second Coming of Christ
My beloved Mother, who was responsible for taking up the Chalice of accepting My existence, at the moment of conception to herald a new beginning for mankind, will also herald My Second Coming.

I will redeem all those who turn to Me for Mercy. My Mother, sent by the Eternal Father to bring Redemption and Salvation to the world will stand by Me this second time.

My Beloved Mother, the Angel of Light, will now triumph to deliver My Mercy and herald My Second Coming on earth. My devoted Mother, the Immaculate Conception, as Mediatrix, will help prepare the world for My Second Coming. She has been preparing mankind for many centuries but has now, in the last 100 years, been trying to instil love in your hearts to ignite the sometimes stagnate love your have for Me and My Eternal Father.

There was a time when My Mother, who through Divine Manifestation would command attention on earth. Sadly since Fatima and Garabandal, few of My sacred servants take her Divine apparitions seriously. Nor are her visionaries, the chosen few, taken seriously. This time, as the year 2011 commences many, many changes in the world are now about to take place. This is because the world, My children, as you once knew it is about to change.

Secret of Fatima Connection with Future
So many of you innocent and trusting souls fail to grasp the evil that is about to unfold. My children, and I include those reading these Messages for the first time out of curiosity who may feel a gap in your spiritual welfare, listen now.

You and your fellow brothers and sisters are being led into a world dictated by the group, foretold in the last Secret of Fatima, to which you are not privy where you will soon find the following.

1. Your money will be worthless and the only way to trade will be in gold or silver.

2. You will need to pray in groups and find a sacred servant, brave enough, to stand up before the persecution.

3. You must find shelters for prayer because your churches will be sold for monetary gain.

4. Hold onto Scripture, you may never had read them before, but be assured copies will be impossible to buy in the future.

5. Set up prayer groups to pray for the salvation of mankind. In three years time you will understand why this is important.

Media Censorship

To the media I have this to say. As communicators to the world the arrogance you display today will turn to despair when your word is no longer heard. You too will soon realise the importance of prayer when mankind turns from the Truth. Your word today can still represent the important independent truth. But this Gift will now be taken away from you. Instead the Truth will now be hidden from mankind through the dictatorship you are about to witness during the Great Tribulation.

Then your word will be denied just as My Word is.

The 'Secret Channel' of Communication

No one will listen to you because the only word delivered to mankind, which will have any impact will be by the Secret Channel delivered to the world through technology. You will find yourself in the wilderness and will end up trying to communicate to a disbelieving world just as I do at this point in time when your word is not heard.

Beware of Dictators

Have no fear those of you, irrespective as to which path you follow God, just hear Me now. Fight those who impose dictatorship in your world for they are of Satan. Never be fooled by them no matter how much they pay you to report lies. They will face eternal damnation unless they repent. Though time is not on their side. Fight for the freedom to report the injustices you witness. No matter that you believe in Me because when you see this prophecy unfold then you will then realise the Truth of My Teachings.

Book of Revelation

Today in a world that may look battered and bruised because of economic collapse it is easy to believe that things will be okay. Yes, My children in the past that would be a natural assumption but not so any more. The Plot devised by the core group of organizations worldwide in every country joined at the hip of Satanic origin, are now ready to spring. Those among you, who do not believe in Me will now, finally understand the prophecies contained in My Father's Book and the Book of Revelation.

Fear not My children. Turn to Me and speak to Me privately in your own words and I will give you the strength, hope and energy to get through this dark passage in the history of mankind.

Those of you reading this Message think carefully. If you doubt the content then look around you and decide if you dare to consider the signs. Do you notice that your freedom of free will, given to you as a Gift from My Eternal Father, is now being tampered with? I, and My Eternal Father would never interfere with this Divine Gift so Sacred a Gift is it. But if man decides to accept Satan and the flames of Hell, then so be it.

God, My Eternal Father cannot prevent this. Yet Satan will try to take this Gift of free will from you. When you find that your free will is being snatched from you, through powerful forces over which you have no control, then you will know that The Evil One is behind this.

Satan will never win

Please, please keep alert My precious children. Do not give in. If enough of you pray and stand up you will save souls. Satan and his army will never win. They can't. It is impossible. Only God has the power to end this terrible conflict.

I, Your Saviour and appointed Judge urge you now to stand-up, be courageous and fight for what is right in your hearts even if you suffer fear. Fear is given to you by Satan. Fear is never put into your hearts by Me or My Eternal Father.

Put down your guard and open up your heart to love, not fear. Love comes from God. I have told you that love is not something that you feel unless you open your heart. Love and God, the Eternal Father, Creator of this earth go hand in hand. They cannot be separated. When they are then Satan is at work.

Go now My children and make up your minds. Do you want Love to envelope you through My Sacred Heart or fear? It's your decision.

Your Divine Teacher, Saviour and Just Judge of Mercy

How The Warning is a Gift to mankind
Sunday, January 02, 2011 21.45 hours

Why are these Messages frightening?
My beloved daughter when people hear these Messages they will question them, challenge them and pull them apart. More than that they will pour scorn on them and ask the question why do these Messages not speak more of joy and happiness? Why are they frightening? Surely this approach to communicating to the world would not come from Jesus Christ? Surely Jesus Christ preaches love not terror? My answer to these charges is simple. It is because I love all of you that I now show you My Mercy through these Messages. I come first as Saviour for all to free you so that everyone can benefit from Salvation. My death on the Cross was to give you a second chance to enter My Father's Kingdom. This

time I come back as a Just Judge. You are all now, through My Love for you, being shown Mercy by Me first. This Mercy takes the form of an advance Warning to help you get your lives back in order before I return on Judgement Day.

Out of My compassion for each and every one of you I now give you the final chance to open your hearts and live your lives in the way you are meant to.

Joy on Earth cannot be compared to Joy in Heaven

Turn your back on sin, repent and bring prayer back into your lives. It is out of Mercy that I must warn you of the Truth. The joy that you believe is missing from My Messages is due to the fact that mankind has turned its back on true joy. The joy felt in Heaven cannot be compared to the so-called joy you experience on earth. Joy on earth, which comes from true love, will be pure. Joy that comes from worldly goods is meaningless.

My children the joy I should feel from watching you is short lived, unfortunately, because of what I witness on the earth today. All that you hold dear springs from worldly possessions or through the acknowledgement from others who praise you. Little time is devoted to preparing yourselves for the next life.

The Warning is a Gift

My Mercy is being brought to you as a Gift. Accept it. Relish it. Reach out to Me, all of you. I am your life raft in a fiery sea that is full of unexpected currents and eruptions. Save yourselves now or face being sucked into a current of such magnitude that should you decide, at the last minute, to accept a lift into the raft you will not have the strength to climb in.

The Purification in the world continues

I am weary, children. No matter how much I attempt to communicate many of you still turn a deaf ear. Even My priests do not heed My call when I wish to reveal My Mercy. As the Purification in the world continues and increases in velocity now is the time to call Me children.

Earthquakes and other global disasters

Never fear the storms, earthquakes, tsunamis, floods, volcanoes and heat waves, which will descend on the world to help stop the antichrist and his arm. My followers will be safe in the knowledge of that which awaits them in the New Paradise, which will result when Heaven and Earth infuse as one. These things must happen. They cannot be stopped as they have been foretold. These events, however, My children will be short lived.

You, My believers, will be rewarded for your faith and endurance in the face of huge opposition. The joy, then, My children, will be hard to fathom. Those of the Light will be enveloped with the glory and love that awaits you. Those in the dark will not be able to stand the Light. You may wish to do so but it will hurt you so much that you will have to hide. But there is nowhere to go except the den of darkness, which is headed up by the King of Darkness himself - The Evil One. Is this what you want?

How Satan works through people

Do you understand the terror that The Deceiver represents? Do you not realise that he lurks behind every single act of selfishness, greed and love of self? While you live what you believe to be your exciting, fun filled and busy life spending, eating, vanity dressing and constant search for the next entertainment you are blissfully unaware of what is behind your actions.

That secret voice, which you cannot hear but feel - when you feel an urge to act, which coaxes you to seek, seek and seek more fun, thrills, and excitement comes from The Evil One. No matter that your actions, cause you to smile, laugh and clap your hands with excitement. It is of little weight. These strong desires are designed to help you seek constant self-gratification. What good is that? Does it make you feel good when it is over? Of course it doesn't. When you stop and ask yourself what if I could no longer do these things - what then? Would it matter? At first yes, perhaps it would be frustrating but it is only when you are left with nothing that you will need to focus only on keeping yourself alive.

Food will become more important than fun filled material goods. Then when you run out of food and go hungry you will realise that none of those former attractions matter. This is the purification that will now take place quickly in the world. Through this purification, a form of cleansing, you will become whole again. Then and only then will you be ready to accept the Truth.

How Satan leaves you feeling empty

My children you do not see Satan at work. You cannot see him yet he spends all his time trying to steal you from Me. He causes you terrible pain children. All the temptations he puts your way used the worldly appeal of money, beauty, possessions and talent, which are devoured by you because of greed and desire. You believe that when you have amassed all these things that you feel complete. Sadly this is not true. This is the lie that Satan uses to entrap. When those of you who have reached such lofty heights of wealth find that, for whatever reason, you have lost it all then be thankful. For it is only when you come naked of worldly possessions that you can truly allow Me into your heart.

Message to the wealthy

For those of you with wealth - I do not condemn you. Because you have material comforts this does not mean you are not following the right path. But you do have a responsibility to share and look after those less fortunate than yourselves. This is your duty. It is not the wealth or material comforts that are wrong. It's not the joy and laughter that you experience when enjoying life that is wrong. It's when it becomes an obsession and when your desire for luxury living takes precedence over your own faith and the welfare of others that makes this an offence in My Father's eyes.

Your wealth, homes, clothes and possession are like clouds passing through the sky. They are there one minute and gone the next. You cannot take them with you into the next life. It is your soul that will go with you. Look after your soul, show love to one another and those who cause you anguish in this life. Follow My Teachings. Ask for My Mercy. Only then will you join Me in the new earth that is Paradise. Do not forfeit your inheritance and your place in My Father's Kingdom.

Your beloved Jesus Christ.

2011 Year of the Purification

Tuesday, January 11, 2011 00.30 hours

My beloved daughter at last we reunite. It has been a number of days now since you have been in the frame of mind to receive My Messages. Fear not because you will need the time now to heed My most urgent Message given to the world so far.

2011 is the year for the time in which the changes - the purification - will commence and be witnessed by millions throughout the world. Although prayer will help stave off global disasters, it will not be enough now to halt the Hand of My Eternal Father when it swipes down on mankind shortly.

The evil behaviour and the filth of mind, body and soul, which is being revealed in the world at this moment is clear now for all of you to see. For those of you so busy and wrapped up in your lives now is the time to stop and see what is happening before your eyes.

The Evil One, who works through those in the darkness, has created havoc where daily murder is now so routine that mankind has become de-sensitised to the evil perpetrators who carry out these atrocities. Self-love and greed dominate your society. Your leaders and politicians are power hungry and in many cases couldn't care less about your welfare. Suicide, on the rise, is caused by the despair created by The Deceiver, the Evil One, in your society.

He, who never reveals himself to you, hides behind every act of public demonstration, which glorifies sexual immorality and grievous bodily harm to others and oneself.

The constant pursuit of luxury goods, which you prioritise over your families welfare is rampant. As you, My children, chase these worthless dreams you will find in time that you will be without food. Those empty and useless things will not feed your empty stomachs. Nor will they fulfil your empty souls, which are screaming for comfort- a comfort you no longer have at your disposal. This comfort can only be achieved through prayer and particularly organised prayer in groups.

Purification comes before My Second Coming

Earthquakes are now about to strike the earth, as the wrath of My Father's fury will be unleashed. You, My ungrateful children, who have turned your back on the Light of Truth, need to be fearful now. The beginning of the Great Tribulation is about to unfold where the spectacle of ecological unrest will escalate. Man will be powerless. In time, he will realise and accept that My Father exists and that I, His beloved Son, now prepare the way for the world to witness My coming back to earth for the second time. That time draws close now. However the world must undergo this essential purification first. As the number of world disasters will continue to rise, so too will those followers of Satan. Out of defiance they will continue with their miserable evil lives and inflict pain and terror on My believers and those who live righteous lives.

As My believers declare the truth to a disbelieving world more people will, however, sit up and accept that changes are indeed taking place in the world. They will soon, through the prophecies I am presenting to My children through My chosen messengers, understand what they are actually witnessing, because the events that will unfold cannot be brought about by man. They can only happen if and when My Eternal Father gives His permission.

Time has arrived for the seals to be broken

The time, My children, has arrived for the signs as foretold when the seals are to be broken and the trumpets to herald the changes. Evil will not be tolerated by God, the Creator of mankind and will be stamped out in the world for good. No follower of the Evil One, irrespective as to what level of commitment he has for Satan and his empty promises, will be spared unless he repents!

Love, My children, will be shown to all of My followers and those of the Eternal Father when you open your hearts. Satan, however, has manifested himself to such a level of exaltation that his power has now infected so many of My children that they no longer believe in virtues such as honesty, good deeds, respect for life either for each other or for their own families. Brother is turning against brother, sister against sister, neighbour against neighbour, priest against his superiors, Bishops against the Teachings of the Holy Book.

Why do you punish Me with your lack of love?

My children have even turned their back on this beautiful planet - so lovingly presented to you by God the Father, the Creator and Maker of all things. What have you done? Why do you punish Me with your lack of love for your Saviour? Why do you turn your back on your own needs - the urgency of feeding your own souls, of quenching your thirst for knowledge of My Father's Kingdom, Heaven - your promised inheritance? You, My children, are turning your back on your own salvation! Don't you realise this? Please believe that unless you examine your own conscience now and pray for guidance that you cannot and will not be saved?

Priests ignoring Teachings

My sacred servants, the very shepherds appointed to guide My flock have not explained the existence of The Evil One. They, in their quest to appear as modern, open-minded and practical teachers have failed to point out the dangers of ignoring the Teachings contained in My Father's Book. The Book that states clearly the existence of the Evil One and how he works through each and every one of you so that he can take you away from your final but rightful home - the New Paradise which I promised you all when I died on the Cross for you. I did not die for a faceless group of people. I gave up My Life for each and every one of you so that you can be saved.

Remember although My Love for you is all encompassing it also causes Me deep suffering. This suffering comes about because you ignore My existence. You chose, blindly continuing to believe naively that earth provides all you could ever wish for. You forget that life, the life after this, will continue indefinitely.

Prophecies given to you out of Mercy
Signs, message and prophecies have been sent to you children through the years as a result of My Mercy. With the exception of My followers very few of you listen, open your eyes or ponder for even one moment to ask yourselves this question. Could this be really a Divine communication? If it is then what do I need to do? The answer is to listen and accept the Truth of your future options. Decide what path you wish to take. Pray then for your soul and those of your loves ones.

For those of you who arrogantly turn your back in scorn when My Name is mentioned or who wave your hands in disrespect when My followers proclaim My Truth then you are lost to Me. I can only, through My Mercy, give this world signs and Messages to help guide you. Because of the Gift of free will given to mankind by the Eternal Father, God the Creator and Maker of all things, I cannot force your hand. While a message of love and compassion will always be My underlying reason for communicating with you so too will My sense of hurt and distress.

My suffering pain and hurt is intensifying as My children jump into the open arms of Satan. This means that I now have to show clearly to all of you what fate lies ahead of those who reject Me and My Eternal Father.

The reality of Hell
Choose the lies promoted by The Deceiver - the main one being that God, the Eternal Father does not exist - and you are doomed. On entering the Gates of Hell you will then realise the horrible mistake

you have made. Believe Me, My children, if you could just witness the shock and sense of horror of those souls when the final Truth after death is revealed to them you would not be able to withstand even just one moment of this torment. Should you witness just a glimpse of this place now, in human terms, you would drop dead with sheer terror of the fate that befalls those who chose the path of sin.

This pathway, which looks pretty, appealing, enticing, glorious and full of wonder, changes when you get half way down it. The changes you come across mid way shows you that you are not being satisfied. This strange empty and disappointing feeling continues unabated for the rest of the journey. You cannot understand why you feel like this. Your experiences, pleasurable on the exterior, are full of unexpected disturbing, nasty feelings which are mixed with anger, frustration, loneliness and fear. It is only when you meet your idol at the end of your journey and look into his wicked eyes, which dance with condescending amusement that you will scream until you are hoarse. It's not until that final moment that you will scream for My help. But it will be too late. There will be no turning back at that stage. You will have made your choice in this life. And although I will cry bitter tears of deep sorrow for each of My lost souls I cannot save you at that stage. Your free will, where you choose your own destiny, will be completely out of My Hands.

Through this Message, harsh though it is, I am giving the world the final Warning, out of Pure Love for each of you. I plead with you finally to hear My Voice now so that you can save your souls.

Your beloved Jesus Christ

Saviour of Mankind and Just Judge

The Warning, Second Coming Close, Chance to Save your souls
Wednesday, January 12, 2011 15.00 hours

My daughter My Message yesterday was harsh. Many reading it will say, "this is not the way the Lord speaks". But how do they know? It is because of the suffering that is being endured by My beloved children at the hands of others that I must speak out. I speak out because of My Divine Mercy in order to help save you My children so that we can be united as one Holy Family in the New Paradise. I do not want to lose one single soul to The Deceiver. It is important that My voice is heard.

Non-Believers find it so difficult

I understand that for many of My children, especially those non-believers, they find it very difficult to believe in the next life. They are so conditioned by worldly matters that, in their struggle to survive, they have neglected their spirituality to such an extent they don't believe that there is another life at all. They now need to consider. They believe that all ends after death and that the only world they need to worry about is the one they live in right now. How I am distressed for these misguided souls. If they could only experience a glimpse of what Paradise provides, they would spend their days in prayer and Adoration to Me and My Eternal Father in praise and thanks.

This New World that I have promised them is a reality. Praise to the believers who have never forgotten this fact and who still pray to Me every day. How I love My followers. But how I suffer for them too. These devout followers do everything they can to convince others of My existence. Then they are laughed at and scorned on My behalf. How this breaks My Heart.

How the departed pine for all those left with no faith

How your loved ones pine for you all on the other side non-believers! For those of you, whose loved ones are at peace in My Father's Kingdom, they constantly pray to intercede on your behalf. What you do not realise

is this. If you take time to speak with Me privately - in your own words - and ask Me for guidance, even if your faith is lukewarm, then I will respond. And you will know that I have responded. Turn to Me now children. In your own words and ask Me to restore your faith.
Consider My Teachings through these Messages and through the Bible and remind yourselves what way you must live your lives. I will, through My Mercy, reveal to you your grievances against My Teachings and every sin and offence you have committed throughout your life very soon.

Not Judgment Day but a taste of what it will be like
This is an act of Mercy on My part. You will see your sins and understand immediately how they appear to Me. Instantly you will understand clearly how offensive they are and wrong. This is your chance, children, to repent. This is not Judgement day but a taste of what it will be like.

Out of Mercy you are being given the greatest Gift of all before Judgement Day - the chance to repent and change your life before the Final Day - the time when I arrive back on this earth. I come, as you know, not as a Saviour then, but as a Just Judge. That time is now close My children. Do not fear. I love you all. You are in My Heart. Allow Me to enter yours now and let Me guide you to My Father's Kingdom. Never fear death. Death will simply be a doorway into a new beautiful life of blissful eternity full of love, peace and happiness.

Life on earth only a passage in time
Your life on earth is simply a passage in time. It can be full of love, joy, pain, rejection, fear, anger, despair, frustration and sadness. But it is only when you turn to Me that your pain will ease. Blessed are those who suffer and especially in My Name for you will be glorified in My Father's Kingdom. Blessed too are those who turn back to Me for there will be great rejoicing in Heaven.

You will be welcomed into My New Paradise. Pray for your souls and those of your families now. The Warning will take place soon. Then you will know the Truth. You will then have the chance to redeem yourself in My eyes.

I love you all. I rejoice because I know that so many more of My children will now turn back to Me and God, the Eternal Father as the time for the end times draws very close now. Be prepared.

Your Loving Saviour

Jesus Christ

How to enter Heaven, role of suffering

Friday, January 14, 2011 10..0 hours

My beloved daughter the way in which I communicate with you is beginning to change. While I have, in previous Messages, warned My children of the urgency to repent in order to achieve salvation, My next communications will focus on helping souls to aim towards spiritual perfection.

Paradise, My daughter, although the rightful home for each and every one of you, is not easy to enter. The entrance is small and only so many can enter at a time. In order to enter souls must show humility and place themselves fully in My Hands. They must push aside pride, strong will and the eagerness and attachment they have for the material things on this earth if they want to enter Heaven.

All My children who are starting on their spiritual journey towards Me now that they understand the Truth need to work hard now and understand the qualities essential to enter My Father's Kingdom.

Importance of Humility

Humility is a term many of My children understand through My Teachings. While many of My followers understand why it is important they are confused as to what it really entails. Humility means sincerity. It means accepting, with dignity, the trials, challenges and abuses you will find yourselves facing especially when you come in My Name. My best advice is this. Think of yourself as a child, a simple innocent child with no knowledge of the evil society that you would normally experience as an adult. Communicate at all times in your prayers to Me through the eyes and the heart of a child.

Keep prayers and communication simple. I do not expect you to recite all prayers handed down out of love to the world. Look up and share your problems with Me. Share your sufferings. Give them over to Me. You will be rewarded greatly when you accept sorrow or suffering in your lives for Me. You may not realise this but when you do you are saving many souls and are paving the way for them to enter Heaven. This fact will not be revealed to you until you, too, enter Heaven where you will experience the glory of your generous gift to Me.

Do not lose your temper when defending your Faith

When showing humility this means accepting what goes on around you, painful though it may be. Show dignity at all times even when My Name is being scorned in your company. By all means defend - and passionately if you so desire - but never dismiss the abusers by publicly scorning him.

Explain the Truth of My Teachings calmly. Do not lose your temper. Do not show fear of the abuser either. Be firm. Defend yourself but only by reiterating My Teachings. Never be afraid to speak the Truth openly. Do not confuse humility with cowardice. Some of My followers who understand the importance of humility and its relevance in sanctifying souls confuse this by staying silent when My Name is mocked in public. Yes, you should never judge the person who ridicules Me or My Eternal Father or, indeed, My beloved Blessed Mother, but you should stand your ground in defence of the Truth.

Sorrow a Gift from God

When speaking to Me as a child, understand this. If you open your hearts and place all your trust in Me I will direct you when you suffer sorrow in this earth. Do not turn your back on Me. While it is excruciatingly painful My children consider sorrow a Gift from God. A Blessing.

Because it is through sorrow and suffering that purification takes place. Offer your sufferings to Me. By doing so you are relieving the torment I endure, when I experience the pain of My Passion on the Cross over and over again each day as I witness the horror in the world today.

The Purification which takes place when you accept sorrow or suffering, no matter how bad, when offered up with joy for the salvation of mankind cannot be truly understood by you My children. But as you draw closer to Me by opening your hearts, abandoning your will to Me and completely surrendering to Me you will understand more. You see it is only by doing this that you will be in union with Me. And when you do, your trials and suffering on earth will ease. In time you will accept suffering with joy in your hearts. Especially when you offer this as Gift to Me.

Suffering is a Gift from God and is permitted. The souls you will help save guarantees you a place in My Father's Kingdom.

These Teachings are not new My children. It is just that you have not been reminded of the simple Truth. My Messages and Teachings have never changed. They are simple and are summarised in the Gospels and in the Ten Commandments. Just remember when you give yourself to everyone you give yourself to Me. Show love to your neighbour and you show love to Me.

Treat him the way in which you would expect to be treated yourself. And never forget that when you find yourself becoming angry with others and are tempted to do them harm or punish them in any way that I am present in them - even in those who hate Me. Inflict damage on any of My children and you do the same to Me.

In time, My children, all these graceful actions will make sense. Pray every day for the strength to live your life in My Name. Know that every time you forgive another, although he may seem like the enemy, you expand My Heart of Love and Mercy. For that you will receive eternal happiness in Heaven.

Pray for perseverance. Imitate My Life. It won't be easy. But your actions, no matter how small, will help souls.

Your beloved Teacher and Saviour

Jesus Christ

One with God the Eternal Father and the Holy Spirit

Carrying my Cross, How to Live your Lives

Sunday, January 16, 2011 15.00 hours

Yes My beloved daughter it is I. It has been a long learning curve for you and you will continue to be fed with the knowledge of the Truth through the Gift of the Holy Spirit, which fills your soul.

My daughter, please ensure that these Messages, which are a mixture of forewarnings, prophecies and a summary of My Teachings, are spread to every corner of the world. It is vital that My children understand the ways in which they can prepare their souls in order to redeem themselves in the eyes of My Father.

Spiritual Renewal Taking place in the world now

There is an emerging devotion and honour of Me, My Eternal Father, the Holy Spirit and My beloved Mother, taking place in the world right now. Although it is not clearly visible yet, this powerful spiritual renewal will help protect My children, even those who turn their backs on Me everywhere. The Gospel will now be revisited, as people will begin to experience the hunger pangs for the Truth. As the purification steadily increases and becomes more widespread around the world so too will these souls, empty of love for Me, open their hearts again.

As the love unfolds through the light of My followers, the effects of the Evil One and the behaviour of those he infests will weaken. The Evil

One will retaliate.

Satan's Days are numbered

As his days on this earth lesson by the hour he will attempt to inflict as much damage as he can. His followers will quicken their activities and rise immediately to spread wickedness everywhere. Their actions, which will be terrible to bear witness to, as they manifest themselves before your astonished eyes, will be short-lived.

Faith, My children, strengthened through regular daily prayer will stamp out these atrocities. Go back My children and re-discover My Teachings. Bring Me back into your lives. Take Me into your hearts once more so that I can hold you in My arms. Let Me guide you towards spiritual perfection so that you are prepared for Eternal Life when Earth and Heaven emerge as one.

Imitate Me, My children, in your daily lives. Take up My Cross even when the burden of doing so may seem too much. Never fear to accept My Cross, as I will only allow you to carry what you are capable of.

Meaning of suffering in this life

When you suffer in this life, you are carrying My Cross. You have two choices. If you reject My Cross, moan and are bitter because of it then the suffering increases unabated. On the other hand if you accept the Cross and offer up your suffering to save souls then this is a wonderful gift to Me. If you accept this suffering, the trials and tribulations with joy then your load will become lighter. I will help you carry it. The pain will then ease and peace, love, joy and pure happiness will reign in you.

Lead simple lives

Live simple lives, children and do everything in moderation. When you eat, drink, sleep, rest and relax ensure that it is done in moderation. Once your physical needs are met you should not continue to seek more as its saps your spirit. Penance, My children, is vital to your becoming closer to Me. By this I mean personal sacrifice. Fasting is just one example of penance. I preached the importance of Penance during My time on earth. So too did My precious prophet Saint John the Baptist.

I, by fasting for 40 days, did so to show you an example. It is only by fasting, children, that you will help drive out the Evil One.

My dear children, you have so much ahead of you. You do not understand yet what will be required of you in the years ahead. It is important, in the meantime, to draw closer to Me so that you are prepared for the trials ahead that face Christians throughout the world.

Go in Peace.

Your Loving Saviour

Jesus Christ.

How Easy is it to Sin

Monday, January 24, 2011 22.00 hours

Today, My beloved daughter, you have finally understood the dangers posed by The Deceiver when you let down your guard. Prayer to My Eternal Father, through the Divine Mercy Chaplet, is important in sanctifying your soul.

Sin, My beloved daughter, is hard to avoid. It is harder to achieve My special graces than it is to avoid sin in any form. When you have been called to do this Sacred Work you will always be a target of the Evil One who sets out, at every opportunity, to create negativity in your life. He will use those around you as a means of attack, which is why you must always be on your guard against him. Never let him win because when he does he succeeds in infesting souls and causes terrible pain, anguish and suffering. He causes friendships to disintegrate, confusion, despair, and instils false thoughts in the minds of his targets. Then when My children feel guilt at their own weakness for succumbing to temptation they experience a form of wretchedness that brings desperation misery and distraction into their lives.

My children you will always be tempted into sin. Perfection of your souls is extremely difficult to attain and requires a tremendous discipline and determination on your part. If and when you fall prey to the Evil One's seduction and commit sin, you must immediately pray from your heart and seek forgiveness.

Regular confession is a Sacrament much misunderstood. It is only by weekly attendance in the confessional that your soul can remain in a state of grace. When your soul is sanctified in this manner and through daily prayer only then can you can keep the Deceiver at bay.

The guilt of sin

If you suffer guilt as a result of sinful action, irrespective as to how grievous the offence is in My Father's eyes, don't fret. Turn back, open your heart, and ask for forgiveness. Guilt is a negative feeling. And while it serves as a form of guiding your conscience, it is not healthy to remain in this state. Ask for the graces, through prayer, to attain the purity of soul required to serve Me. Patience is important. Never let sin drive you away from Me. Guilt must never stand in the way of seeking redemption.

Remember children that because of original sin you will always fall victim to the temptation of the Evil One. It is through prayer, fasting and dedication to the Holy Eucharist that you will become closer to Me. This does require time which must be set aside.

Go now My children and remember one thing - never be afraid to turn back to Me when you have sinned. Never be embarrassed to ask for forgiveness when you are truly remorseful. But remember also that when you don't you will attract The Deceiver again and again and your soul will plunge into darkness. Darkness attracts dark. Light attracts light. I am the Light.

Turn to Me now and let My Love shine through your poor lost souls. I love you so much My children that when you turn your hearts towards Me, no matter how much isolation you feel, you will never be turned away.

Go in Peace and Love

Your Divine Saviour

Jesus Christ

Prepare for The Warning, the Illumination of Conscience
Friday, January 28, 2011 00.15 hours

Tonight, My dearly beloved daughter, you were given the graces to make you stronger to continue with this Sacred Work. Through the devotion of My beloved and cherished followers who have been praying hard for you, you My daughter will forge rapidly ahead to complete the Book of Truth. No matter how much you are distracted you still find it hard to reject your duty to Me. This is pleasing to Me but we don't have much time.

The world, My daughter, is being given this special Gift - the Book of Truth - to show My children what they now need to do in order to prepare for The Warning, the Illumination of Conscience, which is being given to mankind to help prepare them adequately for My Second Coming.

For those who don't believe in Me they must still be given the chance to read the Truth. When this event takes place, after these Messages are given to the world, people will understand the authenticity of My Words given through you, My daughter, to save mankind.

Mystical Event to be experienced by all over 7 years of age
Don't feel hurt when people dismiss these Messages, My daughter. Just be thankful that they are being given this Gift. They will understand

the Truth of this prophecy after this Mystical Event, which will be experienced by all of My children over seven years of age everywhere throughout the world, takes place. Those who live after this event will be more cautious about the contents of this Sacred Book. They will find it difficult to ignore even if their faith is weak. Others who don't want to know the Truth still need to be reminded of the contents of this Work.

Never give up My child when it comes to saving souls. All My precious children were born out of the Love of My Eternal Father. When they lost their way it did not matter. God, My Eternal Father still loves each and every one of His children.

Faith, My child, can be re-kindled by the faith of others blessed with the Holy Spirit. My chosen children, sent to spread My Word now to the world, have the ability to bring tears of joy into those poor souls screaming out for direction in their empty confusing lives.

Look at everyone through My Eyes

Always look on your friends, family, neighbours and work colleagues through My eyes. Always look for the good side. Show love to them and they will feel My Presence. They will be drawn to you and won't know why.

Through My example, imitate Me and you will help Me convert My lost children. By praying hard for them you can draw them nearer to Me. Through sacrifice and the acceptance of suffering in union with Me you can save souls. This includes those souls yet to leave this earth as well as those awaiting Judgement in Purgatory.

Let Me remind you finally that you have two choices. Believe in Me by opening your minds to the Truth contained in the Gospel. If you have lost all faith then read just a portion of My Teachings. Then ask Me to show you the Truth in your hearts. Then you will know which path will lead you to Me in Heaven. Alternatively you can keep your eyes closed and refuse to listen. Only prayer, by believers can help you then. Prayer by My followers, combined with the recital of My Divine

Chaplet of the Divine Mercy Gift, given to Sister Faustina in the 20th Century can save your souls at the time of your death.

Pray the Divine Mercy
Pray, pray, pray My Divine Mercy for your own souls and those of non-believers now. Prayer groups will help spread the Truth, instil faith in those who have lost all sense of who they are and where they came from. It will be instrumental in igniting the spread of evangelical enlightenment which will now be felt in all parts of the world as the time approaches for the prophecies in relation to My Second Coming on Earth begin to be revealed as they unfold before a series of global events.

Be prepared children at all times. Keep in a state of grace and keep your hearts open to My Teachings of love and peace on earth. If My children all followed My Teachings then there would be no wars, greed, hatred or poverty in the world. You need to sit down quietly every one of you for just half an hour each day.

Go through the psalms, the parables and ask yourself "does this lesson apply to my life in today's world?" You know the answer is, of course, yes. Pray for the strength to change your attitudes and views on life after death. Remember this important lesson. Earth is simply a brief passage in time. The only true happiness and Eternal Life is with Me in Heaven, Paradise - My Father's Kingdom.

Your Loving Saviour

Jesus Christ

Love is way to Salvation
Saturday, February 05, 2011 11.50 hours

My dearly beloved daughter you have been given extra graces today to enable Me to draw you closer. For it is only by being close to Me that you will be able to experience peace, love and joy in your heart. It is only through prayer and by handing Me over your troubles that you will become in union with Me. When you surrender My daughter and trust in Me then you will understand the love I hold for you in My Heart. And when you do, your love for Me will grow stronger. It is only when you offer up all your concerns and place them in My Hands that they will be taken care of.

You can only show real love to others when you love Me. It is through love that you will be blessed with the gifts of looking at other human beings through My Heart, which is full of love and compassion.

It is only when you show Me true love that your life will change and joy will surge through your daily life. Never fear My Love children. It is there for you all in abundance if you could only turn to Me and ask for it. Once you receive this Love be generous with it. Spread My Love everywhere so that all of you, especially lukewarm souls, can invite Me into their souls. This is the only way to salvation.

Your Loving Saviour

Jesus Christ

Global Conversion about to happen

Sunday, February 06, 2011 13.40 hours

Dearly beloved daughter this is one of the final Messages to be inserted in My first piece of Sacred Scripture contained in the volume "The Warning."

My beloved children you will soon be made aware of My existence through Chastisement. Very soon now, believers in God, the Almighty and Atheists alike will be given the final Gift before the glorious day when I return to Judge.

This Great Event will open up your hearts and you will look in awe at the wonderful Love that I show you in this Act of Mercy. Many of you do not release that I, or My Eternal Father, exist. For so many of you innocent souls you should understand that My Mercy extends to you during The Warning.

No matter what Name you will want to give Me it will be then that a new understanding will embrace your souls. Be grateful when this happens because this Chastisement will be your Salvation.

Once this event is over all those believers along with those who will convert, because they will finally understand the Truth, will form My new army on earth. Each one of you, who will have sought forgiveness when your sins will be revealed to you, will seek to spread the Truth to those in darkness.

This Gift will, My children, bring you hurt when you are mocked in My name. Be thankful when this happens because then you will know, painful though these experiences will be, that you are a true disciple of Mine. You will join Me in Paradise when the time comes. Never fear your Faith My loved ones. For if you were to glimpse, for just one moment, the sheer splendour that My Father has created for you in Paradise your human eyes could not withstand the Light and the Glory. Once glimpsed, your attachment to this earth, beautiful though it is, because this too was created by God, you will beg for the time when you can join Me in Paradise.

Message of Love for Atheists

Remember one final lesson from Me. Atheists everywhere listen to this Message now even if you find it hard to do so. Every one of My children on this earth feels love at some stage in their lives. When you feel love in your hearts you cannot see it, touch it and may find it difficult to describe. There is no scientific method available which can evaluate it. Love makes you humble. Love makes you generous of heart. Love can help you to make big sacrifices. Love is confusing but passionate. Love is not man made. It is a Gift from God. Love comes from only one source. Love is God. God is Love. It's that simple. Open your hearts to the Pure Love that I, and My Eternal Father, hold for each and every one of you. Look to Me as a child would look to its parent. Call Me and I will fill your hearts. When that happens you will never turn back.

Your Loving Saviour

Jesus Christ

Publish My Messages across the world

Monday, February 07, 2011 22.00 hours

My daughter you strayed a little and now you ask for the strength to give you the confidence and courage to carry out My instructions. This is good. Give Me your time as My Beloved Mother requested because your souls must remain pure when communicating My Word.

I must now ask you to start planning the release of My precious Warning, a Gift for every single person in the world. They must be given details of this by the end of February over the Internet and across the world. Hurry child do what has to be done so that as many people as possible are given a chance to hear it. Give this time My beloved daughter because it is now urgent. This request is not meant to frighten you. It is to emphasis the urgency so that as many people as possible in the world are prepared. Then they can seek reconciliation when their sins are unveiled before their eyes.

By preparing they will benefit greatly. It is because of this piece of Scripture that they will survive The Warning. Then they will be pure and with the blessings they will receive will then be ready to face the trials that will follow.

Embrace this Gift, My daughter. Do not feel frightened or disillusioned. This is a Gift for mankind. Your accepting this call has meant that you have suffered but not in the way you expected. Your suffering came about because of temptation. Your doubts have stopped you from accepting the peace and joy in your soul that is yours if you would allow Me the freedom to take you and guide you. It is time now, My daughter, to surrender all to Me. Offer Me your free will as a Gift and I will give you the biggest and most cherished Gift of all. Peace, joy and a tremendous love for Me in every part of your being. Come now My daughter. Be Mine. Finally join in union with Me. Give Me all your love, suffering, worries and concerns. Just release them now. Then, and only then, will you be truly free and light of heart.

This Work will require strength My daughter. You are not just what you term a visionary. I am giving you the Gift of prophecy. Why? Because you, My precious prophet, will be instrumental in spreading the Good News to the whole world about My Second Coming when I return to earth.

I realise that this news may come as a shock but you have been preparing for this role for a very, very long time only you did not know it. To help you with this task I have assigned a number of saints to help you. They include Saint Benedict, Saint Augustine, Pope John Paul II, Saint Faustina, Saint Malachi and Saint Theresa of Avila. I will reveal others in time. All are working now to support your task, which is one of the most important ever given to mankind at this crucial time in history.

Do not fear My daughter. You are more than capable of this task. Why do you think I demand such discipline from you? You still have some way to go in your spiritual development but that will come in time. I will continue to communicate privately with you while the first Volume goes public. I love you My daughter. I know you love Me. I know that it can be very difficult for you with all your pressures. But you will persevere get stronger and stronger. Your energy and quick pace of mind will ensure that this important series of Messages goes out to all My children everywhere. All countries.

That's all for now. Thank you for taking the time to meditate and respond to Me this evening.

Your Loving Saviour

Jesus Christ

Message from the Holy Spirit

Saturday, February 12, 2011 15.30 hours

The time has come to rise up now and take this Cup - drink from it for it is the Cup of Salvation. By drinking from this Cup you will now be prepared to share this Cup with mankind. You now prepare to unveil the Words of Christ so that souls can be saved during The Warning.

Do not waste one single moment as the time now draws near for this Great Event. You will have only a short time for the world to read the contents on the Internet. But this period will be instrumental in saving millions from the fires of Hell.

This is a big responsibility but you are now ready.

Go now in love and peace

The Holy Spirit

Rise of Arab World, 3 World Leaders to be assassinated

Thursday, February 17, 2011 23.45 hours

My dearly beloved daughter I am full of joy today now that this important series of Messages are being prepared for release to all mankind. You will find soon that all countries will search out these Messages. Don't worry about your safety, as I will protect you and your family at all times.

Although I am full of love for you My child, My Heart is breaking with deep sorrow for the suffering, which is being inflicted by the cunning society plotting to take over countries.

They will do this by cleverly removing Leaders. Then they will offer help. Then they will buy the friendship of new regimes until they control them. This new control will be worse than the power hungry dictators who were toppled in the name of freedom.

Watch now, My daughter the speed at which the Arab world will unite against My people, the Jews. Watch how all their allies will fall away leaving them exposed.

My daughter, when the Warning takes place, My Word will be heard more readily after the conversion takes place. This will be the time for My holy followers to unite defiantly against the tyranny that will emerge in the Western World especially in Europe. Fight for your right to pray. If you don't it will not be a religious war but a war of genocide.

There will be three world leaders assassinated shortly one by one. Remember that each one will be assassinated through the plotting of the Evil Group - the sub cultural organizations that rule in all nations though you cannot see them because they are cowards. But not for long will they hide. When control is in their grasp they will strive for your attention and demand respect.

The Warning will help save all My children everywhere. Conversion, a Gift from Me, will be given to even those who plot and scheme to win control over God's earth. If they could only understand that this power will never be theirs they might stop. But they are blind.

More of My angels who now infiltrate the earth as human beings will help show these poor misguided souls the Truth. Many will convert. Others wont.

My daughter, go spread the Word quickly. You have only weeks. Use every tool available to you. Show courage. Do absolutely everything to allow all of My children, all nations to understand the meaning of My special Gift - when My Hand reaches out from Heaven to save their souls.

Those who do not convert at first will do so before the Persecution when more and more souls will turn back to Me. This will be a very difficult time for all. But be patient there are good times ahead when peace will return to earth. My children will, after this wake up call, see the Love that I hold and will come running back into My Arms. Then when that happens My Arm will form and defend My Kingdom against The Deceiver whose reign will be very short.

This is a turning point in the history of mankind children. You will understand this very shortly. By then any sceptical thoughts you have at time of The Warning - when it happens you will open your hearts to the Truth.

Go now My daughter in Peace and Love for all Mankind

Jesus Christ

King of the Jews

Prophecies La Salette, Fatima and Garabandal now unfold

Saturday, February 19, 2011 15.00 hours

My dearly beloved daughter you are trying hard to obey My instructions to sanctify your soul and this is greatly pleasing to Me. Please give Me one full hour of your day in silence with Me and let Me draw you closer to My Sacred Heart.

You will feel much stronger when you do this. Start from today to spend this time in My company so that I can enlighten your heart and ease your load.

Today I wish to unveil to you My wish for mankind to start evaluating their lives in preparation for The Warning. My daughter those of you who fail to prepare need prayer and much of it.

The Warning, the Great Gift will now be presented to the world. All will be given the opportunity to savour the joy when they will finally realise the Truth, the Truth of My existence. Pray for everyone My child that they will have the courage to seek My forgiveness.

At last My daughter My children everywhere are beginning to open their eyes. They are now realising that the world is changing. The world as they once knew it has shifted into a new phase. This new phase will lead to a number of stages before they, My children will finally be ready for the New Paradise.

The parasites of The Deceiver will fight stubbornly to the bitter end unfortunately. Pray for those poor delusional souls now that a spark of light will flood their hearts when they come into contact with My devout followers. You, My followers are being given the graces to help convert all those souls lost in the wilderness and confused state caused in their souls by Satan.

Prophecies La Salette, Fatima and Garabandal now unfold

All of the prophecies given to the Blessed visionaries at La Salette, Fatima and Garabandal will now unfold for all to see. For all the thousands of believers who know and accept these prophecies, know that now I your Saviour call on you all to pray for the souls of all mankind. Open your hearts once more to these new Messages - the last prophesies of their kind to be bestowed on all of My children before I come back to Judge.

Call on all Ministers of the Churches

I call too, My sacred servants of all denominations who honour My Eternal Father to listen now. Do not allow The Deceiver; through his False Prophet deceive you into believing the lie that will be perpetrated in his name shortly. This will be a very difficult time for those of you who love Me because you will be very confused.

The False Prophet and the antichrist

Just watch with clear eyes the False Prophet who will attempt to lead My Church for he does not come from the House of My Eternal Father. He will seem like he does. But this will be false. Watch too for the friendship he will display with the antichrist for they will be two of the most deceitful followers of Satan - dressed in sheep's clothing. They will have powers, which will seem like the miracles of old but these powers will be Satanic. You must keep in grace at all times in order to defend your Faith. Pray for My holy servants, who lukewarm in their faith, will be drawn into the arms of the Deceiver. He will appeal to them because he will offer excitement, passion, so called love, which will be ego-driven and his charismatic appearance will be difficult to resist. Go down this path, My sacred servants and you will be lost to Me forever.

You may ask why should these events present such difficulties. You will then wonder why I allow these things to happen. Surely Jesus, in His Mercy, would not present such obstacles? Well I must permit them because it will be through these challenges that the final battle between My Eternal Father and the Evil One can take place. Without a final confrontation he, Satan, cannot be thrown finally into the abyss of Eternal Hell.

Be alert to this deceit. Do not allow your souls to be lost in this way. Pray, pray, pray for the graces of discernment so that you may see this False Prophet for what he truly is. A demon sent to distract you, from the depths of Hell. Be thankful that you are his targets. Because of your allegiance to Me you will be put to the ultimate test, the test of your faith. Never again will you have to face such a test. So be prepared. Turn to Me all of you My sacred servants now before it is too late.

Your beloved Saviour

Jesus Christ

Part 2.

First Volume

Messages 50 - 99

Thursday, March 03, 2011 to Monday, May 30, 2011

Democracy to Disappear - Priests will be Martyred
Thursday, March 03, 2011 23.00 hours

O dearly beloved daughter it is with joy that I welcome your attention this evening. Your absence has pained Me somewhat but I knew you would turn back to Me soon.

Please listen carefully. While I realise that you are busy with your life you must understand the sheer urgency of this Message. My Word is being given to you in the most historical era since the beginning. For it is in this time that the world will now experience changes never witnessed by mankind to date.

Get ready now My children, wherever you are in the world. For very soon one of the most precious gifts, out of My Mercy, will now be given to each of you. My Warning, which is being given to you will spread conversion everywhere. When this takes place, after that moment in time when the earth will stay still, Love through the acceptance of the Truth will be widespread.

Satan's followers will find it difficult to defend their wicked behaviour before the love and light that will shine through you. But although the great event, which will startle you, brings much conversion you must still prepare for it.

Accept that this prophecy will take place. Very few will deny it both during and afterwards. Yet many will still continue to turn away from Me. The Great Persecution will follow

Priests will suffer

My army of beloved followers will rise bravely and defend My existence. Yet even those who you least expect, including My Christian church leaders, will side with The Evil One and his parasites. They will be seduced due to their weakness of faith. You will find that those holy vicars of Mine, My loyal sacred servants, will have to defend their faith. The cruelty, which will be shown to them, will be similar to that I faced by My executioners. Heed this all of you who follow Me. Do not be tempted to follow the path of the traitors even if you are frightened. Never fall for their false promises. Be brave. Pray for strength.

Persecution won't last long

Brace yourselves believers for even those closest to you will turn away from the Faith. You may find yourself isolated, laughed at and publicly ridiculed. Ignore their taunts. I will guide you all and protect you, because this time won't last long. The most painful suffering you will experience will be their disloyalty to Me, to the Truth.

Non-Christian Nations will control

Prayer can help diminish some of the catastrophic events, which will unfold. The persecution, which will be inflicted on those of you who believe in Me and My Eternal Father will be by the nations who are empty of love. Love for God. The only love they hold in their hearts is for the power over less fortunate countries. Control is their primary aim. Glory, and the pursuit of wealth and ownership over you, your country and those of you who refuse to denounce Me. Give in My children and you will find it very difficult to back track or retrace your steps towards Me. This will require tremendous courage in the face of powerful adversity but win you will. Should you suffer because of the passion you feel in your hearts for the love of God, My Eternal Father, then you will accept this with joy in your souls.

Rise of new dictators

Sudden changes in global situations, which up to now seemed like trifle unrest will now emerge as all out wars. Wars will lead to shortage of food. Democracy will diminish quickly and wicked dictatorships will rise. These dictatorships will, however, be very careful how they are perceived. They will come as peaceful negotiators and as 'saviours'. In return for feeding your mouths they will control your possessions, which will then become theirs. You will have to get permission to feed your families. In order to travel you will need a special form of identification and will be asked to accept the Mark - the Mark of the Beast. Run My children. Hide. For that's not all. They will dictate how you pray because it is not to God they turn. These, My children, are Satan's armies and they want to steal your souls.

Those of you who believe in Me get ready. Go back to your churches immediately. Pray to God, the Eternal Father. Gather in groups and pray, pray, pray. Ask for reconciliation now so that when you witness The Warning you will accept, with humility, the state of your souls. You will have nothing to fear.

Pray too, for your family and friends, your children, your neighbours. All of them need to prepare. So many will then be converted when they witness the Truth of My existence. So many will not be able to withstand the shock when they see how they have offended Me. Others simply won't care. The hours are ticking now.

Ask Me to Help You

Signs, all of which have been foretold, are around you children. See them and accept them for what they are. Uprisings. Earthquakes. Floods. Climate change. They will now escalate. Money is now becoming scarce so too will your food. Do not believe that all is lost for when you ask Me for help your prayers will be answered. I will hold you all by the hand and help you through this turmoil. But you must open your hearts. Block any attempt to seduce you into joining in the Evil One's plotting. Retain purity of heart and mind. Be humble in your outlook. But never be afraid to defend your right to believe in Me.

Time to prepare your souls

The time is ready. Go now My children and prepare your souls. Seek, through the Sacraments, the graces needed to sanctify your souls. Then ask Me to take you in My arms and ask for salvation. My love and compassion for each and every one of you is beyond your comprehension. The Warning, one of the most gracious gifts I can give you all before the Final Judgment even takes place, must be welcomed by you. Be thankful that you are being given this wonderful gift. Because when conversion takes place in every corner of the world you will then be truly ready for the New Heaven and Earth, which will then merge as one - My Paradise and the glorious inheritance each one of you is entitled to share should you so chose.

Await My Warning now My children. For the time is drawing very close now.

Your Loving Saviour, Just Judge and Merciful Jesus Christ

All Christian Repent Now, Catholics Pray for Pope Benedict XVI

Saturday, March 05, 2011 10.00 hours

My beloved daughter we are united once more. You have been busy these last few days. Have you noticed the strength I am giving you both in faith and body? This is because your work is so pleasing to Me. As you continue to publish these Messages please encourage as many people you know to seek reconciliation quickly now for their sins. It does not matter which Christian faith they belong to. They must show their humility and allegiance to Me through the act of seeking redemption.

This simple act will make them stronger during the event I refer to as The Warning. Repent all of you to save your souls. Prepare for The Warning immediately because for those of you who are not in the state of grace you may not survive it.

My beloved daughter, I want you to continue to move quickly to spread the Word regarding these Messages. I have explained to you before that they must be given to as many people as possible in the shortest possible time. As this event looms so too will an event regarding the Holy Vatican.

Ask everyone to pray for My beloved Holy Vicar Pope Benedict for he is surrounded by the enemies of My Eternal Father. Pray for the priests who have never wavered in their faith to Me or My Eternal Father.

Rise of the False Prophet

They need to pray hard now as the outcome of this attack on My Holy Vicar will be witnessed by you all. Pray, pray, pray that the False Prophet will be identified for what he is. Watch out for his demeanour. His attention seeking agenda, the way in which My misguided sacred servants will drop in awe at his feet. Then listen to what he has to say carefully. His humility will be false. His intentions mischievous and the love he exudes will be all about him. He will be seen as being innovative, dynamic - a breath of fresh air. While he is driven and energetic, his powers will not come from God, the Eternal Father. They come from Satan, the Evil One.

Pray, pray, pray. For you My children need to be on your guard. You need Me to guide you now as these prophecies are revealed to mankind. Be strong, loyal to My Teachings. Pray in groups. Pray the Holy Rosary to seek protection from the Evil One.

Remember one lesson. My Teachings never change. They are the same as they have always been. As I said before it is when you find that they are tampered with, toned down, or as will be the case, distorted in a way that seems strange or at odds with My Teachings, turn away and pray to Me for guidance.

Your Divine Saviour

Jesus Christ

Words of Comfort regarding those who question these Messages

Sunday, March 06, 2011 15.00 hours

My daughter, stay strong. You must not torture yourself by reading the comments on the Internet, which prove the hatred that many, many of My children feel towards Me. My rejection did not begin and end at My Crucifixion. It continues today as a direct result of the hatred spread by Satan through My children. You will suffer in My Name so too will My beloved followers who dare to defend Me. This, My beloved daughter, is not new. It is just shocking for you to witness it.

Even those of My followers who claim to believe in Me will find these Messages hard to digest. In time, when the proof will be revealed, all of those who proclaim to hate Me will re-evaluate their views. Some will cry when the sweetness of the Truth is shown to them. Others will still question and question because they make the mistake of trying to come to their decision through human reasoning.

Go now, pray for all those who question these Messages. It is only right that they do. For those who come in My Name, must accept that they will be challenged, and rightly so. So, therefore, all messages should be looked at carefully.

Go now in peace and love. And remember I love all My children including those who profess to hate Me.

Your Loving Saviour

Jesus Christ

Judge of all mankind

Mankind is being punished
Friday, March 11, 2011 15.30 hours

My beloved daughter the Purification, which will be suffered by mankind through wars, earthquakes, volcanic eruptions, tsunamis, heat waves and mud slides is continuing because of the sins of mankind.

Only those who turn to Me, their Divine Saviour and their Creator, My Father, their Father, can be saved. Never look on My Father with fear for He loves all His children. Yet He will apply punishment to those who refuse to accept His existence. His patience now, as evil, lack of faith and man's obscene love of himself continues, is coming to an end.

My Eternal Father, God the Maker and Creator of all, loves all His children with a tenderness that parents feel for their children. But just like parents, responsible parents do, their children are punished if they commit acts, which are aggressive or unacceptable. So too now will the wrath of My Father be released in the world at this time. This, My daughter, is as I have told you the Year of Purification.

People everywhere will understand that these events are not natural. They are caused by Divine Intervention to make man understand, finally, the Truth of the Scriptures.

Pray, pray for conversion.

Your Beloved Jesus Christ

Earthquake in Europe & World War
Friday, March 18, 2011 00.00 hours

My dearly beloved daughter it is with great love that I come to communicate with you this evening. For I know the torment you have been suffering. The suffering, which you have now offered up for souls means that they would have faced damnation had you not done so with joy.

My daughter, these Messages are authentic but you must only communicate with Me during prayer or after prayer. This is important because The Deceiver can sometimes try to intercept unless you are in quiet prayer with Me.

World War

My daughter, the prophecies about which I spoke are about to happen. My beloved Vicar does not have much time left in The Vatican based on events, which took place in March. Other events now to be witnessed by mankind include an earthquake in Europe, which will shock many. But this purification will help unite people, which will be for the good of everyone. Other global events including the volcanic eruption will occur now, (*details of location and month with visionary) while war in the Middle East will involve other nations. The other nations from the West will provoke a reaction from Russia and China. All will end in a World War.

Prayer will dilute severity of these events. Prayer will create conversion. Conversion will dilute, through prayer, the scale and severity of these events.

Suffering will bring Humility - Humility will save souls

My daughter as the world continues to experience these upsetting events they who suffer will be humbled. Through humility they can be saved. All of this is necessary to prepare the world for My Second Coming. This time is not far away. It will be, My daughter, a day of great glory for believers. Keep this day at the forefront of your minds because any previous suffering you have endured in My Name will have been forgotten by then.

All prophecies foretold in the Book of Revelation now present themselves to the world. For those who do understand the significance of these events please, please explain the importance to others of the need to ask God for the forgiveness needed to cleanse their souls.

Doubting My Messages
My daughter, always, always listen to My Messages with your heart. You know they come from Me, your Divine Saviour though others will sometimes have you convinced they don't. This hurts Me so much. I understand many of your own doubts stem from a concern that you would hate to mislead people. You must now finally dismiss all such thoughts.

Surrender your will to Me
You, My daughter would be stronger if you were given the spiritual support you needed from a priest. Sadly not one of them will take up My Cup properly - a fact which I find deeply insulting. So you must now trust in Me completely. Surrender your will to Me finally and everything will seem much clearer. Pray My Divine Mercy as I have asked you before every day as well as the Holy Rosary. Also attend Adoration at least once a week in a Church. All of these little gifts to Me will bring you closer to Me. The closer you become the easier and simpler will be your tasks.

Defend these Messages
Respect this Most Holy Scripture. Defend it. Accept it will be attacked and torn asunder especially by those who profess to be experts who will seek out sections, which they say contradict My Teachings. The only contradiction will be their own flawed interpretation of My Teachings. This is where they have twisted and misinterpreted My Holy Word because it suits them to do this.

Importance of remaining in state of grace
My daughter I have missed you and your close communications with Me from the heart. Ask Me for the graces to keep you strong and you will be given these. I have plans for you My daughter. They are very important. This is why it is essential that your soul be purified and that you remain in a state of grace at all times. As your final transformation takes place towards spiritual perfection you will, My daughter, suffer. But I will prepare you for this. The opinion of others should not concern you. Those who are not in the Light who upset you - ignore them. But pray for them. Be

aware, however, that they can draw you so far away from Me, without you realizing it, that by the time you do you will have closed your heart to Me.

St Augustine and St Benedict are both working with you. Invoke their help and you will find everything much easier. Doing My Work, carrying out those tasks I require of you is difficult. Every single step of the way attempts will be made to trip you up. Anger, frustration and arguments will spring up around you and intensify. All are designed to weaken your will if you allow it.

You must bless your home and carry Rosary Beads, a Benedictine Cross as well as Holy Water at all times now. Be brave now. Trust Me fully. Finally let go. Offer Me your free will now and I will bestow you with all the graces needed to carry out My Work to perfection.
I love you My chosen daughter. I will continue to make your stronger than you are. I will guide you. For this to be truly effective you must surrender to Me in body, mind and soul. But the offer must come from you and be given as a precious gift to Me. I cannot just take this away from you because your free will is a special gift from God, My Eternal Father.

Go now My daughter in peace. Hand Me over your worries and concerns. Free your mind, body and soul. Then when you surrender your free will you will finally become in union with Me. This gift to Me will ensure that My Word is heard more effectively around the world.

Your beloved Saviour of Mankind

Jesus Christ, Just Judge

Pray for those who cause you pain

Monday, March 21, 2011 23.00 hours

Tonight, My beloved daughter, you feel a peace, which you have not felt for such a long time. You, My daughter, have been tortured by The

Deceiver and now, through the graces that I have bestowed no loaffects of such attacks.

I have sent you a clean soul full of love to help guide you. He will hold your hand and lead you towards Me and the Truth. You, My beloved daughter, now understand what it is like to suffer in My Name. You know what it is like to be mocked in public, ridiculed behind your back, accused of wrongdoing of which you are not guilty and all, in My Name. Rejoice My daughter for this means that you have now become closer in union with Me. Prayer, as you now finally understand, will keep you in a state of grace and peace.

My daughter, do not judge those who cause you pain. Pray for them. Forgive them. But you have already done that haven't you? Now you understand the Truth of My Teachings. I will make you stronger and stronger My daughter. Never fear. As I have told you before The Deceiver will never steal your soul. I hold you close in My arms and vow that should you stray I will always draw you back to Me.

You must now gain the strength and courage to communicate My Divine Messages to mankind. They are urgent. You know what to do. Call Me into your heart every minute of the day. I love you My brave precious daughter. I am proud of you in the way you calmly defended the Truth and did not deny these Sacred Messages, because you now know the Truth.

Your Loving Saviour Jesus Christ

Significance and Power of Prayer
Thursday, March 24, 2011 23.00 hours

My dearly beloved daughter it is with great joy that I reunite with you this evening. You are now filled with the grace of discernment and are very clear as to the right path you must follow.

Finally, having surrendered in union with Me you are now free. Free of doubts clear of conscience, stronger than before and ready to reveal to the world My Promise. My Word will convey the urgency needed to be prepared to open up your hearts to the moment when all will be shown their sins.

By being prepared and forewarned many, many more souls can be saved. The higher the conversion the weaker then will be the persecution, which will follow. My daughter, never become complacent, neither should you be fearful of future events. All will pass and, in its place, a happier world with greater love everywhere.

Messages simply to remind all of God's existence

Tell My people everywhere that these Messages are simply to remind all God's children that He exists. They must also realise that their souls are the most important part of their human make-up. To look after their souls is vital if they are to share in the wonderful future that awaits all. People simply need to remind themselves of the Ten Commandments and honour them. Then all they need is to follow My Teachings and live their lives as I have told them.

The reason I give prophecies is to prove to My beloved followers that a Divine Intervention is taking place. By doing this I hope they will open their hearts to allow the Truth to sink in.

Divine Love Brings Peace

Many people pay lip service to My Teachings. For others they find them boring and tedious. By imitating Me they are afraid they will miss out on the comfort they believe that material things will bring into their lives. What they fail to understand is that the only real comfort they can possibly experience is Divine Love. This love can only come into your life by drawing closer, through simple prayer, to Me and My Eternal Father. Once you experience this peace, you will find yourself free from worries and stresses.

No amount of false stimulants can match the euphoria that comes about when you become close to My Heart. Not only does this love pierce your entire body, mind and soul it enables you to live a freer life. You will experience a deep contentment unknown to you before. Then you will be taken aback at how little the world of material luxury appeals any more. You will lose interest in these things and this will surprise you.

O children if you could only try to come close to Me you will finally become free. No longer will you feel an empty despair in your soul. Instead you will be calmer, in less of a hurry, have more time to show interest in others and feel at peace. This will radiate from you. Others will be naturally drawn to you. You will wonder why. Don't be afraid for this is the Grace of God at work. When you are filled with grace it is infectious and then it spreads to others through love. Then the cycle continues.

Please remember children, therefore, the significance of prayer. The power it yields and the speed at which it travels to envelop all those fortunate souls who are drawn into this cloud of love.

Satan's Web of Deceit causes fear

Just as prayer and love for one another gains momentum so too does the hatred that spews forth from Satan. The Deceiver, working through these people who have no faith or who are dabbling in dark spiritual games, spreads his deceit. His web of hatred traps even those on the farthest parameter who may feel that they are living a reasonably good life. This subtle web can entrap anyone who is not careful. The one common denominator all those who become trapped feel is unrest, anxiety, despair and fear. This fear turns into hatred very quickly.

Run to Me, all of you. Do not wait until your life is turned upside down by unnecessary grief. Because I am always there, watching, waiting, hoping that each of you will let your pride fall away so that I can step in and embrace you. Go into your church and pray to Me. Speak to Me at home, on your way to work. Wherever you are just call out to Me. You will know fairly quickly how I respond.

Wake up - Open your closed hearts

Wake up children. Don't you realise by now that you need Me? When will you finally open your closed hearts and let Me in? Do not waste valuable time for your own sakes and that of your families. I am Love. You need My Love to quench your dehydrated and malnourished souls. My Love, once you experience it, will lift your spirit and allow you to feel real love again. This love will then open your mind to the Truth - the promises I made for each one of you when I died for your sins on the Cross. I love you children. Please show Me the love I implore of you. Don't remain lost to Me. There is little time children to turn back to Me. Don't delay.

Your Loving Saviour

Jesus Christ

Hand of My Eternal Father will now fall on this ungrateful blind world

Monday, April 04, 2011 19.00 hours

My dearly beloved daughter time is not on our side now. Push. Push these Messages as far afield as you can. The time for The Warning is very close. Tell My followers, out of their faith for Me, to help convert non-believers to prepare for The Warning.

My daughter while you may still be questioning these Messages you are losing precious time. Time is not available for My beloved souls who are craving redemption. Sin, My daughter, is rampant and spreading like a virus in every corner of the world. Satan is playing havoc with mankind. He is everywhere. He is tormenting good souls as well as those who are lost to Me. He has got to be stopped. Prayer and the spread of My Word will help. Tell My followers how Satan is infesting mankind. Not only is he present through global unrest he is infecting those who believe they are acting out of a sense of justice. He is even present in the young carefree society in their music and celebrity culture.

Save souls now by praying My Divine Mercy. Spread this prayer as a matter of urgency. The sense of panic, horror, unrest and bitter hatred that is now being experienced in the world is felt deeply by Me, man's Divine Saviour Who cries endless tears for these lost souls.

Surely mankind cannot fail to see this hatred for themselves at every corner? Don't they know that this is Satan, The Deceiver, at work? As the evil hatred and sickening atrocities spread like wildfire so too will the Hand of My Eternal Father now fall on this ungrateful blind world. As the human atrocities continue, where man inflicts terror and murder on each other, so too will the ecological disasters increase in punishment for man's sin against man. This Chastisement will now befall on the world.

The battle to save souls has begun

The battle to save souls has begun. Pray for yourselves and your families hard. For many innocent souls will be caught up in this calamity. Fear not because those loyal to Me and My Eternal Father will be saved. If My Eternal Father does not interfere now, then man will inflict genocide on such a scale that the world's population will be depleted in huge proportions.

Divine Mercy

Hold on to your faith all of you, because without your faith your suffering will be difficult to endure. Praise to My Father for granting Me the Gift of Divine Mercy. My Mercy knows no bounds and this will now be proved to all of you. This ocean of pure undiluted love will be poured over all of My children to help save you from the hatred and evil which is being spread by The Evil One. Wash your souls now in My Love through prayer because the time is close.

Remember I love all of you. My Gift of Mercy is for all, even those sinners in mortal sin. They will be given a chance to repent, to defeat Satan, to join My ever-merciful Kingdom to come.

Look towards Heaven. Let Me hold you all and embrace you.

Your Loving Saviour

Ever-Merciful Judge

Jesus Christ

Never Judge other Religions, Creeds or other Sexual Persuasions

Wednesday, April 06, 2011 00.05 hours

My beloved daughter the torment you are enduring is because The Deceiver is constantly trying to tempt you to give up this most Sacred Work. He is tearing you apart. Accept this. Never doubt My Divine Word no matter how difficult this may be for you. You will be rewarded with the spirit of peace when you truly surrender to Me. Keep telling Me this every day. Throughout the day and ask Me for the graces to fill you with joy as soon as The Deceiver attacks you. Keep strong My daughter. Never give up. Keep your mind free of clutter and concentrate on My Messages for the world. They are the most important Messages for mankind today. They are being given to instruct mankind to find the right path towards Me once again.

People are confused by My Teachings

Many people are lost now. They are confused by My Teachings and the numerous ways in which they have been interpreted. Watered Down. Changed. Added to. Taken Away. My children need guidance now so that they can seek the graces needed for them to become strong again and light of heart. This can only come about from prayer and by adhering to My Teachings.

I do not exclude one single soul in the world

My children who are converted know this and become closer to My Heart through the Sacraments. However for those wandering lost children they must start right at the beginning and remind themselves of the Ten Commandments given to the world through Moses. Many, many children today are not aware of these. I do not exclude one single soul in the world irrespective of which religion they practice.

Warning to Believers who look down on other creeds

If My believers differentiate themselves and place or exalt themselves at the expense of those who are unaware of My Teachings, then they are behaving just as the Pharisees did. Shame on those who consider themselves above those souls who need enlightenment. Shame on those who, although they are aware of the Truth, pour scorn on those of different faiths, who believe that by being privy to the Truth, and who benefit from the most Holy Sacraments, that they are more important in My eyes. Yes I receive great comfort and joy in My Heart from those devout followers. But when they condemn or judge others because of their faith they offend Me greatly.

Followers of mine open your eyes to the Truth of My Teachings, at the most simple level. Judge not others. Do not look down on those whom you believe to be sinners and who reject My Teachings, because they are equal to you in My eyes although you have been given the Gift of the Truth. It brings Me great heartache when those followers, though well meaning, dictate to those poor lost souls how to live their lives. They go about it the wrong way.

Never tell those of different creeds or sexual persuations they are doomed

To push My Teachings in a manner where you tell those who are not followers that they will perish or come to harm by brandishing their ways as 'evil' will simply render them weaker than before. Many will simply turn their backs on you. Then you will have failed. Instead of lecturing, show compassion. Teach through example. Never tell or attempt to say to these people that they are doomed in My eyes, because they are not.

I love every single soul of all religions, of all persuasions, of all creeds, of all sexual preferences. Each one is a precious child, no one better than the next. While sin will always be there - you are all sinners remember that - it will be up to each one of you to follow My Teachings and spread My Word.

Embrace each other. Show compassion to each other. Don't exclude anyone irrespective as to whether they are Catholics, Other Christian denominations, Islam, Hindu, Jews, Buddhist - even those new cults which have emerged who do not believe in God, The Eternal Father. Pray for them. Teach them the importance of opening their hearts to the Truth. Teach through example. Spread conversion. But never ever inflict judgment on others or attempt to differentiate yourself from those who do not understand the Truth.

Never believe because you have been given the graces from Heaven because of your allegiance to Me that you are better than your brothers or sisters. Yes you bring joy to My Sacred heart but you must deal with others in a loving but not dictatorial manner.

None of you is worthy to judge others

Remember this lesson. Not one of you is worthy to judge or assess others. No one has the power or Divine Knowledge to make any moral assessment of others. Keep an open mind always and remember the day you believe you are more important in My eyes than those you deem to be sinners is the day you become lost to Me.

I will not exclude any creed from these Messages

My Word is now being given as a Gift to mankind, each and every one of you. I will not, through these communications, focus on just one group of devout followers. For those of you who understand the Truth let Me remind you. All My children the world over, especially those most hardened sinners and-those who do not believe in the existence of My Eternal Father, God the Creator and Maker of all things, are now a priority. It will be up to you My followers to pray very hard and show love to those who are blind. But do this in the way I am instructing you. Remember finally I love all of you.

Your Loving Saviour

Jesus Christ

King of all Mankind

Millions of Souls will be saved through these Messages

Thursday, April 07, 2011 22.00 hours

My beloved daughter the Gift of the Holy Spirit was bestowed on you today along with special Divine Graces. You, My daughter, having surrendered your free will, will now move on to do My Most Holy Will. You will now realise the importance of full obedience to Me. In your thoughts, words, acts, behaviour and attitude. You will now follow My guidance and seek it out before you take any action on My behalf.

Finally you are ready to follow My instruction. You now need to devote at least two hours to Me in prayer every second day. In addition you must follow directions from the most holy spiritual director sent to you from Heaven. He will speak to you as I instruct him to. Do exactly what he says. You must ensure that you communicate with Me every day because I have much to tell you.

My daughter, hear only My Voice from now on. Only write what you receive from Me. Never take meanings about these most Holy Messages from others. There is only one mouth with which I communicate to you and that's Mine. Trust Me My daughter. Trust in Me completely. Never question these Messages because it is Me speaking with you. Always remember that. Now that you trust in Me you will be much stronger. Let Me assure you that you will now be able to deal more effectively with the attacks from The Deceiver

Feel at peace. The love for you, My daughter, is surging through My Heart while your devotion and love for Me fills you and makes you weak. This powerful love is pure in its entirety and cannot be compared to anything you have ever experienced before in this world.

Heaven rejoices at your final surrender. But now you will have to prepare yourself to help save millions of souls. My daughter the task I ask of you is enormous in human terms. You, My daughter, will be the messenger to the world of the largest volume of My Holy Word for the world to prepare for My Second Coming.

They, My precious children whom I love with a deep passion beyond your knowing, must be drawn back to My most Sacred Heart before it is too late. You My daughter will be expected to deliver My Word to mankind. This is no easy task. You will suffer because of it but you must understand that this now is your duty to Me. You are being called to ensure that through the Word from My Divine lips that millions of souls will be saved from the fires of Hell.

Communicate with Me properly now. I will guide you all the time. Peace be yours, My daughter. My Most Holy Spirit is now flooding your soul. You are now full of love and joy and ready for the next stage of this Divine Mission.

Your Saviour

Jesus Christ

My pain is even greater today than it was during My Crucifixion

Wednesday, April 13, 2011 23.00 hours

My dearly beloved daughter I cry with great sadness tonight at the sins of mankind, which have increased with great intensity as the time for the world to commemorate My Passion on the Cross draws nearer. My pain is even greater than it was when I was first crucified. I am now reliving the agony I endured as the sins of mankind pierce My Heart like a sword that is longer, sharper and more painful. Hear My pleas. Hear My cries. All of you, comfort Me in this deep agony I endure today. I have to witness, daily, the deep sorrow, the pain and torture inflicted by man on man, by man on children. These murderers suffer no remorse so infected are their dark souls by Satan, The Deceiver. He shows no compassion for any of you because he has no soul. Yet man foolishly succumbs to his temptations like blind men. So slavishly do they allow themselves be sucked into this terrible darkness that I have to rely on those of you believers to pray hard to salvage such souls.

My pain intensifies daily. Sin is not seen by man for what it is. At its most basic level it is a love of self. At its worst it is a love of all things that damages others through dishonesty, violence, abuse and murder. Why do people turn a blind eye when they witness such atrocities? Those victims are people such as yourselves. Pray hard for these perpetrators because they too are victims. They My children have been ensnared by The Deceiver, yet many do not even accept he exists. The time is drawing close now for My Word to be truly heard again on earth. Please, please explain to all that My Mercy is now about to be witnessed on earth during the forthcoming mystical event. It is important to tell as many people as possible to ask God, the Eternal Father to forgive each and every one of you for past sins committed. Do it right now and quickly. Save your souls and those of others. While conversion will be rampant some unfortunate souls will not survive the shock. Pray, pray that they will not die in mortal sin.

Please remind yourselves of My Passion during Lent by considering the Sacrifice I made willingly for all of you so that you could be saved . Then understand that The Warning, the Illumination of Conscience is My next Gift of Mercy for mankind.

Spread conversion everywhere. Help defeat The Deceiver by praying My Divine Mercy to save souls.

Trust in Me now and bring Me back into your hearts. Unite together to save mankind through love.

Your Divine Saviour

Jesus Christ

Son of God, the Almighty Father

Creator and Maker of all things

Special Graces promised for calling on Jesus for just one day

Thursday, April 14, 2011 11.00 hours

My beloved daughter, thank you for devoting more time to this most Sacred Work. The time has come for all of you to open your hearts to Me for just one day to enable Me to fill you with special graces. These graces will now be bestowed on those of you who have forgotten that I exist as the time draws nearer to Good Friday.

As the time for the powerful Novena of the Divine Mercy draws close this time will be used to flood your souls with a special Gift from Me. Do now as I say and pray, in your own words, to Me today. The graces I will give you will not only bring you closer to My Sacred Heart but will fill you with the Holy Spirit. Pray My Novena from Good Friday and include as many souls as you can and I will save every single one.

For those of you who fall back, even after devotion to Me, I will lift you up again and again. Never be afraid to turn back to Me if you stray. I will never forsake those who keep coming back to Me. As sinners this will tend to happen. Never fear I am standing next to each of you ready to embrace you every time. Sin can be forgiven. Never feel guilty for sin if you need to turn to Me to ask for forgiveness. I am always there.

My children use Holy Week to remind all of the Sacrifices I made for sinners. My compassion is still strong. It has never diminished for souls, even those whose sins cause Me deep offence. If a soul seeks forgiveness then that sin will be banished. My Novena of Divine Mercy will instil the most powerful graces when recited from Good Friday in the lead up to the Feast of Mercy nine days later. By reciting this you will not only save your own souls but millions of others. Do this for Me.

Your Ever-Loving and loyal Divine Saviour

Jesus Christ

I am Present in the Eucharist despite the misinterpretation of My Promise

Thursday, April 14, 2011 00.05 hours

My dearly beloved daughter do not worry you are improving in the way you are setting time aside in prayer to Me. Now it is important that man understands that in order to come closer to My Heart he must understand the need to receive the Sacrament of the Most Holy Eucharist.

Many people, including other Christian groups deny My Real Presence in the Eucharist. Why they have decided to deny the promises I made at My Last Supper, where I promised I would give My Flesh and Blood as food and nourishment for your souls, is unclear. What is clear is that the miracle of the Holy Eucharist, present in all tabernacles all over the world exists today and is there to fill your poor undernourished and empty souls with My Presence. This Presence will strengthen you in ways that were you to miss receiving Me, once you get used to this, you will feel lost.

Many Christians ignore one of the most fundamental promises I made during My Crucifixion where I would be present in Bread and Wine and leave a permanent mark to help nourish souls. Too much human reasoning has meant that I have been rejected by even well meaning Christians. These same Christians cannot receive the Holy Eucharist in its true form. The Most Holy Eucharist was given to you all as a great Gift for your redemption and salvation. By rejecting the fact that I am present means that you are forfeiting special graces, which are part of a pact to bring Me even closer into your hearts. Remember when I died for you it was to lead you to towards Eternal Life and salvation. Receive Me as the Living Presence and your souls will alight in ways you would not have believed possible. Turn back to receiving My Body and Blood. Let Me remove your doubts. This is one of the biggest mistakes Christians have made by denying Me entry to their souls in this way. It greatly offends My Eternal Father because of the Sacrifice involved to save your souls. Let Me bring Light and nourishment into your lives. You will be more inclined to accept the Truth of My Teaching after The Warning takes place.

Remember what I promised during My Last Supper that when you take the bread and wine it will become for you My Body and My Blood. Any other interpretation has been distorted by human logic and reasoning. Now understand and accept the Truth.

Your Loving Saviour

Jesus Christ

How to ensure your family and friends can enter Heaven
Friday, April 15, 2011 15.30 hours

My beloved daughter I rejoice because so many good and devout followers of Mine join together during Holy Week as one to honour the Sacrifice I made for all. A Sacrifice I would willingly give up again and again were it to save every single one of you. My Love is deep for every individual in the world each of whom was created through the Holy Will of God, the Eternal Father, Creator of mankind. All of you hold a very special place in My Heart even those of you who don't know Me.

If you were promised a life on this earth offering you wealth and happiness many of you would jump at the chance. So desperate are you to satisfy your aspirations of the body. If men were offered Paradise in Heaven they would find it hard to envisage. I understand this. For the lukewarm soul he would need to have a vivid imagination to fathom this glorious place. He will always struggle to envisage this glorious entity. The only souls who can are those with a strong faith in the existence of God. The only way to truly understand the jewel that awaits each one of you is to strengthen your belief. The only way to do this is to pray hard to see the Truth, the Light, the glittering future that awaits all those who honour God, the Father Almighty. Believers you must pray for your friends, spouses, relatives, parents, brothers, sisters and children who have little faith. My prayer of Divine Mercy, when recited by you on their behalf will save their souls. That is My promise to you now.

Your Loving Saviour

Jesus Christ

Wake up to the Truth before it is too Late
Friday, April 15, 2011

My beloved daughter you must tell the world that My most Holy Will must now be adhered to if mankind wants Eternal Life. This world will, although it has much to offer, never satisfy your hunger. Were it not for the sins of your first parents Adam and Eve then, yes, it would have been possible to live in eternal happiness with no obstacles in your way. Because The Deceiver is everywhere he will not let any of you plan your life towards Me. Cunning, a liar, he will strive continuously to ensure that you fall into sin through various means of seduction. He will find it very difficult, however, to target you if you are in a state of grace achieved through Confession and the Blessed Sacraments.

The Holy Rosary is especially effective against Satan because of the powers given to the Blessed Virgin, My Mother, by God the Eternal Father. She has tremendous power over The Deceiver. He is powerless against her and he knows this. If you allow My Holy Mother to guide you towards the graces she can intercede for on your behalf then you will be immune to his influence.

While people today strive towards happiness and peace on this earth they look for a secret formula. This is where they spend time trying to unlock the secret of happiness, material gain and peace in their lives. They come up with new ways, ideas, all of which are promoted through get rich schemes. Irrespective of all the arguments they put forward, most of which are based on psychologically driven idealism, it is simply not possible to attain peace and joy in your lives if you do not believe in God, the Eternal Father. He is the only giver of life. Without becoming close to Him you will be empty of spirit. Those of you who invest considerable amount of time trying to disprove My existence waste your time chasing dreams, which will never come to fruition. Your stubborn refusal to acknowledge your Creator, the Supreme Being Who Created this world will lead you into an abyss of eternal darkness. Many people like you who went to extraordinary length to deny the existence of God in their lifetime, by spreading the lie that there is no such thing as God the Father, are now sadly in the depths of Hell by their own choice. Don't you allow this to happen to your souls where those who do end up in Hell burn as if they were still made of flesh. How Satan laughs at your ignorance. When you deny God you are denying your right to eternal happiness. This same eternal happiness is what you seek relentlessly in this world. But it cannot be attained on earth.

Never live your life on earth as if this is the only part of the cycle of your existence, because it is not. Your real home will be in Paradise with Me.

Your Loving Saviour

Jesus Christ

What you will experience during The Warning and Prayer for instant pardon

Saturday, April 16, 2011 10.00 hours

My beloved daughter move quickly to escalate awareness around My Message for The Warning is almost upon the world. Tell those souls who refuse to pray to push aside their pride and distaste and turn to Me now to ask for forgiveness. Be clear that many, many souls will not survive this imminent event. Many of these souls are simply lazy and while they may, behind it all, believe in God, the Eternal Father, they think that at some time in the future they will then deal with their spiritual beliefs. But it will be too late.

Tell the world this event is going to save them. Many will repent during this mystical experience. They will feel a burning sensation, not unlike that experienced by souls in purgatory. This will give them an insight as to what souls, who are not fully clean, have to go through before they can see the glorious Light of Heaven. By simply accepting that this event may take place they can survive it. Turn to Me and say "Please guide me towards the Light and Goodness of your Great Mercy and forgive me for my sins" and I will pardon you instantly. Then after The Warning you will experience a deep peace and joy in your soul.

Young people find it embarrassing to pray

Many people in the world today refuse to pray. Many young people in particular find it embarrassing and old fashioned. They mistakenly believe that yes, while they do hold a belief in God, that prayer is not necessary. This is not true. It is essential in order to enter the Paradise you will desperately crave after death. If you remain in sin you cannot taste this glorious feast. Just as those of you who keep fit, look after your body, watch what you eat carefully and keep trim so too must you prepare your soul in this way. Without paying attention closely as to the state of your soul it will become weak and lacking in the nourishment needed to ensure that it is in perfect shape.

Prayer to say to convert others
Because of the weakness of faith among those in the world who are believers those of you who are strong in your faith have a huge responsibility now. You must pray this conversion prayer for the others.

"I urge you Jesus, in your Divine Mercy, to cover those lukewarm souls with your Precious Blood so that they can be converted." Say this short prayer on behalf of those whom you believe need it most.

Remember children My glorious promise. I will triumph in the end. Satan, The Deceiver, simply cannot survive. Please let Me protect you and take you with Me. Don't give Satan your soul. I love you all. Keep asking Me to strength your belief every day.

Your Divine Saviour

King of Mercy and Compassion

Jesus Christ

Even small prayer groups of Divine Mercy can save millions

Saturday, April 16, 2011 22.45 hours

My beloved daughter the time for The Warning is now close and it will happen quickly in the blink of an eye. All will be stopped in their tracks as they witness My Great Mercy. Pray for all those in mortal sin as a priority. They need your prayers for many of them will drop stone dead from shock when they see the horror, as seen through My eyes, of the sinful atrocities they have committed. Praying The Divine Mercy can save millions even if it only a small group of devout loving followers.

I will not give you a date My daughter for this great event. But be assured the time is now upon the world, as the evil continues to grow unabated across the entire world, so too will the Hand of My Father now fall everywhere. He will not stand back and allow these evil sinners in league with Satan to destroy or infect My children any longer. Shame on those self obsessed sinners, whom I still love despite the evil stain of their sin. I ask you to pray for the forgiveness of their sins now.

As The Warning will now take place, so too will the ecological disasters befall mankind. Prayer is your only weapon now My children to save yourselves and mankind from the fires of Hell. Once The Warning is over peace and joy will prevail. And then the persecution by the New World Alliance will commence. Their power will be weakened if enough of you spread conversion and pray hard.

Don't be afraid My beloved followers you will work closely together to pray for the salvation of mankind. And you will save millions of souls in the process.

Your beloved Saviour

Jesus Christ

New World Order Plan to control your money and food
Sunday, April 17, 2011 09.00 hours

My beloved daughter, tell the world that they are about to witness a number of ecological disasters now. They will occur in the most unusual and unexpected places and will be severe in their intensity. Man's sinful behaviour has brought this about. Repent all of you and remember these climatic disasters will wake you up from your blind slumber and lack of faith. They are also taking place to dilute the impact of the evil group of global alliances and their wicked stupid activities. These groups under what I will term as a New World Government in waiting are planning to spring now under the leadership of the antichrist. These same groups have brought about the collapse of the banking system and will now destroy currencies everywhere. This is so that they can control you.

My daughter when I first shared this Message some months ago you thought that the Messages seemed bizarre yet you wrote down what I told you. The wicked evil plan these serpents, followers of Satan, has been plotted for some time now. Some of their cunning schemes are already being revealed yet many people believe that the world is simply going through yet another financial crisis. Wake up all of you now. Look around you and see for yourselves. Stop trying to imply that the world is simply in the throes of a depression caused by a slump in the economy, because this is not true. These people will now control each of you through a global currency and your country's indebtedness. No country will escape their clutches. Please heed My Word. Your money will be worthless. Your access to food and other necessities will only be possible through the Mark, the identification I spoke about. Please, please do not accept this Mark because you will be lost to Me. This Mark will kill you not just physically but spiritually. Remain outside of this jurisdiction. Start planning your food stockpiles, blankets, candles and water now if you want to avoid receiving The Mark, The Mark of the Beast.

He the antichrist who will head this New World Government believes he will steal the souls of the human race. But he won't. Just as many will fall under his influence so too will My followers remain steadfastly loyal to Me their Divine Saviour.

For all of you who will pour scorn on these prophecies listen now. Fall under the influence of this global power and you will be lost. You will need strong faith to survive. Prayers you request will be answered. I will protect you during this fearsome period on earth. Prepare now for group gatherings where you will be able to pray in peace and secrecy. They, the New World Order will also be in prayer in their own vile churches. These churches exist everywhere although they have been set up in secret. They hold sacrifices and pay homage to their idol Satan. These cults are rampant now and all share the one ludicrous goal, to control mankind. They will do this by attempting to control your money, food supplies and energy. Fight them in the best way you can through prayer and the spread of conversion. Pray too for these deluded people who have been made promises of great wealth, technology, longer life and miracles. How wrong they are. They have been truly deceived. When they find out the truth they will have been plunged into the depths of Hell and it will be too late.

Pray, pray all of you My Divine Mercy and the Most Holy Rosary every day as often as you can to alleviate the impact of this devious and demonic plan. Pray too for those souls who will be lost in the imminent global ecological disasters brought about by the Hand of God, the Father. They need your prayers. Please heed My plea for prayers for they will be answered.

Your beloved Saviour

Jesus Christ

Wrath of God to descend on New World Order

Sunday, April 17, 2011 19.00 hours

My dearly beloved daughter it is with great sadness that I must tell you that pending ecological catastrophes will result in a huge loss of life in Asia, Europe, Russia and the United States of America. The wrath of God, My Eternal Father will fall swiftly on this Global Alliance who are plotting underground organizations to inflict death on the rest of the world for their own gain. They are responsible for creating wealth farms and new technologies, which would dazzle you, were they not so sinister in their aims. These people from every first world country are rich, powerful, talented and control banks, military, world humanitarian organizations, police forces, governments, energy suppliers and the media. None of you can escape their clutches unless I tell you how.

Prayer, especially the recital of the Divine Mercy, will spread conversion and by saying the Holy Rosary this will dilute the work of these evil parasites whose idol is Satan. The interesting thing is this. Many of these fanatics caught up in this deceitful web believe they are being simply ambitious with a natural desire for wealth and do not hold any religious beliefs. What they don't know is that they are being deceived by Satan and are influenced by him daily. In their thoughts, aspirations, words and deeds. How blind they are.

Everywhere they are clustered so too will the wrath of God descend with frightening force. This is already underway. They will be stopped but it will take a little time. It will not stop them entirely but it will dilute the horrific impact their deeds would otherwise have. The Blessed Trinity is now active in communicating to chosen souls all over the world. Believers will have noticed this already. Those who don't believe in God, the Father, think that these people are merely doomsday cranks. While many people in the world today can indeed make false claims please do not ignore them without first hearing what they have to say. Always pray for guidance during these difficult and confusing times. Keep your attention focused on Me, your Divine Saviour, at all times. I will hold your hand and support you through these trials.

Many people, when they witness these prophecies coming to light, will panic and will be terrified in many instances. But there is no need to fear because this period will be short lived. And then will come the New Heaven and Earth where you will all live peaceful, long and blissful lives in union with Me.

The more people turn back and ask God the Father for guidance the less the impact of the evil reign planned by New World Order will be. Go now in peace. Pray to strengthen your belief in Me.

Your Merciful Saviour and Just Judge

Jesus Christ

Sexual Immorality will lead you to Hell
Tuesday, April 19, 2011 23.50 hours

My daughter as the world divides into different divisions - those who live simple and orderly lives, some in wealth and peace, those who are afflicted through poverty and illness or who are victims of war and those in power - all will witness the very same forthcoming events in wonder.

Many will see ecological catastrophes as the Hand of God. Others will say that they are a sign of the end times, while others will say that it all has to do with global warming. But what is most important now at this time is to understand this. Sin, if it escalates to unprecedented levels will cause destruction in your orderly lives anyway. But when it intensifies to the current levels experienced and witnessed by all of you in the world today then you can be assured that such catastrophes will be the Hand of God at work.

God the Eternal Father has already responded and acted in this way. Now as the time approaches to destroy Satan and his followers further ecological unrest will be unleashed by God in His Mercy. He will do this to prevent Satan and all his corrupt human puppets who salivate at the prospects of the riches and glory he promises them through his psychological powers.

Satan instils evil thoughts and actions in souls weak enough to expose themselves to his possessive powers. Such people share common traits. They are self-centred, obsessed with worldly ambitions and wealth and are addicted to sexual deviations and power. All will end up in Hell, if they continue to follow the glorification of the antichrist who is about to make himself known in the world.

Many innocent people do not believe in Satan, the antichrist or indeed in God, the Father Almighty. So they turn a blind eye. Yet they wonder why the very society they live in has collapsed. They don't understand the frightening speed at the collapse of the traditional family unit. They put this down to the ills of modern society. What they don't know is that Satan targets the family as a priority. This is because he knows if the family collapses then society too collapses. Many do know this because it is becoming increasingly apparent in the world today.

Then look at sexual immorality. You wonder how horribly society has been infested with this depravity. Yet again what you don't realise is that Satan is responsible for every single act of obscene immorality in the world. While those of you, caught up in a world of promiscuity, sexual deviation and abuse of others will argue that these acts are a source of amusement and in some cases a form of income - you must know they will be your passport to the eternal flames of Hell.
For every depraved sexual act you participate in so too will your body, even though you will be in spirit, burn as if in the flesh for eternity. Each part of the human body you abuse through mortal sin will suffer the most pain in the fires of Hell. Why would you want this? Many of you poor deluded souls don't realise that you have never been told the truth, the truth that there does exist Heaven, Purgatory and Hell. Many of My well-meaning sacred servants of the Churches have not emphasised these Teachings for a very long time. Shame on them. I cry for their anguish because many of them do not really believe in Hell themselves. So how can they preach about the horror that is Hell? They can't, because many have opted for the easy answer. "God is ever Merciful. He would never send you to Hell. Would He?"

The answer is no - He doesn't. That is true because He could never turn His back on His children. But the reality is that many, many souls blocked by the mortal sin they have been enticed to commit become addicted to their sins time and time again, over and over. They are in so much darkness - comfortable within their own immorality - that they continue to choose this darkness even after death. They cannot be saved then. They have chosen this path by their own free will - a gift from God, which He cannot interfere with. But Satan can. And he does.

Chose which life you want. The path of life towards God, the Eternal

Father to Heaven or Satan, The Deceiver, in the fires of eternal Hell. There is no clearer way of explaining the outcome to you My children. It is because of My love and compassion that I must teach you the Truth.

This Message is meant to frighten you somewhat because unless I show you what is in store for them I would not be revealing My True Love for all of you.

It is time to face up to the future not only for yourself, but, for those friends, family and loved ones whom you influence through your own behaviour. Behaviour breeds behaviour. In the case of an innocent you could unwittingly be guiding and leading them, also, on the pathway to eternal darkness through ignorance.

Look after your soul. It is a gift from God. It is all you will take with you into the next world.

Your Saviour

Jesus Christ

Stand up against the attacks by Satan

Wednesday, April 20, 2011 17.45 hours

My daughter your faith is being continually tested every hour of the day when you are being pressurized by outsiders to dismiss these Messages. This will always happen. It is time to get used to this torment. You can be reassured now, more than ever, that these Messages are authentic and come from Me the Divine Saviour of Mankind, Jesus Christ.

It saddens Me when I see believers, in particular, so influenced by The Deceiver to dismiss My Most Holy Word when it is being presented for the world to witness.

My daughter you are more than capable of ignoring now all voices who claim to speak with the authority given to them by Divine sources. Many false prophets are present in the world today and are not who they claim to be. Only listen to My voice as I have told you before. You do not need the approval of others to continue with this Sacred Work. These volumes of Sacred Messages will be seen for what they are in time. You must never be tempted by misinformed souls that they are not Divinely inspired, because that is not the case. Block out the lies that will assail your ears by The Deceiver, Satan, he, My daughter, wants to stop this Work and will do everything to prevent you from fulfilling this Mission.

Rise now and speak with the authority of the Holy Spirit, which has been bequeathed to you My precious daughter. You are a chosen messenger to deliver, as I have said, the most important Messages for mankind in these times. You make Me so happy with the strength and courage you have shown in the face of the attacks you have had to endure at the hands of Satan. Remember though you must accept this work with the humility expected of you. Receive Me in your soul now everyday for extra graces. I love you My daughter. Heaven rejoices at the speed of your response to My Most Holy will.

Your Saviour

Jesus Christ

Defend your children's right to a Christian Education

Saturday, April 23, 2011 00.05 hours

My beloved daughter today is the time for all those who believe in the Passion of the Cross to help carry it so that My Word can be heard once again in the world. Remind them how I died and why this represents Salvation. It is your duty now to inform those who have lost their way to open their hearts again to the Truth of My Teachings.

Stand up now and defend your rights to be Christians. While I expect tolerance on your part - where you must respect the views of other faiths - never insult Me by pushing your Christianity aside into second place. It is a dangerous doctrine when you mistake tolerance as a substitute for the Truth. Be open to other faiths and treat your brothers and sister equally. However, never feel pressurised into pushing aside your beliefs or denying your children the right to a Christian education. Many schools run by Christian organisations are bowing to pressures to abandon their allegiance to Me. Many governments are trying to ban Christianity with the spread of new laws. Yet you will find that other non-Christian religions will be treated less harshly. Instead, any religion will be tolerated more favourably than Christianity.

Fight for your faith now. Pray for conversion. Pray that those regimes who oppress your right to be a Christian show more tolerance. Failure to withstand these pressures will result in a barren world when fewer Christians will practice their faith.

Take up the cross from today and show example to others. Never be ashamed of the Cross.

Your Loving Saviour

Jesus Christ

King of Mankind

Pledge your allegiance to My Divine Mercy

Sunday, April 24, 2011 16.40 hours

My dearly beloved daughter it is with joy that My children now rejoice in the commemoration of My Rising. This year is important because it marks the beginning of the New Era of Enlightenment due to commence in the world shortly.

My great gift of Mercy will bring huge relief to believers and create a vast sense of euphoria among those non-believers who will convert. When they discover the truth they will be light of heart and they will be filled with love for God, the Eternal Father and Me, your Divine Saviour. Even non-Christians will understand the Truth of My existence. Finally this will create a great sense of joy and love in the world.

The Warning must be followed by prayer

It is important, however, to remember one important lesson regarding The Warning. This great event, when all of you will see not only your sins as I see them but will understand the truth about the next life, must be followed by prayer.

Sadly many will fall back into sin afterwards. Now is the time to prepare to avoid this situation by praying My Divine Mercy Chaplet every day of your lives. By getting into the habit of praying this powerful prayer you will retain the level of conversion and faith which will sweep the world thereafter.

Rejoice, pray and thank Me, your Divine Saviour, for this great Mercy. Kneel and give praise to God, the Father, for the Gift of My Sacrifice. Prayer will help dilute the impact of the persecution by the New World global alliance, which will follow. If enough of you remain loyal to Me, My Teachings and continue to pray as well as receive the Sacraments you can change the course of events, which would follow.

How powerful My Divine Mercy is. So many of you still do not understand the significance of it. Many, sadly have never heard of it before.

For those of you loyal to Me now I must make a very special request of you. I do not want to see any of My children destroyed. This is why The Warning is being given to you. This will show every one of you, including the sceptics amongst you, what will actually happen during the Final Judgment. So to help Me save each soul I want you to pledge your own gift to help Me win over souls.

Create Divine Mercy prayer groups all over the world and use this prayer for every person known to you who may be dying for I will guarantee their salvation if you do. Gather now My people. Follow your Saviour. Pray as you have never prayed before and then more souls will be saved. Then you will all become part of the New World I promised you when Heaven and Earth merge as one. This glorious future is for all of you. Rather than fear this great change open your minds, hearts and souls to the great joy ahead. By merging as one great powerful group all over the world, in each country, in every family, in every church and in every community you will make a great difference.

Your prayers will help prevent much of the persecution, which will happen as foretold. So out of deference to Me, your Ever-Loving Saviour, follow Me now.

I live in each on each of you. I know what is contained in your hearts and souls. By giving Me your pledge of mercy for your brothers and sisters you will receive special graces.

Your Divine King of Mercy and Just Judge

Jesus Christ

Convert others at every opportunity

Sunday, April 24, 2011 20.30 hours

My dearly beloved daughter today is significant in that My rising from the dead has fulfilled My promises to man, that by rising I will help lift all of you towards the Light of Heaven. Rise now all of you and come towards Me and your own salvation.

My children you must convert others at every opportunity. The more you explain and the more you show those weak souls the love in your heart, then the final outcome will be achieved when you convert another soul.

I will shower you with great blessings. This is a very special gift from Me and represents an act of great mercy on your part.

Conversion, My children will save souls. When a conversion takes place this then spreads to those friends and acquaintances of the person who has been converted. Conversion spreads conversion. No matter if you are laughed at or treated as if you are speaking nonsense. It takes much bravery on your part My beloved loyal followers. But each time you stand up and explain My Teachings to others, people will listen. While some may smile at you and appear not to take you seriously, deep down many will listen to what you have to say.

When the Holy Spirit works through you during your work, the recipient will feel a tug at their heart. Yet they won' know why. Then you will draw them closer.

Some people will be slow to respond. But be patient. They will begin to yield by degrees. First they will ask you a question. This will usually relate to whether something is right or whether it is wrong. It will be then that the conversion takes root. Never give up spreading the truth of My teaching. This does not have to be done like a preacher. Rather it can be very subtle. Convert others in your every day lives through ordinary conversation. This way people will be more receptive.

My children you will feel shocked, however, at other people's reaction especially those who are living their lives in denial and darkness. Their response will be aggressive and mocking in tone. You will be asked whether you really believe in such rubbish. Then you will be scolded and insulted. Your intelligence will be called into question. You will be accused of turning to religion because of personal difficulties. You will feel embarrassed from time to time and may find it hard to defend yourself. Stay silent in such situations. Then simply ask questions from time to time.

Ask such souls "Why do you feel like this"? The more questions you ask of them the more these people will begin to evaluate their own answers. You will not convince everyone of the truth. However every attempt on your part will raise you up in My eyes.

Go now My children. Convert in My Name and you will be bestowed with many, many graces.

Your beloved Saviour

Jesus Christ

Arab uprising will spark global unrest - Italy will trigger fall out

Tuesday, April 26, 2011 20.10 hours

My dearly beloved daughter the tears I shed for all My beloved tortured children in the world who are the victims of violence and abuse are never ending. My poor precious children are suffering everywhere all over the world and especially in the Arab world. How I agonise over their suffering, those poor helpless souls. Please pray for them My daughter by offering up your own suffering for them.

The atrocities being committed in the Arab world will sadly continue, as more Arab nations will be embroiled in a series of conflicts. The time for the first of the assassinations I spoke to you about last February will take place shortly. The Arab World uprising will spark unrest indirectly in every corner of the world.

Italy will be instrumental in the fallout which will trigger the involvement of global powers in a war - all these events are inevitable but prayer can ease suffering. Pray My daughter that people will turn to Me and ask Me for help and guidance through these times of turmoil.

I do not want to see My children suffer. But suffer they will until the

Truth is revealed during The Warning. Pray now for those misguided dictators who kill innocent souls.

I call on My sacred servants around the world to accept that the prophecies predicted in the Book of Revelation are now unfolding. Spread the Truth of My Teachings and save your flock before time runs out. Go now. Do your duty to Me. I call on those of you who have watered down My Teachings to stop now. Look into your hearts and tell My people the truth that they cannot, and will not, be saved until they seek forgiveness for their sins. They must humble themselves in My eyes and ask Me to give them the gift of redemption.

You, My sacred servants, must now play the role for which you were chosen. Be brave. Preach the Truth.

Your Loving Saviour

Jesus Christ

Humility necessary to enter Heaven

Friday, April 29, 2011 15.15 hours

My dearly beloved daughter, humility is a lesson, which all those who wish to enter My Kingdom must learn.

Humility declares your littleness in My Eyes where you revere Me, your Saviour the Son of God made man. Without it pride gets in the way. That is of no use if you want to declare yourself fit for My Kingdom.

In today's world humility is not acceptable in an era where assertiveness and a desire to succeed in bettering yourselves, ahead of others, is deemed an admirable trait. Those who do not exalt themselves or push ahead with confidence and arrogance in the world are ignored. Their trait of humility and generosity towards others is considered a weakness - they are not worth bothering about to be included in their company. Yet the opposite virtue to pride is the key to entering the Kingdom of Heaven. So what is considered to be a successful approach to developing the key to wealth and riches in this life is precisely the formula that will lead you to darkness after death.

Humility, where you accept that you must serve your Maker and Creator first, is what is truly important. By declaring your nothingness you proclaim the Glory of God.

Humility is a virtue which is not only precious in My eyes but which is an important part of your spiritual development. It means placing others before yourself for the Glory of God. Yet it is so easy to fall into a state of pride so quickly.

Warning to Chosen Souls

Take those who have worked hard to develop their spiritual lives to please Me. Then consider those fortunate souls who have been given gifts where, through the Power of the Holy Spirit, act as visionaries in the world. Very often, having attained these graces they subtly begin to consider themselves to be more special than their brothers or sisters. They boast of the gifts they possess. Then they become selective as to how they share these gifts. Their self-glory then affects their ability to impart the Truth. What they have forgotten is that all the gifts they are given come from Me. I love everyone. They are given these gifts to share. Just as I give these gifts to such chosen souls for the good of others so, too, can I take them away.

Self-glory prevents you from truly following My steps. Learn to be humble, patient and devoid of pride. If you work towards humility you will be given a special place in My Heart. While I select certain people as chosen souls they should consider this a gift. They must never think they are more important in My eyes, because I love everyone. Yet I will reward good work once humility is shown to Me and your brothers and sisters.

Your Loving Saviour

Jesus Christ.

People all over the world share the same traits
Saturday, April 30, 2011

I rejoice tonight My beloved daughter because of the way in which you obey Me. Your obedience in attending daily Mass and receiving the Most Holy Eucharist is pleasing to Me. You are becoming stronger now in mind and spirit to respond quickly to My most Holy Will. You still have much work to do to prepare your soul, My daughter, towards the perfection that is required of you. Never fear because I am guiding you every step of the way.

My daughter, how I love sinners, how I yearn for their allegiance to Me. I look and I see people with friends and family happy with laughter in the home and I am filled with joy because My Spirit is present there. Then I look into other homes and I see disarray, sadness, anger and in some cases evil in the form of abuse. And I cry. Because I know that Satan is present in that home. Then I watch and see groups of friends working together for the good of others in their day-to-day life and I am pleased. I then look at other groups working feverishly for the good of themselves with just one motive. That is to generate huge amounts of power and wealth. All their actions have one goal, to look after themselves. And this is usually at the expense of others. Then I weep because I know they are in darkness. And then I watch, with fascination, the intelligent educated groups who want to convince the world that God, My Eternal Father, does not exist. They rant and present sophisticated arguments as they arrogantly deny Me too. To then witness believers, of lukewarm faith, be sucked into this den of darkness breaks My Heart, so many, many groups with diverse interests, goals, aims. Very few, sadly, invest the time in communicating with God, the Eternal Father.

Faith has deserted many millions of people in the world today. The result is that many people feel confused, don't know what goals to aspire to, nor look for guidance from My sacred servants.

This whirlpool of confusion will continue unless My children call on Me to help them. Pray for all My children everywhere. Look around you and you will see that people all around the world are the same. They may be of different nationalities, speak in different tongues and have different coloured skin. They do, however, share similar traits. Some are happy, some suffer, others, are full of love, while others are angry and violent. Most people have a sense of humour and experience this at some stage in their lives. So when you look at your own family and friends you will see the very same similarities.

So if you feel the need to pray for those closest to you then I urge you to consider your brothers and sisters in every corner of the world. All of you are My children. By praying the Divine Mercy for all My children everywhere you, My followers, can save mankind from the darkness of Hell. The power of this prayer will guarantee that My Mercy will cover everyone around the world.
Let Me take all of you to My Paradise. Don't call Me to suffer should I have to leave any of you in the hands of Satan.

Pray, Pray My Divine Mercy at 3:00 P.M. every single day and you can save the world.

Your Ever Merciful Jesus Christ

Russia & China to cause disruption

Sunday, May 01, 2011 21.00 hours

My dearly beloved daughter tell the world that preparations are now underway to prepare souls for the New Paradise on earth which I have promised.

The date for My Second Coming on earth is not for your knowing. Be assured though that My promises will always be fulfilled. No one can stop My great Act of Mercy to redeem mankind. Satan does not have this power. He, the Deceiver, is to be destroyed My daughter and cannot survive. His time is very short now. I warn those who follow him through sin that they have few chances remaining to redeem themselves. They must turn away now from sin if they want to be saved. Those of you followers who may have a family member or special friend who are following a path of sin then it is your duty to try and open their eyes to the truth.

Prepare now to avoid taking the Mark of the Beast

Many events both on earth and in the Heavens are now about to take place, which will turn the course of history. Prepare all of you during this time. I have told you before that money will be scare so please try to prepare your families for survival so you won't have to accept the Mark. Please do not ignore My pleas.

Prayer groups are vital now to protect yourselves and save the world from the persecution of global political, banking and so called Human Rights Organisations. Their goal is one of power and control over you My children, although many of you cannot see this. You will though in time. And that time is close. Start preparing for your future survival now and keep in prayer for I will offer My special graces for protection to all of you. Please do not be frightened for all that will really matter will be your allegiance to Me.

As the One World Order takes control of the Middle East you will be astonished at how many countries will be under their control, how many innocent souls will believe that these new regimes will offer them freedom. But this will not be the case.

Russia & China to cause disruption

Watch now as Russia and China become the third entity to cause disruption. Very soon now those of you who have given control of your countries to faceless groups who treat you like puppets will soon see the sinister groups these political forces, not of God, try to dictate how you live. Defend yourselves through prayer. Every day and every hour I will ease your suffering. Receive Me in the Holy Eucharist and you will gain a strength that will sustain you to extraordinary levels during this persecution.

I, Jesus Christ, do not wish to cause panic in your lives. But I cannot stand to the side and not warn you of these events. Out of My Mercy I am giving you a chance to prepare not just for your spiritual welfare but for the livelihoods of your families. To avoid the Mark please prepare carefully.

The Warning will without question, ease any such persecutions because so many will be converted. Pray, pray now for all global conversion and to dilute any torment that will evolve during the reign of the antichrist and the False Prophet.

Your beloved Saviour

Jesus Christ

Satan is wreaking havoc in the world but his days are short now

Wednesday, May 04, 2011 20.45 hours

My dearly beloved daughter it is now with great urgency that the world and all those asleep to the Truth of My Teachings must listen to My Holy Word. As the turmoil will continue to escalate in the world you must now stop and contemplate on the Scriptures - what you have been told about the changes, which will be witnessed on earth if sin continues.

Even for those of you who doubt the existence of God, the Eternal Father, or Me your Divine Saviour, will see sin being committed daily on front of your eyes. Whether this occurs during your personal encounters in every day life, in newspapers, broadcast media or the Internet it is hard to ignore. Even those of you who are tolerant in your acceptance of sin are shocked at the levels of depravity you are forced to witness.

What do you see? What shocks you the most? Is it the vicious violence you are privy to on television viewed from the comfort of your own home? The murders, which are carried out and condoned by governments in the name of justice? Or is it the depravity displayed by obscene pornography, which is presented as art? Is it the lies proclaimed by deceitful fraudsters behind the legal system where they can afford to buy their freedom from punishment? Could it be the hatred shown by man against strangers they meet on the street? Is it the terror felt by ordinary citizens at the hands of their own government? There are so many grievances against the Laws of Moses, The Commandments, being enacted now that it is impossible to fathom all, so much, at once.

Law and order has disappeared. Love and generosity shown by neighbour, to neighbour is disappearing quickly. Even those faithful servants of Mine who act in the Name of God are no longer leading their flock.

This chaos is caused by the King of Deceit, Satan, the Evil One who goes to great lengths to hide his identity from mankind. A coward, he works using his powers to seduce. Make no mistake for he has powers, which he uses to destroy mankind. He turns man against man. Brother against brother. Neighbour against neighbour. And all with one goal. That is to quickly wreak havoc in as fast a period as he can. He will never stop tormenting you, My children. Face up to his reality. Accept his existence. For non-believers it is only when you finally understand the truth of Satan's existence that the truth will sink in, and that is that God, the Eternal Father really does exist.

Just remember that Satan's days are numbered. Don't let him win. Pray for all those in the world so they don't fall into the trap of hatred that he lays down to ensnare God's children. He does this, not just out of hatred for you, My children, but for the hatred he feels towards Me, Jesus Christ and My Eternal Father. He will not rest until he causes the maximum damage.

Pray, pray, pray that his strength will diminish. Especially pray the Holy Rosary for that is the prayer that will crush Satan.

When I return to Earth remember there will be only one path to eternity and that is the one you need to walk down towards Me.

Your beloved Saviour

Jesus Christ

Atrocities of My Crucifixion not revealed to Man in the way they should have been

Saturday, May 07, 2011 09.50 hours

My beloved daughter you must now gather My Cross and help Me carry it on the journey, which I have mapped out for you. My precious daughter, how you have suffered these past few weeks. I allowed this to happen because it has brought you closer to My Sacred Heart.

Many souls are called to impart My Messages to the world. It will be only through the voluntary purification on the part of the soul that will determine the quality of the discernment. In other words, if the soul I chose to communicate My Word to is pure then the Messages will have more impact. They will have a more lasting impression on the soul. They will be full of compassion, yet they will reveal the truth of My Teachings in its raw format.

I have no time for the niceties expected by man who is conditioned to hear My Word in a certain way - in a dumbed down version. Even My Passion, the Cross, and the atrocities committed by man at My Crucifixion have not been revealed to the world in the way in which they were meant to be. So few of you, My children, understand the appalling treatment of Me, your Divine Saviour, at the hands of man. This treatment of Me today, where I am mocked, laughed at, cursed, ignored and abused is still evident. My death paved the way to save your souls from eternal damnation. This is still the case. Don't throw away the gift of salvation for without accepting the Truth you cannot be saved.

Hear this. I am the Truth. I am the key to your salvation. On your deathbed, even if you have ignored Me, My Teachings, denied My real existence, turn to Me and ask for redemption. It is never too late to turn to Me and ask Me to hold your hand and let Me lead you to My Father's Heavenly Kingdom. But you can only do this while you are alive on this earth. This is your only chance to be offered Eternal Life. It will be too late afterwards.

Your beloved Divine Saviour

Jesus Christ

The Holy Spirit has now been poured out over the entire world

Tuesday, May 10, 2011 16.00 hours

My daughter tell the world that a significant Act of My Mercy took place today where the Holy Spirit, one of the greatest gifts to My children, has been poured out over the entire world. This gift is essential in helping mankind to prepare for The Warning. Infused with the power of the Holy Spirit, My sacred servants and followers will be strengthened considerably in their love for Me and My Eternal Father.

This gift of life will bring new impetus into your jaded lukewarm souls, which are screaming for enlightenment. This has been foretold and all, including the most hardened of sinners, will benefit.

My Mercy, as I have said, knows no bounds. Filled now with the Spirit of light and holiness you, all My followers everywhere, must be brave now and proclaim My Word to all you come into contact with. Dismiss the scorn you may experience for it is too important now to ignore My pleas for conversion.

Hear My prayer now to give you the encouragement you need

"Fill me now O Lord with the Gift of the Holy Spirit to carry your most Holy Word to sinners who I must help save in Your Name. Help me to cover them, through my prayers, with your Precious Blood so that they can be drawn to your Sacred Heart. Give me the gift of the Holy Spirit so that these poor souls can revel in your New Paradise."

Say this prayer every day after you recite My Divine Mercy and you, through your allegiance to Me, will help save My children.

Save Me from the torment I suffer in My Heart as I watch with so much sorrow at the way in which My Holy Name is received in the world today. Not content with denying Me, many, many souls react with anger if you, My loyal followers, even dare to mention what I stand for. They are very angry because The Deceiver so cleverly twists their minds to turn away from the Truth. Help these souls all of you. Pray and ask Me now for the strength you will need in this work.

Special Graces for those who spread conversion

For all of you who spread conversion special graces will be given to you and a very special place will be reserved for you in My Father's Kingdom. Go now and allow the Holy Spirit to flood your souls to help Me save mankind.

I love all of you. Each of you holds a place in My Sacred Heart. Not one of you, sinners included, will be excluded from My battle to save souls.

Your Loving Saviour

Jesus Christ

King of Mercy

Note: Final comment by Our Lord Jesus Christ to Maria given at the end of this Message.

"My daughter this event is significant. It will save many souls before The Warning takes place and will continue to be present in the world afterwards to help prevent sinners from falling back. It has been predicted, My daughter, and represents great news. But My followers must work hard now to help Me lead the Battle for Souls."

Message from Virgin Mary regarding protection of Saints

Wednesday, May 11, 2011 22.30 hours

My child you are now becoming much closer to my precious Son's Heart. Your journey has been difficult yet it took place over such a short period of time. It was by the command of God the Father that I was sent to communicate to you your calling for this work. Your response was immediate. You never hesitated. For that is the power of the love you have for me your Blessed Mother. I have guided and coaxed you towards this very special calling. Please keep turning to me, your Beloved Mother, each day for daily guidance. All the saints are still walking with you but you don't know it. You must call on St Benedict, St Joseph, John the Evangelist, St Augustine and Michael the Archangel to give you the support you will need. So much stronger now are you my child that you wonder why. It is because of your obedience to my Beloved Son that you are now receiving the graces needed for this special Divine Mission for which you have been chosen.

Praying my Most Holy Rosary each day is important for it will protect you from the Evil One. St Benedict has been assigned to you at all times to protect you from the attacks from The Deceiver. This is why the worst ones have been kept away from you. Pray to him daily my child for this continued protection.

Accept the suffering demanded of you by my precious Son, Jesus Christ, for this will save countless souls. Your special gift to Him of your free will, will prevent millions of souls from entering the fires of Hell. Keep remembering what your suffering is achieving and the joy that this will bring to my Son's Sacred Heart.

You are now enjoying the special gift of being in union with my Son. The more you completely surrender, show humility and make further sacrifices, the more you will help Him in this task which is so important to Him.

Be thankful my child for being asked to do this Sacred Work for without it millions of souls could not be saved.

Come nearer now to my Heart and let me keep you closer to my Son. I will protect and guide you at all times.

Your Beloved Mother

Queen of Peace

Earthquake in Europe took place today as predicted
Wednesday, May 11, 2011 23.00 hours

My beloved daughter today the earthquake I spoke to you about some months ago took place in Europe in Spain today. Other ecological events, which include a volcano, floods and a heat wave, will follow. Watch out for these events for when they take place this will prove that these Messages are coming from Me, Jesus Christ.

This, My daughter is the Hand of My Father Who is about to unleash punishment on the world to help eradicate sin. Pray and keep praying for more conversion to dilute these disasters.

My Beloved Mother explained a number of important things to you this evening. The need for daily prayer and Adoration is important - as often as you can - for this will yield huge results for you, My Daughter, in your work.

Rest now. You are tired. I will speak with you tomorrow. Go in peace.

Your Divine Saviour

Jesus Christ

Why God, the Eternal Father, is sending new prophets into the world

Friday, May 13, 2011 22.45 hours

My dearly beloved daughter for the doubters, especially My sacred servants, who may dismiss My Word through these Messages this is what I would like to say to them. Increase your faith in Me by acknowledging that My Word was given to the world not only during My time on earth but through the power of the Holy Spirit after that.

Since the beginning of time God, My Eternal Father, has communicated to mankind through the prophets. In this way the Teachings of the Truth were made known to man to ensure that their faith remained strong. Other revelations and lessons in the Truth were also given to mankind through the Apostles, other devout disciples and through the prophet John the Evangelist. After that My Word, My Teachings and everything that man needed to bring him the salvation he needs was in order. Now that the world is facing the biggest shift in its history God, My Eternal Father, has sent new prophets to the world. These prophets, make no mistake, do not bring you new teachings for that is not necessary. Instead they are being sent for three reasons.

The first is to remind mankind of the Truth contained in the Book of Revelation. The second is to make man alert to the times he is living in so that he can rekindle his faith. The third is to help spread conversion so that My followers can form the biggest army of all in order to save souls. I am communicating through this prophet and others so that My Word is heard in every corner of the world.

Remember My Absolute Love and Compassion

Listen carefully to all these Messages which not only proclaim My Word as you know it but which reveal to you My absolute love and compassion for every single one of you. Remember too, My Great Mercy. All sinners will be forgiven once they ask for redemption.

Importance of the Holy Rosary and Divine Mercy

While ecological disasters will occur please remember that prayer including the recital of the Holy Rosary and the Divine Mercy will help avert much of it. Remember My cherished children that you who believe in Me and My Eternal Father and who follow My instructions have nothing to fear. Also let Me remind you that because of the two great acts of Mercy being given to you - the Gift of the Holy Spirit which burst upon the entire world a few days ago and the Great Warning millions will be converted to the Truth. This will be a great miracle and one, which will bring joy to the multitudes.

The Persecution by the Red Dragon and those not of God

While Satan will rise through his poor misguided followers whom he pulls away from Me - their only hope of eternal salvation - this will be for just a short period. It will, I must warn you though, be a frightening period of persecution headed by the Red Dragon and those political entities, not of God. Through prayer and the Sacraments you will find the strength to persevere during these trials. All of these events have been foretold and must come to pass so that evil can be finally stamped out in the world. It is necessary, therefore, that this purification and series of Chastisements take place. Because only then will the world be ready for the New Paradise on earth.

Never ignore My calling. It is only when you see the prophecies revealed to you by My chosen messengers begin to materialize that you will know for sure that it is I Who speaks with you.

Your Divine Saviour

Jesus Christ

Reject the work of New Age Spiritualism
Sunday, May 15, 2011 17.00 hours

My dearly beloved daughter I am calling on all My followers to denounce the work of the New Age Movement, which has gripped the world.

Christianity has always been a prime target of Satan. Because he is so cunning he will constantly try to seduce those with empty and spiritually lost souls. He will always try to present his lies couched in what appears to be love. Then he will try to control My children's minds using ancient pagan tactics designed to free their minds from the so-called stresses of modern living. Beware those of you who succumb to practices, which claim to bring your mental state into a stage of oblivion in the name of meditation. Once you allow your mind to be controlled in this way Satan and his demons can move in so silently that you won't realise it, so smooth will be the transition.

Avoid ancient spiritual practices including use of tarot cards
Many, many souls in the world are starving for spiritual guidance. In their quest to bring meaning into their lives they are unwittingly allowing themselves be sucked into practices which amount to paganism. Any false dogma, which entices you to believe that peace in your heart and soul can be achieved through ancient spiritual practices must be avoided at all times. Learn to recognise them for what they really are.

The use of crystals, meditation, reiki, yoga, tarot cards, belief in spirit guides, metaphysics and so called faith healers are there to entice you to believe in an alternative superiour existence outside of that created by

God the Eternal Father.

Warning about Ascended Masters
Many of you today who are constantly searching out spiritual comfort in the practice of following your angels must also be alert to the fact that once the term Ascended Masters is mentioned you can be sure that these angels do not come from Heaven. Ascended Masters, My children, are fallen angels and come from the dark. Yet you will be told and then be convinced that they come from the light. All of this pagan spiritualism, if you let it take over your lives, will eventually pull you downwards into the pits of darkness when you least expect it. Satan will be so careful as to how he presents these dark lies because at all times you will be told, and you will believe, that these things are all good.

Most of these practices are presented as being good for your self-esteem, confidence, control over your life, all of which is a lie. Not only do these practices drive you away from the Truth, but they bring untold misery once the evil spirits enter your soul as a direct result of these practices.

Bible warns of dangers of magic
The Truth can never be tampered with. Teachings handed down to man in the Holy Bible warn mankind of the dangers of magic, fortune telling and the adulation of false Gods. In today's world these practices are presented as harmless, but necessary, for your spiritual well being. Because of the nature of gentle souls many of them will be naturally drawn to New Age Practices because of the false façade of the love they exude. Nothing could be further from the Truth.

Warning about fanatical devotion to Angels Remember it is Satan and his fallen angels who have carefully and cunningly drawn you into these unsuspecting lies. For those of you who promote an almost fanatical devotion to angels I have this to say. Why do you not proclaim the Word of God, My Eternal Father first? Isn't this obsession with angels just another form of idolatry? Yes, by all means, pray for the help of the holy angels, however, always ask this question. Is your devotion to the angels at the expense of your love for Jesus Christ, the Son of God or God, the Eternal Father? If so then you offend Me, your Divine Saviour, Jesus Christ.

Wake up now to the lies of so-called spiritualism. The angels you attract by participating in such practices will not come from Heaven or from the Light. They will seem to come from the Light but that is the deceit that Satan and his demons use to cleverly camouflage their actions.

Remember one final lesson. Dress up your pagan practices as much as you like to appear as if you are paying homage to the Divine Light of Heaven but it will be a lie. The lie, and those you convince to follow this bizarre journey towards a so called spiritual realm outside that of My Father's will bring you so close to Satan that beyond a certain point there will be no return.

The only Divine Realm of Love that exists outside of this earth is Heaven. Anything else you have been told is untrue. Satan, however, wants you to believe that there is. The reality is that he is pulling all those unsuspecting and superstitious souls into the darkness of Hell with him and all the fallen angels, all in the name of false love.

Please remember that love, true love, can only come from God, the Eternal Father.

Your Loving Saviour

Jesus Christ

Importance of Fasting and Self Denial
Monday, May 16, 2011 11.30 hours

My beloved daughter you are finally realizing that without Me you are nothing. It is through My Graces that you receive life in My Father's Kingdom. Without My Presence in your life it will be barren and devoid of any real meaning. O how I wish all My children would understand the life that I can bring them especially through the Sacrament of the Holy Eucharist. For it is only when you receive Me into your frail souls through the Divine Bread and Wine that you will truly feel My Love. This love will strengthen you, not only in your soul, but in your mind. My Presence will lift you to become true followers of Mine.

A follower of Mine who does not receive Me regularly through this most Holy Sacrament will be like a vessel that is only half full. You need My Body and Blood which was shed for you all to fill you with My True Presence. For without this you will be unable to find the real strength to proclaim My glory fully.

Children you must understand that belief in My existence is just part of your spiritual journey. There is so much more you need to understand. It will only be through your denial of the pleasures of the flesh that you will truly be fulfilled. By virtue of the fact that Satan controls man through the temptations of the flesh so too should you deny him the access to those pleasures you may seek. Fasting is one of the most powerful ways to rid your soul of Satan and his demons. So few people in the world can commit to this sacrifice yet it is so simple and does not damage your health. One day of fasting a week will bring you special graces. By making small sacrifices in honour of Me, your Divine Saviour, you will not only save souls but you will become closer to Me. Other sacrifices where you denounce worldly goods will also bring you closer to My Sacred Heart.

Life, My children, should not be all about the pursuit of material things, if they are surplus to your real needs. By accepting simple needs and by devoting your time to Me you will experience true contentment. Not only that but for the first time in your life you will know the meaning of true freedom. Remember Satan controls man through the desires of the flesh including food, clothes, sex, homes, cars, holidays, luxury living, music, alcohol and idolatry of famous people. By accepting that these are simply illusions you will then understand that your time on earth should not be wasted with such useless pursuits.

Your time on earth Children is just part of your journey into eternity. Life of a different kind will continue for you after death. Irrespective as to whether people believe in God, the Eternal Father or not their soul will still exist after death. Seek now the Light so that your soul will experience true happiness for eternity and an exalted place in Paradise. To achieve this level of spiritual sanctity please make sacrifices of the flesh while are you are still alive on earth. Offer, too, all your sufferings in your life for lost souls and you will reap the rewards waiting for you in the next life.

Your Loving Saviour

Jesus Christ

Honour My Father

Wednesday, May 18, 2011 17.00 hours

My dearly beloved daughter I have missed the time you promised Me yesterday. I realise that you lead a very busy life but remember that I am the Life whom you must seek out above all your day-to-day activities.

Time for man to honestly reflect on his life

The time for mankind to reflect on his life in a truly honest way has come. All My children everywhere, in every corner of the world, must ask themselves this question. Do they or do they not believe that God, the Father, exists? As the end times foretold draw nearer and nearer a number of choices will now have to be made. Do you, My children accept that God, My Eternal Father created you? If you do, then answer the next question. How much time do you spend thanking Him for the gifts of life, your family and friends? The home you live in? The food you eat? If you don't, you are not a follower of the Truth.

Show My Father Respect

For those of you who do believe in God, the Creator of all things do you not know that prayer is vital if you are to benefit from the next glorious life He has planned for you. Speak to Him daily. Show Him the respect He deserves, because by not paying attention to Him you offend Me. For all those devoted followers of Mine, I your Divine Saviour Jesus Christ, call on you now to understand how important it is to honour My Father. He is not being given the attention He deserves. Many people have this image of God, the Father, as being stern, frightening and angry. So in awe are you that you push Him to one side. If you knew how much He craves your love you would drop down on your knees this instant and beg Him to forgive you. Please pray to God the Father. He needs your love. He needs your devotion. Prayer to My Father yields tremendous Mercy when you ask My Father to protect you and to save you in My Name, He rarely refuses your request according to His Most Holy Will. God, My Eternal Father is very loving, compassionate and allegiance to Him will bring the world great graces and salvation.

Pray to My Father to avert global disasters

Pray to My Father to avert global disasters on behalf of His beloved Son and He will hear your prayers. So very few Christians in the world especially call on Him for help any more. He, Who so lovingly created man in His image, has been forgotten about. Show Him the honour that is now required to help alleviate the ecological catastrophes that will occur on earth during the Great Tribulation.

My Father holds the world in His Hands. His children, however, no longer honour or adore Him. They are oblivious to the fact that while Satan continues to steal souls there is only one Power that will withstand eternity and that is the Power of God. In His Mercy He will hear your cries for help. Please call on Him now especially in these times of great change.

Your beloved Saviour

The Son of God, the Father Almighty

Jesus Christ

Responsibility of Parents in the world today
Thursday, May 19, 2011 18.15 hours

My dearly beloved daughter the world has now succumbed to the depths of utter despair in its lack of belief in the existence of God, the Father Almighty. Even little children now gleefully deny His existence. Those empty hardened souls insult not only My Eternal Father but cause Me deep anguish.

So far have you fallen children that you have completely discarded all sense of the spirituality that you were born with. How far do you think your love of the world and its materialism will take you? For those of you engrossed in wealth and the comforts of all worldly attractions you should know that they will soon be taken away from you as part of the purification ahead.

Responsibility of Parents

Why do you teach your children the importance of man-made materialism at the expense of their poor little souls? Your primary aim is to teach your children the importance of creating and building wealth. You rarely teach them the morals they need to equip themselves with the responsibilities for adulthood in relation to how they should show respect for others, to understand the importance of honesty and the need to show understanding towards their brothers and sisters. Unfortunately My children have completely lost their way on the spiritual path required for them to reach the ultimate destination. Have you no shame? When will you learn that your obsessive love of money and all that it offers will end in disaster? It will only be when you are stripped naked of these comforts you crave that you will realise how alone you are.

Listen to Me now while you can. Place your family's needs first for that is good. Provide for them. But please do not encourage your children to become slaves to wealth and a desire for fame for you will be pushing them into the arms of Satan. Your children were born and given life by you physically, but, they were Created by God, the Eternal Father, when they were given their souls. By all means show responsibility as a parent by providing for your children's physical needs. But remember that their souls need nourishment. Teach them the Truth of My Teachings and the importance of looking after their souls. Only then will you be giving your children the true nourishment in body and mind that they need to survive so they can enjoy Eternal Life.

Your Loving Divine Saviour

Jesus Christ

Confusion about what My Second Coming will mean

Friday, May 20, 2011 10.00 hours

My dearly beloved daughter, many people wonder what The Second Coming really means so let Me explain.

I came into the world the first time to redeem mankind from eternal darkness so he could benefit from Eternal Life. God, the Almighty Father, out of His Mercy sent Me so that all His children would have life. For up to then, due to the sins of Adam and Eve, this would not have been possible. I come again, this time to reward all those who follow Me.

Much confusion exists in the world regarding this event. Many people believe that My Second Coming indicates that the end of the world has come. That is not the case for, instead, it will mean the End Times when Satan and his followers who create untold misery in the world will be banished from earth for 1,000 years.

About the New Paradise on earth

This New Paradise I have promised will come about when Heaven and Earth merge to become one. This new life I bring to all My devoted followers is one of love and glory. You, My followers, will have to endure much suffering, however, while this transition takes place. To help prepare the world for this great event I am bringing a great gift of My Mercy beforehand. The Great Warning, which will give each and every one of you the chance to see your sins and how they offend Me, will enable you to see the Truth. When you realise the stain of sin that exists within you only then will you really understand the sorrow that I feel.

A glimpse of what will happen at the Final Judgment

By allowing you all to experience this great act of My Mercy you will be given a true glimpse as to what will happen at the day of the Final Judgment. In this way you are being given a fair chance to turn back to Me once more. You see, I love all of you with such a deep and abiding passion that I will do everything possible to save you from the grip of The Deceiver.

Be warned though that Satan will now increase his activities through your brothers and sisters to persuade you to turn your back on Me even after this great event takes place. You must now open your minds, leave all human reasoning aside to accept the truth of your existence on earth. Every lie couched in scientific human logical thinking will be perpetrated to prevent you from accepting the Truth.

Satan does not want you, My children, to come to Me. His vice like grip must be broken but it can only be done with your help. Do not allow him to cloud your judgment with his lies. It will be very difficult for you to ignore his arguments, taunts and ridicule. For that is the way he works.

Satan will work through other people to discourage you

Many of you will not know that Satan is working like this through other people whose views you may respect. But this is just exactly how he works. He will communicate through those poor souls who are attracted to the dark. He will ensure that their minds are blocked to the truth of My Glory and the Eternal Life that is yours by right. Never ever let his influence affect your love for Me. And remember because he will not win this battle then those poor souls who follow him will be thrown into Hell with him. If you desire Eternal Life then use this time on earth to denounce Satan while you can.

I will rule the earth for 1,000 years

My daughter I will rule the earth for the 1,000 years. Make no mistake for I am now in charge of events as they now unfold in the world. I have now prepared the way for My new kingdom on earth and that time is near, much closer than many realize, rejoice for this news will be welcomed by all. It will bring to an end all suffering in the world. It will ignite a fount of love and glory for all My children to share.

This New Paradise will be beyond your comprehension but hear this. This new life will offer you all of My devout followers a life free from worry. You will want for nothing. All will be provided by Me. Each and every one of you who chose this Glorious Kingdom will be astonished at the Precious Jewel that awaits you. Pray now that your brothers and sisters open their eyes to the truth of the promises I have made so they, too, can enter this new life on Earth.

Your Loving Saviour

Jesus Christ

Forgiveness the pathway to freedom
Saturday, May 21, 2011 10.40 hours

My daughter forgiveness is the pathway to freedom. When you forgive those who offend you or who have caused you hurt you become free of spirit. That is when joy fills your soul. That too means that I am present within you. When you forgive others this is a sign of love, not only for your neighbour, but love for Me your Divine Saviour. For those who do not believe Me know that when they, too, forgive others I am present and walk with them. Yet they have no idea that this is the case.

Forgiveness is love. My Love is endless. But I implore you, My children, to allow Me to forgive you for your sins. If you could only ask Me, to do this not only will you be free but the love and the joy you will experience will surprise you. This act of humility will allow you to communicate with love towards others. Your light will shine and will affect others in a special way but neither you nor they will be aware of this. My Love, after the act of Redemption takes place, will flood your soul. Your clean soul will be like a magnet as it draws others towards you.

To forgive others is not easy My children. Pride and a sense of self-worth prevent this great act of mercy taking place. This is the work of Satan. For he knows that lack of forgiveness leads to other more serious sins against God the Father. When you cannot forgive others first of all build up a resentment which, when it festers, leads to hatred and even murder. In many cases it can lead to war.

If people everywhere forgave one another graciously then hatred would not exist. Murder would be less frequent and love, the love of God, The Eternal Father, would spread.

Learn to forgive one another. Push pride aside and ask for My Mercy. For when you ask for something according to My Holy Will you will be granted your request.

Your Loving Saviour

King of Mercy

Jesus Christ

New Revelations Floods in France this Summer
Sunday, May 22, 2011 14.30 hours

My dearly beloved daughter the revelation given to you on the 18th March 2011 at midnight that the volcanic eruption in Iceland would occur in May has now taken place. You may wonder why you were so shocked when this happened as foretold. So I will explain. Although most of your doubts have been dispelled regarding the authenticity of My communications with you there was still a fear on your part that you were not discerning these prophecies correctly. You must rise now with confidence and let Me allay your fears. Move now and publish, without hesitation, other events I have revealed to you. By doing this more people will understand that it is I, Jesus Christ, Who now commands the attention that is required to help save souls.

When these prophecies are confirmed there will be little doubt in the hearts of My followers of their authenticity. Yet the hardened soul who refuses to believe and who will always provide a logical response when they witness the truth will still not be convinced.

Floods in France, Heat wave in Turkey

Hear Me now. Floods will occur in the south of France this summer. A heat wave will take place in Turkey. Other ecological events, which will cause disarray, include an earthquake in England (but not immediately) some of which will impact on other European states. Expect a rise in sea levels in the Mediterranean, which will shock every one. Earthquakes will also be felt in Norway and in South America. I will, My daughter, reveal other events to you but with only one motive in mind. That is to convert My children. If and when they accept that I speak to them through you then this will bring Me joy. I have no wish to frighten My children but these events will continue to escalate in the world as part of the Great Chastisement ahead. They are a necessary part in the Battle against the Deceiver.

Pray now, My children, to dilute and avert these events because prayer is extremely powerful as a means of pardon.

Go now in peace. Do not be afraid to publish these prophecies for they will occur.

Your Saviour

Jesus Christ

Why I communicate to the world in this way
Monday, May 23, 2011 09.45 hours

My dearly beloved daughter it is now time to reflect on My Sacred Messages and to ensure that as many sinners all over the world take heed of them.

Make no mistake these Messages are being given to the world as a gift to help save all of you, all of My children and including those who follow different paths to God the Eternal Father.

People especially Catholics, will be confused when I do not place them ahead of My other children of different creeds. My choice of Words are designed to be heard by all and not just the chosen few. My Love does not differentiate. For those who question the way in which I speak to mankind, through this messenger, hear Me now. While you, My followers, understand that the Truth has never changed from the time of My Crucifixion know then that I must extend My Love to all God's children. No one is better than the other.

My daughter you must not respond or try to defend My Word when challenged to explain why I would speak in this way. My Word is Divine. It must not be changed or amended to suit those who consider themselves experts in theological law. For My Word will be given to the world in a language, which will be clearly understood by mankind today. Many will ask why these Words do not use the same terminology or expressions used by My prophets and apostles of old and I will answer them now.

Remember My Teachings never change. No matter what language I use today to communicate in a modern way the Truth remains the same, intact.

Be wary of visionaries or seers who claim that they are receiving messages from Me, who use ancient language or extracts from the Holy Bible. For this is not the way in which I would communicate to mankind today. Why would I do that? Would I not alienate a new generation? Those who are ignorant of the language contained in My Father's Holy Book?

Simplicity is the key My children when communicating My most Holy Word. Remember when teaching others of the truth of My existence that simplicity in your approach is essential. If you do not do this you will not reach those lost souls because they will turn a deaf ear.

My Message of Love

The Message of My Love is very simple. I am the Life that My children on earth crave. Explain that I am the Truth. Make this clear. Without Me there is no Eternal Life. Use the prophecies, which I reveal to this messenger to gain the attention of non-believers. For this is why they are being given to the world. Not to frighten them but to prove that I am now communicating today in a way in which My most Holy Word will not only be heard but believed.

Your Loving Saviour and Teacher

Jesus Christ

King of Mercy

The skies will open up during The Warning
Monday, May 23, 2011 14.30 hours

My dearly beloved daughter you are suffering the torment that I endure for the sins of man. This is what it feels like. Now you are glimpsing just a tiny fraction of My suffering which I face every minute of your day. There is nothing to fear, My daughter about The Warning.

The Warning will be a dramatic event
It will shock many people in the world as it will be a dramatic event where the skies will open and the flames of Mercy will shoot up across the world. For many people will not understand what is happening. So shocked will they be they will mistakenly think that they are witnessing the end of the world. Tell them to rejoice when they witness My Glory for this, if you are properly prepared for it, will be the most spectacular example of My Mercy since the day of My Crucifixion. This, My children, will be your saving grace and will prevent those who would otherwise have been condemned from entering the depths of Hell.

All My children everywhere must warn lost souls as to what to expect. Urge them to seek reconciliation by confessing their sins now. It is important that as many people as possible are in a state of grace beforehand as they may not survive this event due to shock. Far better to witness this Divine Spectacular event first rather than being unprepared at the final day of Judgment.

Keep strong all of you. Rejoice if you are a devout follower for you will be shown a glimpse of My Divine Presence, which your ancestors never saw during their lifetime. Pray for the rest of My children. Tell them the truth now while you can. Ignore their scorn for should they take action now by praying for the forgiveness of their sins they will thank you after this Great Miracle takes place.

Go now in peace. Do not be fearful. Just pray for those souls with no faith so they do not die in mortal sin.
Your Divine Saviour

Jesus Christ

If you find it difficult to pray
Tuesday, May 24, 2011 18.00 hours

My dearly beloved daughter I am happy today that so much work has been done to impart My Most Holy Word to the world through your work. You must never feel that you are not doing enough because of the amount of people who reject these Messages. For those of My children who do not accept My Word now they will in time. Then they will be hungry to hear My Voice.

Stay focused on Me now. Don't be led astray by those who pour scorn on these Messages. Never be discouraged for those who are listening to My Word now are, in fact, spreading the truth to others out of their love for Me.

Conversion is a difficult challenge in a world so blind to the Truth of Eternal Life. Perseverance is needed for with the help of the Holy Spirit, Whose power is being felt now everywhere all around the world, My children will eventually come back to Me, but not all. For those who would prefer the artificial comforts offered to them through The Deceiver they will find it very difficult to reject the life they lead. Pray for all of your family and friends now so that you can all unite in your love for Me during The Warning. For if you will accept this event as your route to freedom you will be rewarded with My Great Mercy.

Prayer is not easy

Prayer is not easy for many of My children who find the recital of long prayers repetitive and a little boring. If this is the way you pray and you are struggling then just sit down quietly and communicate with Me in silence. Simply reflect on My life on earth. Reminder yourself of the time I spent there and the lessons of love I gave to all of you. That's enough. Let yourself become quiet of mind and I will sit with you in contemplation. I walk with every one. I am present every minute of the day no matter what you are doing. I am never far away. Remember that I am your crutch in life. Lean on Me. Ask for My support with sincerity and I will hear your call. I never refuse your request if it is according to My Holy Will. However, when you ask for favours, which are designed to bequeath you with worldly excesses, know that I will never bestow these. For I can never give you gifts, which I know are bad for your soul. My gifts are given so that I can bring you closer to My heart, for when that happens you will want for nothing more.

Your Loving and devoted Saviour

Jesus Christ

I would like to thank those who help in spreading My Holy Word

Wednesday, May 25, 2011 16.00 hours

I come now to give courage to all those followers of mine, when having recognised My True Voice, responded with great works of generosity. For those of you who are giving freely of your time to promote and spread My Messages I would like to thank you. You, My precious children, bring great joy to My Sorrowful Heart at this time in history. You, My children are brave, courageous and infused with the Gift of the Holy Spirit. Your loyalty and gift to Me of your time and loving devotion to the Truth will yield great graces in the New Paradise I promised My children.

I will guide your hand during this Sacred Work and you feel My Love. Never be fearful of proclaiming My Word for every little effort made by anyone who promotes these Messages will be rewarded.

Go now, My precious loyal followers. Spread My Holy Word and help your brothers and sisters who need direction.
Your Loving Saviour

Jesus Christ

Message of Warning to World Leaders
Wednesday, May 25, 2011 22.00 hours

My daughter countries all over the world are bubbling under the surface with unrest both in terms of the hatred being shown by man to man as well as pending ecological upheavals. This is where Mother Nature will unleash the unexpected soon to show man that he is not, irrespective of his arrogant assertiveness, in control of anything.

Man has many lessons to learn. Constant efforts to gain power at the highest levels by those in authority is having an effect on the ordinary man who has to rely on those government and business leaders to look after his needs. The help needed by man will only be manifested when those leaders rule with true love in their hearts for their people. Sadly, greed and a lust for power, means that this is not in fact the goal of many world leaders today.

God the Father will no longer tolerate your sinful deeds
My warning to those leaders all over the world, whoever you are, is this. Inflict unfair practices and hardships on your people and the Hand of My Eternal Father will fall swiftly on those countries and locations within which you reside. He will no longer tolerate your sinful deeds. Hide if you will but it will be useless. Your weapons of destruction will be destroyed. Your treatment of your fellow citizens will create a situation, whether you

like it or not, where you will have to answer to God the Eternal Father. Your moral responsibilities must be adhered to because you will be judged by your actions eventually.

Lead your people with love, dignity and respect for their physical and moral welfare. Deny your people the right to religious freedom or inflict dictatorships of any kind which forces them to stop or curtail their religious practices in the name of political unity then you are doomed, not only will you suffer for your actions but judgment will be harsh. Any of you who swears allegiance to your people in the Name of God, the Eternal Father and orchestrates unfair new laws, which deny them the right to food, shelter and religious freedom will face the Wrath and the Hand of God, the Father.

The world is suffering now in every country because of dictatorships although not in places where you would assume to be the case. The world is also suffering from financial difficulties which makes the vulnerable weaker. I say now to those leaders who have any sense of Christian duty to fight for the right to allow My Teachings to influence your decisions, which will have a direct impact on My children everywhere.

For those of you colluding in the corridors of power to suppress a multitude of countries in a controlled manner, which will affect nation after nation and will lead to hardship everywhere, be aware that your actions will be punished. For God, the Eternal Father has been patient up to now in the hope that you would see the futility of your ways. Instead you have pushed forward as an Elite Group who considers itself more important than the rest of the human race. Your actions, be warned, will end in disaster. Your allegiance to wealth, dominance and greed will leave you not just naked and vulnerable but in a worse state than those you abuse through the misuse of power.

The time has come for the battle to rid the world of evil and the rule of Satan. God the Father is now about to unleash many earthquakes, tsunamis and floods in an effort to make you wake up. Your plots to overthrow world leaders, those in power of religious groups and to introduce control measures including a One World Currency will not be ignored. As you witness now these events unfolding you will find them impossible to ignore. These events will shake your blind addiction to power. You will wake up to the error of your ways. And when you do I will be standing waiting. You will run to Me and ask, not only for forgiveness, but you will use your love of Me to make amends. You, My children who have a deep underlying love for Me are My biggest hope in defeating evil and unfair political corruption in the world now. Pray for the graces to help you turn back to Me.

Climate catastrophes not witnessed since the days of Noah
Prayer will as I have said before help dilute disasters in the world as it now heads towards a series of climate related catastrophes, never witnessed by man since the days of Noah. The world, as you know it will suffer so many events all at once that chaos and confusion will be the norm.

Why would you allow this to happen? I speak to those with huge political and financial clout who are privy to what is happening behind closed doors. This is your last chance, given to you out of a sense of love and compassion to man everywhere, to turn now and stop your evil ways. Or face the consequences.

Your Just Judge

Jesus Christ

King of Mercy

Dealing with Financial Hardship
Thursday, May 26, 2011 13.00 hours

My dearly beloved daughter it is My wish that you now begin to fast at least one day a week. For by doing so you will greatly please Me. This sacrifice will strengthen your purity of soul and bring you closer to My

Most Sacred Heart.

My children in the world face many challenges in these times, challenges, which they have never had to deal with before. The biggest challenge now is to deal with the way in which money is becoming scarce. This is very frightening for many who need this to keep their homes and feed their families. The second difficulty is the lack of any meaningful spiritual guidance in their lives, which had, up to now, been seen as important.

Lose your income and you lose your aspirations for luxury worldly goods. For what use is a luxury car when you cannot feed your family? What use is a beautiful dress when you cannot keep warm in a house you can't afford to heat properly? It is only when My children find themselves bereft of the excesses to which they had become accustomed that they understand the reality into which they have now been plunged.

Today your basic needs must be your priority. After that you need to ask yourself what is important now? Once you are fed and clothed what then? One-man upmanship is no longer relevant when you are striving to survive the basic elements. Envy of your neighbour's wealth and status matters no more. It is only now that you will seek out the spiritual comforts that have been missing for so long in your lives.

In your quest to find comfort of mind turn to Me and My Eternal Father, God the Creator of all things. Do not be tempted to seek remedies from spiritual healers unless they represent Me. Do not seek artificial solace in stimulants to ease your pain and sorrow. The only way you will become free of worry and anguish is when you turn to Me, Jesus Christ your Saviour.

I am waiting now. Ask me to help you and I will supply your basic needs. I will always provide you with what you want. But you must ask Me first. Never keep your worries to yourself. Share them with Me. Hand Me over all your concerns. I will respond immediately. For this will fill Me with joy when you trust in Me completely.

I love you all.

Your devoted Saviour

Jesus Christ

King of Mercy and Compassion

Sin will always be sin no matter how you justify it

Sunday, May 29, 2011 17.30 hours

My dearly beloved daughter, how I cry for all of My children who sin because they don't understand My Teachings. Many of them are not aware they offend Me because either they have never been taught the Truth or they have decided to defend their sins. Many of those who sin try to justify their act because they listen to others who use tolerance as a guise to justify sin. Sin will always be sin in My Father's eyes no matter how small the sin. Many of those who commit grievous sin somehow always manage to defend their so-called 'right to sin' by blinding themselves to the evil that their sin represents.

My children are fortunate that I forgive them for their sins

If only My children everywhere knew of My Mercy, they would then realise how fortunate they are to be given this great gift of forgiveness I offer them in this life. If they do not ask for forgiveness regularly then their sins will lead them to continue to sin again and again. The more they sin the further they will remove themselves from Me and the harder it will be to come back to Me. Listen to Me. My Mercy is there for all of you to benefit from. Accept this from Me now. Do not allow the world to trap you by allowing yourself to fall prey to the temptations of sin. Once you sin you become trapped and won't know where to turn. Sin makes you feel uncomfortable deep down and within you.

Tolerance is fashionable today
So many of My children keep shouting aloud of the need for 'tolerance in society'. Tolerance is fashionable today in its loose term. It can be used to distort even the most gravest of sins. Tolerance is cleverly moulded to defend every type of sin known to man in the world today. Everyone claims the right to tolerance. Whatever the sin it will be promoted as a civil right in most instances. No matter how these sins are promoted as 'being right' they will always be wrong. It is time that man faces the truth, to become responsible again. To accept that the acts of sin they are partaking in are morally wrong. To treat their fellow human beings, including those children in the womb, as being equal in all things.

Pray hard for the graces to see the Truth for what it is. And not the doctored version you chose to believe in because it suits your selfish goals. There is only one Truth. In your hearts, every single one of you knows the difference between right or wrong. Accept this now if you want Me to save you from the fires of Hell.

Your Saviour

Jesus Christ

The Swords of Justice will fall now
Monday, May 30, 2011 03.00 hours

Hear Me now My children everywhere. The Swords of Justice will fall on those who fail to prepare adequately for The Warning.

My flames of Divine Mercy, presented to the world to give each of you a taste of what the Final Day of Judgment will be like is going to be misinterpreted by so many of you. This great day of The Warning draws closer by the month so you must now put aside the time in preparing for My Divine Mercy.

Many, many souls will find it difficult to understand what this event really means. So many will, as a result, die of shock, which saddens Me, because for those who do not survive it will be because of the sorry state of their souls. Catholics everywhere seek Confession now if you want to benefit from My Great Act of Love and Mercy. Christians and other faiths speak in silence and tell God how remorseful you are. How much you regret your transgressions and ask Him to forgive you for your sins. Only those who are strong of heart in their love for Me and God, the Almighty Father, will be prepared adequately. Others, because of their strength in mind and character will finally understand the truth and accept Me with love in their hearts.

As for others, so harsh will the shock be, that when their souls are revealed to them in their darkness they will drop dead. By then it will be too late to seek forgiveness. There will be no hope for them. Pray, pray all of you so that as many souls as possible will survive My Great Act of Mercy.

Your Loving Saviour

Jesus Christ

Warning to those who are involved with Satanic Cults

Monday, May 30, 2011 22.00 hours

My daughter you are getting much stronger now and through your obedience to My Most Holy Will can alert the world now to what lies ahead.

When I speak about sin I have not revealed the vile sins, which are committed which, even regular sinners would find hard to fathom. The sickening practices conducted by so called sophisticated western societies behind closed doors would shock you to the core.

The evil atrocities where children are ritually murdered in deference to Satan are a reality in the world today. But they are just some of the intensely evil acts, which are committed by Man influenced by Satan. Go this far, My children, and you will find it impossible to come back to Me. Other acts, which break My Heart include the physical abuse particularly of young innocent children. Let Me spell out for you the kind of sins, which would greatly distress many of you were I to describe them in detail. Satan followers through their cults are savage in their treatment of the human being for whom they have no respect. Sacrifices including human sacrifices, blasphemies cursing and acts of desecration of Me, My Eternal Father and My Beloved Mother are regular rituals. So little shame have these Satanic worshippers that they flaunt their disrespect in public through music, the movies, TV and the arts. Those guilty of such sacrileges will face eternal damnation where they will burn in Hell for eternity.

This is one of the last warnings you will receive from Me, your Saviour Jesus Christ. It is also My final request of you to save yourselves while you can.

I, Jesus Christ, don't make idle threats. I will do everything to save you. But beyond a certain point there is nothing I can do to stop you seeking out the false solace you think you will be offered by the Evil One. Unlock the Satanic shackles by which you are bound and flee to Me now. I will save you but you must ask Me to forgive you while you are alive in this life.

Remember it is your choice. Heaven or Hell. You chose while you are still alive on this earth. Because you won't be able to do this when you pass over into the next life.

Your Ever-Patient and Loving Jesus Christ.

Part 3.

First Volume

Messages 100 - 149

Tuesday May 31, 2011 to Monday, July 25, 2011

Tell them I love them but I want them to talk to Me
Tuesday, May 31, 2011 10.00 hours

My dearly beloved daughter this has been quite an extraordinary journey for you in such a short time. I realise that you are tired now. The speed at which these Messages have been received by you and published in so many languages so quickly shows you the urgency they represent. This also shows you the Divine Guidance at work in its most perfcct format.

These Messages while full of My Teachings are really being given to explain the importance of looking after your souls in this life while you can. Many people will, when they read these Messages, especially those with little belief in God, the Eternal Father will be disturbed by them. Many will be converted. Some will be fearful for their future on this earth and that of their families and friends.

Please tell them I love them

If by opening their minds first to the fact that God really does exist then they will be ready for stage two. That's when they will begin to wonder why such communication is taking place. Why Jesus Christ, the only Son of God the Eternal Father would take such extraordinary steps they will come to the obvious conclusion. It is because I love each and every one of you that I want to save you. I want to cherish you all and I must go to the most extraordinary lengths to bring you closer to My Heart.

I want to touch you in your hearts so that a light will spark in your soul. There is nothing to fear in this world if you will trust in Me completely. I have wonderful plans for all of you who will come closer to My Sacred Heart. The most extraordinary gifts await you. Have no fear of worldly unrest, for I will protect all those who believe in Me and will provide for your needs of the flesh. Trust in Me the Lord of Mankind sent, yet again, to salvage you from eternal darkness.

Turn to Me as innocent children

No need to learn prayers if you are ignorant. Yes they are helpful but all I am asking you to do is to speak with Me. In the way you would normally chat to a friend, relax, confide in Me. Ask Me for My help. My Mercy is full and overflowing just waiting to shower you with. If you only knew the compassion I have for everyone on earth. Even sinners. My children are My children even when sin stains their souls. I detest the sin but love the sinner.

So many of you are afraid to ask regularly for forgiveness. You must never worry. Ever. If you are truly sorry you will be forgiven.

Sin, My children, will be a constant problem. Even My most devout followers sin, and sin, over and over again. It is a fact. Once Satan was unleashed sin became widespread. Many are too ashamed to turn to Me. They lower their heads and turn a blind eye when they have behaved badly. Too proud and embarrassed they continue on as if it will be forgotten about. What they do not understand is that dark attracts dark. So when you sin once it is much easier to sin again. By blocking your conscience the cycle then rotates around and around. Then the sinner will make every excuse to ignore the wrongdoing. They will keep falling further downwards in a spiral. This is because they don't know how to ask for forgiveness. Because they have not understood the importance of humility they find it impossible to turn to Me. It is not complicated you know to ask Me for forgiveness. Never be fearful of Me. I await each of you who has the courage to condemn your own sins. When you get into this habit some extraordinary gifts are given to you. After confessing your sins you will be in a state of grace. Then when you receive the Sacrament of the Eucharist you will feel a surging energy, which will surprise you. Then and only then will you find true peace.

Nothing will faze you. You will be strong not only in your soul. Your mind will be calmer and more controlled. You will face life with a different and more positive outlook. Who would not want such a life?

Come back children to Me during these times of sorrow in the world. Let Me show you the joy that is yours when you turn to Me.

Remember I gave up My Life for you once. My Love knows no bounds. I will answer your call. All you have to do is ask.

Your precious Loving Saviour

Jesus Christ

Prophecy at Garabandal will now become a reality

Tuesday, May 31, 2011 15.30 hours

My dearly beloved daughter we have come a long way in such a short time. That was for a reason. For it was all the time needed to impart My most Holy Word in a world

starving of My Love. Still they do not listen, because they do not want to know. While many of My loyal followers are alert now to the changes coming so many have no interest, whatsoever, in the warnings givens to the world by My Beloved Mother up to now. The prophecies given at Garabandal will now become a reality. Prepare now for this event for you have only a few months left to prepare your souls.

Please do not fear My daughter for I know that these events have made you sad because you are thinking of your children's future. The Warning will change everything. But it will present a fork in the road. Mankind, when having been woken up to the truth of the existence of God will then, through his own free will chose one of two paths, the path of salvation, or the path of damnation.

Chastisement will wipe out much of the world Pray hard that man chooses the first. For if He doesn't the world will suffer the most severe Chastisement with much of it wiped out. Why would My children wish this? Yet, because of sin, man will sadly chose to ignore My promise and follow the path of the Deceiver. I have told you I will not give you a date for The Warning for this is known by only a few chosen souls. For if this date were to be made public people would be tempted to seek redemption out of a sense of false humility. Trust in Me. All will be well children. You are blessed to be given this wonderful Gift of Revelation. The world will now seem to become quieter and somewhat strange in the coming months leading up to The Warning. For when it happens, spectacular though it will be visually in the sky so quiet will this mystical experience be that you will be more prepared for this silent encounter with your own conscience.

Remember the more people that are forewarned of this event the more souls will be saved. Pray, pray My Divine Mercy for those souls who will die during The Warning. They need your prayers.

Your Loving Saviour

Jesus Christ

Pope Benedict's Day are now numbered
Wednesday, June 01, 2011 11.00 hours

My dearly beloved daughter you have just been tested yet again in My Most Holy Name to deviate from the Truth. This will be a regular occurrence for not a day will pass when The Deceiver will not stop to try and take you away from this work by placing doubts in your mind.

You must not look at other visionaries messages or listen to any other person who claims to come in My Name if they give you a message, which is contrary to the Word you receive from Me.

My prophecies are accurately communicated to you My daughter. Satan will continue to chip away and hurt you when you least expect it. So be on your guard at all times. My beloved Vicar's days are now numbered. He will have left the Vatican before The Warning takes place. Trust in Me. Obey Me. You are now progressing well. But never take your eyes away from Me

Do not, however, be afraid to live your life as you would normally as long as prayer and devotion to Me is an integral and important part. I am going to ensure that you are not alone in this work from now on and that only those who are being directed by Me will have any influence on your discernment.

Trust Me when I say Satan will not sabotage My Words nor contaminate these Messages you receive from Me. That will not happen in this instance, for this Mission is paramount and every protection is offered to you My daughter. If you ever feel concerned about any Messages simply ask Me for the answer and it will be given. Do not ask anybody else for their views for they are not qualified to comment on My Divine Word.

Never get involved with other visionary's messages. This is very important for it will damage your Work.

By now you know that I, your Saviour and King of Mankind am in Authority. No man shall sully My Word. Ever. Be thankful you are being afforded the gift of prophecy and obey Me at all times. Never offend Me by doubting. Those times are well behind you. Seek Me out with humility in your heart and soul. Keep silent when My Word is mocked, attacked, denied, contradicted and questioned for it is not up to you to answer for Me. You will learn so much more from Me My daughter if you will sit down and listen to Me. I infuse your mind with the gift of discernment. Accept this gift. Do not doubt. Rejoice with Me.

This is a very important Mission unlike anything I have sent to mankind since the early prophets. It is going to require strength on your part in human terms. What is important right now is to simply communicate with Me through prayer, Adoration and the Blessed Sacraments. Anything else must be kept outside of this. Your family is very important at all times. Everything outside of these two entities falls into a much lower category. Try to relax and feel My Love. Don't waste valuable time worrying. Just join with Me in full union and you will be safe from harm. I love you My daughter and I trust you.

Your devoted Saviour and Teacher

Jesus Christ

Satan recruits young people through pop culture
Saturday, June 04, 2011 17.00 hours

My dearly beloved daughter conversion, as a direct result of My Messages, given to you is spreading the world over. Rejoice for I told you that My Word, when read, would ignite souls everywhere including those lukewarm sinners. When I gave My Word to the world thousands of years ago to My beloved apostles they made a deep impact on mankind. Today, apart from the followers of God the Eternal Father and I His son, Jesus Christ, much of what was taught has sadly been forgotten.

My communications through you, My daughter, is to try and simplify My Teachings. More importantly, the reason I speak now is to remind, teach and instil My Most Holy Word in the minds of My children so that they can be saved from the clutches of Satan.

My daughter I have filled your soul, through the Gift of the Holy Spirit, with the power of discernment. This power is given to you not just so that you can understand these Messages but to reveal to you the evil of sin. Now, when you witness sin you feel sickened to such an extent that it will make you feel agitated. I am giving you now a taste of what I suffer when I see My children infested with sin.

Many of those you see in your day-to-day life, through the media, the movies and on TV confuse you. Sin, when present in souls manifests itself in a way that is clear to see through certain signs. You, My daughter, can now through My graces, immediately discern sin in someone. The first sign you will see is arrogance and pride where one man considers himself more important than another. Other signs presented to you stem from the sin of pride and greed.

One of the most rampant sins in the world today is sexual perversity. When it is presented to the world it will always be camouflaged by humour. This is a clever way of trying to convince others that it is a natural part of your human make-up. You see, My daughter, every person in the world likes to laugh and needs a sense of humour, which is a gift from God. So when sexually deviant behaviour is promoted it will usually be presented to make you laugh. This is when it will demean not just women but where it will influence young children so that they will accept evil decadent behaviour as normal pop culture.

Satan likes to recruit young souls. So he uses modern means to target these precious little lambs of mine. They, My little children, will unwittingly emulate their disgusting behaviour, which will be fuelled even further by peer pressure.

Warning to those in the Music Industry

I warn now all those in the music, movie and the arts industry. If you continue to contaminate My children you will be punished severely. You, My misguided children, are puppets in Satan's armoury. He uses you by first seducing you through the allure of wealth, fame and opulence. Then he invades your soul. After that he will drag you into the depths of depravity where his demons will enter your body so they can act out their own horrible lusts and sexually depraved acts. All along you will think that this is just harmless entertainment. Don't you know that your souls are being stolen? Don't you care? Don't you realise that if you commit these acts of obscene sexual depravity you will be lost forever? As you lustily crave for more excitement when the last act no longer excites you will become insatiable. After that you will self-destruct. Why do you think there are so many of you who are living in this false façade that is celebrity culture committing suicide? Taking drug overdoses? Feeling depressed? Despair tearing through your hearts? Don't you know that Satan wants your soul quickly? The sooner you die in mortal sin the quicker Satan can steal your soul from God, the Almighty Father your Creator.

It is difficult for My children who are caught up in this lie to understand. But think of it like this. Even when you are in sin there is still the light of God present in you. Many sinners, and atheists do not realise this. They continue on their downward spiral of sin moving closer to Hell. Yet it is only because of the Light from God that keeps them sane. Without the Light of God this earth would be in darkness. This darkness, once experienced, will terrorise you. Your sinful acts will not only be repulsive to you but you will want to run and hide. For even then if the Light of God were to suddenly appear you would not be able to withstand the glare or the power.

Without God's Light there is total darkness of soul. Because you My children have never had to do without this Light you would not be able to survive if and when this Light extinguishes.

Nurture your soul - it is all you will take with you into the next life

The Warning will give you a sense of what this feeling will be like. Should you be in mortal sin during The Warning have no fear for it is only that. A warning. Sadly, so shocking will your sins be when you see them in their raw and ugly state that it could affect you physically with shock. Don't wait until then. Do something about your spiritual life now. Consider the dignity of your soul. Nurture you soul because it is all you will take with you into the next life. Your body is of no consequence. However if you use your body, given to you by God the Almighty Father as a gift, in a sinful manner so that you cause others to sin, it will be your body that will cause the downfall of your soul.

Think My children of your future happiness. For your time on earth is only a fraction of the time you will experience in your existence. Failure to look after your soul will guarantee your isolated abandonment into Hell in which no life exists other than eternal pain and torture.

Every day millions float swiftly towards the gates of Hell

Every day millions of souls, at the moment of death, float swiftly towards the gates of Hell, powerful people, leaders, rich, poor, singers, actors, terrorists, murderers, rapists and those who have had abortions. The one common denominator all of them share is this. None of them believed that Hell exists.

Your Loving Saviour and Teacher

Jesus Christ

Two comets will collide, My Cross will appear in a red sky

Sunday, June 05, 2011 16.30 hours

My dearly beloved daughter time is near. The Warning is close now. It is with great sorrow that I must tell you that many souls will not heed these Messages about The Warning. My Word falls on deaf ears. Why won't they listen? I am not only giving them My great Gift of Mercy when I will shower My Graces over the whole world, I am also trying to prepare them for this event. Many millions of sinners will rejoice when they are shown My Great Mercy. Others won't get a chance to redeem them selves in time because they will die of shock.

My daughter you must do everything you can to warn the world because this great event will shock everyone. They will see great signs in the skies before The Warning takes place. Stars will clash with such impact that man will confuse the spectacle they see in the sky as being catastrophic. As these comets infuse, a great red sky will result, and the Sign of My Cross will be seen all over the world, by everyone. Many will be frightened. But I say rejoice for you will see, for the first time in your lives, a truly Divine Sign that represents great news for sinners everywhere.

See My Cross then and you will know that My Great Mercy is being given to each of you, My precious children. For it was with the deep abiding love that I held for you that I died, willingly, on the Cross, to save you. When you see the crosses in the sky during The Warning you will know that this is a Sign of My Love for you.

Pray My beloved followers that your brothers and sisters can rejoice when they, too, are shown the proof of My existence. Pray that they will accept that this is their chance to redeem themselves in My eyes. That this great act of Mercy will save their souls if they will allow Me to help them.

You will be shown what it is like to die in mortal sin

The Warning will be a purifying experience for all of you. It may be unpleasant in part especially for those in grave sin. Because for the first time ever you will be shown what it feels like when the Light of God disappears from your life. Your souls will feel the abandonment felt by those who die in mortal sin, these poor souls who left it too late to ask God to forgive them their sins. Remember it is important that I allow all of you to feel this emptiness of soul. For only then will you finally understand that without the Light of God in your souls you cease to feel. Your soul and body would be just empty vessels. Even sinners feel the Light of God because He is present in every one of His children on earth. But when you die in mortal sin, this Light no longer exists.

Prepare now for this great event. Save your souls while you can. For it will only be when the Light of God leaves you that you will finally realise the empty, barren darkness that Satan offers which is full of anguish and terror.

Replenish your souls. Rejoice now for The Warning will save you and bring you closer to My Sacred Heart.

Welcome the Warning. For then you will be given the proof of Eternal Life and know how important it is.

Your Beloved Saviour

Jesus Christ

King of Mankind.

The keys of Rome now being handed back to God, the Almighty Father
Monday, June 06, 2011 10.30 hours

My dearly beloved daughter, be strong now. The content of My Messages to you are causing you fear, which you must not succumb to. Sometimes you feel so alone in this work yet I stand with you every day and am not far from your side. My Messages, as I have told you before, will not always bring joy to souls. Believers, however, will understand that Chastisement is necessary to help purify the world.

It is difficult I know to digest the content sometimes but you must place all your trust in Me. I am instructing you, once again, not to engage with those people, believers of mine, who challenge, analyze or pick holes in My Holy Word. For neither you nor those souls has the authority to do so. Let those who continue to pour scorn and denounce My Word be, for this is no longer your concern. Yes, of course, you will be criticised when you proclaim My Word. Ignore those now who try to engage with you. Time is too short to waste with such diversions. The people you need to concern yourself with now are My poor children who lack faith or who do not know Me or My Eternal Father. They are the ones of great concern to Me.

So while those well meaning Christians who will always try to discern My Word devote their time to analysis instead of simply following My Teachings and praying for their poor brothers and sisters, valuable time is being wasted.

My daughter, tell the world that the ecological disasters foretold will now strike the earth. All will commence now, so many, so quickly. And all due to the blind eyes turned on thc Word of God the Father by sinners wrapped up in their dens of iniquity.

Believers do not be fearful

Believers pray now. Do not be fearful. I will offer you My Divine protection at all times even when you are ridiculed in My Name. Prayer will give you strength and courage as the Evil One and his minions now pour out their venom on My children. As their heinous acts of warfare on humanity begins to escalate through terrorism, monopoly of world currencies and the poisoning of the earth through deliberate contamination hear Me now. The Wrath of God the Father will now fall and quickly. Prayer must be conducted in groups all over the world because it will help avert some of these events.

Pray for My beloved Pope Benedict. He is surrounded by very powerful enemies of God, gluttons for power and control of My Church. Prayer can help delay his imminent departure when he will be forced to leave The Vatican as foretold. Pray, pray, pray for this period in time for it will be the darkest ever to befall My sacred servants, Bishops, Cardinals and all true followers of Mine. The keys of Rome will now be handed back to God, the Almighty Father.

The time has come for the battle against Satan and his evil followers. Their attempts to sabotage mankind will be dealt with most severely for they will endure great suffering for their evil acts.

Rise now, My children. Place all your trust, confidence and devotion to Me as a priority. Daily prayer, Mass and The Eucharist will help Me, and My Father, stamp out this evil. Follow Me. Take up My Cup, for when you do this you will enjoy Eternal Life.

Your Loving Saviour

King of Mankind

Jesus Christ

Message from the Virgin Mary regarding her lost children

Tuesday, June 07, 2011 14.45 hours

My child these last few days have not been easy. When you obey my Son that is all that matters. Please do not allow doubts or fears come into your heart at this stage for when they do it is because the Deceiver is at work.

Open your heart to allow the graces to flood your soul so that you can become closer to my Precious Son. You are now close to your Blessed Mother who supports you and guides you at all times. This part of your Mission is hard to deal with but remember that working for my Son is never easy. You will become stronger, despite your hesitancy, because you still follow His instructions so this is good. Pray now for all my lost children everywhere for they are empty of love, the real love that my Son offers them. This love is their salvation. So please offer up all your prayers for these poor lost souls.

Go now in peace and continue to do everything my Son asks of you at all times.

Your Blessed Mother

Mary Queen of Heaven

Message to priests, Bishops and Cardinals about False Prophet

Tuesday, June 07, 2011 15.50 hours

My dearly beloved daughter you have suffered because The Deceiver is tormenting you. You must pray hard to resist his attacks on you. Place all your trust in Me and then let Me deal with these. Instead you are getting upset when you must offer this suffering to Me with joy in your heart.

If you keep reminding yourself that it is because you are in union with Me that these sufferings come about and that you are truly blessed as a chosen soul then you will feel differently.

Many of My followers are now beginning to realise what is happening in the world and through the Graces of the Holy Spirit they are rising to the challenge of defending My Word. This army of the faithful will become stronger now and will fearlessly lead sinners towards salvation.

My Holy Vicar Pope Benedict needs your prayers. Pray for him daily for he needs protection on every level to take him through the torment that lies ahead. It is important that My followers keep alert to any new pope that may come forward for he will not be from God. Please urge all My sacred servants to prepare for the terrible challenges, the most daunting they will ever have to face in their ministry. It will take great courage to stand up to the Truth of My Teachings. So many of My sacred servants are blind to the promises I made when I said I would come again. When did they think this would be? So used are they to reciting My Teachings that they have forgotten that they may witness these events at any time and, perhaps, even in their own lifetime? For this is one of the greatest challenges today.

If I sent prophets into the world thousands of years ago then, of course, I will send them again in the period to prepare the world for when I will come again.

Wake up to the lessons you teach your congregation. Realise that it is I who speaks to you now. Many will come in My Name but few will speak the truth. This Message comes from Me your Divine Saviour. Pray for the discernment to recognise My true voice when it is given to you. Open your hearts now and listen to what I have to tell you. The time has come, to inform you, that the prophecies contained in the Book of Revelation are about to unfold before your eyes.

You, My beloved servants must fight with bravery through your love for Me, against the obstacles, placed by The Deceiver that will challenge you to the end of your endurance. You must acknowledge that the False Prophet is about to seduce you. Charm you. Convince you that he represents the truth. You must now show your allegiance to Me, and My Eternal Father. Please do not despair. For although these events will frighten you and disturb you, your allegiance and loyalty must be to Me.

For the first time in your ministry your faith will be truly tested now. The Church of Peter is My Church. But when the keys are handed back to God the Father, which they will be now, the Church becomes part of My Kingdom. I am the Truth. Follow the Truth at all times.

Pray to Me now for the graces required to ensure you will rise above the deceit of Satan in time. Otherwise the False Prophet will ensnare My beloved children through his charismatic charmful ways, the ways of The Deceiver with whom he is entangled. Satan will not win over My Church if My servants are alert to the deceit and see it for what it is. A diabolical lie from which, if you become involved and swear allegiance to this new abomination, there will be no return!

Hear Me now. Turn to Me for guidance and the special graces required to lead My flock back to Me and My Heavenly Father. For when you do I will bestow such graces that it will not be long before you will find the strength to defend My Word at all costs.

I love you all and yearn for your support during these End Times.

Jesus Christ

Prepare your family to witness My Cross in the Sky

Wednesday, June 08, 2011 16.45 hours

My dearly beloved daughter I must share with you the feelings I am enduring now. The first is one of happiness because I am to bring so much Mercy to My children during the Illumination of Conscience, which is close. And then there are My tears of great sadness for those oblivious to this event and who are unprepared. My children will need to tell as many of their friends and family of this great event in order to save their souls. No matter if they smile and ridicule your claims for, afterwards, they will thank you. Tell them the truth. Ask them to open their minds. They should be made aware of what they will witness because when they see My Cross in the sky they will be prepared. That is all they need to understand. Then they will accept the discomfort they will endure when their past lives are played out before their eyes. Tell them to review their life and remind them of the harm that they may have inflicted on their fellow brothers and sisters.

Spread My Word after the Warning

My children, as soon as The Warning happens and when conversion takes place move quickly to spread My Most Holy Word. There is an urgency to this because this will be a crucial period. That is when, through the work of My beloved followers everywhere that My children will stay on the right path. It will be the time when prayer and conversion can dilute the impact of the havoc, which will come about through the reign of both the antichrist and the False Prophet.

Accept the truth now for what it is. Do not fear the truth. Embrace it. For when you do you will be set free and your confidence in Me will enable you to defend My Word properly. Fear will hold you back My precious children. Courage will win souls. Your battle on My behalf will ease My suffering and bring Eternal Life to so many more souls who desperately need your help.

My Love for you, children, is all encompassing and never waivers in its intensity. My Cross is heavy but when you take it up with love in your hearts your load will be light. You My beloved followers, sacred servants and lay people, are My future army to help defeat Satan. Pray now for the strength to deal with the challenges to your faith. Lead by example and the gift I am bestowing on each of you who pledges his or her allegiance to Me will create instant conversion when you speak My Most Holy Word.

Remember I am with you all the time now. Many of you who have been close to Me for some time will now experience a stronger sense of the Holy Spirit and the power of discernment, which will astonish you. Accept this as one of the greatest gifts being given to man today. I have not bestowed a multitude of such Graces since My apostles were given the precious gifts through The Holy Spirit.

You, My followers, including My sacred servants are My True Church. I will, with the help of God, the Eternal Father, lead you so you can march with all My children towards the New Paradise, which awaits you all.

Your Loving Saviour

Jesus Christ

Message of Love to all My followers

Wednesday, June 08, 2011 21.00 hours

My dearly beloved daughter today I rejoice at the faith shown by My beloved followers all over the world who are hearing My Call through these Messages. I rejoice because of the deep faith shown by My beloved children in a world that rejects Me. My precious children, those who believe in Me, bring tears of joy to Me in times of sadness. Were it not for those with a deep devotion to Me I would not be consoled.

My children who love Me must listen to Me now. Let Me embrace you in My arms and explain to you the importance of your faith. Your faith is like a flame in My Heart, which never dies. It may flicker from time to time but I will instil in you the energy to keep this flame aglow. You, My children of the Light, will devour the darkness but you must stay together as one to fight the antichrist.

Satan cannot win for this is impossible

Always understand this important fact. He, The Deceiver, cannot and will not win for this is impossible. Therefore, you must always accept that My Light and that of My Eternal Father will never diminish, for it is not the Light that will extinguish. But it is the dark that will attract those poor souls who will be drawn towards it. Those poor misguided children are in My Heart and mean just as much to Me as you do. You, My children, as in any family must look after your wayward brothers and sisters. No matter how grave their sins never judge them. Bring them back to Me. Talk to them. Pray My Divine Mercy for them so they can be saved from the clutches of The Evil One at the time of death.

Shout now from the hilltops. Remind everyone of the truth. Ignore those taunts. But when explaining to My children how much I love them do not force your views on them, Instead simply explain that they were created by God the Father. Tell them He sent Me, His only Son to save them, to give them a chance to live Eternal Life. And then tell them I love them and that I walk with each one of them every minute of the day. Even when I witness their rejection and the evil they do onto others I am still there beside them. Hoping they will turn to Me and ask for My help, for when they do I will embrace them with tears of joy and relief. Help Me save those precious souls. Do not let the Deceiver take them from Me. They are your family. My family. We are one. Just one lost soul is one too many.

Thank you My beloved children everywhere. Know that I am with you now in a much stronger Presence through the Holy Spirit than at any other time in History. Hold My hand and walk with Me towards the New Paradise on Earth, which will be your glorious home in the future.
Your beloved Saviour

Jesus Christ King of Mercy

My Spiritual Guidance will block Satan's Acts of Destruction

Saturday, June 11, 2011 15.30 hours

My beloved daughter it has been another testing week where My Word, on the one hand, has been embraced by so many while, at the same time, denied as outright deception by others. Have they who deny My Word not read the Truth? The Truth contained in My Holy Book? The Book of Revelation was given to all My children to help them understand the turmoil which will be caused towards the end times by the spread of lies created by Satan and his demons. Unless you understand the Truth contained in the Book of Revelation then how can you possibly understand the Messages I am bringing to you today?

Do you think that I would turn My back on you and leave you at the mercy of Satan and his evil army? Did you not realise that I would try to warn you and then help you?

My great Mercy will destroy the effect that Satan has over My children. I come yet again to save you from his clutches. My gift of The Warning will dilute the terror that would have continued to gain momentum were this not to take place.

I communicate to you now not just to prepare you for all this great Act of My Mercy but to guide you through the maze of destruction planned by the evil group whose king is the Evil One. My spiritual influence will block Satan's acts of destruction significantly. Hear My Word. Follow My instructions. Lead and support each other in your faith and you will be given the help required to follow the path swiftly towards the promises I made to you.

Many of you, My precious children, will be frightened but please do not let fear block the truth. Satan will use fear to stop you from accepting My Message of Love. Much of what I tell you now is very difficult for you to understand. But understand this. Were I not to come now and show you the Truth then you would be lost. You would find it a very difficult period to live through. As I prepared you through My prophets before I will now prepare you today, through this messenger, for the time when I will come again.

This is a gift borne of My deep love for all of My children to deal with the forthcoming reign of the antichrist and his ally the deceitful False Prophet who will mislead My Church on earth.

Let down your defences. Open your eyes to the Truth. My Word today is given simply to remind you of the Truth of My Teachings. My Holy Scripture is the Truth. The Truth is reflected in My Holy Scripture. If I remind you today of the promises made to you before and of the pathway to salvation then this is only a repetition of My Holy Word. The Truth will always remain the same. It can never be changed or adapted to suit mankind. It will always remain the same.

Let Me help you understand what is happening now. Don't cower in fear. I love you all and simply want to hold your hands children and protect you. My goal is to ensure that every one of you will live life with Me in the New Paradise on earth.

Your Ever-Loving Saviour

Jesus Christ

'Liberators' in Middle East want to control The Jews

Saturday, June 11, 2011 22.00 hours

My dearly beloved daughter it is with love that I speak with you tonight because very soon now more and more of My cherished followers will unite as one to fight The Deceiver. Right now He and the wealthy influential groups behind whom he hides, are plotting to gain as much control over you all but you cannot see this.

They will be stopped sooner than you think. Many of them will convert during The Warning. This will weaken Satan's One World Group to such an extent that many will wonder what path to take, so confused will they be. Many will then turn back to Me children for they will seek redemption.

Revenge, control, power and hatred combined create the biggest threat to man's survival. All of the wars you see taking place in the Middle East and beyond have been orchestrated. They are not a coincidence. Understand that so many countries at once did not rise up on their own, they were helped by the Evil Group in all governments, those governments who control the World. These leaders in the Middle East are now being removed to make way for the liberators, those who will proclaim justice and peaceful means to help My children. But that is not their intention. Their intention is to control of My beloved people, the Jews who are under threat now on all sides.

All of these events will be interrupted by The Warning. All of those involved with this evil global group will also have to face Me one by one when I will show them how they offend Me. Many will fall down on their knees and beg for redemption.

This, My children, is very important for the more sinners, everywhere and especially those who control your livelihoods turn back to Me the greater will be My Mercy. Pray that all those who witness the Truth when, during The Warning, they will realise that I love them will convert.

Prayer, My children, is very powerful. When you pray to God, the Father in My Name for the salvation of these and other souls He will not refuse you.

Your loyalty to Me, and daily prayer is needed urgently to loosen the grip that Satan holds over My children who are rightfully Mine.

Your Ever Merciful Saviour

Abundant Love at Adoration makes you stronger and calmer

Sunday, June 12, 2011 19.00 hours

My beloved daughter the graces received by My children at the Eucharistic Adoration are powerful. They not only give you the graces to cope with life's suffering they make you stronger in your love for Me your devoted and loyal Saviour.

The love that is poured out over souls during the Adoration is given in abundance. The soul feels this flood of My graces in so many different ways. The first gift is one of peace in your soul. You will feel this instantly after you have completed your time in close union with Me.

So many, many of My children are denying themselves the many gifts I have to offer at Adoration, where you spend one hour of your time before My Presence on the altar. While Catholics are aware of the power of the Eucharist many do not acknowledge the importance of this most important time with Me in contemplation. They simply ignore this Gift. It bores them to have to spend this extra time with Me.

O if only you knew how strong this would make them. Their fears and worries would be dissipated were they to just keep Me company in quiet intimate reflection. If My children could see the light that envelops their souls during this special Holy Hour they would be astonished.

Children it is during this hour that you become very, very close to Me. This is where your voice, your pleas, your pledges of love for Me will be heard. Many wonderful graces are given to you children at this time so please do not ignore My pleas to spend this time in My company.

The rewards will make you free of worry

The rewards will make you free of worry, light of heart, mind and soul and calmer in yourself. When you receive Me during the Eucharist I will fill your soul. But when you come to Me in Adoration I will envelop you to such an extent that the floodgates of My Merciful Love will saturate your mind, body and soul. You will feel a strength, which will yield a quiet confidence that you will find difficult to ignore.

Come to Me children now. I need your company. I need you to speak with Me when My Divine Presence is at its strongest. I love you and want to pour all My graces on you so you can fuse your souls to My Sacred Heart.

Your Loving Saviour

Jesus Christ

Hand Me over your troubles and I will ease your burden

Monday, June 13, 2011 18.00 hours

My dearly beloved daughter prayer is increasing now at a stronger pace due to the Gift of the Holy Spirit, which has penetrated the souls of all My followers the world over. Their ears are now alert to My Most Holy Word.

Pray for all My poor tormented children who are suffering great hardship in the world as a result of the horror of the acts to which they are victims, all because of the sins of mankind.

Let Me remind all My children everywhere to recite My Divine Mercy chaplet every single day. Pray too, and I include all Christian faiths, the Holy Rosary to My Beloved Mother for this powerful prayer will weaken Satan's power over My children.

All I ask is for all of you who are in sorrow with trials and worries to hand Me over now all these concerns and allow Me deal with them. Trust in Me and your burden will be eased. Let Me guide you into a more peaceful state. Relax My children and allow My Peace to flood your delicate starving souls. The darkness you feel stems from fear. Fear stems from lack of trust. When you lose trust in Me, Satan plants doubts in your minds.

Never underestimate what he does when he constantly plays games to turn you against your neighbour. This deceit is always primarily directed at My most devout followers. He hates you if you love Me. He will never rest until he unsettles you. He laughs when you falter. Don't give him this power because when you do your faith in Me weakens.

The Prayer to St Michael and the recital of the Most Holy Rosary are your most powerful weapons against Satan.

Go now with more confidence and hand Me over your problems and concerns because I am here waiting for you at all times to bring you into the Light.

I love you all children. Trust in Me more.

Your Loving Saviour

Jesus Christ

My followers must show courage to prepare others for The Warning

Tuesday, June 14, 2011 19.00 hours

My beloved daughter much work needs to be done by My followers to tell people what they must expect during The Warning.

Give them details in advance so that when they see the red sky flare up, a reflection of My Great Mercy, they will know that there is nothing to fear. Instead they must rejoice for here, at last for many of My children around the world, will be the proof they have been seeking all their lives.

Great rejoicing amongst My children is what I yearn for not tears of sadness. When you see My Cross you will all know then the Passion of My Love for all of you.

Many will weep tears of great joy for they will know I have come to flood their souls with the Grace of Redemption. For others who don't know Me they will be frightened for then the true realization of the graveness of their sins will become apparent.

Follows of mine everywhere I call on you to show great courage by telling My children that they must not fear when they witness this divine spectacular display of My Great Mercy for mankind. Bring them back into My fold by preparing them. If they will not listen pray for them.

Your Eternal Saviour and Redeemer of Mankind

Jesus Christ

Intellectual Religious Snobbery offends Me

Wednesday, June 15, 2011 10.00 hours

Today My daughter I want to warn those devoted followers of Mine who publicly proclaim My Name, to follow the truth of My Teachings and to thread carefully.

I love all My followers and especially those who show humility at all times. I become frustrated, however, when solemn and earnest Christians who speak My Word try to analyse My Teachings in a loud and dictatorial manner. Not enough is it to spread My Word they feel they must bring

My Teachings into a human intellectual debate, which serves only one purpose. To prove to others that they are more qualified to understand My Most Holy Word. So intent are they to prove that they are right in their discernment that they divide My true followers. Their solemn and earnest devotion to Me can often render them impotent in their real love for Me, which should always stem from humility.

They must keep their loud voices, full of intellectual criticism, quiet. They must stop, listen to My voice and resist the urge to prove their knowledge of spiritual matters to others. When they do this they are guilty of the sin of pride. They do not know Me at all. Because they do not take the time to stay quiet and humble themselves before My eyes which are all seeing. Until these solemn followers of mine become little in My eyes and lower themselves before Me I will not be able to draw them to Me.

Glorify Me. Honour My Word. Follow My example. Never persecute others in My Name especially your fellow Christians.

Your beloved Teacher and Saviour

Jesus Christ

Communicate to a young materialist and fickle society

Wednesday, June 15, 2011 23.00 hours

My dearly beloved daughter the trials and spiritual dryness you are enduring at present are allowed by Me to bring you even closer in union with Me.

Sometimes when you suffer I have to turn to one side so I won't have to witness your sorrow. Yet as you endure each trial and move onwards to the next stage you will become even stronger than before. The deeper your suffering from the cruelty and abuse of others who ridicule you because of this Sacred Work becomes, the more graces you will receive.

How to suffer in My Name

To suffer in My Name, however, is not enough. You must not complain openly about these torments. You must, to satisfy Me, suffer in silence My daughter. To the outside world you must appear to be joyful. Only then will your soul be fortified and brought to the level of sanctity that I require of you for your Mission. For when you evolve in this way the fruits yielded when you speak My Word means that My Messages will be heard more effectively in every corner of the world.

This time, as I prepare all My children for the greatest challenge since My Crucifixion, it is vital that as many people hear My Most Holy Word. The Truth now being revealed will be heard not only by believers but by those who do not want to know Me or who don't want to accept the Truth of the existence of God, the Eternal Father.

Communicate to a young materialist and fickle society

My daughter you must use methods that will communicate My Word to a young, materialist and fickle society. Ensure that you communicate in a way that they will understand, pay attention to and talk about. For what good is this work if it is simply just reinforces My Holy Word to believers only? Yes, it is important that My followers are reminded of the promises I made when I said I would come again, but it is those souls with no knowledge, understanding or interest in My Compassion for mankind who I must reach at all costs.

You My daughter and My followers have a duty to inform agnostics, atheists and a whole young generation of the truth now. Speak to them in gentle tones. Never be aggressive. Use words of encouragement. Make My Word interesting.

Not the end of the world

Talk to them of the promise I made for the New Paradise on Earth. It will not mean the world will end but, rather that a new Era of Peace, joy and happiness will now evolve. They cannot, and must not turn their back on this Glory. Pray for them. Bring them to Me and you will receive special guidance and graces.

Simplicity and the Truth should be your weapons of choice. Lead by example. My daughter you must plan now to use different and new methods of communicating My Word. Help will be sent for you to achieve this.

Spread My Word using modern communications

Modern communications methods must be utilized to ensure that My Word is spread rapidly. Pray now. Ask publishers in as many countries as you can to produce the volumes in as many languages as possible. Use audio, video and other methods to spread My Word quickly. Call on volunteers to forward My Messages to the multitudes.

For this, My daughter, will save souls. I love you. Your strength and determination to succeed in this work, which stems from the pure love you have for Me and My Beloved Mother, will bring souls - who would otherwise have gone to Hell - back into My Arms and eternal salvation.

Ignore those who show disrespect for My Name

Be brave. Ignore abuse. Do not respond to those who show disrespect for My Name. It will be My followers who will hurt you the most. For many, well-meaning true disciples of mine fall into error from time to time. Their knowledge of My Teachings can create a sense of pride, which leads to arrogance. Then intellectual pride creeps in. Those poor loving and solemn souls of mine whose love for Me is not in question must never look down on those they may feel are on the wrong path. They must not fall into Satan's trap of assuming a position of superiority and solemn rigidness. This then becomes a battle of wits to see who, in human terms, is more knowledgeable than the other or who has a better understanding of the Truth of My Teachings.

Remember what I taught you all. The Truth is simple. The Truth is Love. In your quest to prove your interpretation of My Holy Word if you do not show love and patience then your version of the truth is not of Me.

Love each other. You are all equal in My eyes. But for those of you who go out of your way to help bring My lost souls back to Me then you will be risen in My Eyes.

Your Divine Saviour

King of all Mankind

Jesus Christ

My Children will face Me for the first time during The Warning

Monday, June 20, 2011 11.45 hours

My beloved daughter, prepare My children now for very soon they will come before Me in all My glory and compassion. I will show Myself to every single man, woman and child over the age of reason very soon.

This wonderful day when I will show them My Mercy as opposed to My Justice must be welcomed by all. Rejoice for you will all, each and every one of you face Me for the first time.

For many they will be full of love and happiness for this is a wonderful reunion. For others they will be fearful. But there is nothing to fear for I love you all. Sin will be the only division but if you repent and accept the truth of your offences against Me, and My Eternal Father, you will realise the wonderful Mercy, which is being afforded you. For those who will be fearful I have this to say. Fear stems from sin. With sin in your soul you will be distanced from Me. Accept your sins for what they are, a human weakness. Then look to Me and I will lead you to Eternal Life and the Truth.

My Great Mercy brings wonderful news

My Great Mercy brings wonderful news to My children the world over.

For when this, The Great Warning takes place, you will be given a chance to change your lives for the better. When the truth of My existence is revealed then conversion will be widespread.

Then, and only then, after The Warning takes place will the world be given a chance to withstand the Great Chastisement, which will follow if sinners do not repent in their multitudes. For then the Hand of My Father will fall everywhere on those who refuse to hear the truth - those who turn their back on love, love for Me and your brothers and sisters. For your sinful ways will be, at that stage, no longer accepted. For this would be the final straw. For Satan's powerful influence will not be allowed to retain its vice like grip on mankind. Those who stubbornly follow the wicked path where they persecute My children will be stopped.

The Great Chastisement

A Great Chastisement, the likes of which has not been witnessed since the time of Noah, will be unleashed by God, the Eternal Father. My followers who may say that this is not the way in which Jesus speaks need now to ask yourselves this question. If Jesus is full of Mercy why would He, or God the Father allow Satan's army to continue and inflict terror on My children? It is out of love for all of God's children that this Great Chastisement will take place. Repent all of you. Reject the empty promises of Satan. Reject the false empty life he offers you. Accept that when you hear My Name being rejected in the world today that this comes directly from the influence of Satan. Until My children turn away from him then there can be no peace in this world.

Accept this Warning as a Message of Pure Love. To those in power I say this. Reject the lies to which you have paid allegiance or suffer the consequences.

The Great Mercy I will show you during The Warning is the solution for a New Era of Peace. Accept it and the Chastisement will be averted. Reject it and only those followers of Mine can be saved. It will be too late for the rest of you.

Your Loving Saviour

Just Judge

Jesus Christ

Message from Virgin Mary about communicating to Young People

Wednesday, June 22, 2011 18.00 hours

(after a private apparition in which she appeared to the visionary for over 30 minutes)

I come in the Name of Jesus Christ. I am the Mother of God your beloved Mother Queen of all the Angels.

My child, you have just been tested because of the work you do for my beloved Son and you have become stronger as a result. You know now what has to be done so that as many young people as possible understand Who my Son is. He, the Most Precious Son of mine, Saviour of the World, will do everything to save all of those who walk the earth in ignorance of His Mercy.

Those children who stubbornly refuse to listen must be told the truth and very soon. Please tell young people all over the world that Jesus walks with them every second of the day. He cares so much for them. They have no idea of the depth of His Love. He wants to embrace them into His Sacred heart so that they will enjoy the New Era of Peace on earth. If only they would respond.

My child it is so difficult for people to understand the truth of the existence of God, the Father. To convince them of the truth of His Beloved Son's Sacrifice is very difficult. This, my child, must be your goal. Go in Peace and Love.

Your beloved Mother

Queen of the Angels

The Warning will prove that God Exists

Wednesday, June 22, 2011 19.00 hours

My dearly beloved daughter, strong now, having endured the worst trial so far, you will move to impart My urgent pleas to the whole world.

They, My beloved children, need to know that when I come soon they will come face to face with Me. How I long to show them that I really do exist and how I await the joy on their faces when they witness My Love and Mercy.

For many of My children will fall down and cry tears of relief, tears of joy and happiness, tears of wonder and love. For, at last, it will be possible to live a New Life thereafter where all can follow the Truth of My Teachings. My children will not realise the significance of this Great Act of Mercy, the greatest Gift ever bestowed on mankind since My Crucifixion. For it will be through this Gift of The Warning that man's eyes will be finally opened to the truth of their entire existence on this earth and beyond.

Those who are alive in this world today must understand how privileged they are to be given the proof of the existence of God, the Eternal Father and I, His beloved Son, although this is beyond your comprehension.

After the Warning do not turn back to your old ways

I urge all of you that when you have seen My Presence and shown how sin, not only offends Me but propels you down the pathway to Hell that you must not turn back to your old ways.

The period after the Warning is crucial for world peace and your salvation. Do not reject this gift. Grasp it with both arms. Let The Warning bring you as one in Me. When you do this and pray for guidance you will be rewarded with the New Paradise on Earth where you will want for nothing.

Rejoice. Listen to Me. Heed My Message and allow My Love to envelop you towards My Glorious Kingdom.

I love you all. The next time you feel a stab of love in your heart for another fellow being remember that this gift comes from Me. Without love there is no life.

Your Divine King of Mercy

Jesus Christ

Son of God, the Eternal Father

Ordinary People, Good People Turn their Backs on Me

Thursday, June 23, 2011 21.10 hours

My dearly beloved daughter the joy you feel today is as result of the graces bestowed on you during Adoration yesterday. Now you know how important it is to allow Me to pour such graces on souls during this most special time when in My personal company.

How to identify lost souls

Today I want to talk to you about lost souls in the world and how to identify them. My followers often mistakenly believe that lost souls are those in mortal sin. This is not necessarily true. A lost soul can be a person who does not believe in Me or My Eternal Father. A lost soul can also be those children so caught up in their day-to-day pursuit of earning money, building wealth, careers and craving after material things. All because of the joy they believe that these things will bring them in their future lives. These are ordinary people, good people but who turn their backs on Me.

Many of these children of mine are good at heart. They can be full of love for their fellow men, their family and friends. They may be popular and well liked. And yet they can be lost souls. How is this you may ask? Because they do not believe that their soul is just as important as their physical needs and so they neglect it. By neglecting their soul they are prone to temptations thrown their way each day. They find it hard to resist worldly goods without considering that the time they invest in their ambitions could be spent showing love to others through the art of sharing. In their pursuit of money they can become proud. Pride makes it difficult to behave like a true follower of Mine.

Children if you spend all your time chasing the dreams that you believe this world has to offer - wealth, possessions and positions of power - there is little time left to pray or nurture your souls for the next life. So many of My children can never understand why worldly goods leave them empty inside. They do not listen to those followers of Mine who know the truth. By failing to acknowledge the existence of God, the Almighty Father, they cannot succeed in pleasing anyone other than themselves. On the outside these people live active, healthy, fun-filled lives without a care in the world. But this kind of lifestyle cannot be achieved in the right way without believing in Eternal Life. Humility is missing in their lives.

You may say, in their defence, but they need to feed their families and look after others who rely on them and so they work towards these goals? My answer is no they don't. They are not aiming to feed their families. In many cases they are aiming for excesses to satisfy their lusts. The more they do this the more they become lost to Me and My Eternal Father.

Unless My children wake up and recognise the ways in which Satan uses all the glorifying attractions of the world to suck you into a false sense of materialistic security you cannot come to Me. Time must be spent in this life in praise of your Creator. In looking after your neighbour through charitable works. In putting others needs before your own. By following in My footsteps.

Unless My children who do not believe in God the Father or who do believe in Him but who chose conveniently to push any homage to Him aside because they are more concerned with worldly matters they will find it hard to enter the gates of Heaven, the True Paradise they crave. Earth is just a phase in your entire being. Heaven, even a glimpse of what it offers, cannot be experienced in your lives on earth. None of those worldly attractions are worth chasing if it means you have to forfeit the jewel that is Heaven.

The essential traits to enter My Glorious Kingdom are faith, love, humility and a desire to please Me.

Your beloved Teacher and Saviour of all Mankind

Jesus Christ

People don't know what their soul is - the answer is simple
Saturday, June 25, 2011 01.30 hours

My dearly beloved daughter your voice, while being heard finally by My sacred servants all over the world, falls silently in those quarters oblivious to the existence of God the Almighty Father.

You may say, they don't listen, but they cannot listen if they don't hear. Be brave now talk to as many as you can. Ask people to publish the news of My Word. Call them. Ask them. Explain that they must read My Messages before they dismiss them. For it will only be when they feel the strength that comes from My Divine lips, when My Spirit will attract their spirit that they will finally understand that it is I Who is communicating to the world.

I am sad, My daughter, because of the deep barricades and divides which today block out every attempt by My Blessed Mother and I, her precious Son, to speak through visionaries to the world. In the past humility was a little more prevalent. Today, this important trait has disappeared. In its place is a world where everything that exudes human intelligence, allure or physical appeal is accepted as a priority in people's lives. Their spirituality has died. They are, My daughter, merely empty shells. Shells that when cracked are nothing. Substance of soul is what My children must strive for. This is difficult for many people and especially those whose minds are full of human wisdom where little space is left for spiritual wisdom.

Such is the lack of spirituality, fuelled by the power of Satan, that people have fallen prey to leave open their souls to commit sin. A lack of spirituality or belief in God, renders a soul to contamination by The Deceiver. The King of Deceit leads souls in the belief that only the body and mind alone are interwoven to become whole. Sadly, you cannot be whole without your soul.

What is your soul?
Many people don't know what their soul is. What it feels like or how to recognise it. Is it your mind, your conscience? The answer is simple. Your soul is you. It is who you are, your conscience, your beliefs, your understanding, whether this represents the truth for what it is or the truth for what you want to believe it is. It is not a separate part of you, dear children, something that belongs to another world. It is present within each human being.

Your soul can be looked after by following My Teachings. It can be neglected through sin, which is very difficult to avoid, but it can be replenished by confessing or expressing remorse and starting out again. Or it can be destroyed. Some deliberately destroy their soul by sinning for the pleasures or vices of this world, in the full knowledge of what they are doing. Others deny they have a soul. Their arrogance convinces them that they know all. That life begins and ends on this earth.
And then there are those young souls who, through no fault of their own, were reared by parents in times of plenty where they wanted for nothing in the materialistic sense. Their religion is based on material gain. By

striving for more stimulus their ambition continues to increase until, eventually, there is nothing else they can strive for until death faces them. Then they are lost. Puzzled. Confused. With a deep sickening feeling inside they know something is wrong. The soul is telling them but they don't know how to respond. They are the ones you need to save.

I call on all of My followers everywhere to help Me save all of My poor children. I know I am asking for an extraordinary act of generosity on your part. It is a huge responsibility. But by obeying My Most Holy Will you will help Me save much of the world from the grip of Satan and the terror he wields.

Go forth now, My followers, all of you and spread My Word to a jaded, misguided and disillusioned world. My Graces will pour forth over each of you for even just one conversion. One soul that can escape the horror of hell. I love you all. I embrace you My followers, My precious children everywhere. How you bring Me daily comfort. How you console Me. Now bring Me more souls.

Your Divine Redeemer

Saviour of all Mankind

Jesus Christ

Virgin Mary - Satan loses his power when My Rosary is recited

Saturday, June 25, 2011 15.00 hours

My child, always keep focused on my Son for He needs your attention. You must place all your trust in Him and never let anyone take your eyes off Him.

He, my child, has chosen you as one of the important messengers for these times so that lost souls are saved. Tell people to pray my Most Holy Rosary, even non-Catholics, for this is the greatest weapon against the influence of The Deceiver who groans in pain when it is said. His power is weakened when my children say this prayer. The more my children pray the Holy Rosary the more souls can be saved.

You, my child, have a very difficult Mission, much harder than any of the prophets in history. This is because of the darkness of spirit in the world. Never before has such a darkness descended when My children turn their back on my Son, He who died a terrible death to save them. Yet they have not only forgotten this but choose to deny His very existence. Prayer to me, your Blessed Mother, hurts the Evil One who cringes and loses his power when my Rosary is recited. This is the weapon that has been given to me so I can help save lost souls before I crush the serpent's head finally. Never underestimate the power of the Rosary for even just one group of people dedicated to the regular devotion of my Holy Rosary can save their nation. Tell my children to be careful when turning their back on prayer for when they do this they are leaving themselves wide open for The Deceiver to ensnare them by his charming but dangerous path to darkness. Bring my children into the light by spreading devotion to my Most Holy Rosary.

Your Beloved Mother

Mary Queen of Peace

First Message from God the Father - The time has come now for Me to reclaim My Glorious Kingdom - New Paradise on earth will last 1000 years

Saturday, June 25, 2011 16.00 hours

Note from Visionary "Just before I received this Message I had just finished reciting the Divine Mercy when suddenly the Holy Spirit announced to me that I was to receive a Message from God the Father.

I was trembling with nerves. I then asked the question "In whose Name do you come?" This was the response.

I come in the Name of My beloved Son, Jesus Christ, Saviour of mankind. I am God the Father and I am speaking to you for the first time. My chosen daughter I speak to you today so that I can inform mankind of the Love I have for all.

Many do not know Me. They think they do but for millions of My children I am merely a faceless entity. So little do they know of My desire to allow them to let Me Love them in the way in which it was meant to be.

My Name is used loosely in the world by many who don't acknowledge that it was by My Hand that the world and its creatures were made for those that do they are confused as to Who I am and are somewhat fearful of Me. I am not to be feared for My Love is Pure for all of My children. So much do I love you that I made the greatest Sacrifice of all to bring you back into My Arms and give you the opportunity to be saved from the deceiver. I sent My beloved Son, Jesus Christ, into the world so that you could understand the Truth of Love. This Love, when you accept it, will save you all.

My Heart is broken by the way so many of you will not turn to Me and show Me your love. I yearn for you to simply turn and ask Me for help. There is no need to fear My Love for it was through My Love that you were given your first breath. I created each of you in My Likeness so that I could have a family. I created the world out of Pure Love so that you, My children, could share this Paradise with Me. So lovingly was this created that every single detail was so carefully constructed. So happy was I when Paradise on Earth was created that the angels rejoiced and Heaven was alight with the flames of love that no human being could ever possibly fathom. And then it was destroyed by sin caused by the serpent.

My children let Me explain. The time has come for Me to reclaim the

Paradise I lovingly created so that we can, again, become one family.

A family that will become close because of the powerful bounds of love that will hold it together.

This New Paradise on Earth is now being planned for all of My children.

It will last 1,000 years on earth and no one must be excluded for that would break My Heart. My beloved Son, Jesus Christ and the Holy Spirit are trying hard to bring you back into My loving fold so that the Paradise, created in the beginning can, once again, emerge as the greatest gift of all for My children to enjoy.

This Paradise will be a place of love, beauty, glory, and will be home to all who are pure of heart and soul. It is for every single soul on earth and is the goal that is contained within each and every single soul on earth, including those who do not realise this.

My Son speaks to the world and prepares to show His great Mercy during The Warning to give all sinners a chance to enjoy the New Paradise on Earth

You must hear My Voice. I call on all of you to pay attention. Turn back to Me. Accept that I exist, that I am the source of all life, all creation, all glory. When you do you will be welcomed into My Paradise on Earth which offers everything you could ever dream of. Listen to My Son and the Message He gives to the world to convert you all. For those who will not listen, even then, or who continue on the path of heinous sin, no Mercy will be shown.

I am the God of all Creation. I am the God of Love, of Compassion. I am also the God of Justice. My Hand will fall on humanity, who through the evil allegiance to the Evil One, refuse to follow the path of Love and Truth.

For the time has come now for Me to reclaim My Glorious Kingdom which no man, through sin, will stop. Should they try they will be lost forever.

I am your God, your Creator. My Love never dies. It is aflame and full of deep tenderness for you to bring you back to Me, to the inheritance I so lovingly created. Because of sin many of My children will have to forfeit their right to this inheritance and step back to allow those who truly love Me to enter the doors without hindrance.

Please children do not dismiss My plea to mankind. Accept the Mercy now being offered by My beloved Son.

Accept it with open arms.

God the Father

Creator and Maker of All Things

The Warning is a manifestation of My Divine Mercy given to St. Faustina

Sunday, June 26, 2011 18.00 hours

My dearly beloved daughter time is close now. There is very little time to warn and prepare all those poor souls who will be so shocked during The Warning that they will not realise what they are witnessing. They must be told so that they will know what to expect. If they open their hearts to this great moment of Divine Mercy they will be given the chance of Eternal Life.

This great Warning is the manifestation of My Divine Mercy given to Sister Faustina. This great Act of My Mercy was foretold and it will be during The Warning that My Great Mercy will envelop the whole world. My Blood and Water will gush forth so that you will all know the truth at last. Tell those who do not believe in Me, or My Eternal Father, that this event will happen. Then when it does they will be able to withstand the shock of My Mercy, which will save millions of souls during The Warning from the grasp of Satan. The truth, when revealed, will save so many from the fires of Hell.

The Holy Spirit thereafter present in My children everywhere will help defeat the works of The Evil One. All of you must spread the Word about how mankind needs to prepare their souls in advance. For even believers must understand that they too will find it emotionally disturbing to view their own past sinful behaviour as it appears to Me.

I call on all of you now to seek Confession. For those other Christians you must kneel down and pray for redemption. For those who are unsure of this prophecy please keep your hearts open for when you witness this ecological but supernatural event it is important that you understand that this is the greatest miracle you will ever see and that it is My Great Gift to you all. Consider this. This is how the Final Day of Judgment will unfold only this time you will not be condemned. You will be given a new lease of life when your soul will be saved to enable you to restore to the level I desire of it.

Believers pray for others with all your hearts now that they will be saved.

Yours Saviour

Jesus Christ

Continue to spread My Word - I am sending you many volunteers

Tuesday, June 28, 2011 19.30 hours

My dearly beloved daughter the hurdles are getting higher, over which you must jump when you suffer for Me. The attempts by The Deceiver to pull you from this work have never been so powerful. You must stay strong and stand firm against such attacks. Know that he, The Deceiver, will never take you away from Me yet he will try and keep trying. This is one of the most difficult phases in your Mission. It is lonely, difficult and causes you deep physical as well as pain of the soul. You must trust in Me to help you deal with these attacks and recognise them for what they are.

Now My daughter, listen to Me. You must continue to spread My Word quickly around the world using every help that is sent to you. I am sending you many volunteers and, already, their work is bearing fruit.

All you need to do now is to keep communicating My Word to save souls. Never give up. It is tempting I know and the abuse you have to withstand is not easy for you. Let Me hold your hand tightly and lead you now towards the strength that is required of you. My blessings have been dispersed around you to strengthen your armour so that nothing will stand now in the way of ensuring that the world can hear My Voice.

Your Loving Saviour

Jesus Christ

Confess your sins now - do not be frightened

Wednesday, June 29, 2011

My dearly beloved daughter the help I have sent you will now spread My Word rapidly around the world using modern communications. My Heart is ablaze with the love for My special children who arose to My Call, for they are the army who will lead My children.

All My blessings envelop each of those who help carry My Cross for the good of mankind. The Holy Spirit is bestowed on those to enable them to spread these Messages virally and with real impact.

My children and all My followers just remember the one thing that I want you to focus on. Warn the others to seek redemption before The Warning. They must confess their sins now and must not be frightened. Instead they must rejoice. There are only a few months left for this Great Act of My Mercy. Do not waste time. Go in love and peace. Do not flinch in this work. It is for the good of all My children. All of those who work to spread My Truth will be rewarded for their devotion and faith. My Blessings will protect each of them and their families.

Rejoice now for the time is ripe for the world to finally hear My voice in the way they should.

Your beloved Saviour

Redeemer and King of all mankind

Jesus Christ

Don't allow the human failings of My Church to turn your back on Me

Thursday, June 30, 2011 20.00 hours

My dearly beloved daughter I smile this evening with joy in My Heart for, at last, younger people are hearing My Word through the Internet just as foretold.

In this way more people will be able to tell the world how to prepare for The Warning. My Heart bursts with joy when I see the love that My children have for Me in every corner of the earth. My Love never dies. They, My beloved followers are full of My Love, which they feel in their hearts. Now they can tell the world, including the cynics, how much they revere Me by praising My Glory to all. For those courageous and loving creatures of mine will now attract those who resist Me to the truth as to why they are on this earth in the first instance.

Heaven rejoices with those who openly proclaim their love for Me on the Internet. My Love for them surges forth so that My Graces will be showered over each of them stretching from one corner of the globe to the other.

I now come to save you before the Day of Judgment

Remember one lesson Children. The Truth of My Teachings never changed. Human error, the sins of My sacred servants and those who have abused the Truth to suit their own ambitions may have soiled My Name but they never changed Who I Am. I Am the Saviour of mankind. I came the first time to save you to allow for the forgiveness of sin. I now come again to save you before the day of Judgment.

Because My Love is so powerful it will now permeate throughout the world by the power of the Holy Spirit to draw you back into the fold of My tender Love. Feel My Love now children. Don't allow your disappointment with the human failings of My Church to turn your back on Me, Jesus Christ or My Eternal Father.

To those who turned their back on Me because of the sins of the Church

It is because of sin that you were tempted to block out the truth. Those of you who blame the Church for your lack of belief in Me are not being honest with yourselves, for if you truly love Me you would not make excuses. Satan is everywhere in the world now children trying to convince you, at every opportunity, that your Faith is not relevant, not important, that your faith will not guarantee you a place in Heaven. In some cases you believe that the Mercy of God is endless and that you can be saved once you live a life where you do not cause harm to others. You very often challenge Me when you blame Me for the evil in the world. This is when you become angry with Me and God the Eternal Father. How can God stand back and allow such evil to manifest itself in the world? Where murder, rape, abortion, torture, greed and poverty exist? You must stop now and hear Me.

Remember that sin, caused by Satan who most people today do not believe exists, can infest every single one of you because of the gift you were given by your Creator, God the Father. This gift of free will is given to everyone. Some use this gift for good works where they show love to all while others abuse it to take advantage of others. When Satan attracts those, through their weak free will, then they become capable of committing great atrocities. Free will is yours children. When it becomes contaminated through sin, havoc in the world results. God, the Father cannot force you to stop doing something whether it is right or wrong, for He will not interfere with your free will. He will always encourage you to pray in order to receive the graces needed to avoid sin. It will be through your free will that you will make one of two decisions. Turn to God or allow yourself to be seduced by the lies of Satan who will twist your mind away from the Truth.

Remember I am the Truth. Satan does not want you to see the Truth. He will use your intelligence and present sophisticated arguments to seduce you. He can even convince you that something is evil when it is good. So when you believe that it is hypocritical to turn to prayer in praise of God the Father because of the sins of the Church you must recognise this deceit for what it is, another way to encourage you to turn away from Me. The Truth. Now children show Me your love by standing up and defending My Name in a disbelieving world.

Very soon you will encourage others to hear your views. Just as those who claim they don't believe in Me shout aloud how much they hate Me, you must now tell the world that you love Me. Only then will massive conversion be stirred in the world. Let Me raise you up now so you can prepare My children to enter My New Paradise on earth. Remember only those who believe in Me and My Eternal Father can enter this Paradise.

Go now and bring Me the multitudes.

Your beloved Saviour

Jesus Christ

Prayer can avert disharmony in the world
Friday, July 01, 2011 23.00 hours

My dearly beloved daughter prayer and devotion to Me is like water given to a thirsty man. When you lack water your thirst will continue so that eventually without water you will die. For those who know Me, love Me and show devotion to Me you must understand one thing. If you do not continue to receive My Body and pray to Me regularly you will very quickly lose your desire for Me. Without this desire you will distance yourselves from Me until your heads will be turned by the temptation of sin planted in your minds by Satan. Without Me truly present in your lives you are nothing My children.

Be on your guard at all times. Prayer protects you from sin. Your devotion to Me may attract the Deceiver who will taunt you more often. However, without regular devotion to Me you will walk aimlessly in this world.

Believers understand that prayer can avert much disharmony in the world. Already prayers said through this visionary and other seers has eased the immediate dangers facing Pope Benedict but not for too long. Prayer to My Blessed Mother can move mountains, dilute the impact of evil atrocities including those foretold and convert sinners.

Remember this lesson My daughter prayer acts as your armour against the Deceiver. You, most of all, must learn the necessity of regular prayer in your Mission. You need to spend more time in silent reflection with Me. For when you do not do this your discernment of My Messages becomes weakened and errors can occur. Be careful, My daughter, when referring to dates of the prophecies given to you. If I say months that could be anytime within a year. Never confuse human interpretation with those of the timelines given to you by Me. I have not given you any specific dates for events only guidelines. These prophecies will take place but only by the Hand of My Eternal Father. Trust in Me more. Your prayers and those of My followers can help delay, or in some cases, avert disasters. Always remember that.

Pray, Pray, Pray. For when you do this from the heart your prayers are heard. Pray especially for those world leaders whose lives will be ended soon through hateful evil acts. They and those with hardened hearts guilty of the crime of inhumanity need your prayers most of all. Always pray for sinners because I love all My children and I need your prayers to save them from the fires of Hell.

Your ever-merciful Jesus Christ

Battle which Satan is mounting to discredit thcsc Messages is intensifying

Saturday, July 02, 2011 10.00 hours

My beloved daughter this period is going to be difficult for you as the Messages infiltrate the world. More people will attack these Messages and when they do ignore them.

My Holy Word is being spread as I have said. Now I want to proclaim the main points of My Messages even further. You already know how to do this so begin today. What I am asking of you is challenging but you will be given further help to do this.

Meanwhile you will need others to pray for you because the battle, which Satan is mounting to discredit these Messages is intensifying. You must pray for protection against the hurt he will inflict on you through others.

Accept that this series of trials are essential in keep you in a state of humility. Know that you are My voice to the world. Promote My voice and do it as soon as you can.

I love you My daughter. Lean on Me completely and I will carry you through this.
Your Loving Saviour

Jesus Christ

Atheists and Scientists will say that The Warning was an illusion

Sunday, July 03, 2011 18.30 hours

My dearly beloved daughter you must move forward, look straight ahead and follow My instructions. Do not turn to the side when you are being assailed by the Evil One every minute of the day. Focus on Me only. You must learn to understand that time spent in My company especially at Adoration is essential if you are to keep on top of this Mission. The length of time spent in prayer is also important because the longer you spend in close communication with Me the more graces you will receive. Failure to do so will mean that you are leaving yourself wide open to attacks from The Deceiver.

My Word, My daughter, is being ignored by many who do not want to listen. There are many reasons for this. Many of My children today have closed their eyes to the truth of their spiritual existence. They embrace the world and all it offers as a substitute for the Bread of Life. Many are also wary of false prophets for this is the age in which false prophets will emerge everywhere.

This is the confusion that Satan wants to cause so that those genuine messengers of mine go unnoticed. Because of the humility required by My chosen visionaries they cannot exalt themselves in the eyes of the world for it is not in their nature. The false visionaries will push themselves into the limelight. Their focus will be centred on themselves. Their messages may seem authentic and full of flowery language featuring extracts from the Holy Bible where it suits, but there will be two key aspects to their messages that will expose them for the untruths they impart. The first is that they will be central to the messages and will enjoy all of the attention they receive. Then finally you have the messages themselves. They will be confusing, hard to read and will not leave a lasting impression on the soul. Sadly, My daughter the Church tends to ignore the authentic seers because they must show responsibility in these matters.

It is, therefore, far easier for My Church to support those messages, which include extracts from the Holy Bible to declare these to be authentic. Not so easy is it for them to accept the simplicity of My Teachings especially when today much of the truth hides behind the mask of tolerance. Not easily accepted either is the reminder of the End Times when, through fear and ignorance, those sacred servants of Mine refuse to take up My Cup and act responsibly.

This is the most important time in the history of the world. All the signs have been given to My visionaries throughout the last century yet they are ignored and shoved aside as they bury their heads in the sand. It is precisely at this time that My sacred servants must preach about the importance of My return to earth. They must prepare souls by reminding them of the consequences of failing to redeem themselves while they are still on this earth, for they cannot ask for forgiveness after death. I call on My sacred servants now. Why won't you emphasize this to your flock? Why do you not actively discuss the repercussions for My children during the Great Chastisement? Don't you know that many of My children will lose their souls to the antichrist who is already here on this earth ready to spring as he waits in the wings? My children must understand that The Warning, while a Great Act of Mercy, is only the first phase in what will be a very difficult and challenging time for all My children. For after that those hardened sinners and followers of Satan will deny My existence.

Atheists will say it was a global illusion. Scientists will look for a logical explanation but there won't be one. Meanwhile My followers will be torn in two. Many millions will have converted but they will be confused by the lies spread by the Evil Group, the One World deadly organization whose goal is to destroy the little people for their own financial gain.

Children if enough people cannot stay on the true path then it will not be possible to avert the impact of the Chastisement. For this is when God the Father will move to stop sinners from destroying His Creation and His children. He will unleash earthquakes on a magnitude never experienced before; volcanoes in the most unlikely places and the earth will be tossed like a ship in rough waters with no anchor to hold it in one place.

Please children allow The Warning to save you all. Accept that this miracle will help save millions who, otherwise, would have been lost. But for those who do not want to change their lives they will choose the house of Satan. Without prayer there is no hope for them for they will forfeit the keys of the New Paradise on earth. Instead they will burn in the fires of Hell. If they knew where this the Evil Path is leading them do you think they would change their ways? Children please help them by telling them the truth. Pray to save their souls if they won't listen. For that is all you can do.
Your beloved Saviour

Just Judge and King of Mercy

Jesus Christ

For My Followers who denounce these Messages

Tuesday, July 05, 2011 14.30 hours

My dearly beloved daughter today is a special day for it pleases Me to tell you that those whose faith has been strengthened by My Messages can be assured that their daily recital of the Divine Mercy is saving souls.

My children must never forget that prayers, when said with sincerity and from the heart, will always be heard. Prayers are always listened to and any special intentions are fulfilled according to My Most Holy Will.

Children please continue with your prayers because they will help ease the period of the Great Chastisement. My Father is now ready to take over His Holy Kingdom and commence His Reign once again when the New Paradise on Earth emerges. The evil in the world right now has never been so intense. Because of the huge world population and the works of the Evil One, war is everywhere. The hatred shown by man to man is palpable. Whether this hatred is manifested as political greed or control over other countries by another, it is all the same. Satan has many followers. They, his followers, in many instances are not aware as to how he influences every thought and deed at all times during any one day.

If My children could only see the amount of demons present in such men they would be sickened. They possess many of My children the only visible signs being through their evil deeds. Pray, pray now My followers that those poor lost souls can be saved during The Warning.

Between now and The Warning all I ask of you children are your prayers and especially the recital of The Divine Mercy. My Father will save souls if you dedicate yourselves to saying this once a day, preferably at 3 o'clock in the afternoon.

For those of My followers who denounce these Messages I implore of you to pray to the Holy Spirit to ask for the gift of discernment before you dismiss My Holy Word. To those of you who insult My visionary and recipient of these Messages you must ask this question. If it is Satan who you believe influences these Messages then why would he ask you to pray, to seek forgiveness, to receive the Holy Eucharist? Then you will know that this is impossible.

The deceiver will influence My followers firstly to encourage them to deny My Word because he knows that it will be their rejection of My Most

Holy Words of Love that will hurt Me most.

Reject Satan and his wicked ways now. Turn to Me. I implore you for you must not allow him to influence you in this way. Your prayers are needed now to save My poor children who will not survive The Warning.

Your Loving Saviour

Jesus Christ

Importance of Sacraments - Marriage and First Holy Communion

Wednesday, July 06, 2011 15.30 hours

My dearly beloved daughter watch now as the faith of My children begins to grow and blossom. While there is much darkness in the world the light of My followers becomes brighter by the day because of the flame of the Holy Spirit, which has descended over the whole world.

Today My daughter I wish to remind all of My followers of the importance of prayer to ease suffering in the world. Your prayers are now helping to avert many global disasters foretold. Prayer is the most powerful mitigation and when said on behalf of others they will be answered.

While I am happy with those of strong faith I am still fearful for those who are adverse to My Divine Light, The Truth. Many people now wander around the world as if in a stupor. Nothing brings them peace. Nothing brings them joy. No amount of material comfort eases their pain. Their empty souls are lost. Please pray for them.

My daughter please pray for My Vicar Pope Benedict for he is surrounded by Masonic forces who are now making every effort to dethrone him, these evil forces have been infiltrating My Church since Vatican 2 and have diluted My Teachings. Many laws were passed which offend Me especially the presentation of My Holy Eucharist by lay people. The lack of respect shown to Me and My Eternal Father, through new laws introduced to facilitate modern society has made me cry with sadness.

The Most Holy Eucharist must be received on the tongue and not soiled by human hands. Yet this is precisely what My sacred servants have done. These laws were not passed by Me in Spirit. My sacred servants have been led down a path not in line with the teachings of My apostles. Today My Sacraments are not taken very seriously especially those who seek the Sacraments of Matrimony and the First Holy Communion.

The Vow of Matrimony is very serious for remember it is a Sacrament and is made in the presence of God the Father, yet for many it all about materialism and the exterior trappings. Many who receive the Sacrament of Matrimony do not acknowledge its importance thereafter. Many break their vows so easily. Why do they do this? Why pay lip service to this most Holy Union only to part soon afterwards? This is a mockery of one of the most important unions Blessed by the Hand of My Eternal Father. Many people do not pay any heed of My Father's Will that no man shall pull asunder such a union thereafter, yet many people divorce which is a law not recognized by My Father. Divorce is an easy way to run from your responsibilities. All marriages are made in Heaven. No man can destroy a marriage without offending My Father.

First Holy Communion
Receiving My Body in the Sacrament of the Eucharist for the first time is another example as to how I am mocked. So many parents pay no heed to the importance of their children receiving the Bread of Life. They are more concerned as to how well dressed their children are rather than the wonderful gift they are receiving. This Gift will lead them to salvation. Yet the materialism, which surrounds the event, has nothing to do with their souls. For Me the saddest part is that these little children are not being told about Me. The love I have for little children is all encompassing. When they receive the Holy

Eucharist, in the full knowledge as to what they are receiving then their souls become pure. The more they receive Me in this way the stronger will their faith be.

Remember without the Sacraments your faith becomes weak. After a time if your soul is bereft of My Special Blessings it becomes dormant. All faith in Me and My Eternal Father disappears in time with only a tiny flicker of recognition flaring up from time to time. Return to Me through the Sacraments. Show respect for the Sacraments in the way you are supposed to and you will truly feel My Presence again.

Remember the Sacraments are there for a reason for they are the nutrients you need for Eternal Life of the soul. Without them your soul will die.

I love you all. Please embrace Me properly by respecting the Sacraments given to you as a Gift from God the Almighty Father.

Your Loving Saviour

King of Mankind

Jesus Christ

Narcissism an evil epidemic present in the world today
Thursday, July 07, 2011 21.00 hours

My dearly beloved daughter I want the world to know that My Love for them infuses My entire Being as I prepare for the Great Warning. I am full of joy because I know that My children, especially those who do not know Me, will finally accept that I exist during My Great Act of Mercy.

One of the most disturbing traits, which have infested My children is that of narcissism, self love, in this world. This evil epidemic is prevalent in every level of society and is one of Satan's favourite attacks as his demons enter the souls of My children everywhere. They can be seen preening and posturing so that others will adore them. Their first love is for themselves only and then when that's not enough they crave the attention of those around them to encourage them to openly adore them.

Today Satan's infestation is so great in the way in which these poor souls present themselves it is difficult to ignore. Their obsessiveness as to how they look means that they will even go as far as damaging their bodies and do whatever is necessary to satisfy their love of self.

When Satan is present in such souls it is easy to spot. These people will be full of vanity and will tend to be seen in places of influence. The sin of narcissism will intensify during the End Times where many will ensure that their looks, their well being and selfishness will be at the expense of their friends and even their own families. Love of self is considered an admirable trait in today's world. This pursuit of self-gain can never be satisfied because Satan will ensure that these people will strive for more and more.

Children, the sin of pride is one, which is intensifying in the world now. Do not accept this form of behaviour as part of your day-to-day life. So many young people use these figures of so called physical perfection as a goal to aim for. Yet their demeanour is to be pitied if you open your eyes and see it for what it is. It is a breach of the First Commandment and should such people persist on this pathway they will be pulled by The Deceiver into further disarray.

Narcissism is seen in all areas of life including politics, fashion, the media, cinema, and even within My Own Church. Humility cannot be achieved if you suffer from narcissism. Without humility you cannot enter My Father's Kingdom.

Your Loving Saviour

Eternal Father will prevent New World Order from final persecution of His Children

Friday, July 08, 2011 15.30 hours

My dearly beloved daughter I realize that this work is taking its toll on you and that you need to rest for another week but listen to what I have to say.

Tell My children to wake up now and see the turmoil in the world where financial crises abound. Tell them that while people's greed was partly responsible for plunging them into debt, that the banking crisis was deliberately planned by the One World Order.

Many reading this Message will smile and question this fact but they should also know that unless they stand up and defend their rights they will be forced to accept the Mark of the Beast to access their money.

New World Currency will be presented to an incredulous world

The New One World currency, which will be presented to an incredulous community is designed to control you. Then once that happens they will try to deprive you of food. Unless My children accept this reality now they will be defenceless when they are under the control of a New World Order led by Masonic forces. Prepare now My children because although The Warning will convert millions, including those loyal to the One World Order, it will not be enough to stop these evil slaves of Satan and the antichrist. With control of your money you will find it hard to defend your right to property, food and health, the three things which they will be in charge of if you do not start shouting your opposition now. Stop your leaders in their tracks. Don't let them bully you. If enough of you are alert to this evil monstrous plan then you can warn others.

Plan your food supplies now

Plan your food supplies now. Grow and buy seeds that will keep you alive. Buy silver coins or gold so that you can buy what is necessary. Most importantly find locations where, as a group, you can meet to offer the Holy Sacrifice of the Mass. For in time your churches will be burned to the ground.

Satan's minions are like ants they multiply in their thousands

Never accept the Mark, the chip of the Beast. Pray, pray that your home will be given the special blessings to safeguard you from the army, which will try to put you out of your home. Satan's minions are like ants. They multiply in their thousands by the hour. You, My children, must pray now and fight this series of atrocities being planned by the New World Order who salivate at the prospect of controlling the world. Plan to have blessed candles in your home. Stock up now for they will keep you in the light of protection. Unless you wish to become a slave to this hideous doctrine then you must plan now.

Buy gas stoves, blankets, dried and tinned food, water purification tablets and candles, along with religious images to sustain you and your families during The Great Chastisement, which will follow the Warning.

Prayers are already diluting the impact of the Great Chastisement but you, My children, must be alert at all times. By being careful in your preparations you will be able to survive the great bombardment being orchestrated which will be worse than what happened to the Jews under the reign of Satan's disciple Hitler.
Heed this warning calmly. For by preparing in advance you will spare yourselves from the indignation being planned by the New World Order. For those of you who are involved with the New World Order hear Me now. Repent. Heed The Warning for what it offers you - a chance to turn your back on Satan and the flames of Hell.

Advice for Servants of the Church

For My sacred servants this is what I must inform you. Fix your eyes on Me now and pray to The Holy Spirit to keep you on your toes so that you will recognize the False Prophet as soon as he shows himself within your midst. Then you need to gather in groups to ensure that My children will be able to receive the Most Holy Eucharist during the persecution.

My Father's Hand is ready to fall now with great force on those wicked arrogant leaders of banks, Western and Eastern powers who plan in secret how they aim to control all of you. My Eternal Father will destroy everything in their wake to prevent them from the final persecution they are planning against His children. He won't stand for it. Remember children, God the Eternal Father wants to protect you all. His patience has finally run out. He will, up to the very last minute, accept those who turn to Him for forgiveness. However He now has to stop those evil regimes from the horror they inflict on the rest of His Creation.

It is because of the love of His children He does this. For those who say God, the Father, cannot be angry for He loves all know this. Yes, He is angry and his anger is justified because of the evil injustice, which is being perpetrated on His precious family. Once again He will unite all His children to live in peace finally for all of eternity.

Remember children to see the signs all around you, the multitude of wars, lack of money, lack of food, lack of healthcare and accept that this is the work of the Evil One. It is not the work of God the Eternal Father. He will no longer accept this behaviour. Be thankful He is taking action for if He did not His Creation would be destroyed. And He will not allow that to happen.

Your beloved Jesus

Saviour of Mankind

Redeemer of the World

Let My sacred servants know the content of them so they can prepare their flock
Saturday, July 09, 2011 16.00 hours

My dearly beloved daughter just as you forge ahead confident in your discernment of My Messages you then stop and feel the torment of doubts. These doubts, at this stage of My communication may puzzle you. For every step backwards you take this is a test of your faith My daughter. For no man can assume that they will always be worthy of Me. Accept this suffering My daughter for these trials will always assail you in this work. Trust in Me and surrender your free will on a continuous basis to help you become stronger in this work.
My daughter there are at this time a number of visionaries with whom I communicate with the help of My Blessed Mother, Michael the Archangel and the Holy Trinity but they are fewer than you think. Some of the apostles will be hidden from view, their work known only to the saints in Heaven. Then there are those who the world will eventually recognize as My messengers. You are one of these. It will not be an easy Mission, My daughter, so that is why I am allowing you to suffer setbacks, trials and errors. It is only when you get used to these episodes that you will continue to become stronger and stronger until, eventually, you will not care one way or the other what others think of you. You are walking with Me every step of this Mission and you must never forget that.

It is important you ensure that as many poor souls as possible are given the Truth of My Word. You must let My sacred servants know the content of them so they can prepare their flock before The Warning. It is not important whether the Church authenticates these Messages because time is not on their side. They, My sacred servants, will take many-many years to accept My Messages so just keep going.

You, My daughter, will make many enemies in My Name. This is something you will have to accept so do not allow those obstacles stand in your way. My Messages are converting thousands of lost souls already. It is vital then that you obey Me at all times, so that more souls can be saved.

I realize that this work is lonely and frightening for you but remember I only pick those with an open heart who are strong enough to impart My Word. In turn the strength you will find will help fast track these Messages to a wider audience. So please never feel down hearted. For while you strive to feel joy in your heart when carrying My Cross this is rarely the case. You will suffer always in My Name and will find it will take time before the full force of joy will be experienced. Your suffering is saving millions of souls so you must be thankful for this. All the saints are working on this side to keep you strong and to protect you from Satan who will do everything he can to stop you. But he will never achieve that because the Hand of My Father will strike down on those who attempt to sabotage My work to save as many souls as I can through you. Lean on Me and I will propel this work so that My Messages will be heard by millions, believers and non-believers in every corner of the globe.

Your beloved Teacher

Saviour of Mankind

Jesus Christ

Do not be frightened, conversion will create a great sense of love and peace

Sunday, July 10, 2011 12.10 hours

My dearly beloved daughter for many of My children who are frightened by My Messages and find them hard to face up to then please listen to Me now. The evil that is escalating in the world is by the hand of mankind through sin. This cannot continue. Please do not fear for it will not change the plans now underway by the

Evil One World Group. You My children need to be made aware of what is happening. It is important that everyone is warned about the actions of this Group and their sinister plans which they have created to control you.

Please welcome The Warning

My Warning, the Great Act of Mercy is such a great Gift of Love so please welcome it for it will result in much conversion. Conversion will be so widespread that it will create a great sense of love and peace when My children have been humbled by this great event. Then there will be strength in their numbers. The more people who believe in The Truth the weaker then will be the impact of the New World Group. Prayer and much of it can avert much of the damage they will attempt to inflict. So please never forget to pray the Holy Rosary and the Divine Mercy for both combined will help wipe out much of this pending evil. Go now do not fear. Look with enthusiasm for a new beginning, a new peace where evil will be stamped out for good.
That is My Promise to you children.

Your Loving Saviour

Jesus Christ

Call on high profile personalities to spread My Word

Wednesday, July 13, 2011

My dearly beloved daughter when you turn your back on Me afterwards you will find it difficult to find Me again. I realize that you believe I make difficult demands of you but My Word, to be imparted to the world, is of such urgency that you must obey Me as I have requested you. Remember you surrendered your free will to Me My daughter, which was a wonderful gift. To honour that gift is not easy for you because you are only human after all. I now call on you once again to hear My call and to spend more time in My company. I need you to feel My Love, not just the love that I have for you, but that I hold for every single child of Mine on this earth.

I want My followers to spread My Word of Peace and Harmony all over the world. They must volunteer everywhere to remind every one of the need to promote My Messages of Love. Please ask singers, the media, personalities or anyone whose voice is listened to and respected to hear My pleas. Take up My Chalice of Love. Drink from it for it will bring you the salvation you crave not only in this world but in the next life. Share this with your own followers.

How you do this is up to you for those who respond to My call will be given the gift of the graces needed to do this most Sacred Work. Children remember this. The more of you who rise now to spread My Most Holy Word and tell everyone the truth the easier it will be for My children to pass through the Great Chastisement as well as the persecution being planned by the New World Order.

My Message to mankind must be listened to, assessed and action then taken to remind all that they must open their minds to accept the existence of God the Almighty Father, the Holy Mighty One, for when they do peace will reign again.

For the sake of the Sacrifice I made for you all through My death on the Cross hear My call and do whatever you can to let everyone you know understand that I am communicating to the world just as was done by My Father through the prophets before My time on earth. Be strong. Be brave. Pray to Me for guidance during your crusade on behalf of Me and My Eternal Father.

Jesus Christ

King of Mankind

Saviour and Redeemer

My Messages will bring tears of conversion

Thursday, July 14, 2011 14.30 hours

My dearly beloved daughter you must never forget that those who speak in My Name will be mocked laughed at and made to look foolish. This is the cross I speak of. Never be disillusioned when this happens.

Many now challenge My Sacred Word. Some take the form of genuine questions, which stem from a love for Me while others are designed to make My Word seem foolish and a nonsense. My children must accept that I will now increase My communications to you all because of the lack of time. No matter that My Word is challenged instead be joyful for you know that it is when I communicate to My children in this way that obstacles will present themselves. This is when you will know that it is I. If when reading My Messages My children feel tears then they will know that these are the tears of conversion - a gift to each and every one of you through the power of the Holy Spirit.

Many of My children feel confused because when My Word is given to the world in this way I can upset their normal routine. My Word will not bring happiness to every soul because, sometimes, the truth can be frightening. If they will first sit down and allow My Peace to flood their souls by submitting themselves to My Holy Will they will experience true contentment. Trust in Me children. Do not block Me out. Listen carefully to what I say and I will take you on My journey to everlasting salvation.

Remember God the Father is now in charge of His Kingdom, which no man can tumble. Any attempt to do so will result in failure. As sinners continue to insult Me and My Eternal Father His Hand will be ready to fall quickly. Because of The Warning He will hold back until conversion has been achieved. Meanwhile all those who do not accept the truth you must know that you have little time now to prepare your souls.

Pray for each and every one of you so that souls can be saved.

Your Loving Saviour

Jesus Christ

King of Mankind

Execution, Euthanasia, Abortion and Suicide

Friday, July 15, 2011 17.30 hours

My daughter it is when My children feel love in their hearts that they can be assured that I am present in their souls. My Love will keep My children strong when they least expect it. This is also true of hardened sinners whose outward shell hides, very often, a tender heart.

Every single person on earth is a child created by God the Father. Because of this the Light exists within each person although it may be very weak when souls are drawn to the darkness. Nevertheless My Light is still present. For without it there would be complete darkness where they could not function. It is when souls reach a terrible state of darkness that they very often resort to suicide. This is when because of the weakness of soul and spirit that Satan steals their souls by convincing them to end their lives. Many of My followers do not understand the state that such darkness can have on a soul so they must pray hard for these children who are in this state of despair.

God, My Eternal Father is ever merciful and will always help these souls many of whom are suffering to such an extent that their minds cannot function in the full state of reason. A mortal sin can only be committed when a person, in their full mental capacity, has clear intentions when he or she knows that what they are doing is wrong. So please do not assume that such souls are completely lost for many do not know what they are doing.

Be aware that euthanasia is frowned upon by My Father and is not tolerated for no man can knowingly take the life of another. No reason can be put forward to justify this in the Name of My Father. Tolerance may be presented along with the argument for humane treatment to justify this deed but no man, except the Father Almighty can decide on the date of death for it is not man's right. He will never be given the authority to commit this mortal sin.

Every excuse is offered by man when taking the life of another yet none of them will be accepted as being right in any circumstances. This applies to execution, the sin of abortion and euthanasia. Sit up now all of you and remember you will be judged harshly should you break the most Sacred of all My Father's Commandments. Thou Shalt Not Kill. Remember there is only one God and only He can decide when life is to be taken. Break this Commandment in the full knowledge as to what you are doing and you will suffer the torment of Hell for Eternity.

Please I implore you do not cave in to the pressures of Satan who constantly encourages the taking of life so that he can steal souls who otherwise would be destined for My Father's Glorious Kingdom.

Your Divine Saviour

Teacher and Redeemer

Jesus Christ

Unite your families to enjoy the New Paradise on Earth

Saturday, July 16, 2011 23.00 hours

My dearly beloved daughter when souls are lost they can seem, on the outside, to be full of joy living life to the full. Yet they can be lost to Me and this brings Me great sadness. So many in the world go about their daily lives, full of things to do, so busy that they forget that this earth is made of clay. That time spent here is so short. Those personal belongings all turn into nothing eventually. That people when they die turn to clay. Yet their souls remain alive and will never die. The soul will continue to exist for eternity.

I am saying to you now, My children, to unite your families and friends as one close to My Heart for when you do you will enjoy the New Paradise on earth for 1000 years still united. This is My promise to you all. Live your lives responsibly. Always put your families before everything also on this earth. Always place your trust in Me.

Bring your families to Me. If they won't come willingly pray to Me and I will give them the encouragement they need. I will always answer prayers which request the saving of souls.

Your Beloved Saviour

Jesus Christ

Any man who claims to be Me is a liar for I will never manifest Myself in man

Sunday, July 17, 2011 15.40 hours

My dearly beloved daughter one of the most confusing times will emerge shortly when not only will those who claim to come in My Name be false, but there will be those who will claim to be Me. My children must understand this. I came the first time as man to save mankind from sin. This time I will come to judge. While many will come face to face with Me during The Warning I will not come the second time until Judgment Day.

Any man who claims to be Me is a liar. Such souls, and there are many of them My daughter, do not mean harm. So deluded are they that The Deceiver convinces such people that they not only have Divine Powers but that they are the Son of God Incarnate. But this is untrue for I will never manifest Myself in another human being on this earth. This could never happen. No man is worthy of such an honour for this has not been foretold.

Many will now come forward and claim that they are Me, Jesus Christ the Son of God. For those poor souls I say this to you. Drop on your knees now and ask God the Father to protect you from The Deceiver. He wants to confuse you so that you, in turn, will not only confuse My children who await My return to earth but will exacerbate the ridicule extolled by atheists. Not only do you bring shame to My Name but you are unwittingly turning people against their belief in God the Almighty Father.

I also wish to warn those who claim to perform miracles. Anyone who makes such claims to hold such powers will not be from God for there is only one God and only He, or I His Beloved Son Jesus Christ, can bring about such things. Satan on the other hand also possesses powers. He can create illusions. In the case of miracle cures Satan can bring about, through those so-called faith healers whose powers are sought from the occult, temporary solutions where miracles may seem to have been achieved. But they will not last long. Satan will also bring about so called miracles including visions, seen by many in the skies. Again they are illusions and not of God.

Children you are, while trying to show your allegiance to Me, being tempted by the forces of evil every single day. You must only focus on Me and My Eternal Father. And remember I do not walk on this earth as a human being. I may be present on earth in Spirit but I will never manifest Myself in any man.

Pray for guidance every day and for the discernment to be able distinguish lies from the Truth.

Your Loving Saviour

Jesus Christ

Your weapon of choice is your love for Me

Tuesday, July 19, 2011 23.45 hours

My dearly beloved daughter thankfully you are now settling back into a routine having taken a small break. You will become stronger as a result but please remember that you still must focus on Me at all times.

My Love for all My children is very powerful and is quite different to the love one talks about loosely in this world. My children feel My Love when they open the door to Me when I knock. When I come to their door they have two choices. They can either open the door and allow Me in or they can shut Me out. When they do allow Me to enter their souls My Love penetrates their being. It is a Love they find that can make them feel weak with surprise so intense is it or joyful to the extent they cannot stop telling others their good news.

For My beloved followers who love Me know this. Because of your love and devotion to Me I allow My Love to radiate from you so that it becomes infectious and spreads to embrace other souls. Once you allow Me into your hearts I will fill you with the Grace of the Holy Spirit so that you can tell everyone what it is I need to tell you now.

First of all I love you with a deep tenderness in My Heart. Secondly, because of My Love I will now eradicate evil in the world so that I can bring all My children back into the embrace of your Ever-Loving Creator, God the Father.

Please, none of you My devoted followers, must allow fear to enter your hearts as The Warning draws closer by the week. For when this great Act of My Mercy takes place you will rejoice. For My Gift to you is that you will become closer to My Heart than before. This will make you so strong that you will sail, without hesitation, towards the New Paradise on earth, so smooth will the transition be.

My Love is now more powerful than ever as you, My beloved followers, do all you can to spread My Word. Use what means you can to tell people to prepare for The Warning. You are brave My children and you bring joy and happiness into My sorrowful Heart which yearns every second to save all My lost souls.

I am relying on you now to pray as hard as you can for sinners who will not withstand the test that The Warning presents them. Go now My strong loving army. Your weapon of choice is your love for Me. You will know in your heart it is I who speaks and that it is I who now knocks on your door. You must now knock on the doors of My sacred servants all over the world and make sure they read My Holy Word.

Your beloved Saviour and Redeemer

Jesus Christ

You are now in the middle of the Tribulation

Wednesday, July 20, 2011 23.00 hours

My daughter you are, as you know, the most unlikely visionary because of your lack of knowledge of Holy matters. Yet you are the chosen messenger. You must understand that you will be unable to defend My Messages with any real authority so therefore keep silent when asked to define My Messages.

You will be provoked and challenged to become involved with religious and especially eschatology arguments but you must no longer respond or provide your own interpretation of the answers. Because of this work you will be disliked. Spiritual jealousy will arise among My followers especially theologians and those who have studied Scripture all their lives, so keep silent for you do not have the knowledge nor, as I have told you before, the authority to do so.

Just follow My instructions and keep to yourself. Respond to prayer requests by all means and help bring My followers and devotees who have pledged their support to this work together.

Time is short now. Everything is going to happen quickly. The Warning is close now so there is not much time left to pray for those poor souls who will be lost. By reciting My Divine Mercy dedicated to those particular souls many millions will be saved.

You are now, My children, in the middle of what is called the Tribulation as foretold in My Holy Book. The second part, the Great Tribulation will commence as I have said before the end of 2012. This is not meant to instil fear in you My daughter but to make you aware of the urgency for My children to pray for My Help.

Already through the prayers of My visionaries all over the world the power of the New World Order, driven by Masonic forces is beginning to dilute and unravel before your very eyes. Many more of these power hungry global organizations will be brought to their knees in humility as they answer, not only to God the Father, for their wickedness but to those to whom they have a responsibility on this earth.

Watch now as the clusters of powerful groups try to outdo each other, cover up their own sins and hide the truth from those they fear in high places. Prayer, My children, is bringing this about. God, the Father is striking out now to punish these people before they can inflict the evil plan they are preparing to control My children.

This is a painful time children for Satan's influence has never been so powerful in these last days of his reign on earth. Fight his evil ways, children - all of you. Just look at the havoc he is causing when he turns brother against brother, country against country, creates hatred amongst all of you and disrespect for each other's lives. And then there is the sheer hatred he instils in My children for Me, their beloved Saviour. The hatred he stirs up for My Father has reached epidemic proportions. The most powerful form of hatred shown to My Father is for man to deny He exists.

How you must feel the anguish children that you have to face in the world today. No man can ignore the deep disquieting unrest spurred by Satan and his millions of demons infiltrated throughout the world. My Love will now be proven to you all. Through My Warning I come once more to save you through the Mercy of God the Father. Believe in Me and My Eternal Father and you will have nothing to fear. Ignore what is happening and you will fail to prepare adequately.

Your beloved Saviour

Jesus Christ

No man will fail to hear My Son's Word before the time comes for His return

Saturday, July 23, 2011 17.15 hours

Sccond Message from God the Father

I come in the Name of My Beloved Precious Son Jesus Christ.
My chosen daughter while you sometimes falter in your attention to My Beloved Son's call to hear Him speak, you have risen in My eyes because of the gift you have given Him. Your gift of becoming a victim soul to help save millions of souls makes Him weep with joy and relief. For so many souls are being lost to the fires of Hell every day, every second and for every breath you take.

My Son requires your total submission now My daughter. Do not hesitate to obey His every command. Your heart is full of love and compassion not just for My Precious Son but for all My children. Touched by the Holy Spirit you will now feel instant love for strangers in whom you will see My Light. You, My daughter have now been given the graces to see both the love and evil in all. You will also be able to quickly discern sin in poor misguided souls.

For this work now means that you must surround yourself with every protection. I will, My daughter, protect you and your loved ones, for now you will be targeted more forcibly by the Evil One. Pray and ask Me for this protection every day now and you will be spared the intensity of the persecution. You must now call on Me to help you spread these Messages so that My Son's voice is heard and revered in the way it should.

My messenger, My daughter, you have little understanding yet as to what is required of you. Only so much information can be given to you at a time. You will now be inspired by Me and you will fulfil, with My guidance, the prophecies foretold when My Son's Word will be spread just like the Holy Gospel to mankind. No man will fail to hear My Son's Word before the time comes for His return. You have been given this task and for this Gift you must bow your head in appreciation of this Glorious request from the Heavens.

My daughter you will be assisted in every way but you must obey My Son at all times. Rise now My daughter for man needs to hear the Word of Warning that My Son imparts so that souls do not have to suffer the torments of Hell should they die in mortal sin without first being given the chance to be redeemed by My Son during The Warning.

Let My peace flood your soul now. My Heart surrounds every move you make. Never feel you are alone in this Work for you are being guided every minute of the day.

God the Father

August 2011 - Salvation of Souls month
Saturday, July 23, 2011 17.30 hours

My beloved daughter you make Me so happy. Your total surrender now means that I can save more souls everywhere. A victim soul, My daughter is not entirely clear to you as to its full meaning but, in time, it will be. By then you will be so strong that to suffer for Me will bring you joy not sadness. It will not be easy but then working for Me, your beloved Saviour, cannot be easy.

It was by the inspiration of God, My Eternal Father that you were encouraged to make this final sacrifice for Me. This is a very special Grace My daughter although it won't appear to be in human terms for My Graces are not always about bringing joy and happiness into your life. They can bring suffering but, at the same time, provide you with a real insight into My Glorious Kingdom.

Many, many people in the world form My precious army. They will through prayer, personal suffering and the spread of My Word save souls. The stronger My army is at saving souls the less the impact will be of the Chastisement.

I ask all My children to spend the month of August praying the Divine Mercy daily for the lost souls who will not survive The Warning. One day of fasting a week is also required as well as daily Mass and the receiving of My Most Holy Eucharist.

If enough of you do this in which I call "Salvation of Souls" month then millions of souls will be saved throughout the world. Do this for Me children and you will become part of My Glorious Kingdom. Your souls, at the point of death, will join Me in Paradise. That is My most solemn promise.

I love you Children. Now go and form the most powerful army in the world, the Army of Love, the Army of Salvation.

Your Loving Saviour

Redeemer of Mankind

Jesus Christ

God the Father will destroy the plot to overthrow currencies

Sunday, July 24, 2011 23.00 hours

My dearly beloved daughter My followers' devotion and allegiance to Me and My Eternal Father is already making a big difference. You, My children, must know that your devotion burns flames of such magnitude in My Heart that it feels like it will burst with love for you. Heaven rejoices now at the way you, My beloved children, honour Me with such a passion and devotion. You know in your soul that it is I who speaks. It is I who brings a feeling of such love and tenderness in your heart.

I have a Message for all of you, children, who follow My most Holy Divine Word on this website. In a modern world this is how I must communicate. This and other communication channels will be used to ensure My Word is heard and felt by all believers, non-believers and those who don't know Me at all.

Please know that every effort you make out of your love for Me is having an impact. I hear every single one of you. I know the joy that I have brought to your soul. I welcome the way in which your work is spreading My Word. I will reward each and every one of you with specials graces and favours. Please ask Me to hear your prayers. Come to Me. I will hear your call.

Already the work of the New World Order is beginning to fall apart at the seams. This is down to prayers - your prayers. God the Eternal Father will destroy those who continue to inflict their hideous plot to overthrow currencies in the world as well as those political leaders they are trying to dispose of. His Hand will now continue to strike out to protect you, children.

Please, I call you all to tell as many influential voices, including the media, about these Messages. Many will consider you to be delusional when you speak of these Messages. Have no fear for the graces you will receive in doing this work far exceeds the initial abuse you will endure.

Go forward now My beloved children with love and joy in your hearts. For My Word is to be welcomed. At last you know that I walk with you so that I can strengthen the bonds of love for all My followers whom I chose to become close to My Sacred Heart. My Precious Blood spilled so willingly for each of you so that you could be saved covers you every single day.

You are My beloved army and together we will rise to bring all your brothers and sisters back into their rightful glorious home again.

I love and cherish each of you children. Never forget that when you pray to Me each day say this prayer:

O my precious Jesus embrace me in your arms and allow my head to rest upon your shoulders so that you can raise me up to your glorious Kingdom when the time is right. Allow your precious blood to flow over my Heart that we can be united as one.

Your beloved Saviour

Jesus Christ

Satan is powerless against My devoted followers
Monday, July 25, 2011 09.00 hours

My beloved daughter it is with great joy that I once again tell you of the conversion now taking place in the world, as more atrocities are being committed by man through the influence of Satan more of My children are beginning to question the levels of murderous intent now prevalent in your world. As more evil is presented to you so too will the realization that Satan does, in fact, exist. For those who do not believe he exists then let Me explain how you can spot his evil works.

Every time My children witness murder, suicide, war, corruption of governments and those in power, greed, arrogance and injustices know that these deeds are the manifestation of Satan. The Evil One has become desperate now to poison My children's minds, he will do everything he can at this time in history, so intense is his rage. You, My children are his targets. While he finds it easy to infect souls who leave themselves wide open to his influence - those who continually seek self-glory on earth - he is finding it increasingly difficult to dampen the spirit of My devoted followers. So blessed are they through the Gift of the Holy Spirit that he, Satan, is powerless against them.

For all those who obey My instruction of prayer they will become stronger in mind and spirit. Then they will not care whether Satan lashes out at them in fury for their shield of armour is so strong. This does not mean he will not use every method to seduce you through the desires of the flesh. This does not mean he will not hurt you by whispering into the ears of those close to you and those whom you love. Stand firm My followers for it will be through your strength that he will be crushed forever. He, My children, will become powerless as conversion spreads. For how can he get you to drink from his evil cup of hatred for mankind when you do not thirst for all his empty promises? The stronger you are the less he will bother you.

Know now that when you witness global unrest it is The Deceiver at work. My followers now know instantly the wickedness of Satan when his works are so glaringly obvious. Pray that your brothers and sisters will also bear witness to his evil works and recognize them for what they are. It is only when non-believers finally accept that Satan exists that they will turn to Me for refuge.

Pray now for global conversion, the conversion that will come about, not just because of The Warning, but because of the Truth.

Your beloved Teacher and Saviour
Jesus Christ

Call to priests and nuns in the Roman Catholic Church
Monday, July 25, 2011 21.00 hours

My dearly beloved daughter word is now spreading rapidly as foretold regarding The Warning.

My poor sacred servants are suffering My daughter. Please ask all who read My Messages to pray hard for all those sacred servants, priests, nuns, pastors and all those who head up Christian congregations all over the world.

The Catholic Church is being persecuted beyond its endurance. Satan and his army have attacked the Roman Catholic Church through infestation. It is his desire to undermine My Church through the wickedness of clerical abuse, which has led to this terrible situation.

The poor children who suffered sexual abuse were attacked by the minions of Satan who were present in those sacred servants who allowed themselves to be seduced by the Evil One.

Satan walks in My Church because he wants to bring about its downfall.

As for My poor innocent nuns and priests they too are victims of the prejudice at the hands of those who blame the sins of others upon them.

My pleas to My beloved priests, nuns and sacred servants are this. Do not give up. Remember, by your trials you will be raised in My eyes if you can endure these prejudices. Let Me wipe away your tears now for you are being persecuted in a way never before experienced by My Church. You, My beloved servants are My apostles and must never give in to these external pressures. You must never give up your calling to follow Me. For remember I am your Church. I weep tears of great sadness for you. You are now suffering for the sins of your brothers and sisters who succumbed to the Evil One. Pray, pray, pray for courage now to stand up with dignity to impart My Holy Word.

I need your support, more than ever. I need you to administer the Sacraments to a starving and disillusioned congregation. Please do not desert Me especially at this time when Satan has infiltrated the Christian Church with his followers.

Turn now and pray hard to salvage yourselves from the False Prophet who walks in the corridors of power within the Vatican. He will rise shortly. Do not turn to him or you will be lost to Me forever. This is My promise. Kneel down in humility and call on the Holy Spirit to enlighten your soul so that you will be able to discern the Truth from the lies, which you will be forced to swallow by the False Prophet.

Never be disillusioned with the trials you endure. Accept them for what they will offer you - strength of mind and soul. Then you will lead My children to the end times with humility, dignity and strength. Be brave now. I am guiding you. Turn now and pray for extra graces to make you stronger in your Divine Mission.

Your Loving Saviour

Jesus Christ

Part 4.

First Volume

Messages 150 - 199

Thursday, July 28, 2011 to Wednesday, September 21, 2011

Message from Virgin Mary - 'Victim Soul'
Thursday, July 28, 2011 14.25 hours

My child it is with great joy that I come to help guide you in your Mission to help my beloved Son, Jesus Christ, to save even more souls. Your final surrender to offer to the Most High, God the Father, your agreement to become a victim soul is accepted with great joy in the Heavens.

You, my child, are now going to help save those souls who would otherwise have been destined for the pits of darkness. This offering will be rewarded with special graces to give you the strength to endure trials with greater ease. Your spirit, my child, will now be strengthened so that matters pertaining to the materialist world will matter little in your eyes.

Always call on me your Mother and mentor, to bring you into the bosom of my precious beloved Son, Jesus Christ and God, the Most High. Pray now to prepare adequately to consecrate yourself properly for this important challenge.

I will always cover you with my Holy Mantle and you, my sweet child, will always be close to my Heart.

Your beloved Mother

Queen of the Angels

Pray for the souls of those facing damnation who will not survive The Warning
Thursday, July 28, 2011 15.30 hours

My daughter the spiritual dryness you have been going through over the past few days when you found it impossible to pray was The Deceiver trying to pull you away from Me.

Now that you have given your final pledge to become a victim soul to My Eternal Father to help Me save souls you will now be offered extra protection to prevent The Deceiver from distracting you.

The time now has come for a great amount of prayer in this your final chance, children, to help save those souls who will not survive The Warning. Please heed My call to pray hard for those poor lost children during the month of August designated Salvation of Souls month. Spread the word to prayer groups everywhere to follow My instruction for daily Mass, daily Eucharist and one day's fasting a week for the entire month. Do not underestimate the power that your prayers will have when it comes to saving souls.

Start by praying for those members of your own family who are in sin or who are non-believers. They include close friends and acquaintances who have turned their back on My Teachings willingly and who inflict injustice on others. They need your prayers now.

Now is the time for quiet reflection as the day for The Warning draws nearer. Silent, uninterrupted prayer and devotion is called for and I command that My sacred servants everywhere lead My children to pray for the souls of the damned. Only prayer can help them now especially the recital of My Divine Mercy Chaplet.

Unite in love for Me.

Your beloved Saviour

Jesus Christ

Note: when the visionary took down this Message she assumed that the term "souls facing damnation" was the same as saying "souls of the damned". Jesus has since requested that his children understand that ALL souls facing damnation can, in fact, be saved through praying the Divine Mercy on their behalf. He has instructed Maria to change the phrase "souls of the damned" to read "souls facing damnation".

You do not belong to Satan you belong to Me and My Eternal Father

Saturday, July 30, 2011 15.30 hours

My dearly beloved daughter there are times when you think you will not be able to endure the trials you receive because of My Messages but you must not fear. Fear is not something that you need to feel. If you can first let Me take away your fears by trusting in Me completely you will be free.

O how My children have forgotten the power of the Divine Realm My daughter. If they could only, for one moment, put down their shield they would be able to see clearly parts of My Divine Plan for mankind unfold. This shield, the shield of human intelligence driven by human logic, which in turn is ignited by the advances that man has made through science, is nothing but hay. It seems solid but it is empty of substance. Yet man believes that it provides protection against the Truth, the Truth of God's Divine Presence.

Your shield, My children, which blocks Me and My Teachings from your life will be your downfall. It will, in time, offer you no protection and will burn so fast, so instantly, just like straw, that you will become naked. Your nakedness will eventually reveal to you the deceit of Satan and all his empty promises of worldly security, which does not really exist. Man's stubbornness to accept the existence of My Eternal Father will be the cause of his banishment into the darkness.

When you see My Light, the flames of My Love, materialise in the skies shortly let you be in no doubt. This will not be an illusion. It will be a reality and you must humble yourselves to open your eyes to the Truth. Do not turn your eyes away or cower in fear. My Presence must be greeted by you as your last chance for salvation. It is I who comes to envelop you in My Arms. It is I, your Saviour, who once again comes to bring you back from the brink of darkness and despair. I have told you I will never forsake you. I will never leave you at the mercy of Satan for you do not belong to him. You belong to Me and My Eternal Father your Creator.

When you see My Flames of Glory in the skies be joyful. Any doubts you ever had about the existence of God the Father will disappear. To benefit from the graces that The Warning will bring to your soul so that you can be saved you must appear little in My eyes and ask Me to forgive you for your sins. My Love will then flood your soul and you will come back to Me and your rightful home. Resist My Mercy out of arrogance or intellectual reasoning and you will be lost.

Await now My Mercy with joy and enthusiasm for you will become whole again. You will be reborn.

Your beloved Saviour

Jesus Christ

Be prepared at all times
Monday, August 01, 2011 23.00 hours

My dearly beloved daughter you are now truly in union with Me at last. Now you will see why there is an urgency to help people to open their eyes so that they can convert in order to enter My Father's Kingdom.

So many men today mock Me. When My Name is mentioned by believers in a revered manner, they too are mocked, sneered and laughed at. Then there are others who become angry when challenged in My Name. There are also others who not only deny Me but who also hate Me. Never before has there been so many people in the world who have turned their back on the Faith.

So many souls chose to dismiss any thought that I, or My Eternal Father, exist. They think it does not matter whether or not they believe and that it is irrelevant in their lives. Many of those lukewarm in their faith casually dismiss My Teachings, which they merely pay lip service to. They believe that they will have plenty of time later on in life to devote the time they need to their faith. This is especially true of the younger generation who think that their faith is not something they need to bother about just yet. They believe that they have many years ahead of them to honour Me their beloved Saviour and My Eternal Father. This is why older people tend to re-kindle their faith at a later stage of their lives when they begin to think about the hereafter.

What man fails to grasp is that they can die at any moment, any time, any age from birth to old age. It does not matter. He must be prepared at all times.

I implore all believers to pray for the discernment to teach young people everywhere of the urgent need to open their eyes to the Love that I and My Eternal Father has for each of them. Help to open their eyes to the promise of Paradise. It is your duty to Me now so that I do not lose My younger children to the lies that Satan spreads in the world today.

Help Me save all those who believe that time is plentiful for them to pay attention to their souls in preparation for the New Paradise on earth which is drawing nears and which will become a reality in the blink of an eye when most of you least expect it.

Your beloved Teacher and Saviour

Jesus Christ

Questions to Jesus
Monday, August 01, 2011 23.30 hours

After receiving the Message entitled "Be Prepared at all times" the visionary saw an image of Jesus in which he appeared sad. She then asked Him a number of questions to which He replied.

Question to Jesus: "Are you sad?"

Answer: "Yes and weary. The sins of man are tearing My Heart in two."
Question to Jesus: "What will help?"

Answer: "Prayer and much of it. The devotion of My followers through the daily recital of the Divine Mercy and the Holy Rosary will save My children. They, My followers, must persevere even if this is hard."

Question to Jesus: "What upsets you most?"

Answers: "Those who not only hate Me but who chose to worship Satan in obscene rituals where they cannot see how they are being lied to."

"My sacred servants who have lost their love for Me."

"Those who persecute others."

"Those murderers with no regard for the lives of My children."

"Abortion, the worse form of genocide. I spill tears every single moment for My little souls who never get to take their first breath."

"War and the ease in which it is inflicted usually by those who, if they were to be placed in the middle of a battlefield, would run away in cowardice. Many of these people who declare war only do so to gain power. They offend Me greatly."

Question to Jesus: "What makes you happy?"

Answer: "The faith of My followers and those who are determined to help Me save souls. I Love them with such tenderness and compassion. They will be rewarded greatly in My Father's Kingdom."

God the Father: One of most urgent Messages to mankind
Tuesday, August 02, 2011 20.15 hours

I come in the Name of My Son Jesus Christ. I am God the Father and wish to communicate to the whole world. It is My intention to put a stay on the severity of The Chastisement to give mankind a chance to open their hearts to the Truth of My existence. They, My precious children, must know that I am a God firstly of Mercy and then of Justice.

My Mercy has been stretched to extraordinary limits. I will, because of the power of prayer, hold My Hand back in Mercy so that man can alleviate the hatred that is manifested in many souls throughout the world.

Beware My children when I warn you that failure to stop sin from spreading will result in a chastisement that will destroy much of mankind. Such a chastisement will not have been witnessed since the days of the flood that destroyed the earth in the time of Noah.

I will no longer allow you My ungrateful children to destroy those who have shown allegiance to Me. Nor will I stand back and allow the One World Order to contaminate My creation, My children, My earth.

Heed now this, one of the final warnings being given to mankind. Turn away now from the way of sin and you will be saved. Turn away from your blind devotion to the lure of Satan and his seductive charms, which attract you by means of love of oneself and of material wonders. Should you continue to desecrate this beautiful world created out of Love for you in the way you do it will not be there for you to inflict any further damage.

I am the God of Love, slow to anger, but My patience is running out. Those who continue to maim and destroy My children through war and control of the world's finances know that your days are numbered. Your chance of redemption now will be your last. Should you not respond appropriately during the great Gift of Mercy that is The Warning then you and your minions will be destroyed.

My Glory will be known to every man, woman and child. Those who chose the path to My Kingdom will have ever lasting life. Those who do not will experience a darkness the like of which they could never imagine nor want.

Followers of Satan who knowingly idolize his wickedness hear now My Promise. You, My lost children will be offered the Hand of Love and Peace once more during The Warning. Grasp it for it will be your lifeline back into the bosom of My Love. Ignore My pleas and you will suffer for eternity never to return to the fold of My cherished family.

This now, My daughter, is one of the most important warnings to save your brothers and sisters from the torturous fires of eternal damnation.

King of the Most High

God the Almighty Father

Note: For those who do not understand the term "put a stay on the severity" this means hold back - postpone for the present.

Message from Virgin Mary - I will appear only a few more times in the world

Wednesday, August 03, 2011 09.45 hours

My child there is no need to fear in this Work for it has been foretold that conversion will take place. Sadly not all men will or can be saved. They who persecute my Precious Son in the world today are worse than those who executed Him during the Crucifixion. Because my Son died to save mankind from sin a lesson was learned throughout the world of the need for devotion to my Son. Many who know the Truth chose to ignore this.

I have been sent so many times to encourage prayer throughout the world and, yet, my warnings to children throughout time have been forgotten. Today when I make myself known through visionaries in various countries not only are they ignored but they suffer ridicule. My presence and the signs I show in the skies and other manifestations are rejected. Even priests and bishops ignore my warnings. They, too, have turned away from a belief in Divine Interventions. How blind they are to reject help from me their Beloved Mother.

My Son suffers so much it is heartbreaking to see Him in agony today because of the evil of sin. My children have no idea how He suffers the torment He has to witness in the world when He sees the cruelty of man.

My child, remind my children that I will appear only a few more times in the world because the time has come for the final battle when I will crush the head of the serpent.

My children must know how much they are loved and cherished by my beloved Son. I urge them to open their hearts and show Him the love and compassion He deserves. He, your Saviour, who willingly accepted death in its most cruel form to save you, wants now to save this generation from the snares of Satan.

He, The Deceiver, smiles my child because he knows he has succeeded in stealing precious souls. Pray, pray, pray now that my Son will be heard during The Warning and that His Gift of Redemption will be accepted with humble and open arms.

Remember, as your Mother I will always plead for clemency for my children. My tears have flowed for those who do not want to hear the Truth because it will only be through constant prayer that these unfortunate souls can be redeemed.

Your beloved Mother

Our Lady Queen of the Sorrows

My birthday is a very special Feast day

Thursday, August 04, 2011 20.30 hours

Tomorrow, my child is a very special Feast for me, your Beloved Mother for it is my birthday.

My Heart is heaving with sorrow because of the abuse, which my beloved Son is suffering for the sins of man. I smile to see my devoted children doing all they can to save souls but my tears still flow because I cannot bear to see the suffering in your world.

My child do not turn your back for even one moment when spreading the Messages from my Son Jesus Christ and God the Most High for time is running out. Devote as much time as you can to this Work. Keep going my child. I will cover you with my Holy Mantle at all times.

Your beloved Mother

Queen of the Heavens

Time for waiting - tell others to know what to expect

Thursday, August 04, 2011 21.40 hours

My dearly beloved daughter the world each day falls into further decay. Among My children there is a mixture of hope, worry, anger and despair because of war and the lack of money to feed and clothe your family properly. But heed this. You will not have to fend for yourselves much longer for very soon now, after The Warning, there will be a more positive feeling of Light and Love in the world. All is not lost, My daughter.

Pray for those who convert during The Warning that they will stay on the path of Truth. Pray that love for Me and My Eternal Father will become stronger among those followers who already know the Truth.

As long as My children embrace the Gift of The Warning then there is nothing to fear.

For those who do not stay on the path and who turn back to sinful ways they have much to fear. My Father will not allow them to infest others through their wayward and wicked ways. They will be stopped. Sadly, many will turn away from the Truth and try to continue to inflict power and control over the rest of My children.

Pray that the Chastisement will be diluted. Your prayers will help to convert and avert such situations. This is now the time of waiting, praying, preparing and ensuring that as many people as possible know what to expect.

This month of August "Salvation of Souls month" is so important children. Please persevere in your devotion this month for the souls you will save will be in the multitudes. Heaven rejoices at the love and generosity of heart and soul of all My followers who have made this commitment, a precious gift to Me, so that people be saved during The Warning.

Go now My daughter and spread My Word. Go now in peace and love.

Your beloved Saviour

Jesus Christ

God the Father - the role of suffering

Sunday, August 07, 2011 14.45 hours

I am the Alpha and the Omega. I am God the Father Creator of Man and the Universe.

My precious daughter I now finally accept your gift to Me to help save souls. Your gift is accepted with love and joy. This will not be an easy road but you will be protected once you ask Me for My help every single day.

Your suffering will be mental and a darkness of the soul. As it gets worse keep reminding yourself of those creatures who will be saved because of your suffering.

Go to Adoration as often as you can to gain the strength required for this Work. The Messages from My beloved Son will continue. They must be posted as before for His Messages to the world will increase not decrease. You are being helped by many saints who intercede on your behalf.

Keep praying to the Holy Trinity for the graces required to stay strong. Never feel abandoned, as this will seem to be part of your suffering. Rest your head. Keep silent and appear joyful to the outside world. Ignore those who will hurt you. Rather, remember it is because of the Divine Light that will shine through your soul that will draw out the darkness in others. Then and only then will you realise the torment that sears through the Heart of My Son when He sees sin in the world. Your suffering will be just a fraction of what He suffers every minute of the day.

Accept now the Gift that you too have been given by being called to become a victim soul.

Remember, you My daughter, are in My Heart at all times. I watch over you and protect you. Smile now. Have no fear for this Work will bring great rewards for you and your family and loved ones in My Glorious Kingdom.

Your Beloved Father

God the Creator of all things.

Children do not become discouraged by tales of despair facing mankind

Monday, August 08, 2011 19.45 hours

My dearly beloved daughter it is days since I communicated with you. This was to give you a chance to listen to the advice of My Beloved Father, God the most High to help you understand the role of suffering to save souls.

The days now are getting shorter as the time for The Warning draws nearer. All is set for the flames of My Love, which will envelop the whole world as one. The angels, the choirs in Heaven await now the Day of Glory when I return to give man his last opportunity to accept My existence and that of My Eternal Father.

Children do not become discouraged by rumour or tales of despair facing mankind, instead look to Me now and confide in Me your fears. Mankind will be given such a wonderful Gift. Not only will man encounter Me face to face but they will be overjoyed to learn and see the Truth presented before their very eyes.

This is to be a great day in history when Hope and Love will be shown to all of you. Even hardened sinners will fall down and weep tears of remorse. This is good news, children, for all can be saved if they abandon their pride and ego. All, through their own free will, are to be united to allow Me to enter their hearts so that they can be guided towards the Light.

For many sinners in mortal sin this Light will burn their eyes and their soul. It will be painful. If they can only endure the fright of seeing how they offend Me they will become strong and will convert.

So children of My army I say to you now. Smile for the event will be the most extraordinary in your lives and your existing love for Me and My Eternal Father will infuse your soul. So much love will infiltrate your minds, bodies and souls that you will be renewed in spirit forever. Pray now for all of you for the time is short. The world is being prepared now for The Warning so that all will be ready for My Great Gift.

Continue My children with the devotion this month of the Salvation of Souls for by the end the of August millions of souls will be saved through your efforts.

Remember children I am present in your lives every day. Watching. Guiding. I love all of you. Remain loyal to My wishes to save tortured souls.

Jesus Christ

Turmoil in the world caused by the lack of love for Me

Tuesday, August 09, 2011 20.30 hours

My beloved daughter the time has come for turmoil in the world where man will rise against man, brother against brother and neighbour against neighbour as foretold. Events will erupt now one after another. Many countries will experience this. There is much anger in the world, disappointment and fear amongst My children. Tell them that these events are ignited by Satan and that further turmoil will erupt and intensify before The Warning.

This, My daughter, has been foretold as just one of the signs that mankind will experience during 2011 the year of Purification. My children will witness, with shock, the evil that exists in the world in the souls of those driven by sheer hatred and anger for each other. There are no winners, My daughter in this battle which will continue to rage. It is by the hand of man that these atrocities come about. It is because of their lack of love for Me, and My Eternal Father that they become willing accomplices of Satan.

Pray My children for all those who will suffer because of unrest in the world. For few countries will escape these outbursts of fury and destruction. This war of hatred will be seen within various countries and nations. Confusion, terror and sorrow will be felt by many.

Please trust in My Father, God the Eternal Father for His Hand will help stop these calamities children. Keep strong, alert and loyal to Me your beloved Saviour. All will improve in your world when you realise the importance of love in your lives and the importance of harmony and caring for your neighbour. Prayer will help reduce the impact of evil unrest.

Remember war, violence and murder, are not of God, they are created by Satan. His anger has now reached unprecedented levels and his fury is being wielded upon My children by the infiltration of those who are weak in spirit with no love in their hearts.

Hear me now. Love one another as I love you. Reject Satan, his minions and his puppets now. Pray to St Michael the Archangel to protect your community. Pray to Me for guidance. Pray to invoke the Holy Spirit to descend on your countries.

Your Merciful Saviour

Jesus Christ

Fear of The Warning is not something I encourage

Wednesday, August 10, 2011 23.00 hours

My dearly beloved daughter the speed of global events leading up to The Warning, as foretold, continues to escalate. Prayer, My children, is essential now as My followers all over the world, filled with the graces of the Holy Spirit, forge to form My army. This army, while quite small in that many of My followers still have to understand that each of them plays an important role even now, will rise and lead My children up to the very end.

All My children need to listen to Me now. For every atrocity committed by man against man in these times you must pray for the perpetrator in each case. Prayer for the sinners is now called for. By prayer you can invoke the Holy Spirit to bring Divine Light into these poor souls. Many of them are so blind to the Truth of My Father's Love that they wander around aimlessly plunging from one crisis to another so that everyone they come into contact with is hurt. If more of you ask for My Mercy for these sinners then the impact of the Evil One's deed will weaken considerably. This is the secret, My children, in diluting Satan's hatred as it spews forth like the fire from a dragon's mouth in an attempt to engulf the world in its hateful vapour.

He, The Deceiver, and his demons are everywhere. Because the faith of My children is so weak on a global scale, Satan's evil deeds have gripped mankind in a vice that is difficult to disentangle from. If My children everywhere believed in the existence of God the Almighty Father this would not happen. Then Satan's grip would be weaker especially if My children prayed for help and asked for My Father's Mercy.

Prayer is your armour now children between now and the time for The Warning. Use prayer to save souls in darkness. After The Warning your prayers will be needed to help My children retain their devotion to My Eternal Father and to praise His Glory.

Patience, silent prayer daily, the formation of prayer groups, daily recital of the Divine Mercy Chaplet, fasting and the Holy Rosary to My Beloved Mother combined, act as the perfect formula for saving souls.

Fear of The Warning is not something I encourage. Pray now for your own and other souls through the act of redemption and before your face to face encounter with Me your beloved Saviour.

I smile with joy and happiness when I think of the moment when this Great Gift of My Mercy is revealed to My children. It is a homecoming the likes of which cannot be described. For this will be when your hearts will be filled with My Divine Love. Your souls will be enlightened finally in preparation for the New Paradise on earth. I will then bring you the comfort missing in your lives up to now when you will become in union with Me.

Remember children the reason why I communicate to the world now. It is My desire to ensure that all of My children are saved from the clutches of Satan. It is also My deep unfathomable Love for each and every one of you that I must reach out My Hand so that you can join with Me to prepare you to come home again to your rightful home.

Fear does not come from Me. I love you children. I am bringing you this glorious Gift out of My Love. Rejoice, smile and welcome Me when the Sign appears in the sky. Raise your arms and sign praise to God the Father for allowing Me this last chance to save you.

Your beloved Saviour

Jesus Christ

King of Mercy

Pray for those who cannot see beyond material gain

Thursday, August 11, 2011 00.05 hours

My dearly beloved daughter you must persevere in this suffering because by doing so you are saving souls. Your suffering now reveals the torture I endured by the hand of man's sin.

The greed of man is now heightened to such an extent that morals no longer apply in your society. Man's sin of greed means that he does not care who suffers by his hand as long as his lusts are satisfied. Let Me tell you that those who torment others through greed and avarice will not escape My eyes. I watch. I see. I cringe as I witness the ugly path that man chooses to go down in order to gain wealth at the expense of others.

They, My daughter, will be stripped bare of material goods unless they beg for My Mercy. Their money will be worthless. For the man who succumbs to torturing souls by stealing what is rightfully belonging to his brothers and sisters know that you will be left with nothing but ashes. Pray for those who cannot see beyond material gain because if they do not turn their back on these evil acts they will be cast aside and will not enter My Father's Kingdom.

Do evil onto others in this world and you will be thrown away and cast into Satan's den. What may seem like your rightful claim to wealth gained at the expense of others will bring you torment for eternity.

Drop your weapons of greed and gluttony now. Seek redemption for when you do peace will return to society.

Your Saviour

Kind of Justice

Jesus Christ

My followers have now been given the gift of intercession

Friday, August 12, 2011 23.45 hours

My beloved daughter the love of My followers keeps me sustained. I cry tears of joy when I witness the love of those of My followers who surround you and embrace you with their prayers.

They, My daughter, through the gift of the Holy Spirit, have been called to proclaim My Most Holy Word to the world through these important Messages.

If only those other souls who follow Me and who know that I am communicating through various visionaries would open their eyes and listen to what I have to say. Then their prayers would benefit those poor souls who have are prepared for The Warning.

My Love shines through My loyal children throughout the world. The Light of My Love, which shines through them is creating much conversion in the world right now. This month, although My children may not be aware, millions of souls are now being saved because of the devotion of My beloved followers. They, My precious children, followed My command for prayer and devotion during this August, Salvation of Souls month. Tell My children that their prayer and fasting has created much happiness in My Father's tender Heart. An abundance of graces now flow over those dear holy souls so that they are empowered with the gift of interceding for lost souls from this day forth.

How I yearn to hold each of them in My Arms close to My Sacred Heart so that I can show them how much I love them all. So brave, so loyal and despite sinful diversions from time to time, so good. Their hearts and souls are now infused with My Compassion and the Holy Spirit will guide My precious army as they march to victory to help Me claim more souls.

Your beloved loyal Saviour

King of Mankind

Jesus Christ

God created the world – No other planet can be inhabited by man

Saturday, August 13, 2011 17.00 hours

Conversion, My daughter, needs to be a priority now for My children as they tell others about My Messages to the world. Just one soul a day brings Me great joy, My children, when others begin to open their eyes to the Truth.

My beloved daughter when man is so busy each day there is little time for prayer in his life. Prayer, My children, can mean a moment, an hour, a word or any kind of communication with Me. It does not matter where man calls on Me. It can be in the home, in the garden, in the car, at Work, as well as in My Church. Where you talk to Me is not important although you can please Me more when you are speaking with Me in My House.

Many people mistakenly believe I can't hear their thoughts, feel their pain, their sorrow or their joy. Don't they realise that they were created by My Father, the Almighty, Creator of ALL things? He who knows everything calls on all of you to stop for just one moment a day. Ask for My help to strengthen you. Just one moment is all I ask, this one precious moment when you call to Me to enable Me to enter through your soul by the power of the Holy Spirit. Even just a whisper when you call out for My help will be heard. If you don't call Me I can't respond for I would never interfere with your free will.

I am like a Father looking down at a group of children playing, all busy, running, chatting to each other, some laughing and in other cases fighting amongst themselves. Most children respond to the adult when called to attention. But some are stubborn, turn their backs and refuse to do as they are asked. Some children are affectionate, some not so. Few will show absolute hatred however at so tender an age. Yet when I look at those children of Mine in the world today, I see hatred and even worse complete indifference to the existence of Me, Jesus Christ their beloved Saviour. For many they even hate the sound of My Name.

The times you are living in children have seen an unruly group of My children with little discipline who believe that the world is theirs to rule, control, abuse or even damage as they see fit. Little reverence is shown towards the Father, Creator of All things. So arrogant is man today that he believes he has emerged from an even higher hierarchy than that of My Eternal Father. So he continues to seek out more about his origins even though the Truth has been there for him to see all along. So much time is being wasted on worthless pursuits. Worthless dreams all of which are fabricated by the minds of those scientists whose pride in his own intelligence, a gift from God the Father, means he believes he will find new facts about his origins.

Why don't these children realise that earth was created for man? No other planet can be inhabited by man, for that is not part of My Father's plan. How foolish man can be when trying to fulfil the emptiness of spirit within his soul. All the nourishment and fulfilment can be his if he sits down and accepts the Truth. The Truth of the existence of God the Eternal Father the Creator of the universe.

Your beloved Saviour, Teacher and Just judge

Jesus Christ

Enjoy the glorious life that awaits you for 1000 years

Sunday, August 14, 2011 14.25 hours

My dearly beloved daughter you continue to defend My Word when, in fact, there is no need.

My Word will pierce the hearts of believers like a sword when they contemplate on My Messages given to you for the world. They will know the Truth when they read My Word for My Divine Light will impact on them in a way they will find difficult to ignore. Many question and continue to question just as they did during the time of Noah. They were warned but would not listen. They blocked out the voice of My Father when He sent Messages through Noah and the other prophets. Only those who listened and obeyed were saved.

Hear My Messages now. Open your hearts and allow My Word to speak to your souls children. Ignore worldly distractions. Just focus on My Voice. By doing so you will save your souls.

Those who won't listen because they turn their backs will, in time, come with hungry mouths to devour My most Holy Word after The Warning takes place. For then you will be ready to follow My guidance so that I can steer you properly towards the New Paradise on earth where you, your family and your love ones will enjoy the Glorious Life that awaits you for 1000 years. No disease. No shortage of food. No worries. Just love in its most pure form, a glorious entity that is your rightful inheritance.

Please pray hard now for the discernment to accept My Holy Word when it is presented to you children. Consider it one of the greatest gifts in your lifetime. Embrace it body, mind and soul. For only then will you find True Peace.

Your beloved Saviour

Jesus Christ

Help Me Save all Young people – the most vulnerable in your society

Monday, August 15, 2011 00.05 hours

My dearly beloved daughter as My Eternal Father, God the Most High, prepares the world for the changes ahead He is laden with sorrow for the man who is still blind to the Truth of His existence.

When My Father sets about now to ring in the changes to prepare for My return to earth He sees so much sin in the world that He weeps with sorrow for the inevitability of souls who will become lost to Him eventually. Prayer to save those still alive in the world today who willingly turn away from Him in pure defiance, although they know and accept His existence, can help save their souls. Continue to pray and make personal sacrifices for those souls My daughter for without prayer you must fear for their future.

I am relying on My followers to pray for the lost souls. The time left to convince the blind of faith to open their eyes to the Truth of the existence of God the Father is short now.

Link hands My children of the Light so that your circle of love and devotion to Me is strong enough to draw those souls who do not believe or accept the existence of Me or My beloved Father. Do not break this chain of faith when you can reach out to save your brothers and sisters who no longer follow the path to the Truth of Eternal Life. Instead, because they are weakened by the seduction of worldly pursuits, they will need firm guidance to help them.

Do not bully those who don't believe in God. Coax them gently, tell them about My Crucifixion and how My Eternal Father made the ultimate Sacrifice to save His children by giving them the Gift of the Grace of Salvation through the forgiveness of sin.

My Father calls now on all those reading these Messages for the first time. You must read each Message carefully. Then pray to the Holy Spirit for the grace to be able to see that these Messages are of Divine origin. Open your heart to receive My Word. Feel Me in your soul by asking of Me the following:

"Jesus if this is really you, please flood my soul with the Sign of Your Love so that I can recognise You for who You are. Do not let me be deceived by lies. Show me instead Your Mercy by opening my eyes to the Truth and the path to Your New Paradise on earth."

Remember children it is only because of My deep tender Love that I come to the world by communicating with you in this way. It is not to shock you. Impress. Create controversy or debate. It is to help save all souls especially a young generation who have no interest in religion so busy are they with their lives where God holds little place. It is by talking to them in a language they understand that I hope to alert them to events about to unfold. They are one of the most vulnerable in your society children. It is vital that I reach out to them as quickly as I can.

Gather now My children with Me to save all young people in the world today. Help Me to embrace them into My Kingdom so not one single precious soul is lost to Me.

Your beloved Saviour of all Mankind

Jesus Christ

How to ask Me to help you resolve your worries

Wednesday, August 17,

My dearly beloved daughter the graces poured out over you are being given to make you even stronger in this Work by giving you extra confidence.

Confidence in Me children is very important. Yes it brings much joy to My Sacred Heart when I feel your love for me. However it is only when you truly confide in Me and let go of all your worries by passing them over to Me, so I can take care of them, that you can feel a sense of True Peace.

So many of My children pray for special intentions. I listen to every single one. But you must, when praying to Me for something very important to you, let go of your fears. Fear is not from Me. It is given to you by Satan as a means to torment you. Don't you understand this? When you fear something, which you feel has a grip over your life, the more you fear the more the problem festers.

It is only when you stop and say to Me:

"Jesus I hand you over all my concerns in this matter in confidence so that the problem is now yours to resolve according to your Most Holy Will."

that your mind can be at peace. This is what I mean by confidence children.

Confidence in Me means that you display a great trust. Trust in Me. I died for your sins - every single one of you alive today even in this age. Why would you not trust in Me?

I love you like no other creature on this earth. No one will or can love you like I do. Remember this at all times.

Go now in love and peace. I am at your side morning, noon and night just waiting for your call.

Your beloved friend and Saviour

King of Mercy

Jesus Christ

Great Tribulation is being mitigated through prayer
Thursday, August 18, 2011

My daughter those followers of mine who are well read in matters of Holy Scripture tend to get carried away with their own human interpretation so that the lesson I have preached to love one another is so easily forgotten. Love one another. Honour your mother and father. Honour your Creator, God the Father, and live as I have told you in love and fear of My Father.

So many learned men, caught up in their analysis of My Teachings forget one thing. That is when I will come again to judge. Never for one moment do they consider that this time may well happen in their own lifetime and not in the distant future. Why then do they search and continue to search for further meanings in Holy Scripture when the Truth is so simple. Why do they not remember that love is all I ask? Love for me, your Saviour. Love for God the Father and love for each other?

For those intellectual experts who proclaim to be able to analyse My Teachings and then go as far as attempting to predict a date for when I will come again I say this. If you try to assume that you have been able to discern the year for My return then you are sadly mistaken. No one will be given this date not even the angels in Heaven or My Beloved Mother. But this I can reveal. The Tribulation started some time ago. The Great Tribulation will begin at the end of 2012. This terrible period is being mitigated through the prayers of My dearly beloved followers. It will also be diluted through the conversion achieved after The Warning takes place. This event is good news My Children. It is to help eradicate the slavery by man to the Evil One.

Religious experts display an arrogance, which I find repulsive

Many sadly will ignore My pleas to prepare so caught up are they in this so called intellectual religious debate based on human reasoning, one trying to outdo the other to prove that he or she is more knowledgeable. These experts display an arrogance, which I find repulsive. They are no better than the Pharisees were. Their ignorance blocks out the Truth when it is presented before they very eyes.

My Word is being ignored by My sacred servants

My Word has fallen on deaf ears. My Word is ignored by My sacred servant as I attempt to communicate with them at this point in history. Yet after The Warning there will be no excuse for them not to sit up and listen to My instructions. For then they will hold out their arms pleading with Me to guide them through the Great Chastisement. For when this prophecy is unveiled to those who doubt My Word, through this messenger, I urge you then to take up My Sacred Cup, drink from it and fight to save souls.

I urge all of you, including those self-proclaimed Scriptural experts, to sit down in humility and ask this question. Why would I encourage simple believers to become embroiled in an argument over My return to earth? All that matters now is that I am coming. Be prepared at all times. Never judge others in My Name. Seek out the gift of humility at all costs for it will be your passport to Heaven.

Your beloved Saviour

Jesus Christ

What is it that encourages young people to be so ashamed of Me?

Friday, August 19, 2011 23.00 hours

My dearly beloved daughter My Love for young people especially those in their teens and early adulthood is very deep. Like their parents I feel love, happiness, worry and sometimes anger as I watch them grow up. O how My Heart breaks when I hear them say they do not believe in God, My Eternal Father. They, My little children, have been conditioned to deny Him so they can be seen to fit in with their friends so as not to appear different to them.

The fact is that it is no longer easy for a young person to own up to their love for Me even if they do accept My existence. This admission can cause them embarrassment when a belief in Me, Jesus Christ or My Eternal Father, is scorned in favour of a so called 'higher being'. What is it that encourages them to be so ashamed of Me? Why do they feel they need to conform to a world empty of spirit or concern for the soul?

Music and the arts have a huge influence on these precious little souls who have not been told the Truth of Heaven or Hell. They like all of My other children, who persist in avoiding any mention of Me, My Teachings or the existence of My Eternal Father, are just as likely to be lost to the wilderness.

Parents I call on you to tell your children the Truth of their existence on this earth. Where they came from and the destiny that awaits them after this life. It is your duty to help them open their hearts to My Love. Take them to Me gently but use whatever means possible to help save their souls. Do this out of love for them. You may have shirked your duties over the years but now is the time to make amends. By praying The Divine Mercy for their souls you can help them. It better if they walk towards me with the hands held out to Me in this life on their own accord.

To the young people I say this. If you believe in Me don't be afraid to acknowledge this in public. Do not deny Me for I am your lifeline without Whom there is no life. When others see how strong your belief is they will be more inclined to open their own hearts to Me. This requires much bravery on your part but the graces you will receive from me will far outweigh your fear. Once you tell people that I do exist, once you show them respect and love and draw them to you they will respect you for speaking of Me. It may seem odd to be talking about Me in one breath and worldly matters the next but you will become stronger in your faith when you do this. Not only will you experience such a wealth of love in your heart for Me it will save the souls of your friends.

Use the Internet to spread My Message. Talk about them. It does not matter who ridicules you. Because when you do this many, many young people around the world will have Eternal Life because of the conversion created as a result.

Go forth now My precious young army. It is time for you now to pluck up the courage to spread My Messages which are being given to this generation in the world to remind them of who I am, why I saved you all from the depths of Hell and why I am now reaching out to save you once more.

This is the time for Me to reach out to take your hands in Mine.

I love you.

Your beloved Saviour and Friend

Jesus Christ

Money and too much of it corrupts the soul

Sunday, August 21, 2011 23.00 hours

My dearly beloved daughter I visit you tonight as the world begins to erupt in continued violence as nation after nation bombard each other to seek power and glory. Pray for all those souls who will perish in this violence so they can find favour in My Father's Kingdom.

My daughter the world will now undergo the changes foretold to cleanse them so that man can be made worthy of My Promise. They will continue to be allowed to be stripped bare of material things by those greedy people responsible for their sudden demise. As these trials intensify these children will be free of the shackles which bind them to the empty promises of Satan, he who seduces the wealthy by promising them even more will now continue to parade the obscenity of ostentatious vulgarity for all the world to see. He will do this so that My children will not only envy the rich and famous but will do everything they can to imitate them. By drawing My children into this nest, where the trappings of significant wealth will appear to be an important goal to aim for, he will succeed in taking them away from the Truth.

Once bare and naked I will clothe you again children only this time it will be a cloak of armour designed to protect you from the wickedness of evil men. Once armoured you will be ready to enter the world again with a different view of life. A life when love for your neighbour counts as being your number one goal. When you show love to one another you prove your genuine love for Me.

This facade of wealth and riches, which very few of My children in the world have access to, is only that. A front, for there is no substance behind it. You will be taunted to seek out similar wealth when the deceiver convinces you that you must aspire to great riches and fame. The Truth is that while you are busy chasing empty and meaningless desires you will be ignoring your duty to Me.

Never allow the parading of wealth and fame to seduce you children for know that money and too much of it corrupts the soul. Those who have so much money where they are unlikely to be ever able to spend it in this life must give it to those unfortunate people who have little to eat. Do this and you can save your soul. If you hunger after excesses, when you already have enough to feed and clothe a nation, then you will starve. The food of life is your humble acceptance, that love for one another is what I taught you. Loving your neighbour means looking after those who have nothing.

Wake up and accept the Truth before it is too late for you. It is more difficult for those with immense material riches to find favour with My Father unless you share with others. Remember this. To those who have little and who envy those who seem to have every material comfort they wish for you, too, must be careful. There is only one mansion you should try to gain access to and that is the mansion that awaits you in the New Paradise on Earth. Only those humble in heart, mind and soul will be given the key.

Your beloved Saviour

Jesus Christ

Evil is presented as being good while good is presented as evil.

Monday, August 22, 2011 20.10 hours

When man questions his faith he needs to think. If he is in doubt then he must ask Me to open his eyes. If he is finding it difficult to pray he must ask Me to open his mouth. But if he won't listen to the Truth then he needs the prayer of others.

My children I am deeply concerned at the way in which evil is presented as being good while good is being presented as evil. Everything in your world is back to front. For those of you without a deep devotion to Me you will be none the wiser.
Actions are now being perpetrated in the world at every level of government, church and state in your name and you are oblivious to this.

Bad laws are being introduced and presented to mankind as being in their best interests. This includes new regimes, medicine, foreign aid, vaccination and the preaching of new religious and other doctrines. Never has there been so much confusion amongst My children.

On the surface everything is seen as being controlled and in order and in a way it is. But the only real order that exists is by the hand of those who control world events hidden in the comfort of their wicked ways behind closed doors.

Do not be deceived children. You must turn to Me for help so that the wicked events planned by secretive global powers can be weakened. Your only route to real freedom is when you rekindle your faith in Me. This will happen soon, My precious children, when I present Myself to the world during The Warning, which is getting closer and closer.

I urge you to pray for those who have eyesight but who are blind to My Most Holy Word. Pray for those who persist in twisting My Teachings and for My sacred servants who, through cowardice, are giving in to the demands made of them by governments.

There is only one ruler now who is in charge of the future and that is My Eternal Father, God the Creator and Maker of everything. Pay allegiance to Him above all and you will find a firm footing when moving forward on the path of Truth.

Your beloved Saviour

Jesus Christ

No sin is so grave that it cannot be forgiven

Tuesday, August 23, 2011 23.45 hours

My daughter you are now beginning to understand the Truth of suffering. When I ask chosen souls to suffer they suffer as I did during My torture at My Crucifixion. Just as My death saved man from sin then your suffering too can save man from eternal damnation. By offering your suffering, willingly, you make a sacrifice so that the souls of mankind will be shown God's Mercy.

If I were to ask more souls to do this they may show fear and would decline. Yet many souls suffer who are not aware that they are also chosen souls. Many children of mine may ask why do some people suffer and not others? My answer is that I chose the kind of heart those who display humility in this life, those who place others needs before their own. The soul of a tender heart takes up the role of suffering for Me. This is a Gift from Me. It may not seem like a Gift but when you are given this Gift you are saving thousands of souls every day on My behalf.

I now want to ask My followers to make one sacrifice a day akin to suffering to help me save souls in mortal sin at the point of death during The Warning. Please ask me for this Gift. For those humble of heart I will also ask them to make one personal sacrifice in My Glory. For those who feel they cannot do this, then, I will bless you with My special Graces because I know that your existing love of Me, and your prayers, are already saving the souls of your brothers and sisters.

My children know this. My army of followers is growing daily because of these Messages. This will grow into an army of millions soon. I call only on those who are brave enough to take up My gauntlet. Bravery stems from love. One man's interpretation of bravery will differ to another's. I simply ask you to tell the world of My Love. Remind them of the Truth contained in the Holy Scripture. Tell them I am returning to offer the Great Gift of My Mercy soon. For if I were to come to judge so soon in your world Heaven would be deserted so widespread is sin today.

Spread My Good News. Remind them that when they feel love, genuine pure love for someone, even if it be only a passing glance or a good deed you witness, that I am then present.

Tell them that without love they will shrivel up and become nothing.

Tell them that when I see them, they are naked without worldly possessions in My Eyes. I see only their goodness and badness in the soul.

For those poor frightened souls ashamed of their lifestyles tell them that I am forgiving, all merciful and will welcome them into My open and Loving Arms. All they have to do is walk towards Me and ask me to help them. I will never turn away from the pleas of sinners, no matter how dark their sin. I forgive all of those who are truly remorseful for any previous offence they have committed.

Their hearts will be lighter and My Love will bring Light back into their lives. I will come again in Glory children not to frighten you but to bring you My Gifts, these same Gifts denied you through the works of Satan.

Come. Bow your heads. Push your shame aside and ask Me to forgive you now. Nothing shocks Me children. No sin is so grave that it cannot be forgiven by Me if true remorse is shown. Do not delay. Seek redemption now before it is too late.

Your Loving Jesus Christ

Redeemer of Mankind

Prophecies foretold through this prophet now unfold
Wednesday, August 24, 2011 16.38 hours

My dearly beloved daughter every nation in the world will strive to read My Messages given to you. For it will be when they witness The Warning that they will then seek My Guidance to give them strength.

You are tired now My daughter as the suffering increases but you will be given a reprieve in a few days. All this is required of you because I need the suffering to help Me redeem those people in terrible sin. Try and see the benefits that it brings for one day you will rejoice with me when you witness the Fruits of this Work.

March forward My children in strength for as the prophecies foretold through this prophet unfold now so, too, will belief be in the authenticity of this website.

Pray now My children that you, My army increase in numbers and unite as one to fight the spiritual battle that lies ahead.

Your Loving Saviour

Jesus Christ

Climatic Chaos will now be experienced by a number of countries. My Father is Angry
Thursday, August 25, 2011 20.00 hours

My dearly beloved call on all My prayer warriors to pray for the others. They include the non-believers and those ensnared in violence and hatred. They wander desperately trying to find love and peace in their lives and find it impossible. You must pray hard for these because without your prayers they will plunge into the fires of Hell. Do not let this happen. If they can just be encouraged to walk a little towards Me and be prepared to listen to My Words they will be given the Graces so that I can take them in My Arms.

My daughter the world must now sit and heed Me. Very soon they will witness a series of earthquakes and floods. Chaos will be experienced in a number of countries through climatic catastrophes. These are the punishments cast down by My Father on mankind. Sin will be punished My daughter and those countries which are guilty of promoting abortion will not escape the Hand of My Father as it will fall. Prayer has averted many such acts of punishment yet man continues to sin and offend My Father with vile and disgusting acts by man against man including innocent children in the womb.

I urge you to pray now for My children in the countries, which will not escape this punishment. My Father is angry. He will no longer sit back and watch as man destroys mankind. The Earth would implode if man is not stopped. He, My Beloved Father, will withhold much of this punishment until after The Warning. After that, despite man's conversion thereafter, man will still continue to turn back to sin. Punishments meted out are to show man how harsh My Father can be. He loves all His children but He created this world and man will simply not be allowed to destroy it.

Pray now, My children, for all your brothers and sisters.

Jesus Christ

King of Mankind

Message to the Clergy - do not allow bullying by secular societies

Saturday, August 27, 2011 00.10 hours

My daughter if only more priests and members of the Christian Church would open their minds and accept that I am speaking to the world now through these Messages then My Heart would be lighter.

It is My devout followers who hold the candle of light as they forge ahead to spread My warnings to the world to encourage My children to redeem themselves in My Eyes. O how it saddens Me to see how closed the minds are of those sacred servants who profess to communicate My Word, My Teachings, to the world. They break My Heart so hardened have their own hearts become.

My Teachings espouse the fact that Divine Revelations do take place and have taken place since the beginning of time. Did they think that My Mother or I would not communicate to My children over the centuries? They are happy to pay attention to the word of saints gone by, long after their Messages were given to the world, but not so today. The difference during this time is that no time will be afforded to them to enable them to digest these Messages after the event. Because time will be no more as you know it.

I call on you, My sacred servants and My Holy Vicar to read My Words to mankind now. Never before have you needed My Intervention in worldly events as you do now. Remember that I rose from the dead and promised I would come back. How prepared are you now? How often do you remind My children of the need to redeem themselves in My Eyes? How often are you willing to hear the sins of My children when you are so busy? The time is not being afforded to the hearing of Confessions. You have let me down My sacred servants and for that you offend Me greatly. To deny My children the right to the Sacraments is unforgivable. Wake up now and follow My instruction. Do your duty to My children as you promised Me through your Sacred Vows. Please do not turn your back on My Teachings.

Faith, and especially that of My beloved sacred servants is weakening considerably. This is brought about by the curse of Satan who has walked among your midst for some time causing havoc within and outside of My Church. Remember this My sacred servants. This is

Satan at work. You must never give in to his torments so that you pull away from your duty to Me.

Hear Me now. Heed My warnings and prepare my flock so that they can seek redemption for their sins now. Move then so that My Church will continue to fight for the Truth of My Teachings and not allow the bullying from secular societies to push you into a corner cowering with fear. For if you do that you will be succumbing to the temptations of the Evil One whose lies have already destroyed much of My Church.

You are My lifeline My sacred servants and I need you now to help Me Save My precious children as they face the torments which twist their minds to the Truth of My Teachings and the existence of My Eternal Father.

I call on you now to listen to Me when I call you.

Your Beloved Teacher

Jesus Christ

Many souls are perishing in Hell because of the sin of pornography

Sunday, August 28, 2011 17.00 hours

My dearly beloved daughter hear My most Holy Word as I warn mankind of the urgency to beg My Father for the forgiveness of their sins.

Time is short now as The Warning is almost upon us. Never put off until tomorrow what you need to do today. Remorse for your sins is crucial before you ask for your sins to be forgiven. For without genuine remorse it is useless.

So many blackened souls do I see in your world My daughter. There is little Light and were you to witness the depths to which man has fallen you would be shocked. So many millions of My children are plunging daily into an abyss of sinful corruption from which they will find it impossible to pull away unless you pray for them. They are blind to the Truth and even if they were to be shown My Light now they would squirm and hide from Me. Pray for them.

My children who are guilty of hateful sin enjoy the fact that their evil behaviour is applauded for its entertainment value. Pornography seeps into so many homes around the world by TV channels which present these evil atrocities as harmless humorous fun. These same channels which refuse to speak My Name. Violence also is glamorized not only on TV but in games making them so acceptable that people now consider the act of violence a natural thing.

Satan's demons, when they enter souls, begin to manifest in the human body so that their acts become clearly visible to My followers who cringe in horror at what they have to bear witness to. The human body, infested with satanic demons will behave grotesquely. Their physical movements will be distorted and will emulate satanic messages used by The Evil One to seduce like-minded weak people. Weak souls, empty of Love for God, will be drawn towards them and will eventually emulate them so that they, too, will honour Satan and all he stands for in the way they too behave.

Children can you not see how Satan works? My followers you must tell those who do not understand how he works in the pornographic business. This is when Satan sets out to destroy souls and suck the participants into eternal fire. Those guilty of sexual deviant behaviour and those who flaunt their bodies in an obscene immoral way will suffer excruciating pain for eternity.

Help save them now children for they have no idea how their immoral impurity disgusts Me. They are covered in darkness. Bring them to Me so My Light can embrace them and save them from the fires of Hell. Sins of the flesh are abhorrent to Me. So many souls are perishing in

Hell because of the sin of pornography and sexually deviant acts. Let them know what their fate will be unless they show remorse.

Your beloved Saviour

Jesus Christ

Those who proclaim My True Word through visionaries will be ridiculed

Sunday, August 28, 2011 23.00 hours

My dearly beloved daughter Satan and his demons are trying to torment you now. You must acknowledge this fact and then turn your back. Do not respond or engage for when you respond you give The Evil One more power over you. Ignore his taunts and hold My Hand as I stand beside you to protect you from such harm.

Tell My followers that as they take up My Chalice and march forward to spread the Truth of My return to earth that they, too, will suffer. They will be insulted, laughed at and made feel foolish as they speak in My Name. Tell them that when this happens that any doubts they may have had in relation to these Messages will disappear. My children always understand that those who proclaim My True Word through genuine visionaries will suffer ridicule just as the chosen soul, whose role it is to impart My Divine Messages to the world, does. You, My army will be no different. This will be a difficult lesson for you to absorb. Know that you will always suffer in this life when you walk with Me. Know too that only then will you realise that you carry My Cross. For only then will you be qualified to speak My Word. No prophet, no apostle of mine has found this road an easy one. You must pray for the strength to endure these trials, which will test your faith to extremes.

When you hold My Cross to ease My load you will be laden with the burden. If you will trust in Me completely, enfold your arms in mine I will hold you to give you the strength you need for this journey. A journey so laden with thorns that your feet may bleed yet your faith will be so strong that you will not be able to live your life without My Pure Love.

You My beloved children are My precious army. One day you will line the pathways in Heaven in glorious wonder where the angels will sing in praise of the Work you have carried out for Me in your lifetime on earth. I reward all My devoted followers for their loyalty and unfaltering love for Me. You are blessed My chosen souls that you have been given the gift to see the Truth when others simply turn their backs.

Remember you are now being given the Gift of the Holy Spirit and as a result you will be unable to deny Me. This road, however, will be full of rocks that may hurt your feet, boulders which will trip you up and those who will stand defiantly to block your way by bullying you and threatening you to turn back the way you came.
Lift your hand in gentle admonishment and say

I will never deny the path of the Lord. Nor will I ever deny the existence of Jesus Christ whom mankind has tried to destroy not only during His suffering on the Cross but afterwards too. I am at one with Jesus Christ. I speak in His Name. I walk with Him. He lifts Me up so that I too, in my humble way, might help open your heart to the Pure Love He holds in His Heart for you and you alone.

My precious army, rise now when I lead you along the bumpy but Divine Pathway to the New Paradise on earth that awaits you. Please ensure that you gather as many of My wandering children with you along the way so that we can be united as one family.

Your Loving Jesus

Redeemer and Leader of all Mankind

God The Father 'My Hand will fall with force on nations who legalize abortion'

Monday, August 29, 2011 00.05 hours

I come in the Name of My Son Jesus Christ. I am the Alpha and the Omega, God of the Most High. I wish to give My children the world over this Message.

My Hand is being withheld from punishing man for the sins he commits through the power of prayer. I will cast down a severe chastisement if man does not turn away from the sin of murder and abortion. Already you, My children, have seen My anger through earthquakes, floods, tsunamis and other ecological turmoil. I must chastise you children for you cannot avoid punishment for your offences against your fellow man.

The sins of abortion will be punished when My Hand will fall with force on those nations, which condone this abomination. You will not be allowed murder My helpless Creation and should your governments continue to pass laws, condoning this cowardly practice you will see My anger descend with such force that you will beg for the mercy of life. Yet you never stop to think of taking the life of the unborn.

Murder will no longer be tolerated by Me. You will be stopped and soon. Pray for the souls of these helpless beings and ask for redemption. Do not accept such laws passed by your governments, run by heathens, who have no respect for life.

My punishment on countries guilty of legalizing abortion will wipe out nations. Your countries will divide into little pieces and fall into the ocean. Your vile clinics and hospitals where you carry out these practices will close and you, the guilty among you, will be cast into the fires of Hell for your heinous crimes.

I come to give you this Warning now. Never condone abortion. Put your foot down in your countries and fight to prevent this global genocide from continuing. If your governments continue to inflict their act of horror on My Creation you will be dealt a powerful reprimand.

Heed now this, one of My most urgent warnings to the human race. Take the life of My unborn and I will take yours. Pray hard children for the faith of all My children as they continue to ignore the Teachings given to you since the beginning of time.

God the Father

Choose people you know and come before My Father's throne to save them

Tuesday, August 30, 2011 14.30 hours

My dearly beloved daughter My Heart is heaving with sorrow as I look at My precious children who are oblivious to the changes which lie ahead.

I love them so much that I cry with a deep sadness when I see them wander around seeking Me out but unable to do so. They know that there is a missing link in their lives but cannot identify what it is. That link is love. I am Love. I am what they are looking for but they don't know where to look. Yet I am standing there waiting and waiting patiently for them to turn to Me.

So much time is being wasted My daughter. My children look in all the wrong places seeking out the contentment and peace that they crave. But they won't be able to find this unless they acknowledge it will only be through humility that they will find this possible.

Until My children realize they cannot exist without love for My Father, God the Most High, they will die empty of love and peace in their hearts. I am weary My daughter. If only those who have shut Me out would turn to Me. If only they stopped their quest for power, money and glory from earthly possessions then they would know the Truth.

I need all of you My followers to keep praying for the blind souls who are lost. Never give up for your prayers will be brought before the Throne of My Father. Please recite the following

God, the Most High, I come before Your Throne this week to plead for the souls of my brothers and sisters who refuse to acknowledge Your existence. I urge you to fill them with Your graces so that they will open their hearts to listen to Your most Holy Word.

Please chose those souls who are known to you and who do not want to know God the Father and place their names before My Father. Your gift of prayer will be rewarded with their salvation. Go now My army and prepare for the next stage in this spiritual warfare against The Evil One.

Your beloved Saviour

Jesus Christ

My army will swell to a group of over 20 million
Wednesday, August 31, 2011 21.00 hours

My dearly beloved daughter, the love I have for you and My followers surges through Me and brings Me such joy. How I love you all. Your dedication, humility, trust and pure love for Me, is getting stronger by the day. Can't you feel this? This is My Gift to each and every one of you My pure souls who have been plucked from your daily lives to follow Me on the Path to Paradise.

My children who have been awakened by the Holy Spirit, which was poured out over the world in May, will now feel a devotion to Me not known to many of them beforehand. I am gathering My army quickly now and this will swell into a group of over 20 million souls soon. The larger the army the more powerful will be the Holy Spirit in bringing My children together as one to fight The Deceiver. My Divine guidance is now instilled in your souls whether you realise this or not. It is like as if you have an internal switch. When My love calls, you will respond naturally to convert others. This is the power of the Holy Spirit and it is now being felt in every corner of the earth.

All religions, all creeds, all races and all nations will respond to the Light of the Truth now. They are all so precious to My Eternal Father. He is now reaching out to every man, woman and child so they will hear His call. Satan will be unable to withstand the prayers, which are recited by My followers. His grip will loosen and soon. Prayer and the faith of My followers, is making him furious. Because he is powerless in his attempts to place doubts in the minds of My faithful he will switch his attention to weak sinners. These children are so confused already and destroyed by mortal sin that they will be drawn towards him. Because of the darkness of their souls they will be unable to defend themselves. Pray hard that their souls can be saved.

This is an age where My Church, although facing extraordinary obstacles brought about by sin, will now be rebuilt by My followers on earth. This will take time but when it happens, My Church will return to its former Glory and will be renewed in strength.

It will, along with all My chosen people merge into My Father's Glorious Kingdom. The sweetness of this event when the world will be rid of Satan and all things evil is to be welcomed children. This is the New Era of Peace that you have to look forward to on earth. Times may be difficult ahead of you children. Focus on Me and you will survive. Then will come the peace you are waiting for.

Your beloved Saviour

Jesus Christ

How hard it is to climb the Stairway to Paradise

Saturday, September 03, 2011 23.50 hours

My dearly beloved daughter do not be under any illusion, The Deceiver has turned your head away from Me for the last few days. You put this down to the fact that you were busy but this is not quite true. So cunning is he that he deliberately interrupted every single minute of your time. During this time you were aware that you were not devoting time to Me isn't this so? You felt distracted and lost and then you realised that you were empty inside without Me. Close by you the entire time I, nevertheless, allowed you to feel abandoned by Me. For now you have experienced the despair felt by souls whom I reject because of sin. All of this is important for your spiritual development. While it may seem pointless that I allow this, it is part of your training towards the holiness that I require and demand of you. You, My precious daughter, will continue to feel a form of abandonment from time to time as will many souls who are on this same path.

The stairway to spiritual perfection is a very long one. Souls will take one, two and more steps backwards for every single step they take towards Me. I ask you My daughter to tell all My followers to prepare carefully for this stairway, which is essential before the top step is reached. In My Message of November 24th 2010 when I first told you about this stairway I explained how some people climb these steps much too quickly. But you know that would be a mistake. Be aware that it is I who guides you along the steps the entire time.

Children of Mine you must now climb every step of the spiritual stairway before you reach the top steps to the door of Paradise. Be patient. Do not be disappointed when you fall. Simply stand up again and begin climbing all the way.

Children I will hold you by the hand and take you to the top if you allow Me.

Your beloved Saviour

Jesus Christ

Virgin Mary Message - Abandonment as a victim soul
Sunday, September 04, 2011 21.50 hours

(This Message was received after Maria recited the Holy Rosary and after an apparition where the Blessed Mother appeared for a period lasting 20 minutes in a private prayer room)

I come in the Name of my beloved Son, Jesus Christ. I am the Holy Mother of God.

My child you are suffering for my Son and the last week has not been easy as you battle the force of evil in order to remain loyal to my precious Son. I come to you tonight to try to explain what is happening. As a victim soul you will experience periods of abandonment when thoughts of my Son are banished from your mind. Then as you try to devote time to pray you will find you cannot do this. After this you will be confused and then the loneliness for my Son's Presence will cause you anguish. Do not fret because, hard as this is, it is a form of suffering which you must experience as a victim soul.

Please pray for courage and for the graces to accept this new form of suffering which will confuse you. Keep to your daily Mass and receiving the Most Holy Eucharist no matter what lies ahead. You will be goaded by The Deceiver to turn your back on this Work. You will soon, once again, begin to allow the doubts to invade your soul. Ask all to pray for you now. For you gift to My Son is continuing to save souls everywhere. Never forget this no matter how difficult your suffering is.

My child I will always communicate with you when you lose your sense of direction for I am your beloved Mother. I will always be here to protect you and guide you towards my Son so that His wishes are adhered to. Go in love and peace.

Your Beloved Mother

Queen of Peace

Loving your neighbour as yourself is much more difficult than you think

Sunday, September 04, 2011 22.00 hours

My daughter this is now the time to listen to My instructions to alert My children of the times ahead in terms of preparing all My followers of their need to stay in daily prayer. They must also receive My Body in the form of the Holy Eucharist and pray for the saving of souls.

My children are taking more heed of My Messages as they join together to pray for all My children every day before The Warning takes place.

Look on your brothers and sisters through My eyes, which sees them as miracle creations bestowed by My Eternal Father as a gift to mankind. Every soul concerned is loved equally. No difference is made in the eyes of My Father.

If you, My followers, love Me you will Love My Father. In turn, if you are genuine in your love for My Father, you will love your brothers and sisters. You must especially show love to those who may offend you through their behaviour. Some will insult you, mock you and damage your reputation, which may hurt you and your family. They may be known to you personally or they may hurt you by their actions, which can badly affect your ability to clothe and feed your families. No matter how much people hurt you I ask you, in My Name, to follow My lead. Pray for them especially those who harm you. For when you pray for them you dilute the hatred spewed by Satan, a hatred that could spring forth thoughts of revenge.

This is one of the most difficult of all My Teachings. Love they neighbour as yourself. It is much more difficult than you think. When you can achieve this act of great generosity you will help Me fulfil My plan to save more souls.

Your beloved Teacher and Friend

Jesus Christ

Hold Divine Mercy Vigils now - The Warning is Close
Monday, September 05, 2011

(Note: Two Messages were received this evening from Jesus Christ. In the first Message, a private revelation, details of the period when The Warning will take place were given to the visionary. The publication of these is at the discretion of the visionary who has decided not to publish them at this point. They have, instead, been given to a priest for safekeeping. This Message will be published after The Warning takes place. The second Message is a Message for the world right now)

My beloved daughter the time is close now. Prayer has helped My beloved Vicar Pope Benedict withstand the internal battle he faces from evil forces. His time in the Vatican has been extended.

I urge all My followers to hold prayer meetings and Divine Mercy vigils for all My poor children who have wandered away from Me and My Eternal Father. They urgently need your prayers. Prayer, and much of it, is needed now to save them. Have Masses offered up for those who, because of the state of their souls during The Warning, may not survive physically. They need your prayers. Unite. Hold hands in unison with Me.

Your Beloved Jesus Christ

Virgin Mary: Always listen to your heart
Tuesday, September 06, 2011 20.20 hours

I come in the Name of my beloved Son Jesus Christ. I am your Blessed Mother.

You, my child, are being persecuted. Every attempt is being made by The Deceiver to trick you. You my child must obey only one Voice and that is the Voice of my precious Son Jesus Christ.

Arm yourself now my child for attacks on you will increase as too will your suffering. You, through the graces I will bestow, will get through this. Stop your fearful thoughts and put aside all doubts.

Do not allow distractions for they come from the work of the Deceiver. They do not come from my Son.

Always listen to your heart. Then you will know the Truth. I, your beloved Mother, love you so please allow me offer you all my protections from the evil one.

Go in peace and love.

Your beloved Mother

Mother Queen of Peace

As the faith of My followers becomes stronger attacks on them increase

Tuesday, September 06, 2011 20.30 hours

My dearly beloved daughter how you suffer for Me and how strong you have become as a result.

My protection is all around you. Do not fear. As this Work continues to convert souls, so too, will the attacks by Satan. Accept this. Do not let it bother you. Rise above the challenges and keep your eyes on Me at all times. For when you do, nothing else will matter.

The same suffering will be felt by all My followers as the Holy Spirit continues unabated to attract the souls of all My children everywhere, as their faith in Me becomes stronger, so too will the attacks on them by others increase. They, My followers, will notice that they have to face arguments, deal with unusual and abusive comments and reactions from unbelievers which will be difficult for them to deal with. Please tell them to expect this now as the time for The Warning draws near.

Satan and his demons, invisible to the naked human eye, are trying to destroy the love in My children's souls. He inspires distrust towards one another. He causes arguments and plants doubts. He is full of hatred for mankind. He will cause war between countries, fellow countrymen and friction within families. These are all his favourite tactics and are always a sign of his devious work.

Recognize this for what it is - Satan at work. Fight him children by being strong. Ask My beloved Mother to protect you as she is his greatest adversary. Satan's power will loosen if you call on her to help you.

These times are challenging for all My followers everywhere. Every attempt, from every kind of source, friends, family and colleagues will be made, through the work of the deceiver, to encourage you, My children, to turn your back on Me.

Stop him as I have told you. Prayer and devotion to the Immaculate Heart of My Blessed Mother will be your armour.

Be strong now. I love you all.

Your beloved Saviour

Jesus Christ.

Do not be fearful of The Warning - Await it with joy
Wednesday, September 07, 2011 23.45 hours

My dearly beloved daughter, tell My precious children that they must not be fearful of The Warning. Many will feel frightened and this is understandable. But they must listen carefully to Me. I will come to each of you. You will see Me and feel Me in your heart and soul. My Presence will flood your souls with the Purest of Love and Compassion so you should be joyful. At last you will see Me and your soul will be enveloped with love and excitement.

For sinners and unbelievers most of them will simply be relieved that I exist. For their witness of My Holy Presence will be the blood that is needed to flood their souls with the nourishment missing for so long. Many will suffer the torment, as I endure, when they see their sins unroll before them. Heartbroken when they see how they have offended Me they will beg Me to forgive them.

Children over the age of reason will also see how they, too, offend me through sin. In many instances those children who deny My existence, although they are aware of the Truth, will run to Me. They will ask Me to embrace them and will not want Me to let them go.

Even the most hardened sinners will not fail to be affected by this supernatural event. Children you must ignore rumours. Ignore stories, which are sensational. There is nothing to fear. The Warning must be awaited with pure joy in your hearts.

I await the time with so much love in My Heart when I will pour out My Divine Mercy over each of you everywhere throughout the world. This is the moment when, afterwards, you will realize how fortunate you, of this generation, are. How can you not recognise the Mercy that will be shown to mankind? In the past so many souls died in grievous sin. Now, all sinners will finally understand the Truth at last.

It is not easy for My children to acknowledge the existence of Me or My Eternal Father. Without proof of a material kind many do not want to get to know Me. Many have no interest or belief in the Divine Realm. This event will open their eyes to the simple fact that life does not end on earth. It continues for eternity. That is the reason why they must prepare their souls.

The Warning will show them what they must do to rectify this. Remember children I am your Saviour. I love you all in a way that is beyond your comprehension. Await My arrival with love and calmness. Fear not the dramatic spectacle in the sky and the colour of the rays, which will be spread everywhere to herald My arrival. This will prepare you for the moment.

Please pray that all mankind will feel joy in their hearts for this event will mean salvation for mankind on a magnitude that will save so many souls and enable them to enter the New Paradise on Earth.

Your beloved Saviour

Jesus Christ

Never threaten others in My Name
Saturday, September 10, 2011 15.30 hours

I speak with you today, My dearly beloved daughter of the need to obey Me in all things. My daughter all My followers, in order to be worthy of My Love and devotion, must honour My Father's Commandments. While they may falter from time to time they must strive at all times to follow the Rule of Love. Love one another and put your neighbour before you own needs. Then everything else will fall into place.

Those who call themselves My followers must be very careful as to how they spread My Most Holy Word. If they fall into the trap of arrogance, self-righteousness or when they condemn others in My Name they offend Me greatly. Never threaten others of the punishments they can expect from Me. Never tell someone else that I will punish them because you feel angry with them for whatever reason. For when you do this you will be guilty of denying Me because you will be twisting the Truth to suit your own agenda. Never feel superior to others because you are privileged to know the Truth.

Children I love all My children even when they err and stray. Pray for them at all times if you claim to be a true follower of Mine. By all means preach the Truth. Tell them always about My deep love for My children. But you must never judge them. Never tell others that their sins, or those you deem to be sins, that they will be punished by Me in a certain way because you have no right to do this.

My Message today is simple. When you love Me and speak in My Name you must never exalt yourself because of this. You must never threaten your brothers or sisters or cast aspersions in My Name.

Remember because you are My followers you will be targeted by The Deceiver precisely because of your faith. So you must be careful that he does not trick you into making your sin against your brothers or sisters.

You must keep strong My children. I give you this Message to guide you and to keep you on the right pathway towards Me.

Your beloved Jesus

King of Mankind

No matter what your religion there is only one God

Sunday, September 11, 2011 19.15 hours

My dearly beloved daughter when My children feel despair, frightened or lonely tell them they must turn to Me. Never before have as many of My children throughout the world feel such emptiness in their lives. With no direction they become more distracted when they are fed on a diet of junk. Daily media feeds them with stories, which show the evil present in the world with so many countries in turmoil. Then there is the lack of spiritual food and, in its place, a diet of lies when you are told of the wonders of worldly ambitions. All of which, should you attain such things, will disappoint. Then as you strive towards such goals you will be anxious to reach these heights, again, you will be disappointed.

Remember I am your food, children. It will only be through Me that you will find true peace, contentment and pure love in your hearts. It is not possible to gain this kind of peace anywhere else.

Turn to Me now each of you who are suffering sorrow in your hearts. Let Me hold and comfort you. For you, My children, are My lost but precious souls. Many of you have wandered off and do not know your way back to My flock. Some of you have chosen a different flock - a flock not of Me.

Listen to My Call for when you hear My Voice in your souls you will know the Truth. I am your pathway to My Eternal Father. Remember that many of you who give different names to God the Almighty Father may still be worshiping the same God. There is only one God. The time is close now for the time when his Glory will be revealed to the world. No matter what your interpretation is God the Father is Love. His Mercy is all embracing. Come, turn to Him now wherever you are in the world. He is waiting for your call.

Your Beloved Saviour

Jesus Christ

Chastisement can be mitigated through prayer

Monday, September 12, 2011 12.00 hours

My dearly beloved daughter very soon now the world will stop and the period after The Warning will change the way man will look at the world. No more will material pleasures and excesses excite. No more will people treat, as gods, the idols they make of celebrities and wealth. No more will they be so quick to condemn or treat their neighbour cruelly.

The new world, after The Warning, will be a place where love for Me and God the Father will be revered with respect. Many leaders in countries, not of the Christian faith, will pay homage to My Father. Those in places of power who control people's finances will repent in their droves. Many more will peel back their layers of power and share with their brothers and sisters the bread that comes from God the Father. For this bread is for all and is meant to be shared equally.

Many good things will evolve as a result of The Warning. However many souls will not be strong enough in their faith. They, sadly, will go back to their old ways. Seduced by the promises of power, wealth, control and love of self, they will reject God the Father. They will know the Truth yet it will still not be enough for them. These poor weak sinners will be a thorn in your side children. Without your prayers their sins will cause havoc in a world, which will have been recouped during its new purification.

Prayer, My children, is so important. You must ask God the Father to accept your request to quash the persecution, which is being planned by these people. Enough prayer can, and will, avert much of the horror these sinners will try to inflict on the world. So many of you are blind to the plan, which is being plotted behind your backs. The signs are being revealed consistently but you fail to recognise them.

My children as your faith grows pray that the Holy Spirit can be spread to these sinners and engulf their souls. I, your precious Jesus protect you My beloved followers. Under My command I instruct you to pray not just for these fallen souls but that the persecution of ordinary men, women and children will be eliminated. Should these perpetrators, who will defy My Father, continue to terrorize innocent people through the new controls they will unleash on the world they will be punished.

These sinners are being given the greatest Mercy possible since My Crucifixion. They need to embrace The Warning for this is the last time they will be offered the chance of redemption. Otherwise they will face a terrible punishment. This punishment, which will be brought about by the Hand of Divine Justice through My Eternal Father is not desirable. While this great Chastisement has been prophesied it can be mitigated through the power of prayer.

Your beloved Saviour

King of Mercy

Jesus Christ

Changes to be introduced in the Church, which will contradict the Word of God

Tuesday, September 13, 2011 15.15 hours

My dearly beloved daughter it is I Jesus Christ who came in the flesh.

My Most Holy Word must now be heard by My sacred servants everywhere. All My followers must share these Messages with My sacred servants of all Christian denominations. It is vital that they are encouraged to hear My Word at this crucial time before they are torn asunder and split into two camps.

The work of the deceiver has infiltrated My Church on every level. Very soon now, slowly but surely, you will see Holy Masses being reduced. You will see the removal of special prayers and some of the Sacraments such as Confession begin to diminish. I call on My sacred servants now to listen to Me and pray for discernment. It is I who calls you now so I can save your flock. It is I who wants to open your hearts so you can plan for these end times, which will herald a brand new beginning for the world.

You will be asked to show allegiance to the False Prophet very soon. See him for what he is and judge his works in order to see if they bear fruit. For the fruit that he and his slavish devotees will yield will be rotten to the core. One bite will destroy your allegiance to Me. Two or more bites will drive such a wedge between you and My Sacred Heart that you will find it almost impossible to enter My Father's Kingdom.

Watch carefully now the changes you will see creeping in within your own ministry. Some of these adjustments will not seem to be a problem in the beginning. But as time moves on certain changes will be forced upon you and you will be made to swallow lies. The lies will come from Satan and will be dressed in sheep's clothing.

For those pure of heart you will know instantly and will recognize the evil cunning in place, which is being designed to destroy My Church on earth from within its own corridors.

My Truth will cause gasps of indignity throughout the world when My priests will say surely this prophecy is a lie? The only lie that they will have to bear witness to will be the one they are forced to approve which will be in direct opposition to My Sacred Scriptures given to mankind right from the start. Never allow yourselves to accept any other Truth other than that contained in the Holy Bible.

Many changes will be introduced which will contradict the Word of My Eternal Father. These changes, My sacred servants, won't be of Divine origin and you must reject these untruths if you want to remain loyal to Me.

Wake up. Stand up to those lies you will have to face. Never accept them. My Eternal Father's Word will never change. It can never be adjusted by mankind. Many of you will be so distraught that you will find yourselves isolated from your fellow sacred servants. Fear not for there is only one side you can choose. That will be side where I stand. There is no other side.

Your beloved Saviour

Jesus Christ

Ask for the Gift of Suffering
Wednesday, September 14, 2011 00.10 hours

My dearly beloved daughter your suffering has eased and I wish to thank you for this gift. It will return but you will be able to accept it with much more joy in your heart. I need your suffering because it saves the souls of sinners who would, otherwise, end up in Hell. One day you will look into their souls and will be overwhelmed with love and joy when you see them sit next to Me beside the throne of My Father.

Sinners will always be embraced first when they repent. They will always be in the front line much to the surprise of My followers. These souls have been brought to Me through the prayers and suffering of My followers, and My chosen souls. My followers will understand this because they will, through their union with Me, rejoice at the salvation of such souls.

I now need many more souls to be saved My daughter. Please pray that you and other chosen souls will learn how suffering can increase the numbers who will enter My Father's Kingdom. I ask them to request the graces required to be given the gift of suffering. Remember when I bestow suffering it is a special grace and one which will bring many more souls into the bosom of My Heart.

Your beloved Jesus

Saviour of Mankind

The Truth is usually treated with extreme caution and outright dismissal

Thursday, September 15, 2011 23.50 hours

My dearly beloved daughter you are now witnessing more details of the pain I suffered during My Crucifixion. Abandonment. Rejection. Isolation. Dismissal by the mocking wave of the hands of authority and especially from devout followers of Mine. Even My own apostles rejected me at My time of need. So you must not be surprised that this is happening to you too.

You were also shown tonight a vision of Me standing before My executioners to whom I had to listen when their vile lies condemned Me and the Truth of My Teachings. So too will you and My followers be treated at the hands of those who cannot accept the Truth or who find it distasteful.

The Truth, My daughter, is usually treated with extreme caution, outright dismissal and considered blasphemous at times. Never fear. For the Words I give you are nothing but the Truth. You must never be afraid to publish what I give you. Why would I give you untruths? Why would I try to undermine these Messages by allowing an untruth to enter them at any time? For this would be contrary to My Father's will. Even Satan will not be allowed interfere with these Messages no matter how hard he tries.

As these Messages become more intense they will become the subject of much debate and ridicule. Yet many will be drawn to them because beneath it all they will not fail to be moved by the Holy Spirit, which moves their souls.

In time they, My children, will thank Me for helping them plough through the disarray of thorny brambles which will block them from reaching the Gate to Paradise because without My guidance now, at this time, they would be lost. They would not find the strength to be taken safely through the Gates of the New Paradise, the New Era of Peace on Earth, which awaits all those who obey Me and My Teachings.

Your beloved Saviour and Teacher

Jesus Christ

Times of Peace and Glory almost here

Saturday, September 17, 2011 18.50 hours

My dearly beloved daughter you are finally realizing that when you feel rejected then this is simply a mirror of My own Agony. When you are in union with Me, as you are, this will become part of your life from now on. When people reject the Messages you publish they are rejecting My Most Holy Word. When they challenge them and find fault with them they criticize Me. When they look down on you they ridicule Me. When they laugh at these Messages they Crucify Me.

What you are feeling is but just a fraction of My Suffering as I watch in sorrow at man's blindness to the Truth of the existence of My Eternal Father. The pain and sorrow I feel, when I have to witness the sins of man, including the sins of believers, is most intense. This torment barely ceases but is relieved by the suffering of victim souls. It is also eased by the love that My followers show Me through their devotion to Me.

My daughter, while I need suffering to save other poor unfortunate souls, it is not something that gives Me pleasure. I find it painful to watch but feel comforted by it. So many things you must learn My daughter, which are difficult for you to understand, the Ways of the Divine Kingdom could not be understood by mankind. One day they will understand.

Know this My children that the difficult times, which man has had to endure for centuries is coming to an end. This is good news for the man who shows love for his neighbour and, as such, who loves Me. It will also bring to an end, at last, My Suffering, which is endured because I love you all. This Love is powerful and ever yielding and will be the cause of your final salvation.

Go now My daughter and accept the suffering with more understanding in your heart. Rejoice for the times of Peace and Glory are almost here.

Your Loving Friend and Saviour

Jesus Christ

King of Mankind

Classic error made when trying to become closer to Me
Sunday, September 18, 2011 18.50 hours

I come in the Name of Jesus Christ, the Son of God the Most High. I am He.

My dearly beloved daughter why does man continue to seek answers to his existence through science? They search and search but the answers they come up with are untrue and so far away from the true existence of the spiritual realm of My Father's Kingdom that you must pray for these souls.

I know that to accept the Truth of My Existence and that of My beloved Father, is very difficult children. For every time your eyes glimpse the Truth, Satan turns your head the other way. Most of the time he will use logic to convince My children that My Father's Kingdom is just a figment of people's imagination. He will then use the comforts of the material world to convince you that they must be your priority.

Then there are the souls who do understand the Truth. They make a classic error when trying to become closer to Me. It is easy for them to ensure that once their material goods are secured they can then move forth on their own spiritual journey. But that is not how it works. You must, by all means, protect your families and your homes. You must feed those who depend on you. After that you must put Me first before all worldly goods. That will be your passport to Heaven. Man is nothing without God. No material luxuries will, or can be, substituted for the love of God. Nor can they be retained or the same value placed on them if you want to really embrace Me in your heart.

Trust in Me and the rest will be taken care of. If you try to do everything on your own and hold on to wealth, so you can have the best of both worlds, you will be disappointed.

Remember My Love for you will feed your souls. Material wealth will feed your bodily desires but they will decay over time and you will be left with nothing.

Please children, no matter how difficult it is, let Me steer you on the True path to Eternal Happiness. Just ask me for My help and I will respond.

Your beloved Teacher and Saviour

Jesus Christ

The most important Event since My Resurrection
Monday, September 19, 2011 20.15 hours

My dearly beloved daughter it is My intention to bring every man, woman and child into My New Paradise on earth, For if just one soul is left behind it would break My Heart. This is why the number of messengers I now send into the world has increased. It is so they can spread My Holy Word to encourage conversion.

I do not send messengers to frighten My children. Instead the role of My messengers is to prepare every person on this earth so that they are ready and worthy to live in this New Paradise.

My children the times you are living in are not pleasant. Law and order has broken down. Greed has meant that your financial stability has been stolen from you. Self-glory and obsession with ambition has meant that your Faith has also been taken away from you.

Like a household where there is no parental control
You, My children, are like as in a household where there is no parental control. Like spoilt children you are provided with all the material comforts you crave without having to earn them. You are provided with food, which you don't have to toil for. Everything that dissatisfies you is replaced with yet another novelty, another stimulant. Yet nothing

satisfies for long. Then rows take place among the children, each seeking to control the other to get their own way. Physical warfare can then break out. But no one is in charge and so they hurt each other sometimes with grave consequences.

This is how I view the world. My children are unhappy, lacking in spiritual comfort but refuse to be guided by My Church. My Church, today cannot control such an unruly population who do not find devotion to me to be as stimulating as the creature comforts of the flesh.

War is destroying mankind and spiritual decline has created a vacuum in the world which most of you, by now, feel the effects of in your hearts. Nothing is as it seems. Material glory glitters on the exterior its light appealing to those starving for comfort but there is nothing but darkness behind it.

I am the Light that is missing in your lonely confusing and somewhat frightening lives. This is why the time is close for Me to step in and take charge. You, My children, must welcome this and prepare for My Great Mercy.

You must pray for your brothers and sisters and look forward with open arms to welcome My Intervention. Be positive. Be hopeful. Be confident that even the most hardened sinners will be relieved at the Advent of this Great Event, the most important since My Resurrection.

Your Beloved Saviour

Jesus Christ

Doubts make you stronger in your love for Me

Wednesday, September 21, 2011 22.00 hours

I come in the Name of Jesus who came in the flesh and was made man.

My dearly beloved daughter you are now so very close to My Heart yet you can feel so far away. At times you think you have been separated from Me when in fact you have only drawn closer in union with Me.

So strong now, My daughter, I am building your confidence so that you can continue to proclaim My Word to mankind. This is a very important Mission. Because of the demons unleashed in their millions by Satan in these times they are attacking you on every corner. The first people they will use will be believers who will queue up to throw the first stone at you.

As My Great Act of Mercy for mankind gets closer so too will the demons try to block out the Truth and prevent people, good people, from investing the time I need of them to save the souls of My children with no belief at all. Do not allow cruel slander, which is gathering momentum to distract you from My Work.

Heed now My Prophecy. For every man who repents at this time three more souls can be saved per man. Think of it like this. The blessings bestowed on man who seeks forgiveness will be given to these people's families. Every soul who prays to Me now and asks Me to save their closest family and friends will receive My Mercy in abundance.

Prayer is your salvation My children. The more you pray the more I will open your hearts and reveal My Truth. My favours have now been extended in a way not witnessed on this earth before. However I cannot pour out these Powerful Graces unless you ask for them.

My daughter, be advised that a viciousness, which will startle you will now be seen in a mounting attack on these Divine Messages. Ignore them. Close your eyes. Block your ears. Instead pray that such souls will see enlightenment.

Doubts My daughter are trials experienced not only by you but by My beloved followers. While they can be unsettling they are allowed by Me to make you all stronger in your love for Me.

Relax now My children. Accept My Word. Live your lives as I expect you to. Put your families first before everything. They must never be neglected on My behalf. Pray now with quiet confidence and be assured that My Prophecies will unfold at the Command of My Eternal Father. They will happen according to the perfect timing laid down by My Father.

Never forget My children that many secrets given to My visionaries and seers foretelling future events to come have been mitigated through prayer. Many, many ecological disasters have been averted because of the devotion shown to My Blessed Mother. Her devotees have averted many earthquakes, floods and tsunamis because of their prayers. Prayer can be very powerful. One person's prayers and suffering can save a nation. Remember that.

I love all My children. The power to save each other lays in your hands children. Don't forget what I have said before. Prayer is your armour against evil in this world. Prayer can mitigate global disasters. Keep praying for peace in your world. Pray, too, for an easy transition to the New Paradise on earth, which awaits all My children who seek redemption.

Your beloved Jesus

Fortune telling does not come from Me
Wednesday, September 21, 2011 23.30 hours

My daughter this journey for you is escalating. You are ready more than you will ever know. Do not be fearful for your Mission will help save much of mankind. Your role has been prophesied and is being orchestrated in

Heaven. You are an instrument. I am your Master.

You will succeed in this most Holy Task for it cannot and will not fail. You may feel, at times, very disheartened, lonely and lacking in courage. Accept this. Your suffering is delivering precious souls to Me at the moment of their death. These souls now pray for you. Rejoice for if you saw the love they exude for you, you would weep with joy.

My saints in Heaven guide and protect you from the evil one and you are, therefore, granted many reprieves, which surprise and delight you. Never hesitate in this Work. This is one of the greatest Missions of My Work on earth. Be strong, brave and confident but retain humility at all costs. The stage is set now. The events I spoke of will now unfold. As they do so too will your confidence return. For you will have all the proof you need. Yes, Satan has intercepted this Work on a few occasions. I have allowed this because it ensures that you remain humble at all times.

Do not publish dates. Do not ask how the future will turn out for people who make demands of you. Fortune telling does not come from Me. The only future I reveal is connected with the spiritual welfare of My children. Be thankful that you have been given this most special gift. While you never wished for it willingly you were moulded for this Work from your very first breath and you will fulfil My Most Holy Word to your dying breath.

Go forth in My Name and help Me to save the souls of all mankind with love and joy in your heart.

I love you My precious daughter. I rejoice in your heartfelt love for Me and My beloved Mother.

Your Jesus

Part 5.

First Volume

Messages 200 - 249

Thursday, September 22, 2011 to Monday, November 14, 2011

Virgin Mary: Pray for my protection all over the world
Thursday, September 22, 2011 21.00 hours

My child you must ask my children to pray to me so that I can cover them with my Most Holy Mantle in these times. The Deceiver's work is increasing and spreading like wildfire, the evil control you see all around you is being managed by him and his army of demons. They cause much suffering and pain in the world. Praying my Most Holy Rosary will stop him from causing the damage he intends to inflict on this world.

Pray my children wherever you are for my special protection against the evil one.

Pray to ease the suffering of my beloved Son who is in much need of your consolation. He needs your prayers children as He sets out to save mankind from their sinful and wayward lives yet again.

Pray now as you have never prayed before.

Your Blessed Mother

Queen of Peace

Sorrow at loss of My children who want nothing to do with Me
Thursday, September 22, 2011 21.30 hours

My dearly beloved daughter, prepare your family for The Warning. Ask My children everywhere to seek forgiveness for their sins. Their request must be from the heart. If not they will suffer the burning pain of Purgatory during My Divine Mercy. Illumination when I will face each and every one of you.

The Purification ahead will leave such a lasting and unforgettable impression on yours souls that you will remain in the bosom of My Heart for eternity.

For those of you who know and love Me please prepare now for My Greatest Gift. Obtain blessed candles and Holy Water and be ready so you can join in the prayers with the saints in Heaven to help redeem the souls of all of My children around the world.

For the first time in your lives you will be truly alone in My company. Without a sound you will witness My Crucifixion and for unbelievers they will then finally understand the Truth of My Suffering for mankind.

You, My children, will understand and welcome My Great Gift of Mercy and you will be given a strength known only to the saints in Heaven. This strength will forge the backbone of My new army on earth afterwards. This great army will save millions of other souls from the clutches of the army led by the antichrist. Prayer now will save and help convert millions during this crucial time since the Creation of mankind.

Let me embrace you children in advance. Allow Me give you the courage and the strength to bring Me more souls. I need your love. My wounds are raw. My sorrow is at its peak for the loss of so many of My children who want nothing to do with Me.

I feel desolate and alone. Help Me children save them on time. While My Great Act of Mercy will bring Divine Light into the world, on a magnitude that will take your breath away, it will also be a time of sorrow for those who won't be able to withstand the shock.

Please do not be alarmed. I come with great Love and Compassion for you all. It's because I love you that I now step in to save you from the vile acts being carried out by global powers who want to deplete the population of the world. They want to do this through control. I won't allow them to do this. My Father is waiting. If man accepts the sins of which he is guilty then the world will become a place of Peace and Love.

If he fails to heed the lesson from The Warning he will not be spared. That is when the Hand of My Father will fall.

I am Jesus Christ

King and Saviour of all Mankind

God the Father: The antichrist and a New World Currency

Friday, September 23, 2011 21.30 hours

My daughter while the world may fear The Warning they must accept that the prophecies contained in the Book of Revelation are upon us. The Holy state of the Church is now at risk as is the State of Israel. Prophecies will unfold, as the world will be controlled by the antichrist who will attempt to control you through a New World Currency. When and if you are controlled in this way you will be controlled in every other way.

The Warning will put a halt to this and other evil atrocities being planned by global forces which are beyond the understanding of My children the world over. Innocent pawns in a game not of your making, you will be protected by My Hand of Justice.

Rise, My children and fight this sequence of evil through prayer. The global control and persecution being plotted right at this moment can be averted through prayer. Not all of you can or will be saved such is the grip the antichrist will hold over you.

My children Satan will never win. He has not been accorded the power and as his grip begins to loosen now he will drag as many souls as he can into the pits of Hell with him. I weep with deep sorrow for My beautiful Creation and those precious souls of Mine. O if they would only listen to the Truth.

Scientific evaluation is nonsense, for no science will substitute the reality of My Divine Kingdom. No one person on earth can ever fathom the beauty and the miracle that awaits you all for it is indescribable in human terms.

Soon you will understand the plans I have to salvage the world from the hands of the Deceiver.

I love all of you and will protect My followers at every stage during any planned persecution.

Look towards Me. Open your arms and allow Me to hold and protect all of you.

My children who believe in Me have nothing to fear.

Your beloved Creator

God the Most High

God the Father

Explain the Horror of Hell to those who are blind to existence of Satan

Saturday, September 24, 2011 22.15 hours

My dearly beloved daughter why does man persist in denying the existence of Hell?

Many of My children who consider themselves to be modern in their outlook publicly deny the existence of Hell when proclaiming their belief in God the Eternal Father. They mislead My children when they use the excuse that God is ever merciful. By convincing My children that all will go to Heaven they, unwittingly, become responsible for those who follow their faulty doctrine.

Satan exists and therefore so does Hell. Hell is a place where Satan takes those souls who show allegiance to him on earth. These are the souls who push aside all thoughts of God and promote the acceptance of evil acts in the world. In some cases people can even sell their souls to the Satan in exchange for a life of wealth, celebrity and power. Many in the music industry have done this over the years. Little thought is given as to the way in which their allegiance is made very often through group inaugurations carried out through occult practices.

On the other side there are those who live what they consider to be simply fun filled carefree lives where they constantly crave self-gratification. They are just some of souls who, on arrival at the gates of Hell, are shocked and shake their heads in disbelief at the fate that awaits them. They cannot accept that this terror they face is of their own making. The freedom given to them on earth was abused in favour of everything that offends God.

Children of mine please explain the horror of Hell to those who are blind to the existence of Satan. No matter if they laugh and hurl abuse at you. It is your duty to warn them of the terrifying fate that awaits any poor soul who ends up there.

Atheists who on their deathbed believe that their suffering will end on their last breath hear Me now. For those of you who deny the existence of God on this earth, although the Truth has been revealed to you during your lifetime, your suffering in the fires of Hell will be only the beginning of eternal damnation. You, My poor souls who commit grave sin through your own free will reject Me. Instead you chose Satan. He awaits you after death. I will be nowhere to be found. For by then it will be too late to show you My Mercy.

Pray, pray all of you so together we can save these souls. Satan must not be allowed steal their souls. Help Me save them while they still live on earth.

Your beloved Jesus

I have now sent My prophets into the world
Sunday, September 25, 2011 11.45 hours

My dearly beloved daughter how to convince young people and those caught up in a busy meaningless lifestyle is the challenge I present to you.

Your job is to use every kind of modern communications tool available to convince a young modern society of the Truth of My Existence. I promise that all those young children who are given the Truth, through such means, will feel My Presence as soon as they read My Messages. Spread and convert now, My daughter, in every corner of the world. This is the role for which you have been chosen. By spreading My Word virally more people can be reached. Use the Internet and the media. My followers involved will, in time, spread the Truth everywhere.

This Mission has only just begun. The foundations have been laid. Now according to the perfect timing of My Father the world will now pay attention to these Divine Messages.

I promised I would return. To pave the way I have now sent My prophets into the world including you, My daughter. Many are now responding to My Call in every country in the world although their voices are small. In time, they too will be heard so they can proclaim My Glory to herald My return.

There is some time ahead before this Glorious return takes place. Until then prepare My children. The Warning will convert millions but it is only the beginning. The period after that will and must be spent nurturing souls to ensure that they are adequately prepared so they are fit to enter My Father's New Paradise on earth.

You have much to bear children but O so much to look forward to when you are given access to this wonderful New Era of peace, joy and happiness on earth. Perseverance is now called for. Courage and stamina will be given to those who invoke the Holy Spirit. You then, My army, will lift the souls of those who stray from Me. Don't let one of these souls wander off lost into the wilderness. Pray for them. Show them love and understanding. Never tell them they are doomed or accuse them of sin because this is a grave offence in My Eyes. Instead be firm but kind. Just tell them the Truth. It will be up to them afterwards.

You cannot children win over all souls. You can only do your best.

Your beloved Jesus

Insight into My Crucifixion

Monday, September 26, 2011 22.45 hours

My dearly beloved daughter tonight, for the first time, I gave you an insight into My Crucifixion which surprised you. Yet what I revealed to you is of huge importance.

Many lukewarm believers think that when I was crucified that somehow, because I am My Father's Son, I did not suffer the physical pain that man would. They are also of the opinion that because of My Divine status I was not fearful nor could have been because of the strength I received from My Father.

The Truth is quite different. I felt very alone and frightened. My time in the Garden was terrifying because of My human nature. Remember that I came in the flesh. I had the same feelings of pain and sorrow just like any man. Many people do not understand this.

I felt abandoned by My Eternal Father and was taken for granted in some ways by My apostles who did nothing to comfort me during these terrible hours.

When I faced My executioners I trembled in fear and could barely respond to their accusations. I felt as any human being would when facing a violent execution. My Dignity remained intact because of the Sacrifice I knew I had to make for mankind. A paradox, I know, but I also felt love and joy in My Heart during this suffering. For I knew that My death would save you, My children for eternity. Yet I now want you to ask yourselves how many can be saved by My death on the Cross. Who wants to be saved and do they really understand the significance.

Because of My death they can enter Heaven now. Do they also know that this will be by their own choice and through the free will they have been given? Belief in God the Father must be your priority. Come to Me first and I will lead you to Him. Abide by My Teachings given to you through the Holy Bible. Love your neighbour. Keep your Faith simple. Keep a balanced view of your Faith. Love Me. Pray to Me. Adore Me. Allow Me to Love you with My tender Heart so My Divine Presence can flood your precious little souls. I am yours. You are Mine children. It is that simple.

The more you pray the closer you will become. The closer will your heart entwine in Mine.

Your Jesus

Saviour of Mankind

God the Father: Satan's Days are almost at an end on this earth

Thursday, September 29, 201120.15 hours

I am the Alpha and the Omega. I am God the Father.

My beloved daughter the time is drawing close for the world to witness the Mercy to be shown to mankind by My precious Son Jesus Christ. Many forces of evil abound by those lost souls who pay allegiance to the Deceiver, Satan. They too are prepared for The Warning and arrogantly believe that the power promised to them by Satan will steer them to a new worldly paradise of their own making. This is the greatest lie perpetrated by Satan to which they have succumbed. Their darkness of soul means that their hearts will show no mercy to those who believe in Me God the Creator of all things. The power they wield however is weaker now.

Satan's days are almost at an end on this earth. But he, Satan will not rest until he has ensnared millions of these misguided and delusional souls. Pray for them My daughter for they are aimless. They are disjointed and through their panic they will try all they can to control My children through their worldly possessions.

Heed now My Word. Mankind has no power. The only power will be through prayer, the armour against these wicked people. They, in mortal sin, have insulted Me and My precious Creation and for this they will suffer. So many events will now unfold before the eyes of a disbelieving world. So many of My children will be bewildered and shocked when they feel the sufferings of Purgatory and Hell.

All sinners during and after The Warning will experience what they would were they to lose their lives. Those in sin will suffer the same burning purification as those souls in Purgatory who await entry to My Glorious Kingdom. Those in mortal sin will experience the deep despair and darkness of the fires of Hell. This suffering will not last too long and then they will taste the world that they had experienced before The Warning again. This world will be very different to the one before. For at last their eyes will be opened to the Truth of Heaven, Hell and Purgatory. They will then have to choose which path they wish to follow. You would imagine, My daughter, that they will follow the path towards My Divine Love and Compassion but that will not be the case with so many hardened sinners. So infested will they be by the false empty promises made to them by the Deceiver that they will go back to following his direction. They will fight, struggle and through the influence of the demons unleashed by Satan, set free from the depths of Hell, will allow their souls to be sucked into his evil plan for global domination.

This is an urgent call to urge all of you to seek redemption from your hearts for your wayward lives. You have the time to do this but do it soon.

Prepare to ask for Mercy. I love all My children. The great event is for the good of all My children. So instead of fear allow My Love to envelope you to strengthen you. This way you will withstand the suffering, which is ahead.

Your Loving Eternal Father

God the Most High

Aftermath of The Warning

Thursday, September 29, 2011 20.45 hours

My dearly beloved daughter as The Warning draws closer please ask My beloved followers to pray and rejoice with thanks for the Great Mercy which My Eternal Father has granted to mankind.

It will be because of this Glorious Act of Pure Love that more of mankind can be saved to enjoy the era of peace on earth. Be thankful that you are living in these times for millions of you will be saved who, otherwise, would never have entered the Gates of Heaven.

The preparations are complete. Prepare your homes with blessed candles and a supply of water and food to last for a couple of weeks. The aftermath will be difficult but you must not be frightened. Instead be relieved for the suffering is to be offered in thanksgiving for the eternal life, which is now being afforded to My precious souls who embrace this Great Gift.

Be at peace. Trust in Me for remember I am your Saviour and offer those faithful souls protection at every moment. I walk with you. I guide you. I hold your hands with tender Love. You are Mine and I will never let you go from My Sacred Heart. You, My followers are surrounded with the Graces you need to survive The Warning.

Your beloved Jesus

Saviour and Redeemer of all of Mankind

Hardened souls will not find The Warning easy

Friday, September 30, 2011 21.15 hours

My dearly beloved daughter My task to convert souls increases now in its intensity.

Please warn as many as you can to prepare their souls before The Warning.

Inform all those priests, nuns, bishops and other denominations who believe in My Eternal Father, to listen to My Word. So many of My children are in such darkness that the Light of My Divine Glory will hurt their souls. They will feel real pain because they will not be able to withstand this Great Act of My Mercy.

Some people smile in amusement at these Holy Messages. This makes me sad. Not because they do not believe that I speak to them in this way but because they don't want to believe in Me. For all of you who are worried about your loved ones please pray that the purification facing them during The Warning will bring them finally into My Heart.

I ask that all My followers now protect themselves from Satan. They must sprinkle every corner of their home with Holy Water, wear a Benedictine Cross and keep Rosary beads close. Pray also to St Michael the Archangel. Satan and his army of followers will do everything to convince you that it is not I who speaks. Satan and his demons will start tormenting you and placing terrible doubts in your minds. You, My children, can stop him by following My instructions. Sadly, he will twist the minds of weak souls into complete rejection of Me.

Hardened souls will not find The Warning easy. They will argue about the way they have offended Me. Even the burning fires of Hell, which they will experience during The Warning will not wipe away all the doubts of My Existence.

Many will spread lies about The Warning after it takes place. They, the heathen, who are slaves to Satan will create a lie which they will spread everywhere. Scientific arguments will be put forward to explain away the event. They do not want to hear the Truth. They must be prayed for. So strong has the grip of Satan taken a hold over the world that My Name will not be uttered in public. Discussion of My existence on earth is seen to be an embarrassing topic of conversation.

My Name today is used mainly through the use of bad language or worse by the slip of the tongue when cursing. But hear Me now. My Name will be heard and accepted once more after The Warning by those who will convert. Then My Name will be used when they My children pray to Me.

Your beloved Jesus

Virgin Mary: The Deceiver is also preparing for The Warning

Saturday, October 01, 2011 20.30 hours

My child pray for all those souls who have rejected my Son and who are proud of the fact.

The time draws near as my Son once again tries to save the world from damnation. It is important my child that you continue to be obedient in all things requested of you by my precious Son.

He suffers and wants to save all of you from the grip of the Deceiver. He the Deceiver is preparing for The Warning. While my Son through His Mercy will set out to save the souls of all he the Deceiver will try to convince them that The Warning was an illusion.

Satan must be prevented from snatching those unsuspecting souls. Keep them in all your prayers for they are the ones who need your prayers the most.

Your Blessed Mother

Queen of Heaven

Rejoice when the sky explodes for you will know that I am coming

Sunday, October 02, 2011 15.00 hours

My dearly beloved daughter the weather patterns are now changing as yet another sign that times are about to change. Other changes will be experienced. The sun will begin to pulsate and spin in the lead up to the world as it is being prepared for The Warning.

My Cross will appear first. They will be shocked but this is being given as a sign so that you can prepare your souls and ask for redemption for the sins you have committed. By doing this you will not suffer during The Warning.

Pray, pray, pray, My followers everywhere. Rejoice when the sky explodes for you will know that I am truly coming into the world. At last mankind will not be able to deny Me. My Love will radiate in every corner of the world as I try to draw in all souls everywhere.

So unexpected will this event be that the world will stop in great shock. When the slowly recover many will still be unsure about what has happened. As I come so too will Satan and the demons from Hell who will try to devour the souls of My children. This is why I must urge you all to sprinkle your home with Holy Water and have blessed candles everywhere. You must keep yourselves protected.

In the lead up I ask of you this. Pray for all those who cannot find it in their hearts to accept the Truth of My Teachings. Pray especially for those who go to tremendous efforts to deny Me although they are aware of My Crucifixion to save them.
Remember I died for every single one of you to save you. Remember that this time I came again to save you, each one of you. Not one do I exclude.

Now is your chance, children, to be assured of a place in the Era of Peace on earth. Why would you not want to be part of this? Why would anyone knowingly choose the depths of Hell in exchange for this Great Gift?

Rejoice. Pray, give thanks to God the Father for this Great Warning. Embrace this Gift with love and joy in your hearts.

Your Saviour

Jesus Christ

I will never desert you children. That is why I am Coming.
Monday, October 03, 2011 12.30 hours

My dearly beloved daughter I speak with you today of the need to understand what The Warning is and to dispel any confusion surrounding it. Many people are frightened and believe that this is the Day of Judgment. But it is not. This is to be a day of Glorious Divine Mercy, which will envelope the entire world. My rays of Mercy will be poured out over every single soul, man, woman and child. No one will be excluded. No one.

This is My return to save you once again. Didn't you know that I was always going to be merciful? That I would never wait until the Final Judgment until I tried once more to save you all?

This is the Purification I have spoken about. In the lead up to this great event the world has endured a Purification for the last couple of years. I allowed mankind to suffer loss and gain humility through the global collapse of financial markets although I did not cause it. It was masterminded by global groups in places of power including the corridors of governments all over the world by their wicked greed. Yet because of this suffering millions of people will now be ready to hear My Word and accept My Mercy. They would not have been ready otherwise. There is nothing to fear if you love Me and live by the Commandments given to the world by Moses on the instructions of My Eternal Father.

Await My arrival with anticipation of love and joy and be thankful that that you are alive in the world today to receive My Great Gift of Salvation. I will never desert you children. That is why I am coming. It is because I love you so much that I do this. It is because I wanted to prepare you and bring you close to My Heart that I have given the world My Messages through My beloved daughter.

These Messages are going to continue beyond The Warning to give you as much guidance as possible into My Teachings. My Word, contained in these Volumes, which I refer to as the Book of Truth, will create a new Christian Army who will defend My Name until the New Era of Peace commences.

Be joyful now My children. Let me comfort you for this will be the first time you will come before Me face to face. It will be, for My followers, a moment of great love, peace and happiness. Rise now and be strong. For you are privileged and for this you must offer praise to God the

Almighty Father who has allowed this to happen.

Your beloved Saviour

Jesus Christ

Era of Peace not far away

Tuesday, October 04, 2011 15.30 hours

My dearly beloved daughter the New Era is about to become a reality in the near future.

The Era of Peace will be enjoyed by all of My followers. It will be a period of love, happiness and peace, there will be no disease, pain, financial worries, because everything you will need will be provided by Me. You, My children, will want for nothing as I will nurture and embrace you in My New Paradise just as a parent would nurture an infant. This is to be welcomed. It is a goal for which you must all strive.

There is no use waiting to prepare to enter My New Paradise of Peace. For you may leave it too late. Plan today for you will not know when this will happen. In fact it will happen so quickly and suddenly that you, My followers, will simply find yourselves there in the blink of an eye. That is why you must begin to prepare your souls now for only clean souls can enter.

Time is of the essence. This, My children is one of the last calls to you to amend your lives before The Warning. Prepare each day and trust in My Divine Word as you are now being commanded to follow My pleas for the salvation of souls.

The Era of Peace is not far away now and I urge you to prepare your families so that you can be as one in My New Kingdom.

Your Divine Saviour

Jesus Christ

Global Groups under the domain of the antichrist

Wednesday, October 05, 2011 21.00 hours

My dearly beloved daughter I am pleased with the way in which you have increased the number of hours to Me in Adoration. This is good because My Graces given to you during this special time will strengthen your will to spread My Messages even further.

Now that more of My children are realizing the atmosphere in the world both politically and economically has changed beyond their comprehension they will soon see the Truth. The global leaders I speak of, who through cowardice hide where you cannot see them, are increasing their plans for global domination.

They are building armies, weapons and poisonous substances all with one goal in mind, to destroy My children. Conspiracy theories are denounced constantly when those sharp observers publish the truth. For you must understand, so powerful are these groups, all combined under one united front of respectability that they can sway the truth and hide it from the public eye.

Accept children that the evil group rises in battle against My own followers and leaders in the Church. They have even managed to infiltrate My Church from within. Their venom spews forth like a stream flowing and gushing in all directions. There is a plan to not only deceive you but to recruit you to their way of thinking. On the outside they will be seen to offer the world salvation in the guise of humanitarian efforts. Their creative solutions to make life easier for you will be in the form of unifying your money, your food, your health, your welfare and your religion as one, all under one domain, the domain of the antichrist.

Please reject these evil people's attempts to suck you My innocent children into their wicked plan. They want you, through your own consensus, to reject God My Almighty Father. Once they control you, you are lost. They will control what you eat, what religious practices you participate in and the medicine they provide you.

Pray, pray to God the Father to stop their wicked atrocities now and ask Him to redeem their souls during The Warning. Irrespective of what their devious plans are they are in need of your prayers most of all. They are the puppets of Satan, the poor misguided souls, and do not in many cases know what they are doing or whose orders they are responding to.

Pray My Divine Mercy Chaplet for these souls every day if you can for as long as you can. Help Me save them.

Your Jesus

Your banking collapse was masterminded by the antichrist

Thursday, October 06, 2011 22.45 hours

My dearly beloved daughter pray hard because the antichrist is ready to spring from his hiding hole and will leap upon the world in order to devour My children.

His cunning plan will be hidden behind a handsome charming and articulate exterior but when My children look into his eyes they will see darkness for he has no soul. He was not created by the Hand of God the Father.

Pray My children now every one of you to stop him from destroying all those he controls from within the One World Order.

Prayer can mitigate many of his proposed sickening plans against humanity. Sadly, many will be fooled by him. Never before have I urged My children for so much prayer because without your prayers the schemes he is orchestrating will be fulfilled as foretold in the Book of Revelation.

His presence on earth is felt throughout the world but his actions are hidden from view. He is like a rock which when thrown into the water creates ripples that can travel for miles. He wants to destroy you because you are My children.

My children who follow his every move in a slavish manner are blindfolded. The secret atrocities committed by these people create tremendous sorrow in Heaven.
Children I must ask you to pray to St Michael the Archangel to rebuke Satan during these turbulent times. The antichrist is moving quickly and his influence is speeding up the global plot to unify your currencies everywhere.

Your banking collapse was deliberately mastermind by the antichrist so that when your countries needed help he and his wicked minions would rise to rescue your countries.

Wake up all of you and see what is really happening before your eyes. He is waiting to pounce but your prayers can mitigate his actions and halt him in his tracks. His soiled hands are waiting to grab you into an embrace from which you will find it hard to disentangle.

Remember children Satan's remaining time on earth is short. The antichrist has been sent to steal souls from My Father. These souls come from My Father, God the Creator of all things. The antichrist's promise of an everlasting universe is nonsense. Many souls are now being seduced by this new and sinister doctrine. I watch as they fall into this deceitful den of darkness and weep bitter tears. For once these souls follow this path of deceit they are contaminated. Their attitude to others including their family changes as their hearts turn cold.

Satan's power is strong but God the Father will step in and punish his followers on this earth most severely. The Warning is their last chance to turn their backs on the antichrist.

Pray that My Light will penetrate each and every soul during The Warning so that lost souls especially can be rescued from this terrible darkness.

Your beloved Jesus Christ

Purgatory is not a place you should feel content to enter

Friday, October 07, 2011 21.45 hours

My dearly beloved daughter the reason I send so many Messages to My children is to help them prepare their souls in a way, which was not possible up to now.

Many of My children have not read the Holy Bible nor are they aware of all My Teachings.

More time is spent by My sacred servants focusing on the part of My Teachings where I ask you all to love your neighbour, which is a good thing, no talk is made of the consequences facing mankind should they reject The Father. Why do My sacred servants deny the existence of Hell and why do they paint a rosy picture of Purgatory?

My children have been taught many good things through the churches, which proclaim the Glory of God the Almighty Father. Sadly, though, the existence of Purgatory and Hell are played down to such an extent that My children have become complacent about their existence.

My children are being misled also about the existence of The Evil One. Many of My sacred servants even deny his existence. O how foolish they are to believe that man can strengthen his faith without knowing or understanding the truth of The Evil One's power.

This lack of direction on the part of My sacred servants has meant that evil in the world has flourished in a way that could have been prevented through prayer. Satan has been allowed to roam freely on this earth for some time because of the blindness of My sacred servants. If My children were made properly aware of the havoc caused by Satan then prayer to mitigate his influence would have been much stronger.

The existence of Purgatory

The existence of Purgatory is misunderstood. Many believe that it is simply a waiting period of purification before souls can enter Heaven for those souls who may not have been in a state of grace at the time of death. There are different levels in Purgatory children and all souls feel a burning pain of darkness, which intensifies the further down the level. This means that souls who narrowly missed being cast into Hell suffer the pain of burning the most. Although all souls in Purgatory will eventually enter My Father's Kingdom it is not a place where My children should feel content to enter. This is why you must fight sin and seek forgiveness as regularly as possible to remain in a state of grace. This is why you must obey the Ten Commandments at all times. This is why you must also pray for those souls who are there because without your prayers they cannot enter the Kingdom of Heaven until the final Day of Judgment.

It is time now to face the Truth children.

Pray for the graces you need to be free of sin so that you can enter Heaven. Be ready every day for you do not know of the plans, which are already in place, which await you. I give you this Message so that the Truth is clear. These important Messages have not been presented to you clearly children over the decades. It is important that you are well prepared.

By reciting the Divine Mercy Chaplet every day at 3 P.M. I will intervene at the moment of death on your behalf no matter how much of a sinner you are and show you My Mercy. I tell you this because I love you not to frighten you but to ensure you spread the Truth to your families.

My Word today is simply a reminder of the Truth to which you have been denied behind the mask of tolerance. It is a little like the parent of a child whom they spoil because they love the child so much. If the parent over feeds the child then the child's health will suffer. Yet the parent keeps giving the child the food, which the child has now become used to out of misguided love. This can lead to the child's deteriorating health. This child, in turn, becomes ignorant as to what healthy foods to eat because he doesn't know about them. He has never been told.

Go now and tell your brothers and sister the Truth about Hell and Purgatory before it is too late. Because if you don't no one else will.

Your Teacher and Divine Saviour

Jesus Christ

Virgin Mary - The Sin of indifference to my Son is rampant

Saturday, October 08, 2011 14.22 hours

(Received during a private Apparition of the Blessed Mother which lasted 30 minutes)

My child there are so many souls destined for eternal exile should they not turn back to my precious Son.

My Son suffers greatly in anguish as He watches these children lurch from one evil path to another.

The sin of indifference to my Son is rampant and so many who know of His existence still choose, through their own free will, to disown Him.

Now is the time when they will understand what lies ahead of them if they do not repent during the Illumination of Conscience, which they will experience shortly.

For those of you who love my Son take up His Cross and help Him to bring back those souls for whom He yearns to hold in His precious Loving Arms.

So many of you children who do not really know my Son must understand the gentle tenderness of His Heart. So much love does He have for you all, that were you to see His suffering because of rejection you would lie on the ground, cry and beg for the forgiveness of the sins of mankind.

Please, I urge you to pray hard for the conversion so desired by my Son during The Warning.
Your Blessed Mother

Queen of all Mankind

Era for the multitude of false prophets sent by Satan
Saturday, October 08, 2011 16.20 hours

My dearly beloved daughter, as My genuine visionaries go forth into the world so also will the false visionaries. You will know them by carefully scrutinizing their messages for the world. For somewhere within you will find that My Teachings and the Truth contained in the Most Holy Bible have been tampered with. So subtle are these untruths that only those with true knowledge of the Holy Scriptures will be able to spot them.

Watch out for any hatred, which such visionaries create amongst their followers when they fight, divide and split up families. The cults that emerge from such visionaries' work will now surge forth into the world to cause confusion and anxiety amongst believers.

Wherever My Holy Word is contained you will find love. My Messages breed love and harmony and will not fail to affect your soul. My Messages will always speak the Truth and while stark and frightening at times they are being given to you, My children, out of love.

False visionaries will impart messages that are not easy to read or understand. On the face of it they will exude a sense of authority and create a feeling of love. They will not, however, bring you peace of soul. Such visionaries, many of whom, are not of God, seduce first, then control until finally they suck you into a bed of lies and deceit.

Satan and his army will influence such false visionaries and seers. He can even attack genuine visionaries when he encourages them to wander away from Me in confusion. I urge you children to be on your guard at all times.

Denounce messages, which contradict My Teachings in any way for you can then be sure that they are false.

I only speak through a select number of authentic visionaries and seers in the world today. There are less than twenty and fewer than you think. Each of them, have been given a different role but My Voice and My Instructions will have a ring of familiarity, which you will detect. There will be a purpose to their messages all of which are designed to encourage action on your part to prepare your souls.

Any actions encouraged by those who call themselves visionaries and seers which seem strange or which encourage their followers to take actions, which do not involve the love of your neighbour then turn your backs.

Heed now for this is the era of the false prophet who will make himself known in the world shortly. So also is it the era for the multitude of false prophets sent by The Deceiver into the world to cause confusion and a darkness of soul.

Your beloved Jesus

God the Father - Heed now My final calling on mankind

Sunday, October 09, 2011 15.30 hours

My daughter, tell the world of the love I have for all of My creatures everywhere. Also inform them that I will now mastermind the greatest Act of Divine Intervention seen on earth since the Resurrection of My Beloved Son Jesus Christ

All is prepared for this Great Act of Mercy, which I have sanctioned to help save all of you.

My Love for you means that while I intend to fight the Deceiver in his attempts to destroy mankind I will now allow one last Act of Mercy to convert you. This last Act to redeem you in My eyes means that man can once again learn the Truth of My Existence.

My children please bow now and ask for Mercy for your family and loved ones. If they are not in a state of grace they will find The Warning difficult. You must inform them of the need to meditate on the Truth.

The time is short. The Warning is almost upon you. Once it is over you will have time to decide which path you wish to choose, the path of Divine Light or the path of The Deceiver. The choice will be yours.

After some time if man does not turn his back on his wicked ways I will destroy those countries, which pay homage to The Deceiver. They will hide when My Hand falls in punishment but they will have nowhere to go.

My patience is running out as I now plan to unite all those who believe in Me, the Creator of all things and take them with Me into the New Era of Peace. Those who choose to walk the other way will be cast into the fires of Hell.

Heed now this final calling on mankind. This is the time for you to decide you future. Pray for those blind to My Love for many of them when the Truth is revealed to them once more will defy Me and turn their backs.

Your beloved Creator

God the Father

King of the Most High

Message for America: Embrace your brothers and sisters of all denominations
Tuesday, October 11, 2011 15.30 hours

My dearly beloved daughter I wish to communicate with the American people. My message to them is this. You, My precious children suffer greatly in these times. You are experiencing a cleansing that is necessary in order to purify your souls.

The great sins in America, which torment Me are the sins of abortion and immorality of the flesh. Many of My children are infested by the deceiver who rules hidden behind closed doors your monetary and political systems. So many of you are oblivious to this fact. I now urge you to pray for the relief required from their devious plans to destroy your country.

Prayer, My children will help mitigate the Chastisement, which My Father will unleash in the world against the sin of abortion. Pray, pray and unite to pay homage to My Father. For by uniting together all religions, which honour The Father, God the Creator of the world, you can help your country.

You must pray for forgiveness and trust that your prayers will be responded to according to My Father's Divine timing.

Embrace your brothers and sisters of all religious denominations who believe in God the Father and pray as one to redeem the sins of your country. My children, so vast is your country that it is important that I can save as many souls as possible. I can do this only through conversion, which will happen during The Warning and through your prayers and devotion.

Turn to Me now all of you. Do not discriminate against each other's religions just trust in God the Father and He will answer your prayers. You My precious children are lost. You have been shown so much confusion and presented with twisted truths about the existence of God the Father. You use religion as a façade to wreak venom on those more unfortunate than you. It is time to accept the truth that it will only be through your love of neighbour that as a nation you can return into the arms of your Creator, God the Father.

I love you with a tearing compassion in My Whole Being. I strive to save you so you can be taken into the new and wonderful Era of Peace that awaits you on this earth. To enter this New Paradise your souls must be free of sin. [219.8]

Pray for the graces to seek forgiveness for your own sins and the sins committed by your governments.

I leave you in peace and love.

Your beloved Saviour

Jesus Christ

Virgin Mary: You will come under huge scrutiny and attack

Wednesday, October 12, 2011 14.22 hours

My child this is a time that when you work for my Son you will come under huge scrutiny and attack. You must always honour my Son's wishes and obey Him at all times. Never defend His Most Holy Word for He does not wish you to do this. Do not respond to or engage with those who challenge or misinterpret His Word, which may cause debate and doubts.

You will now come under the attack of The Deceiver but you must pray for my protection and never give in to such taunts. He, the Deceiver, works through others to hurt you should you allow him to do this you are engaging with him and giving him the power that he wants.

Stand firm in these instances my child and turn to me always I will cover you with my Most Holy Mantle to protect you from him and all will be well.

Remain courageous and accept this as a gift from God the Most High for without such strength you could not do this work effectively. Always remember you are not alone in this work because the saints all intercede on your behalf and you are being given every kind of Divine Protection.

Continue in your obedience to my Son and try and become joyful as you accept the suffering He allows for the salvation of souls. You must keep saying the Holy Rosary every day and pray with me so souls can be saved.

I bless you my child. Heaven rejoices with this Most Sacred Work on behalf of my precious beloved Son who loves all of mankind but who weeps in sorrow for those souls who will reject His Hand of Mercy after The Warning.

Your beloved Mother

Never defend Me as it is unnecessary
Thursday, October 13, 2011 00.10 hours

My dearly beloved daughter I must inform you of the need to refrain from defending My Most Holy Word.

Those who question My Word must pray to Me for guidance. I am instructing you now to never attempt to interpret the Messages from My Divine Lips.

I have told you this many times and you have not been given the authority to do so. Instead accept My Messages as they are. Do not doubt them. Do not try to analyze them for man knows very little about Divine plans or timing. Nor does man know anything about the antichrist although he thinks he does. Only these matters of such importance remain known to My beloved Father.

I ask that you never defend Me as it is unnecessary. The Will of My Father to communicate to mankind through you and other prophets is all that should matter. As I have said before you are the writer. I am the Author. You are the instrument. I am the Master.

Obedience to Me at all times is expected of you. Doing as I say is simple. Your work will be easier if you refrain from engaging in an intellectual religious debate regarding Scriptural matters about which you know nothing.

Remember the importance of humility My daughter. Remain as a child, little at all times in My eyes and you will find peace. Trials will be sent to you during this work. Expect them. Don't reject them. Your gift to Me of your free will is accepted but you must learn the importance of not trying to reject suffering because this is important for the salvation of souls.

I love you My daughter but feel the need to remind you of My clear instructions. I do not need to be defended. The Words given to you are uncontaminated and do not contradict the Truth as provided to mankind since time began. Many versions of the Truth contained in the Bible have been twisted to suit man's own agenda. I Am the Truth. I Am the Bread of Life. Without Me there is no life.

Move forward with a clearer insight as to what is expected of you. You are protected at all times. Thank you My daughter for the strength you are now showing, but always allow Me to guide you at all times. That way this journey will be easier.

Your beloved Jesus

I cannot force people to convert or turn back
Saturday, October 15, 2011 19.00 hours

My dearly beloved daughter as more people hear My Word, My Love will infiltrate their souls as soon as they read My Messages. I will speak to their souls and awaken their slumber in order to unite them with Me so that I can save souls everywhere. Strength in numbers will help me achieve the salvation of souls on such a grand scale. Because of the free will given to man as a Gift from My Father I cannot force people to convert or turn back to the faith in God the Father, it will have to be their own decision. Prayer will spread conversion. Of that I promise you. Just think of the gift that awaits souls when you, My children, pray for them.

Don't you know the power of prayer. Prayer said by the multitudes in thanksgiving to My Father and in atonement for your sins can save the world. Such is the power it wields. Never before have I urged you so much for your prayers, which must come from your own lips and with a generosity of heart for hardened sinners everywhere. I need your prayers. Without your prayers these poor souls may not be saved because many of them are in such darkness that the impact of The Warning will have little effect. You My cherished beloved children, all of you sinners, many of whom do your best to show Me your love don't you realize that I rely on you so much to keep Me company. Join with Me in the bosom of My Sacred Heart and ask Me for the graces to save your brothers and sisters. I will save millions of souls when you devote your time to praying The Divine Mercy.

This is the time when the recital of The Divine Mercy will be most effective. Be generous of heart, mind, body and soul. Cast any doubts aside. Allow Me, your Jesus, to lift you up to bring you and all those you pray for into My Eternal Life.

Your beloved Saviour

Jesus Christ

Your time on earth is at a crucial point

Sunday, October 16, 2011 21.30 hours

My dearly beloved daughter why is that when My Word is interpreted do so many of My children find it so offensive? While My children must always discern such messages published by those who claim to come in My Name they must also learn to keep their minds and hearts open at all times.

O how I wish My followers especially would open their eyes and welcome Me into their hearts. It is I, Jesus, who calls you to hear My Voice as I urge you to come to Me in prayer.

Your time on earth is at a crucial point. There is not much time before I herald in the New Era of Peace and because of this I need you to prepare your souls now.

Do not allow arrogance to blind you to the Truth. Don't you know I would never deceive you. Hear My instructions to block the Evil One from clouding your judgment. Do not allow him to keep you at a distance for if you would only hear My Most Holy Word you will know that it is I, Jesus Christ, who calls you.

Children if you knew how much infestation has been laid down upon My precious souls the world over you would be shocked. This darkness even covers My precious followers from time to time. The hurt I feel, especially among those souls who pray regularly and show true devotion, when I witness your doubts brings tears of great sorrow.

Pray, pray, pray for guidance from the Holy Spirit. If you open your hardened hearts and ask for the gift of discernment I will answer your call.

How sad you will be when the Truth is revealed to you during The Warning. It is your prayers to save other souls that I now ask for. Surely if you doubt My Word given through these Messages that you could still find it in your heart to pray for lost souls.

I love you and await your response to My pleas for prayer.

Your Jesus

My return to save you will be felt in every corner of the world

Monday, October 17, 2011

My dearly beloved daughter times are changing all around you. The world is in upheaval caused by the spirit of darkness. You are surrounded with all the evidence of what the evil of sin can inflict on mankind. In this spirit of darkness will shine the Spirit of My Divine Presence as I come to save mankind once again.

You, My precious children who know the Truth must tell the others how fortunate they are to being given this wonderful Divine Gift. My Love will strike the earth in a manner where you will drop down in humility and on bended knees weep with sorrow for the grievance you have caused to offend My Eternal Father.

It is through God The Most High that this Great Act of Mercy is now presented to you. Rejoice for now there is Light in the world, which will draw souls forth and into the Arms of God the Father.

I come again to give you the life you need to enable you once again to raise your eyes in adoration and praise to the Glory of God the Father and thank Him for the Justice He now shows to His precious but lost children.

I, Jesus Christ, now prepare to allow you to bear witness to the Truth of Mercy for every soul including hardened sinners and non-believers everywhere.

The proof of My Existence and that of God the Father will be revealed in all its heavenly glory to every man, woman and child.

My Presence will be revealed in a way that no one will nor can ignore. For the heavens will open, the stars will collide so that My return to save you will be felt in every corner of the world at the same time.

O how My children will rejoice when they bear witness to My Divine Presence. Even those in darkness will feel My Love touch their cold souls, which will ignite them again.

Prepare. Await My Glorious return. Pray for those who have fear in their hearts. Do not fear Me. Await this great event with love and humility in your hearts.

I love you children. This Great Act of My Mercy will prove this to you.

Your beloved Saviour

Jesus Christ

God the Father - Prepare the world for the arrival of My Beloved Son Jesus Christ
Wednesday, October 19, 2011 14.00 hours

My daughter prepare the world for the arrival of My Beloved Son Jesus Christ for He now comes, as foretold, to save mankind once again.

His arrival will be heralded by the trumpets in Heaven and the choirs of angels who will sing in praise to announce this great event.

My Great Gift to mankind is being presented to you in the form of My dearly beloved Son Who is being sent to save you before the Final Judgment.

Prepare your souls for when your sins are revealed to you I command you to fall in humility at the feet of My Son and beg for Mercy. You must ask Him to forgive you and you must accept the punishment required to cleanse your souls.

His Mercy is so great that no sin no matter how grievous, cannot be forgiven, if true remorse is shown. Humility is required of all of you so that you will be worthy to enter the New Glorious Era of Peace on earth the time of which is very close. Only those souls who truly repent and show true allegiance to My beloved Son will be fit to enter the gates. For you must be free of sin to enter this wonderful New Paradise on Earth.

My dearly beloved children I have prepared this Paradise with great love for each of you. This is the Inheritance you have been waiting for. This is the way in which the gift of the earth was originally presented to Adam and Eve.

Any man who rejects this Paradise on Earth, where no evil will exist in any form, is turning his back on salvation.

This is your final chance to free your souls from the grip of Satan and the evil influence he has on your lives.

Embrace this wonderful Gift of Great Mercy. Through this Gift you are being offered a chance of true salvation and a Glorious Paradise, which you could not possibly fathom.

For those poor sinners who reject My Son's offer of forgiveness you will be afforded more time to turn back to your faith. However, you will not be given too much time for My patience is running out.

Await now My Son's return to save you once again from sin and to bring you to eternal salvation.

God the Father

Death of My son Muammar Gaddafi

Thursday, October 20, 2011 15.15 hours

My dearly beloved daughter any remaining doubts you may have had from time to time regarding My Most Holy Words will now have been diminished.

I reveal prophecies in order to prove to the world that it is I, Jesus Christ, the Saviour of all mankind who communicates to My children everywhere at this time.

My intention is not to sensationalize but to ensure that no one is excluded from hearing My most urgent call to the world.

The death of My son Muammar Gaddafi whose soul that you and those close to you have been praying for over the last number of months is one of the first prophecies which will prove to the world the authenticity of these Messages. This is My sign to you My daughter to rid your mind of the doubts, which have been lingering in your mind.

You, My daughter, much as it overwhelms you, have been chosen to prepare mankind for My New Era of Peace. This is the time, which will follow sometime after The Warning.

Go and prepare for the next part of your Holy Mission to help save souls after The Warning. You are being given the graces to keep you strong. My children everywhere are at last hearing My cry for conversion.

The ones who hurt Me the most

Never show fear in this Work for there is nothing to fear. Never falter and allow setbacks or verbal taunts to slow down your Work for Me. I am, My daughter, always at your side. Remember this. If and when you are attacked over My Holy Word remain silent. My Holy Word will always be attacked. Those who hurt Me the most are the holy souls who, through fear and caution, are sadly the first to insult Me through these Messages. Satan knows that it is My chosen and devout followers who, when they turn their back on Me, are the ones who hurt Me the most.

You are now My daughter beginning to feel the physical pain of My suffering but you are now prepared to accept this in union with Me. These trials will not last long but throughout the duration you will feel exactly the torment I feel when I witness sin. This, as I have told you before, is a gift and very few chosen souls receive this. Frightening at times you must understand that not only does your suffering bring you closers to My Sacred Heart but it will save millions of souls during The Warning.

This suffering is going to become more intensive as The Warning draws close. Endure this in silence. For in this way you will help Me save precious souls who otherwise would have been snatched by The Deceiver.

Tell My children I rejoice at the strong faith they are showing. Tell them they are becoming closer to My Sacred Heart. Tell them that I now bless them and bestow great blessing to give them the strength they will need as they follow My guidance through these Holy Messages. They will need the strength as it is not easy for My children to digest the enormity of the changes, which will now evolve in your world.

Pray and unite as one. Together, look to the heavens as little children with a simple trust in God the Father. Ask Him, in My Holy Name, to unite you into His glorious army towards the victory of eternal salvation.

I Bless you children with all My Divine Love.

Your Jesus

The Warning is a form of Global Confession

Friday, October 21, 2011 20.30 hours

My dearly beloved daughter, write this. You are now undergoing intense suffering in order to save those souls of darkness who reject Me and My Father.

So closed and hardened are those souls that it will be only be through the prayers of others and the suffering of victim souls that they can be saved, for they will refuse to seek redemption. Their stubbornness will stop them from feeling enough remorse to confess their sins and beg for forgiveness.

The Warning is a form of Global Confession. It will be the time when everyone will be expected to ask for the forgiveness of their sins or face rejection. So many souls in darkness will refuse My Hand of Mercy. They will turn away from Me. You, My daughter, along with all My devout followers can help save their souls from eternal damnation.

I would never pressurise My children to suffer in My Name. But for those who offer Me, as a gift, their help through suffering I can redeem much of mankind.

Suffering comes about from the attacks of Satan when he torments souls who are close to Me and those who are appointed by Me to lead a Holy Mission to convert souls. Know that when these attacks come you are in union with Me. You will then get to know Me so well. You will know how I feel - My Joy, My Sadness, My Grief, My Pain and the terror when I lose a soul to Satan.

Do not worry. Already millions of souls have already been saved through these Messages.

The prayers of My devoted army are already mitigating global disasters and the departure of My Holy Vicar from the Vatican. Their obedience in reciting My Divine Mercy Chaplet is saving souls right now.

My daughter, make sure that all My children understand that I speak to all religions and denominations through these Messages. I exclude no one, for they are all children of God. There is only one God and that is My Eternal Father, God of the Most High.

Come together with Me children and let us work as one to save My souls all over the world quickly. By prayer alone you can help Me save the world.

Your Jesus

Saviour of all Mankind

I wish to form an army of prayer groups
Sunday, October 23, 2011 19.15 hours

My dearly beloved daughter it must be known that I wish to form an army of prayer groups around the world. I will provide you, My army, with prayers that will need to be recited to save souls. These prayer groups will expand and within its ranks will rise a veritable army of devoted followers to bring forth the Truth of My Divine Promise of Salvation for all.

These groups will form the army as dictated by My beloved Father, which will tackle the darkness of evil caused by Satan and his believers and followers.

Yes, My daughter, hard though it is to understand, but there are many people who not only acknowledge Satan but who pay allegiance to him. There are many souls in darkness who pay homage to and idolize the King of Darkness. Many churches, hidden from the eyes of My children of the Light, have been built in honour of Satan. They bow before him, hold black masses and insult Me with every kind of blasphemy and insult, which would shock and disgust you. Their numbers are growing and many of Satan's dedicated and committed followers work in very respectable senior positions in business, banking and political circles. They unite as one in defiance of God, My Eternal Father in the full knowledge as to what they are doing.

Just as Satan hates humanity because it was Created by God the Father, Creator of all things, these satanic devotees hate mankind. The hatred they feel is so deep that they will try to form an elite army to destroy millions of lives on earth. In their pursuit of power and wealth they will aim to clear the way for their own needs and desire to control mankind.

These are among the hardened sinners for whom I seek your help children. I need your prayers to open their hearts to the lies they have been led to believe by the deceiver. They are lost to Me unless they beg for My Mercy. This is why prayer may be their only saving grace.

This powerful army led by the deceiver will attempt to cause terrible destruction. They are already trying to poison My children in the most cunning ways through your water, medicine and food. Please stay alert at all times.

The Hand of My Father will fall soon after The Warning on these wicked souls if they continue to reject My Mercy. Meanwhile children you must stand up and do not allow your nations to be bullied. Pray for My protection and keep your lives simple. Pray and receive the Sacraments. Ask for My help in all things and I will respond to your pleas according to My Most Holy Will.

Pray, pray, pray to mitigate the evil plans to control the world, which this wicked group is plotting. They are gaining power in the Middle East and are making attempts to control Europe before they target other parts of the world. The enemies they reveal to you in the news media are not the real enemies. They create enemies in order to justify retaliation, which will always have the same goals, to control, to own, to build wealth.

Pray for them to convert for without conversion their wicked deeds will cause much grief and distress. My Eternal Father will however serve down His punishment but they can still inflict damage, which will cause untold suffering among My children.

Your beloved Saviour

Jesus Christ

My arrival will be sooner than you expect

Monday, October 24, 201119.09 hours

My dearly beloved daughter you must not allow those who continue to question and pass judgment on My Most Holy Word to upset you. Ignore these interrogations. Remain silent. Pray for them and move on for there is not much time now.

I call on all of you dear children to sit down calmly and pray to Me for Mercy. Please, you must not panic because I come only to save you not to judge. Don't you know this? There is nothing to fear just trust in Me completely.

My arrival will be sooner than you expect so please prepare your souls. Pray for all souls who may deny Me or reject My Gift of Divine Mercy. You, My cherished souls bring me such comfort and ease the torment and suffering I endure when I see the hatred everywhere in your world.

Come closer to Me children and let Me embrace you to give you the strength and confidence you need to greet Me. You, My special army, are in union with Me and whether you realize it or not you are being guided by the Holy Spirit to fight to save souls.

Sit quietly My little ones and remember I am with you at all times. Rejoice and await My Coming when I will pour out My Graces to cover all of My beloved followers everywhere.

No matter where you live, no matter what part of the world you are from, you are Mine. I love you. Look with open hearts and confidence as we draw closer to The Warning.

Your Jesus

God the Father - You must reject darkness and embrace the Light

Tuesday, October 25, 2011 15.30 hours

My beloved daughter, tell the world that I embrace all My children in My Arms. All will be well. All must now be left in My Holy Hands as it is meant to be.

I command that My Son be once again sent into the world to save man from the ravages of sin. This is My Divine Act of Justice for you, My cherished children, so I can reclaim My Kingdom on earth.

Fear does not come from Me. Fear comes from the darkness. When you fear Me you know that it is the darkness that envelops your soul and not My Divine Greatness.

To be part of My Kingdom you must reject darkness and embrace the Light. This same Light is now being bestowed upon you by My Son's Divine Act of Mercy.

My love for all you children is so great that I will use all My power to redeem souls everywhere. My Hand of Justice will fall on those souls who reject Me but not until every effort is exhausted to unite all My children everywhere.

The Kingdom of My Great Glory will be revealed to the world shortly. Not one of you children will want to reject My Glorious Kingdom, which will reign in the New Era of Peace on earth.

Pray for those who will find it difficult to embrace the Truth.

God the Almighty Father

False Prophets trying to detract from My Holy Word
Wednesday, October 26, 2011 15.30 hours

My dearly beloved daughter please tell My children to be alert to false visionaries who speak in My Name but who promote words that do not come from My Lips.

Many of these self proclaimed visionaries, who appear on the outside as Catholics and with all the mannerisms associated with this and other Christian doctrines are in fact New Age followers.

New Age followers will now infiltrate the world to convince My children that they have been sent to promote My Holy Word. Their words will seem on the face of it to be true. The language they use will be sophisticated, loving, well thought out but will mask a lie.

This is the era for the false prophets to emerge and many of My children will find it difficult to discern Truth from fiction.

You My daughter are now being targeted by these visionaries who have set out to detract from My Holy Word. Do not allow this to happen or My children will be sucked into a darkness they will find hard to disentangle from.

Remember this. These false prophets are also My beloved children so please pray for them. Sadly they have been misguided into believing in an imaginary hierarchy and a universe, which does not exist.

Be wary of those who refer to ascended masters or who talk about a new era of light where God the Father is simply viewed as just another facet. These souls do not take direction from Me. They are espousing beliefs instilled by The Deceiver. In many cases these deluded souls believe they are receiving divine messages. This is how Satan works. His soft, soothing words will yield a stark, cold but convincing litany of words. They do not come from God the Most High.

As I have told you before I speak to the world in a simple way. I have no use for colourful language in the guise of a cold superior voice. I try not to instil fear in your hearts. I simply try to lead you to the Truth and the importance of loving your neighbour.

How difficult it is for you children in these confusing times.

Pray, pray that you do not become victims of a series of falsehoods, which will be spread by false prophets. If their messages seem contrived, are difficult to understand and strike fear in your hearts they are not from Me.

Children stay focused only on Me. I have much to tell you. Do not allow yourselves to be distracted for one minute as it is will prevent you from saving those souls so badly in need of your prayers.

Your Jesus

Await now our glorious reunion
Wednesday, October 26, 2011 22.00 hours

My beloved daughter you must not fret over the constant attacks being made on My Messages from false visionaries.

You must know by now that when I speak to chosen messengers, that they will always be a target of hatred. When you are attacked remember I too am also challenged. My Holy Word is taken apart, analyzed, questioned, criticized and declared not worthy to come from My Lips.

O how little My children know. Fear and suspicion blinds them to the Truth. You will be surprised also at how My Word is dismissed so easily in favour of false messages.

As The Warning is almost upon the world the Truth will finally at last be made known to all of My followers. It will be at that stage they will embrace My Word in order to sanctify their poor souls. How I will welcome them and draw them close to Me as their tears will mingle with Mine in love and unity. Before the Warning they will continue to doubt but they will not deny Me after they come before Me. For once they come before Me and see the Love that I have for them they will not want to leave Me for one moment so deep will our union be.

Await now our glorious reunion.

Your Jesus

You My children are blessed if you suffer in My Name

Thursday, October 27, 2011 15.30 hours

My dearly beloved daughter the increasing number of trials you are now undergoing on My behalf is not by chance. As Satan continues to torment you, only think of the souls you are saving through this suffering. Try to rise above these difficulties and keep Me in your thoughts all the time. Pray to My beloved Mother for protection and recite the Holy Rosary as often as you can.

It is important that all of My followers ask for protection against the Deceiver who waits for every opportunity to create doubts in their minds.

He and his demons are everywhere. They will use every tactic possible to cause havoc in your lives. Know that when this happens that you have been touched by My Teachings and that you are now carrying My Cross.

Never fear children for you are all capable of arising from this wilderness because of the strength I now bestow on each and every one of you, My army. You will triumph over the evil one and his wickedness. The more you pray in unison the greater the wall of armour will be. Not one of My children who suffer persecution as a direct result of working for Me can be touched by the evil one.

You, My children are blessed if you suffer in My Name although you will find it difficult to understand this.

Ignore such taunts. Turn your backs. Do not react. Remain silent. Pray for strength. I am with you.

Your beloved Jesus Christ

Greatest attack on My Church since My Death on the Cross

Friday, October 28, 2011 22.40 hours

My dearly beloved daughter the loyalty of My Church to Me, their beloved Saviour, is going to be tested shortly beyond its endurance. My Church has been asleep and in its slumber has not prepared itself for the arrival of the antichrist. Already he and his minions have crawled into every crevice of My Father's Churches the world over.

The Catholic Church is the antichrist's number one target and he will not stop until he turns the heads of at least half of My Church on this earth. So unprepared are My cardinals, bishops and priests that they fail to notice the subtle changes taking place within their own ranks. It won't be long before the divide within My Church becomes truly evident.

This is the greatest attack on My Church since My death on the Cross. My poor beloved servants, many of them are innocent pawns at the mercy of a dark power, which is careful not to reveal itself.

I ask all My servants to pray hard in order to withstand the abomination, which is on the way. They must pray to Me as follows:

"O My beloved Jesus I invoke your protection and ask for Your Mercy to save my brothers and sisters within Your Church from falling victim to the antichrist. Give me the graces and protect me with Your armour of strength to stand up to the evil acts, which may be perpetrated in Your Holy Name. I beg for Your Mercy and pledge my allegiance to Your Holy Name at all times."

Stand up My sacred servants to this evil and the beast from whose mouth these obscenities and lies will spring.

Watch out for changes in the way My Body and Blood will be consecrated. If the words change which deny the existence of My Body in the Holy Eucharist then you must defend My Divine promise. He who eats My Body and drinks My Blood will have eternal life.

Be brave My sacred servants. Pray for the strength you will need as your faith and obedience will be tested beyond endurance.

I love you and protect you at all times. Only those of you meek of heart and humble of soul will benefit from My Holy Protection.

Pray for all My sacred servants everywhere so that they will not reject the Light of Truth in favour of the spirit of darkness, which is about to emerge within My Church

Your Saviour and Protector

Jesus Christ

Virgin Mary: Open your hearts to the Truth

Saturday, October 29, 2011 16.49 hours

My child you must pray for my protection at all times. You are being guided and you must place all your trust in my beloved Son.

Pray for conversion everywhere. So many lost souls are in need of your prayers. Never forget this no matter how difficult this journey is for you.

The spirit of the evil one is covering much of mankind in a way that has not happened before. The deceiver's actions are intensifying and smothering my children everywhere.

Even those who profess their allegiance to my beloved Son are turning a deaf ear to His pleas to save souls. So arrogant have they become because of pride they forget that My Son's Holy Word is the only life they need. Prayer is vital at this time. Those who exalt themselves in the eyes of others, as they proclaim the Word of my precious Son, yet deny His Call, have hardened their hearts to the Truth.

Children you must hear my Son, Jesus Christ, now. Listen to what He is telling you. The Holy Spirit, if you allow Him, will open your hearts to the Truth as He speaks to you through these Holy Messages.

I weep with sorrow when I see how His Holy Word is rejected today. For those who condemn Him you must realize that He comes now not only to save you. He comes also to comfort you in these days of darkness. If you truly believe He is the Bread of Life then allow Him to awaken your spirit of love.

Pray for conversion everywhere. There is not much time.

Your beloved Mother

Mary Queen of Heaven and Earth

Disbelief of those who profess to know Me, which wounds Me the most

Monday, October 31, 2011 03.30 hours

My dearly beloved daughter My Holy Word, which is being given to a world, oblivious of My existence, will ignite souls soon after The Warning takes place.

At last mankind will hear My Word to enable Me to guide them to My New Era of Peace on earth. I call on all My children everywhere to drop down your gauntlet and hear your Saviour speak.

While I will never reveal to you the date of My Coming back to earth I can tell you that I will return in Spirit now. I come now to save you once again during The Warning so that man will convert. Please allow Me to guide you and allow My Most Sacred Mission to be spread around the world to bring My children comfort. Do not block Me out. Do not reject My Hand of Mercy. Do not allow your pride to stand in the way.

Wake up and accept that I now speak with you so I can bring you into the bosom of My Great Mercy. At last your soul will alight with the Fires of My Divine Graces, which will be poured out all over you.

All doubts will be gone. Satan's power will dilute rapidly although he will not relinquish his grip until the very end.

While you ponder My pleas you must ask yourself this. If you believe in Me why do you reject me now? Why do you show anger and hatred to those who come in My Name? Why do you exalt yourselves in My Church at the expense of My children. Remember that you are all equal in My eyes.

Come to Me now with humble hearts. Because until you do this, you cannot benefit from My Mercy or receive the graces I long to provide you with.

My Voice is calling out now to all non-believers to accept the existence of My Eternal Father.

After The Warning allow Me to help you on the path to eternal life. My Heart aches when I witness lost souls. But know this. It is the disbelief of those who profess to know Me, which wounds Me the most.

Your Loving Saviour Jesus

Virgin Mary: Time for my Son to deliver His Gift of Divine Mercy

Wednesday, November 02, 2011 10.40 hours

My child the time for my Son to deliver His Gift of Divine Mercy is drawing close. As such you must concentrate on your Mission to save souls. You must not allow distractions, which take your eye off the most important task of spreading conversion.

The Heavens rejoice as this Divine Gift will soon be presented with the Pure Love that my Son holds in His Heart for all souls. My child, as this work escalates in its intensity the evil one will continue to torment you through different people at every opportunity. You have been instructed to keep silent and focus only on my Son.

You, my child, are the appointed one to convey in great detail the desire of my Son to speak with mankind in these times. Be brave and courageous for this Holy Mission will succeed. It has been foretold so very long ago and you have been accorded every kind of direction from the heavens. The saints all guide you for they have been gathered in full force to ensure that this Mission will not fail. Nor can it. You must stop worrying when things seem hopeless for that is the deceit you will be confronted with through the work of the deceiver.

I, your beloved Mother work with you all the time. It was through me that you were prepared to come before my Precious Son. The graces granted were to enable your soul to be purified so that you were fit to work for the Saviour of mankind.

It was through my precious Son that you have been brought before the Blessed Trinity. This is one of the most important Missions since my Son was sent to redeem the world from sin.

Never allow yourself to deviate from this Mission. Nor must you give in to the temptation to walk away. Pray to me, your Mother, at all times for protection.
Your beloved Mother

Queen of Heaven

Mother of Mercy

Weather will begin to show strange signs
Wednesday, November 02, 2011 19.40 hours

My dearly beloved daughter the weather will begin to show strange signs as the earth moves to a new state in preparation for My Act of Divine Mercy as I come to save you all once more.

Hatred is intensifying in every nation. Discontent is felt everywhere. Love of one another is weak while love of self becomes not only tolerated but is deemed essential in order to be accepted in today's world.

I will wipe out hatred. I will stamp on man's plans to inflict terror on his brother. I will wipe out the arrogance in your souls. All sin will be revealed to you as it appears in its raw ugliness in My Eyes.

Why must so many kind hearted souls turn their backs today on My Teachings of old? Why now? What it is about love of God the Father that becomes shameful in their eyes? I will tell you. It is because so many of My children have been side tracked by the pleasures of the world. Although many of the material goods they seek out are now beyond their grasp they still reject Me. The souls of mankind have been clouded with a darkness so thick that it will take time for My Light to shine through and penetrate their souls.

How I cry tears of bitter sadness for these lost souls who are desperate for the peace of salvation they crave. They just don't realize that only I can bring this peace into their weary hearts.

O how My Love has been long forgotten. I am but a fragment in their minds of no real consequence. They want peace of mind and heart but they will not ask Me for this. It is only when they ask that I can respond. Don't they know this?

For those of you who do love Me but who hate or resent your brother you too need My help. I do not want your loyalty if you don't treat others with kindness. When you hurt your brothers and sisters for whatever reason, you hurt Me. No matter how you justify your actions know this. I feel the pain of those you abuse. When you hurt Me like this you cannot show Me true love from the heart.

Learn from this. Seek humility in all things before you come before Me to swear allegiance to My Holy Will. In this way you will be pure of soul and fit to enter My Kingdom.

You, My children, are very fortunate because millions of you will become part of My New Paradise. This is because of the times you are living in. So many of you in the world today children can now be saved in a way that previous generations could not have been.

Welcome this news and use this opportunity to accept My Divine Mercy with open and contrite hearts while you can.

Your Saviour

Jesus Christ

My messengers are now with you to prepare your souls

Thursday, November 03, 2011 21.00 hours

My beloved daughter prophecies foretold will begin to be made known and witnessed throughout the world so that no one will be able to ignore them.

So many of My children are unaware of the contents contained in My Father's Book, the Most Holy Bible. Little regard is paid to the Book of John where details of the End Times are given to all the world. This time has now come. Prepare all of you.

The Truth contained in the Book of Revelation is just that - the Truth. Can you recognize the signs? Turmoil in the world will continue to escalate at a ferocious pace. Your monetary system is being threatened by a global group, who want not only your money but who want to steal your souls.

The wickedness of man is evident but much of it is hidden. My messengers are now with you children to help prepare your souls. Whether or not you recognize them for who they are, the Holy Spirit, which reigns in their souls will spread conversion.

Those who denounce My attempts to communicate with you will understand the Truth very shortly. It will be then that My children will unite against this wicked force led by Satan. They will not win. Every obstacle is being placed before them by the Hand of My Eternal Father. His Mercy is so great that He will use His power to defend His children and He will destroy those who insist on following the path of the deceiver.

Whatever your various views as to whether or not I speak with you now it will not matter. It is your faith in Me and My beloved Father, God the Most High, which will count in the end.

Prayer is most urgent children wherever you are, whatever your religion, whatever your views. Join together and pray to the Holy Spirit for enlightenment at this time. Satan is trying to turn your backs on me, your beloved Saviour. Do not listen to the doubts and the fear he places in your hearts. He will use lies to prevent me from flooding your souls with My Divine Light. My Love is so strong for you children that no matter how you ignore Me or turn your backs I will continue to call you. I will do this through the Power of the Holy Spirit. You must pray for this gift by saying:

"O Jesus cover me with Your Precious Blood and fill me with the Holy Spirit so that I can discern whether these Words come from you. Humble me in spirit. Receive my pleas with Mercy and open my heart to the Truth."

I will respond to the most hardened of souls when they recite this prayer.

Allow me the chance to bring you towards Me so I can unite as many of My children as possible before The Great Warning.

Remember My Love for you will never extinguish no matter how much you turn a deaf ear to My urgent call for unity.

Your Beloved Saviour

Jesus Christ

Global Group who destroyed your banking system will fall apart

Friday, November 04, 2011 19.00 hours

My dearest daughter from Me comes True Life, the only life that man will ever need from here to eternity.

Children you must know that this terrible turmoil you are seeing all around you will not last long.

God, My Eternal Father, will not allow His precious children to suffer much more. You, My children are the victims of the work of the Deceiver. He who controls the Global Group is weakening. His powers are being scuppered through the Power of My Father. This group who deliberately destroyed your banking systems to make beggars out of you will fall apart. You must not worry because the Hand of My Father will fall on their wicked ways.

Pray that all those deluded souls who slavishly abide by the wickedness, which is at the very heart of this group will convert during The Warning.

You must never give up hope children. It will be through your love of God the Most High that you will return to the fold of your family. The Blessed Trinity is your home, children. Those of you who accept this fact, brought about through conversion, will inherit the glorious Era of Paradise on earth.

Trust in Me always. Offer your worries, troubles and fears to Me. Allow Me to ease your pain and suffering. It will not be too long now when the world will find relief from the painful birth pangs you endure in these times.

Never lose hope. Trust in Me. Pray for My Graces to make you stronger. Lay your head on My Shoulders and allow My Peace to envelop your souls. Only then will you understand the Truth of My Glorious promise of eternal life.

Your Jesus

Saviour of Mankind

God The Father - Last Call to Atheists

Saturday, November 05, 2011 13.00 hours

My daughter mankind will now be shown the Hand of My Mercy as the arrival of My Son becomes imminent.

To all those tortured souls in disarray I say to you put your trust in Me, God the Father. I who created every one of you with love and compassion want to save every precious child of Mine.

I do not want to lose one of you including those who sneer at Me. Prepare for the Greatest Gift, which is being prepared for you. I will prevent Satan from snatching you if you will allow Me. I cannot force you to accept this Act of Mercy. What saddens Me is that many of you will reject this Hand of My Mercy. You will not be strong enough. Yet when you witness the Truth as it will be revealed to you during The Warning you will attempt to grasp it like a lifeline.

You must ask Me for the strength to allow Me to save you from eternal damnation. I call on atheists especially one last time. Do not reject the Truth when it is proven to you. If you do you are lost to Me forever.

God the Father

Demonic Possession and the sin of Hatred
Sunday, November 06, 2011 18.30 hours

My dearly beloved daughter people do not understand that I relive My Crucifixion daily. The pain and suffering I endure is caused by the sins committed by people every second of the day. I endure moments of deep sorrow when I see those souls who offend Me greatly through the sin of hatred.

Hatred is instilled in the hearts of many and comes about due to the infestation of Satan. Many people talk about demonic possession as if it is easy to identify. So many of My children are possessed by Satan. They do not have to be seen thrashing about for a demonic presence to be in place.

He, the enemy of mankind, uses his demons to attack My children. For those who are in darkness they become easy prey because they attract the evil presence.

Once possessed children it is very difficult to drag yourself away. These unfortunate children will, through the cunning and manipulative infestation of the Evil One then infect other souls. And so it continues.

Evil is usually presented as being good. It will be hard to discern except for this. The behaviour and deeds of an infested soul will never be humble in nature. They will never be generous of heart. They may seem generous but there will always be a catch. This catch will always be about making demands on you, which do not sit comfortably.

Keep away from such souls. Pray for them. Do not allow them suck you into sin. Be alert always to the deceiver because he is everywhere in these times.

Always pray to keep such evil at bay. Prayer will weaken his grasp and his strength as well as protect you.

Think of Satan and his evil works as an infectious disease. Take every precaution to avoid coming into contact with those who carry the disease. Should you know that you have no choice, then arm yourself with Holy Water, the Blessed Crucifix and a St Benedictine Medal. They will keep these demons at arm's length.

These are the times children you must surround you and your home with objects, which are blessed. Many are embarrassed to be seen with such things for fear they will be laughed at. These will offer you protection in your home and are a great comfort during prayer. [242.9]

Remember the demon lives not just in Hell but has now firmly established his reign on earth. Prayer is the only thing that terrifies him and renders him impotent.

Prayer will sustain you children in the times ahead.

Your Loving Saviour

Jesus Christ

You will be hated in many quarters and feared in others

Monday, November 07, 2011 20.50 hours

My beloved daughter you must listen. As My prophecies unfold and when My Holy Word will begin to be accepted and listened to you must be careful. You, My daughter, will be hated in many quarters and feared in others.

My prophecies which will be given to you are to ensure that there will be no doubt in the minds of all My children that the promise of eternal salvation will at last be realized.

My daughter you will feel isolated, rejected, feared and will suffer harshly in My Name.

Without your sacrifice I could not fulfil My promise to save mankind so that every soul is accorded the opportunity to benefit from their rightful inheritance.

I call on My sacred servants to protect you My daughter for it will be their holy duty. In time they will understand what their role is. Meanwhile I call on all My precious followers to pray for your protection against the evil forces, which are led by Satan who want to destroy the world for their own gain.

Be strong. Pray for protection and involve the help of My Blessed Mother at all times.

Your Jesus

Saviour and Redeemer of Mankind

Many will suffer the pain of Purgatory as a Penance
Wednesday, November 09, 2011 15.32 hours

Hear My urgent plea children to Consecrate yourselves to the immaculate Heart of My dearly beloved Mother at this time.

She, the Mediatrix of All Graces, has been assigned to bring you to My Sacred Heart in order to save mankind from the ruination that awaits them should they fail to detach themselves from the works of Satan.

It is now urgent that all of you pray hard for the salvation of souls. All souls will come before Me and for many it will be difficult for them. Many will suffer the pain of Purgatory but it will be their only route to eternal salvation. Far better to understand what this is like while alive on this earth than to experience this after death. When they endure this penance these souls will be purified and fit to enter My New Paradise on earth. Only pure souls will be able to enter. I must urge you to accept this gift and face it with strength of mind, body, and soul. But know it and recognize it for what it is, a route to eternal life, a chance to understand My Divine Mercy.

It is time to prepare your souls now. When you have sought redemption for your sins before The Warning, you must pray for the others. They will need to be strong.

Pray My Divine Mercy Prayer every single day from now on, all of you. It will help save those poor souls who may die, from shock, during this supernatural event. This will now be presented to the world shortly.

Never lose hope children. Believe Me when I tell you that I love you. I bring you this Gift out of this Love.

Your Loving Saviour

Two thieves on the Cross

Thursday, November 10, 2011 15.30 hours

My dearly beloved daughter when I was dying on the Cross two thieves were close by, they too being crucified at the same time.

One asked Me to forgive him his sins and was saved. The other did not. Instead he turned a deaf ear. His stubbornness and refusal to ask for My Mercy meant that he could not be saved.

The same will happen during The Warning. Some of My children will acknowledge their sins and accept that they have offended Me. They, in all humility, will accept their penance and will be saved. They will enter the New Paradise in the forthcoming Era of Peace.

Then there will be those who will not accept their sins for what they are, an abomination in the Eyes of God, the Eternal Father.

I will give these souls plenty of time to repent such is the depth of My Mercy. Pray that they will seek redemption in order that they too can be saved. I want all My children to embrace My Great Gift of Mercy. I want all of you to enter the Gates of the New Paradise.

Pray that hardened souls will soften and accept My Hand. Pray that they will learn how to become humble in My Eyes.

Yours Jesus

Redeemer of Mankind

Signs will appear in the sky first - the sun will spin

Friday, November 11, 2011 16.00 hours

Prayer and much of it is needed to help save souls now. You, My daughter, must prepare your family and tell those in need of My Great Mercy to be ready.

Once again the signs will appear first. Many people will sit up and take heed when they see the changes in the skies. They will witness the sun spin like never before. Then they will see the Cross. This will happen immediately before the stars clash in the skies and when My Rays of Divine Mercy will cover the earth.

Silence will ensue so that each soul will be in a state of absolute privacy when they come before Me. Tell My children what to watch out for because they must not be afraid. This is not an event to fear. Instead you must all welcome this encounter.

All My children must accept that it is I who now comes before them. They must not think that this is the end of the world. For it is not. It is the beginning of a new period in time when all of My children will know the Truth at last.

I rejoice and feel a great tenderness towards every single soul who can be redeemed if they allow me to give them this Gift.

Pray, pray, pray for all souls now and in particular for those who will be so fearful that they may not be strong enough to accept My Hand of Mercy.

Yours Saviour

Jesus Christ

Your moment of glory before My eyes - your moment of salvation

Saturday, November 12, 2011 16.00 hours

My dearly beloved daughter separation from Me is painful especially for those who know Me.

Once souls glimpse the Love I have for them they then find the pain of separation hard to bear. This is even more pronounced when souls who profess to love Me who, because of sin, find themselves in Purgatory after death.

While all souls in Purgatory go to Heaven eventually, the pain of being separated from Me is painful and distressing.

For many souls who believe in God the very mention of Hell brings torment into their hearts. Then for those who find that their souls need to be purified in the State of Purgatory they also feel a wretchedness that is difficult to understand by those alive today.

Children your time on earth is so important because it is during this period that you should strive to purify your souls through fasting and penance. Use this time while you can to save your souls. To do this you must seek humility at all times to ensure that you become little in My eyes. Only the little can pass through the narrowest gates of Paradise.

Welcome, therefore, the Gift of Purgatory presented to you during The Warning when you must be purified as penance for your sins. You will not have to wait children for death to face this purification. You are blessed children for no scar of sin will remain on your souls. Then you can gain immediate access to the New Era of Peace I speak about. This is where all My children who seek forgiveness for their sins during The Warning will be taken.

Open your hearts and welcome Me when I come to you during the forthcoming Warning when you will be able to embrace Me. Allow Me to hold you and to forgive you your sins so you will become Mine in body, mind and soul finally and with the total abandonment that I need from you.

This will be your moment of Glory before My eyes. Then you will be ready for the second stage when you will be able to join your brothers and sisters in the New Paradise on earth, as it was Created in the beginning by God the Creator of all things.

This will become your new and rightful home for 1,000 years. Await My arrival with love, hope and joy. There is nothing to fear. Rejoice. I come once again to save you from the enemy of mankind. This time his power is so weak that it will be difficult for him to snatch the souls of those who welcome Me with open arms during The Warning.

Your Jesus

Redeemer of Mankind

Pray, relax and rejoice for this time is short now
Sunday, November 13, 2011 19.00 hours

My dearly beloved daughter sometimes My Messages confuse you. But this is okay. My ways and those Divine plans orchestrated by My Eternal Father are not easy to understand.

Keep your thoughts on Me. Focus only on prayer and especially those prayers, which will help save hardened sinners from the fires of Hell.

Spend this period of time in quiet contemplation and simple prayer. This is all any of My children need to concentrate on. They must aim to bring their families and friends to Me in preparation for My arrival.

Pray, pray, pray, My Divine Chaplet to secure salvation for those souls so infested by evil that their only salvation will be through your prayers.

Do not try to explain these times to your children for they will not understand. For many it could cause unnecessary fear.

Again I say to all My precious children I am coming to save you. Remember this. Were I not to come at this time you would slip away from Me because of the powers of the force of evil so prevalent in your world.

I am your salvation. Your escape from the horrors you are witnessing in your world caused by satanic influence every way you look. Children you must trust in My Love for you. Don't you know that I would not allow you all to continue to endure this wickedness.

For all of you, My children, I promise you this. You will enjoy the New Era of Paradise as My chosen children. But it will be up to every man, woman and child over the age of reason to decide whether they want to join together as one to enjoy this glorious existence.

Pray, relax and rejoice for this time is short now.

Sing in praise of My Eternal Father for the glory He will bestow on all of those who accept My Hand of Mercy.

Your beloved Jesus

Saviour of mankind

My Word is not rejected out of fear but because of sin of pride

Monday, November 14, 2011 20.15 hours

My dearly beloved daughter why is that people complicate My Teachings? So many of My children misunderstand and underestimate My Great Mercy. Despite the number of times I promise My children forgiveness for their sins they are still afraid that I cannot forgive all sin, no matter how grievous the sin.

Evil in the world is caused by the hatred that Satan has for mankind. Those poor deluded sinners who slavishly follow the path of deceit are My beloved children. I love each of them and I will continue to love them despite their darkness of soul. My Love is ever lasting and will never die when it comes to all souls. I am ready to completely forgive and embrace all. I am prepared to do everything to bring all sinners back into My fold no matter how they offend Me.

Satan will be stopped from stealing such souls, but, it will only be when the shield of pride, is discarded by sinners, that they can turn to Me and become part of My cherished family again. Do not misunderstand. I can only bring souls closer to Me. I cannot force them to love Me. I cannot force them to want to enter My Kingdom of Paradise. They will have to accept My Hand of Reconciliation first through their own free will.

I am as I have told you My daughter time and time again a God of Mercy first. My Justice will materialize but only when every exhaustive measure has been taken to save every single soul on earth.

My daughter this work was never going to be easy for you. Because I have given you this holy task of such magnitude it will require tremendous strength on your part. You are made to be strong. You have been trained for this work since you came from your mother's womb. All your responses to My Most Holy instructions have been according to My Divine plan for humanity. It is because you are in union with me (have you forgotten this?) that you will suffer the same rejection that I had to endure during My time on earth. This same rejection by those who boast of their intellectual knowledge of My Teachings in order to reject these Messages of Mine witnessed by you in the world today. Those souls stuffed with pride and their self proclaimed knowledge of Holy Scripture fail to understand this.

My Teachings are very simple. Add in all the fine language and prose you like, the Truth remains as it always has been. Love one another as I love you. It will be only when you show respect for each other and love one another that you can truly proclaim My Word.

So much confusion exists My daughter. So much terror and fear instilled in My children about their future. If only souls would calm down and pray for Mercy then their prayers would be answered. Disasters will and can be mitigated. Keep hope alive in your souls children. Never get bogged down with judging each other and certainly never do this in My Name.

Who dares to judge another through ridicule, in the name of Christianity, will have to face Me. He who sins against My prophets will also have to answer to Me. My Word is not rejected out of love. My Word is not rejected out of fear. No it is rejected because of the sin of pride.

Your Saviour

Jesus Christ

Part 6.

First Volume

Messages 250 - 299

Tuesday, November 15, 2011 to Wednesday, January 04, 2012

God the Father asks His children to unite in Prayer
Tuesday, November 15, 2011 11.00 hours

I come today My daughter to gather My precious children and all those who believe in Me together, to pray in union to save all souls on earth.

It is My desire that you prove your infinite love for the Blessed Trinity by showing humility in love for one another so that sin can be forgiven for the whole of mankind.

I am the God of Justice but am first and foremost the God of Love and Mercy. My Fatherly Divine Love for you is reflected in My Merciful Goodness. As such it is My intention to salvage all souls at this, the end of times, as you know it on earth. Do not fear children. My intention is not to frighten but to embrace you in all My encompassing Love for every child of mine.

I call on all My children especially those souls so full of love for Me, their Creator, to join with your brothers and sisters and rise against the evil in the world.

Satan and every demon in Hell now roam the earth in defiance of Me during these, the end of times, Children. They are scattered throughout the world persecuting souls and driving them to the brink of madness.

The evil influence is being felt by almost every one of you at this time. It is because My existence and that of My beloved Son have been denied, rejected and thrown to one side that darkness now covers your world. Without acknowledging the truth of your creation on this earth you, My beloved children, have become unwittingly a target for Satan.

You will notice a number of changes in your life since this infestation has gripped your world. Murder, hatred, distaste for proclaiming My Glory or acknowledging My Existence, war, persecution, greed, control and moral deterioration. All such wickedness has been created in your world by Satan and spread by sinners so open to his false empty promises.

He, Satan, tempts first those power hungry sinners and those weak of faith. Having seduced them he then possesses them. They, in turn, infect and cause terrible pain by inflicting abuse on their fellow brothers and sisters.

You My beloved faithful, are now being called by Me to stand up and defend My Holy Word so that mankind can be saved. You will do this in two ways. Firstly through constant prayer and, secondly, by spreading My Most Holy Word. Prayer will not only help save mankind from Hell and the complete abandonment by Me but it will also mitigate against My Hand of Chastisement. This Hand of Chastisement will, and be in no doubt about this, fall on those wicked sinners who have allowed the spirit of darkness to control their behaviour towards those innocent dependents over which they exert control.

I, God the Father, call on My children from the Heavens to hear My Plea when I urge you to rise immediately. Join in prayer by reciting the following:

"God the Most High, in the Name of Your beloved Son Jesus Christ, whom You sacrificed to save us your poor children from the fires of Hell hear our prayer. May we offer our humble sacrifices and accept trials and tribulations as a means to gain the salvation of all souls during The Warning.

We plead with You to forgive sinners who find it hard to turn back and accept Your Merciful Goodness to make the necessary sacrifices as You see fit to redeem them in Your Holy Eyes."

By praying to Me, your Heavenly Father, God the Most High, Creator of the Universe and mankind, I will hear your prayer and grant immunity for all those souls you pray for.

Thank you My cherished children for recognizing this My Divine Call from the Heavens. Thank you for your humility of heart to recognize My Voice when it is spoken.

Remember I am an ocean of charity and love you all with a Fatherly tenderness. I strive only to save each and every one of you from the grip of the Evil One so that we can unite as one Holy Family.

God the Eternal Father

Virgin Mary : Pray for Pope Benedict
Wednesday, November 16, 2011 08.00 hours

My child there will be fierce fighting as the battle for souls commences. Pray for all those poor souls who need the protection of my Son's Mercy.

The Evil One will do all he can to turn children away from my Son's Hand of Mercy.

So many of my poor lost souls have no idea of the battle which has already commenced and which is led by the Evil One. His days are short now my child but you must do all you can to help my precious Son to save these people before it is too late.

You, my child, must continue to ask me for protection because you are now becoming a real thorn in the Evil One's side. Be on your guard at every moment. Prayer is important and you must ask others to pray for you.

Pray for Pope Benedict especially now for he too is under attack. Never falter in your work for my Son for you, my child, must endure to the very end in order to fulfil prophecies foretold so long ago.

Remember I cover you with my Holy Mantle at all times.

Your Heavenly Mother

Queen of the Roses

Note: this message was received after a full apparition of the Blessed Mother, which lasted 20 minutes in which she appeared very sad.

Maria Divine Mercy

Preparations are now complete
Wednesday, November 16, 2011 20.30 hours

My dearly beloved daughter, take heed now. Please reassure all My children that faith will ensure their salvation. That is all that matters now.

Love for Me and one another will be your route to Paradise.

If you love each other the way I love you it must be unconditional. You must accept each other's faults. Forgive children. Fighting does not spring from Heaven. It is caused by the deceiver to create disruption.

Rise now and pray, pray, pray for My Great Mercy as time is almost upon you.

Preparations are now complete.

You simply wait now.

Prepare your souls and pray for one another. Just accept My Holy Will My daughter.

Do not ask for explanations. Follow My instructions and show obedience at all times. Do not fall into traps being set for you to encourage you to fall. Satan wants you to fall so he can trample on you but I must again remind you to keep silent. Suffer any indignation with eyes bent downwards in complete humility.

Imitate Me daughter in all you do. Once you do this Satan cannot engage with you successfully.

Go now and wait, for I am coming soon.

Your Loving Jesus

Saviour and Redeemer of all Mankind

Crusade of Prayer (1): My Gift to Jesus to Save Souls

Thursday, November 17, 2011 21.00 hours

My beloved daughter, please ask My children to recite these prayers from now until The Warning. My followers are requested to recite these prayers which I will give you every day to save souls. This is the first prayer:

My Gift to Jesus to Save Souls

My dearest Jesus, You who loves us so much allow me in my humble way to help save Your precious souls. Have Mercy on all sinners no matter how grievously they offend You.

Allow me through prayer and suffering to help those souls who may not survive The Warning to seek a place beside You in Your Kingdom.

Hear my prayer O sweet Jesus to help You win over those souls You yearn for.

O Sacred Heart of Jesus I pledge my allegiance to Your Most Holy Will at all times.

Your Saviour

Jesus Christ

Crusade of Prayer (2): Prayer for Global Rulers
Friday, November 18, 2011 21.00 hours

My dearly beloved daughter today I urge My followers to offer this prayer to save those poor children who are being tormented by the leaders of their own countries who in turn are being dictated to by global forces, not of God.

My Eternal Father, in the Name of Your beloved Son Jesus Christ, I ask that You protect Your children from the persecution, which is being plotted by global forces against innocent nations.

I pray for the forgiveness of sin of those souls who are the cause of this hardship so that they may turn to You with humble and contrite hearts.

Please give Your tortured children the strength to withstand such suffering in atonement for the sins of the world through Christ Our Lord Amen.

Crusade of Prayer (3): Rid the world of fear
Saturday, November 19, 2011 19.00 hours

My dearly beloved daughter I now provide you with the prayer to rid the world of fear:

O My Lord Jesus Christ I beseech You to rid the world of fear which detaches souls from Your Loving Heart. I pray that souls who will experience real fear during The Warning will stop and allow Your Mercy to flood their souls so that they will be free to love You in the way they should.

Your Loving Saviour

Jesus Christ

Crusade of Prayer (4): Unite all Families
Sunday, November 20, 2011 18.00 hours

My daughter this prayer is important for it will help keep families together so that they can remain as one in My New Kingdom of Paradise on earth.

Unite all families Jesus during The Warning so that they may receive eternal salvation. I pray that all families remain together in union with You Jesus so that they may inherit Your New Paradise on Earth.

Your Loving Saviour

Redeemer of Mankind

Jesus Christ

Crusade of Prayer (5): Praise to God the Most High
Monday, November 21, 2011 19.00 hours

My daughter the world must offer this special prayer in praise and thanksgiving to God the Father for the Mercy He is providing the whole world.

"O Eternal Father we offer You our prayers in joyful thanksgiving for Your precious Gift of Mercy to the whole of mankind. We rejoice and offer You most Glorious King our praise and Adoration for Your loving and tender Mercy. You, God the Most High are our King and for this Gift You now bring to us we lie at Your feet in humble servitude. Please God have mercy on all Your children."

Your Jesus

Crusade of Prayer (6): Prayer to stop the antichrist
Tuesday, November 22, 2011

"O Jesus I pray that God in His Mercy will prevent the antichrist and his vile army from causing terror and inflicting hardship on Your children. We pray that he will be stopped and that the hand of chastisement will be avoided through the conversion achieved during The Warning."

Crusade of Prayer (7): Prayer for those who refuse Mercy
Tuesday, November 22, 2011 20.00 hours

My dearly beloved daughter My arrival to save mankind yet again before the Final Judgment is so close. My joy is tinged with deep suffering because of those souls who will reject My Mercy.

You, My daughter must fight along with My army of those beloved children of the Cross to save these souls. This is the prayer they must say to beg for Mercy for souls in darkness.

"Jesus I urge You to forgive those sinners so dark of soul who will refuse the Light of Your Mercy. Forgive them Jesus I plead with You in order to redeem them from the sins, which they find it so difficult to extract themselves from. Flood their hearts with Your Rays of Mercy and allow them the chance to return to Your fold."

Your beloved Jesus

Crusade of Prayer (8): The Confession
Tuesday, November 22, 2011 22.30 hours

I, Jesus your King and Saviour now present My prayer for Confession.

This prayer should be said to plead for clemency for the forgiveness of sin during and after The Warning.

"Dearest Jesus I ask Your pardon for all my sins and for the hurt and injury I have caused to others. I humbly pray for the graces to avoid offending You again and to offer penance according to Your Most Holy Will. I plead for the forgiveness of any future offence which I may partake in and which will cause You pain and suffering. Take me with You into the New Era of Peace so that I may become part of Your family for eternity.

I love You Jesus.

I need You.

I honour You and everything You stand for.

Help me Jesus so that I may be worthy to enter Your Kingdom."

Your Saviour

Jesus Christ

The world will be changed forever
Thursday, November 24, 2011 21.00 hours

My dearly beloved daughter, do not fear for the time is upon you and the whole world.

This journey has been intense for you My daughter during what has been such a short period of time.

You have obeyed My Holy Will right from the start although you had your doubts. Despite being mocked in certain quarters and, in particular, by those who profess to be holy disciples of Mine and that of My beloved Mother, you have never hesitated in imparting My Holy Word to the world. Ignore all this hurt for it has now passed.

Now that I come with My Great Mercy all My children with true faith will fall in humble thanksgiving to welcome Me and accept My Mercy. The truth will now be revealed.

Rise all of you and await with joy My arrival.

The world will be changed forever.

Remember it is because of My deep love for all of you, including those of you who mock My Holy Word or who deny Me that I come to save you once again.

Your Saviour and Redeemer

Jesus Christ

I do not reveal dates

Sunday, November 27, 2011 15.00 hours

My dearly beloved daughter you must keep calm and composed and place all your trust in Me.

The time for The Warning is almost here and you must be patient. Pray My daughter that all of humanity can be saved through My Gift.

Please do not guess dates for I have told you many times that I do not reveal dates.

They are not for your knowing. Be patient. The time for the Warning will be according to My Holy Will.

Place all your trust in Me and leave everything in My Hands.

Your beloved Jesus

Walk by My Side and you will be spit on

Monday, November 28, 2011 20.00 hours

My dearly beloved daughter you must remember that when you serve Me your life will always be a bed of thorns.

Nothing will be easy but know that when you are a chosen soul that it does not come without sacrifice. On this journey you undertake walking by My side you will be spit upon, tripped, mocked, kicked and tormented when you least expect it. All those who openly proclaim My Word will also suffer the same indignities.

However it will not be until you accept these humiliations and trials, as being part of the cross you carry when you chose to work for Me, that you will mature towards the spiritual perfection expected of you.

Accept, My daughter the humiliations, pain and suffering thrown your way. Surely by now you and all My beloved soldiers who accept My Most Sacred Instructions through these Messages must know that it is I who walks by your side.

Your beloved Saviour

Jesus Christ

Virgin Mary: My gift to defeat and destroy the serpent
Tuesday, November 29, 2011 21.00 hours

My child tell all those followers of my beloved Son Jesus Christ that they must seek my protection at all times. Satan's days are drawing swiftly to an end and many children are vulnerable to his temptations.

By asking me for protection and my special graces Satan will not harm my children or draw them away from my Son.

Everyone is a target of Satan today as he roams everywhere seeking the ruination of souls. His attacks are most vicious when you are a devout follower of God and when you have a strong faith. His hatred for such souls will cause them pain and confusion.

He, the deceiver, only has one goal and that is to seduce all souls in order that they will follow him so that he can destroy their chances of eternal salvation.

Pray every moment you can spare for my protection against the evil one. I have been accorded the great gift by my Heavenly Father to defeat and destroy the serpent.

When you turn to me for help I will always help you turn back to my Son for the solace you so desperately seek and which will soothe your soul.

Pray, pray, pray and recite my Holy Rosary for it is the most powerful weapon to keep Satan away from destroying your life.

Thank you for responding to my call my child for I needed to remind you of the urgency of seeking my help because you are under ferocious attack at this stage in your Mission.

Go in peace.

Your Heavenly Mother

Mary Queen of Heaven

I will save you from the horrors of your world

Wednesday, November 30, 2011 15.30 hours

My dearly beloved daughter those so anxious to prove their love for Me very often find despair in their souls which leaves them feeling empty of My love. This can be so unexpected that it can leave the soul in such a state of abandonment that it feels as if it will never recover from the feelings of helplessness and lack of faith.

Do not fear children. Abandonment is something you will feel when you are close to Me. I felt the same abandonment while on earth by My beloved Father. I felt lost and lonely as I tried to communicate with Him many times. This is a tough trial that you will suffer when you are a true believer in God. It is Satan's way of pulling you away so that after a while he hopes you will give up your search for Me and fall back into worldly ways, which will delight but fail to satisfy.

Don't you know that prayer will prevent this from happening? Don't you realize that I allow this for your own good and as part of your training to gain a spiritual strength that is only achieved through this abandonment?

The Ways of My Father are difficult for you children to understand. Just trust in Me, your Jesus, and call to Me to give you the graces you need to fight with Me to save your brothers and sisters. They must be saved from the wicked plans being orchestrated in your world by those powers seeking to control you through the very things you need to survive.

Remember children I am so close to all My followers that when The Warning takes place My army will immediately surge to become a powerful adversary of Satan.

Hope children must never be lost. I will save you from the horrors of your world, which is in total disarray caused by the lack of belief in My Eternal Father.

All this is about to change when the world will witness the proof it needs to accept the existence of God the Father.

Your Jesus

Saviour of Mankind

Terrible War being orchestrated

Thursday, December 01, 2011 12.00 hours

My daughter a great chastisement will befall the world in order to protect the innocent.

A great evil atrocity, which could create a terrible World War is being orchestrated.

The Hand of My Father will fall and punish those souls ensnared by Satan. They will not be allowed bring their wicked plan to fruition.

Few of you children in the world know what is really happening.

So careful are these groups that what you see enfolding before you when nation attacks nation is not quite as it seems.

There is a deliberate attempt being made to create a war to kill millions.

My Father cannot stand back. He must intervene.

Pray, pray and pray children for the salvation of souls.

Your beloved Saviour

Jesus Christ

Virgin Mary: "Chastisement to take place"
Thursday, December 01, 2011 23.00 hours

This message was received after an apparition, which lasted 30 minutes during which the Blessed Virgin Mary cried continuously much to the distress of the visionary Maria Divine Mercy who said it was heart breaking to witness.

My child my sorrow at the wickedness so evident in the world breaks my Heart when I see those lost souls plunging deeper into the abyss of darkness out of which there is no return.

Satan taunts now my children as he swiftly steals the souls of those who have no love for God in their hearts. It is frightening my child that those same souls have no idea what they are facing after death.

My tears of sadness flow in an unending river of sorrow as I watch also the sheer torment and suffering which my Son is enduring right now.

The Hand of my Heavenly Father is ready to fall in chastisement now in certain parts of the world. Those nations planning a terrible atrocity to kill nations will be punished severely. I cannot hold back the Hand of my Father such is the breadth of His Anger.

Pray for those who face this severe punishment. Pray for their souls. Their actions must be stopped or they will wipe out the lives of millions of my poor children. Their evil actions cannot be allowed yet they will aim to cause terrible destruction on those other nations they see as being their enemies.

Pray, pray, pray before the chastisement to ease the suffering of the innocents.

Your beloved Mother

Queen of Sorrows

My Mercy covers all races, colours, religions

Friday, December 02, 2011 23.35 hours

My dear daughter keep strong and think of the Good News in that My Mercy will bring most of My cherished children back into the bosom of My Sacred Heart.

Those poor unfortunate souls who have pledged their lives to wickedness need your suffering so that they can be saved. While this is extremely difficult to understand and from a human point of view, very hard to take in you must trust Me. Your own suffering and that of My devoted followers goes towards the salvation of souls. None of it is wasted. This sacrifice is a gift to Me. Remember suffering also eases My burden.

Weary from My own suffering My daughter I look forward to embracing My children finally as one with My Eternal Father.

Think of it like this. When any loved member of a family emigrates and returns home after many years how much excitement there is, how much rejoicing. Think of the longing a parent has for a son or daughter they have not seen for many years and how much the reunion means.

I love all of you children with an abiding passion. I am looking forward to our reunion when I can embrace each one of you tightly in My Arms and hold you close to My Heart. My family is ready to reunite at last for the first time since Paradise was created for Adam and Eve.

I pour out My Love and Mercy so that it covers all My children in every corner of the world covering all races, all colours, all religions and all sinners.

Await this great moment in time. Finally the wretched hatred, suffering, unease, mistrust, greed, violence and other evil will disappear for good. Imagine what this will be like children, a new wonderful Era of Love and Peace in the world.

Let no one miss this Life of Eternal Happiness. Would you wish for any of your brothers or sisters not to be included. For if they weren't they would suffer eternal darkness in the fires of Hell for eternity. Remember that children. Eternity. There can be no going back after then.

Pray that all souls can inherit this Paradise. Pray for those souls you are personally concerned for. Pray for all souls.

Your Jesus

Saviour & Redeemer of all Mankind

Prophets to prepare for My Second Coming

Saturday, December 03, 2011 20.45 hours

My dearest beloved daughter it is with great dismay that I watch those followers of mine who reject My Most Holy Word through these Messages. How this saddens Me.

I ask My children everywhere to pray for those who reject God in their lives. However I also urge prayer for those followers of Mine who have ignored or forgotten that My Second Coming will happen and that it cannot be stopped. This is an important event and all of you must be prepared for it.

Prophets were sent into the world to herald My birth. Prophets were sent also by My Father to prepare souls for salvation right from the beginning. Prophets are now being sent into the world to prepare mankind for My Second Coming.

Wake up all of you who profess to know Me. If you know Me then recognize My Voice when I call out to your hearts. So many not only reject these Messages but reject Me too.

Let those who so quickly condemn Me, by denying My pleas given to the whole world through these Messages understand this.

By turning your back stubbornly on My Word given to you now you are denying Me the prayers I so badly need from you at this time. You, of all people, who profess to know Me hear what I have to say to you.

Your cruelty pierces My Heart. Your lack of generosity means that your prayers are not being offered as they should be for the salvation of souls.

Where is your humility and why do you disguise your distaste for My Holy Word with a false humility?

You must invoke My Holy Spirit to guide you to Me so that you will work for Me with complete love in your hearts.

Never be boastful of your knowledge of Scriptures. Never use your knowledge of My Teachings to humiliate another. Never slander, abuse, look down on others or mock them in My Name. For when you do this you offend Me greatly.

Wake up children. Prepare your souls and be generous of spirit for the time is short now.

Your beloved Saviour

Time for My Second Coming is almost here
Monday, December 05, 2011 15.15 hours

My dearest daughter preparations for My Warning to prepare mankind are complete.

I want to thank My precious followers who have, through their love for Me, helped save so many millions of souls.

The time for My Second Coming is almost upon the world. So many however are still not prepared but My Mercy will protect them.

My arrival will be a glorious event and men, women and children will drop down on their knees in joy, wonder and with love in their hearts for Me their Divine Saviour.

Many will experience sheer relief for man could not survive the torment which is being inflicted on him by Satan and his millions of dark angels who are hidden in every part of the world and who are causing terrible pain.

They, Satan's demons so ignored by many of My children because they simply don't believe they exist are causing desperate unhappiness in the world.

They create hatred between men, envy, jealousy and a desire to kill. They do not have much time left children because I, Your Saviour, will return soon as promised.

Pray all of you to save all souls in the world so that they too are ready for the New Paradise on earth.

Your Saviour

Jesus Christ

Call on non-believers to turn

Wednesday, December 07, 2011 04.00 hours

My dearest beloved daughter today I wish to call on all those non-believers and those weak of faith. In particular I call out to those so submerged in the ways of materialism and those living in a cocoon of riches with no time for their spiritual wellbeing.

You, My children, worry me the most for you are so far removed from Me. Yet I love you deeply and hope that when The Warning takes place that you will respond to My call instantly.

How I yearn for you children to know Me and understand how your worldly possessions have placed a veil of armour, which blocks you from the Light of the Truth.

It will be for you that the greatest sacrifices of suffering will be made by My victim souls.

Please open your minds and draw towards Me so I can take you and all those close to you with Me and the rest of mankind into the New Paradise.

Your beloved Jesus

Redeemer and Saviour of all Mankind

Virgin Mary: "I experienced the same suffering"
Thursday, December 08, 2011 21.10 hours

My child when I gave birth to Jesus Christ the Redeemer of all mankind I was like any mother. My love for this child was so overwhelming I cried tears of great joy when I first saw His beautiful Face. Yet I knew that the role I had accepted would not be easy although I never realized, at the time, how difficult this journey would be.

When I looked into the precious Face of my cherished Child nothing mattered only my desire to protect Him at all times whatever the cost.

My Heart was conjoined with that of my Son then as it is today. This same Heart suffered in union with Him through every moment of His life on earth.

Every joy He felt I, too, could feel. His laughter brought a smile to my face. His sorrow pained me deeply.

His torture during His Crucifixion was felt in every bone in my body. Every nail, which pierced His flesh pierced mine. For every punch and kick He received at the hands of His persecutors I felt also.

I experienced the same suffering yet I was not present for much of the torture inflicted on Him, which was hidden from me and His disciples.

Today I suffer with my Son just as it was then, when He is mocked in the world today and ridiculed in public, on the stage and in the media, especially by atheists, I cry tears of bitterness.

When I see my precious Son weeping at the sins He witnesses every day I too weep with Him. I see, feel and witness His ongoing suffering for mankind.

Jesus Christ, the Saviour of Mankind has suffered for all of you but loves all of you very much.

I will do everything I can to fulfil His dearest wish to save every single soul on earth from the clutches of the evil one.

When this Mission has succeeded then, and only then, can I rejoice in final peace when my children reunite as one in the New Paradise.

Pray my child that all those who pray for the salvation of souls that not one soul is excluded.

Go in peace and continue this most important Mission for my beloved Son.

I will protect you at all times.

Your beloved Mother

Queen of Heaven

This message was received after Mass and immediately after a private apparition in front of her statue, which lasted 20 minutes in which the Virgin Mary remained solemn with her veil blowing.

Attempts to introduce World Currency in Europe
Friday, December 09, 2011 22.00 hours

My dearly beloved daughter how I wish My children, especially those suffering in Europe under the oppression would just turn to My Father for help.

The evil group I have referred to time and time again are now moving closer in their attempts to control all My poor children in this part of the world.

They, innocent pawns in a ruthless plan to introduce a World Currency in order to control the whole of Europe, must pray hard now for help from God the Almighty Father.

Never give in children to the persecution, which is being perpetrated behind closed doors. Pray to mitigate these circumstances. Call on God the Father, in My Name His beloved Son Jesus Christ, to avert this crisis and say:

"God the Father, in the Name of Your beloved Son Jesus Christ I beg of You to stop this abomination to control Your children. Please protect all Your children in these terrible times so that we may find peace and dignity to live our lives free from the Evil One."

My daughter prayer can and will bring these sinister plans to an end.

God the Eternal Father will, as I have said, chastise those responsible for this evil plot should they not turn back to the belief in their Almighty Creator.

Trust in Me. Trust in My Eternal Father and pray that this persecution be halted before the real plan to destroy, control and damage these souls is eventually revealed.

Your beloved Saviour

Jesus Christ

Transition into New Paradise will be swift and without suffering

Sunday, December 11, 2011 12.45 hours

I come to you today with great joy in My Sacred Heart as your spouse. You, My daughter have accepted this Most Sacred request to join Me to save souls.

It will be through your humble obedience that much will be expected of you now. Fear will be obliterated as you move forward, as a result of My special bequest, to devote your life to My ardent wish to save humanity from the depths of Hell.

Your work, guided by My Divine Hand, is now completely sacred and free from any kind of interference by the Evil One.

No more doubts will assail you but know this. My Word to you will be violated and torn asunder. Every attempt will now be made to sully these Holy Messages even from those who profess to know Me.

Your suffering will be accepted by you from now on with complete surrender and joy in your soul. My strength, given to you by the Power of the Holy Spirit will startle you. You will rise with complete conviction of heart and with a quiet but determined confidence to deliver My Word throughout the whole world.

No man will or can stop you in this Work. No man can prevent you from this most sacred pure calling from the Heavens.

You, My daughter, are ready to become a lifeline for those souls drifting in the wilderness. They will respond to the call of these message no matter how hardened their hearts are. Many will not know why this is happening to them. It will be by the power of the Holy Spirit, which will ignite a flame of love and joy in their souls that will draw them to Me through these, My urgent pleas to bring My children back into My Sacred Arms.

Thank you for responding to this special request to become My spouse in final union with Me. This contract, when you hand Me over your soul completely will allow Me the freedom I need to conclude this Mission successfully for which you have been chosen.

Go now My precious daughter and help Me to fulfil My Promise to mankind. My return will be to reclaim My precious children and take them into the New Era of Peace. This transition into the New Paradise will be swift and without suffering because of your gift to Me.

Tell My children My Heart is swollen with joy at this time as the time to celebrate My birth draws close.

I love you. Your beloved Saviour and Redeemer

Jesus Christ

God the Father: Promise of Immunity for those who reject Jesus

Sunday, December 11, 2011 15.30 hours

My precious daughter thank you for responding to this important calling from the Heavenly Realm when I asked you to accept the Mystical Union with My precious Son Jesus Christ.

I am present in My Son Jesus as He is in Me United with the Love of the Holy Spirit. Your soul, therefore, is now entwined with Mine and everything will become much clearer to you.

My child you are being moulded into the creature I so desire so that you will be made worthy in full for this Divine Mission. Tears of Divine Intervention were given to you so you could recognize instantly this new unexpected calling. Now that you have shed your tears cry no more for only happiness will reign in your soul from now on.

My daughter it saddens Me that no one recognizes Me any more in the world. Many have forgotten Me completely. I mean nothing to so many of My children.

You must help Me daughter when I manifest My Presence so that I am recognized through prayer.

Please pray that the whole of humanity will accept the Gift of New Life, which will now be given to them by My Beloved Son Jesus Christ.

No one truly understands My concern for those souls who reject Me or the existence of the Saviour I sent into the world.

These poor souls, so full of logical explanations used to arrogantly dismiss My existence are lost to Me at this time. Their only salvation (as many will reject the offer of Divine Mercy during The Warning) will be through the prayer of those children who love the Father.

So many who do not accept Me still know very little about Me. I am a God of Paternal Love, a Heavenly Father who watches over each child of Mine, the strong, the weak, the sick, the good and the wicked. No one is excluded from My Infinite Love no matter how black their soul is.

I urge you children to pray to Me in the Name of My Son in atonement for all the sins of mankind.

My Son will envelope the whole of humanity now and when the Illumination of Conscience is past your prayers are truly needed at that stage. Your prayers children will help save those people who will defiantly continue to reject the Mercy My Son will show them.

My solemn promise children is that all those of you who call on Me on behalf of My beloved Son Jesus Christ to save your brothers and sisters that they will be granted immediate immunity. Special graces will be given to each of you who pledges a full month of prayer for their souls. Here is what I request you to say:

"O Heavenly Father through the love of your beloved Son Jesus Christ whose Passion on the Cross saved us from sin please save all those who still reject His Hand of Mercy. Flood their souls, dear Father, with Your token of Love. I plead with You Heavenly Father, hear my prayer and save these souls from eternal damnation. Through Your Mercy allow them to be the first to enter the New Era of Peace on earth. Amen."

Your Heavenly Father

God the Most High

Note Clarification: the immunity will be granted to those for whom you pray.

Spiritual Jealousy is a terrible thing
Monday, December 12, 2011 19.00 hours

My dearest daughter spiritual jealousy is a terrible thing and afflicts many of My visionaries.

It also afflicts those followers of Mine who feel isolated and somewhat disappointed when I chose certain souls to help Me save humanity. Instead they must know that I love all of them equally.

How it breaks My Heart when chosen souls, especially, feel threatened by other chosen souls.

Each soul I chose is given a different task and asked to follow various paths. The common denominator is always the same. I desire that all of My visionaries, seers and prophets undertake a Sacred Mission to save souls.

I use different souls, humble of heart, to achieve My aims.

Satan will always try to turn the hearts of My chosen souls by taunting them. He knows how to touch a raw nerve in their souls by telling them that other chosen souls are more important than they are.

After that he creates a feeling of hurt in their hearts and jealousy. This means that instead of loving one another and keeping in a state of grace they are tempted to look down on each other. In many cases they immediately dismiss each other and allow the sin of pride to invade their souls.

So many of My followers not only dislike my chosen visionaries and seers, they can treat them with contempt, just the way in which I, too, was treated by the self-righteous Pharisees.

During my time on earth they probed and probed every Word, which came from My Lips. Every cunning challenge was presented to trip Me up so they could prove I was a liar. So too will My modern day prophets and visionaries be treated.

Satan torments those followers of Mine by planting doubts in their minds about My messengers because he wants to discredit My Holy Word. That is his goal.

Pray hard that each of you may be given the graces to respect My Word through the pen of My precious seers.

Visionaries never fall into the trap of succumbing to spiritual jealousy. It is unbecoming and pierces My Heart like a sword.

Love one another.

Show respect and honour for each other in My Name.

That is the most important lesson.

If you find this difficult to do then all other works for Me will be pointless.

Your Teacher and Saviour

Jesus Christ

I can't bear to think of those souls dragged by Satan into Hell

Tuesday, December 13, 2011 20.15 hours

My dearest beloved daughter preparations are important for all of My followers as The Warning draws closer.

All those believers must pray hard for the forgiveness of their sins in order to avoid the pain of Purgatory, which most people in the world will experience immediately after The Warning for a short time.

Pray, pray for all those who will be traumatized when they see the condition of their souls when their sins are revealed to them during The Warning.

They must understand that their sins must be revealed to them before they can be cleansed of all sin so they can enter into My New Paradise on Earth - the New Era of Peace, Love and Happiness which each of My children must inherit.

My Heart is full of joy because I bring this Great Gift to mankind. Yet My sadness lingers because of those who will simply reject the chance of this New Life.

I need so many prayers children so that Satan can be stopped from stealing their souls. He will continue to do this right up to the last minute.

I cannot bear to think of those souls who will be pulled from Me screaming and kicking in protest as he and his minions drag them into the depths of Hell.

Help me children to prevent this through your prayers.

Children these souls must reject Satan and his ways outright if they are to enter the New Paradise. They must either turn to Me willingly or not at all.

They have two choices, the New Paradise on earth or the depths of eternal damnation in the company of Satan.

Never ever doubt the existence of Hell children. Be aware that every blackened soul, upon death, is dragged by Satan's demons into Hell and tormented for eternity. For all his promises Satan has created a horrific state of torture for such souls. Because of his hatred for humanity these souls will suffer beyond their endurance. Yet endure they must for all of eternity.

Don't these souls know what Satan's promises deliver?
Don't they know that riches, fame and seductive materialism will create a clear pathway straight into the arms of the Evil One?

Wake up all of you while you can. Save yourselves and those poor misguided sinners from this terrible end to your existence.

You do not have much time.

Let prayer for these souls begin today.

Your Saviour

Jesus Christ

Second Coming to happen soon after The Warning
Wednesday, December 14, 2011 19.15 hours

My dearest daughter you must always trust in Me and know that not one single message given to you will ever be contaminated.

You are firmly held in My Most Sacred Heart and your hand is being guided by My Hand.

Only My Holy Word can and ever will be written by you to impart My Messages for the whole of humanity.

You must not keep trying to establish the date for The Warning. I cannot reveal this date for that is not according to the Will of My Eternal Father. The Warning will happen most unexpectedly and when man is caught unawares.

Time is very short so spend as much time praying hard to save souls. All souls.

Chastisement has been withheld and will only occur if man fails to repent and returns in large numbers back to his wicked ways after The Warning.

My Father has given permission to herald My Second Coming within a very short period of time on earth. It will happen soon after The Warning. All souls need to be fully prepared.

The next Crusade of Prayer to save souls is as follows:

"O Almighty Father, God the Most High,
please have Mercy on all sinners. Open their hearts to accept salvation and to receive an abundance of graces. Hear my pleas for my own family and ensure that each one will find favour in Your Loving Heart.

O Divine Heavenly Father, protect all Your children on earth from any nuclear war or other acts which are being planned to destroy Your children. Keep us from all harm and protect us. Enlighten us so we can open our eyes to hear and accept the Truth of our salvation without any fear in our souls."

Go in Peace.

Your Loving Saviour

Jesus Christ

My children have been stripped bare in this year of Purification

Thursday, December 15, 2011 20.55 hours

My dearest daughter the year of purification is almost complete and My children everywhere are now prepared for The Warning as a result.

Many of My children have suffered terribly in 2011. Wars, violence, murder and hatred all of which was masterminded by Satan's army have maimed and killed those precious souls of mine. These wicked powers will suffer a terrible punishment if they do not repent after The Warning takes place.

Many of My children have been stripped bare of material comforts and have suffered hardships they have never had to endure before.

These trials were created and inflicted on mankind by Satan but were allowed by Me in order to purify souls. Cruel you may think, My daughter, but it was necessary to prepare humanity and to establish humility in their souls.

Now, more pure in My eyes, their hearts have been opened to accept the Truth of their Eternal Life. This means that fewer will suffer during The Warning because they have undergone this persecution.

My children are now ready to receive My Gift of Mercy. This time is almost upon the world. Be patient My daughter. Never expect Me to give the world a date for it is not for your knowing as I have told you many times before.

Trust in Me completely and you will be at peace.

I will bring My Gift of The Warning when the time is right and when My children least expect it.

Your beloved Jesus

Redeemer of Mankind

Virgin Mary: "End times prophet guided by the Heavens"

Friday, December 16, 2011 22.35 hours

My child I come to you to bring you comfort of heart. You my strong child will from now on be able to bear suffering to such an extent that you will welcome it and therefore prove your endurance while fighting to proclaim the Word of my precious Son Jesus Christ.

You my child are torn. Each day presents new and more challenges in this work, many of which are difficult.

Now is the time to pick up your armour without any fear. March onwards and fight for my Son to ensure that His Holy Word is heard quickly around the world, as quickly as you can. Do not delay. Do not allow distractions.

I love you my child. You are fully protected from harm. Do you not notice how little you are affected now when attacked by others for this work? This is the grace of armour.

Fight the battle against Satan with your army of warriors and help save all of mankind.

You are the true end times prophet guided by the Heavens to help convert the world. Help will be sent quickly. Prepare. Rejoice for this is a Great Gift.

You are being guided every step you take so just trust in Jesus and obey my Heavenly Father at all times.

Be brave, courageous and march without fear in your soul.

Your heavenly Mother

Queen of the Angels

Virgin Mary: Hope must never be shunned in favour of fear

Saturday, December 17, 2011 15.30 hours

My child the world must be told quickly of the Love and Mercy that my Son Jesus Christ holds for every single person on earth.

He loves everyone including those with lukewarm souls and those who do not know Him.

Never doubt that these same people who may be lacking in spirit are very much loved by Him. They will be given great hope when my Son's Mercy envelops them.

Heaven will rejoice when these people open their eyes to the Truth during The Warning. This is when they will accept the Love and Hope which will be given to them. It will be the Greatest Gift they will ever receive in this life on earth.

My child people must never condemn those who do not honour my Father. They must never give up hope for those who also reject my Son. These souls are all loved with a deep tenderness by my Son who only wants to save them.

Hope, my child is a gift from God the Father. It must never be shunned in favour of fear or negativity. My Son's Mercy knows no bounds. It will be given to each and every single one of you soon.

Hope and joy must be at the forefront of your thoughts children because my Son is about to bestow such a Great Gift to His children in order to save the world.

He wants all of mankind to be part of this Great Glorious Era of Peace, which awaits all of you.

Pray, pray, pray that all souls on earth welcome this loving Gift with open and humble hearts.

It will be through The Warning that God's Mercy will be finally shown to humanity.

There can be no doubts after that as to how much all His children are loved and cherished by Him.

Your beloved Mother

Queen of the Heavens

Pray as you have never prayed before
Sunday, December 18, 2011 15.10 hours

My dearest daughter those people who are so far removed from Me are My main concern.

Every effort must be made by My followers to spread My prayer given to you to My Eternal Father begging for immunity for their souls (Crusade Prayer 13)

"O Heavenly Father through the love of Your beloved Son Jesus Christ whose Passion on the Cross saved us from sin please save all those who still reject His Hand of Mercy. Flood their souls dear Father with Your token of Love. I plead with you Heavenly Father, hear my prayer and save these souls from eternal damnation.

Through Your Mercy allow them to be the first to enter the New Era of Peace on earth. Amen."

I urge all believers who read these, My Holy Messages given to the world, to pray as you have never prayed before.

I need your devotion to ensure that all My children accept My Gift with love and joy in their hearts.

They must not be fearful for I come with a Gift of Love and Mercy.

Your Jesus

Redeemer and Saviour of all Mankind

Sinners who turn to Me find instant favour
Tuesday, December 20, 2011 20.30 hours

My dearest beloved daughter why do My children feel so abandoned in the world right now?

Why do they despair from grief and loneliness when all they have to do is to call on Me, their Jesus, to give them comfort?

Each of them must turn and ask Me for help. I will answer each and every prayer. Not one request will go unheeded and their prayers will be answered according to My Holy Will.

So many forget that when they turn to Me I am constantly standing beside them.

Every soul on earth is precious to Me.

If they would only realize that it gives Me great joy when they turn to Me for help.

It gives Me even more joy and happiness when sinners ask Me to forgive them and show sorrow for their sins.

These are the souls who find instant favour. Tell them they must never be afraid to turn to Me, for I am Ever-Merciful. The relief they will feel afterwards is a Grace I bestow on those with warm sincere hearts.

This is the time of the year when My Mercy is poured out over the whole world the most. So turn to Me now for the strength and the graces needed to help you endure your trials in the world.

Your Jesus

Saviour and Redeemer of Mankind

Even the sin of murder can be forgiven
Wednesday, December 21, 2011 20.10 hours

My dearest beloved daughter it is I.

Tonight I come to offer comfort to sinners who believe they are not worthy to stand before Me.

I call on those of you, poor tortured souls who believe that your sins are so repulsive that I could not forgive you. How wrong you are.

Don't you know that there is not one sin I cannot forgive? Why are you so afraid?

Don't you know that even the most grievous sin of murder can be forgiven? All sins can and will be forgiven if true heartfelt remorse is shown.

I am waiting. Open your hearts to Me. Confide in Me. I am probably the only true friend you have in that you can tell Me anything and it will not shock Me.

Sin is a fact of life. Very few souls including chosen souls can remain in a state of grace for any length of time.

Never feel that you cannot confess your sins, irrespective as to how serious they may be.

If you fear Me and continue to turn your back you will distance yourself from Me even more.

Many of My children do not feel worthy of My Love. Yet I love everyone including hardened sinners. I do not condone the sin. I could never do that. But I love the sinner.

It was because of sin that I was sent into your world as a Saviour so that you could be pardoned.

To be pardoned you must ask for forgiveness. When you seek forgiveness you must be humble first. For without humility there is no true remorse.

I, your Saviour, beg you to stop and think about how you live your life. You either love God by your good deeds and love of neighbour or you don't.

You do not have to know Me in order to love Me children. By your works, your love of each other, the kindness and generosity you show others you demonstrate your love for Me without realizing it.

It will also be through your humility of heart, when you show true remorse for all the wrong doings in your life, that you will also prove your love for Me.

How else do you think you can become close to My Heart?

You must never be afraid to approach Me. I am never far away.

Come to Me now so I can nourish your soul and give you the peace you crave.

Your beloved Jesus

Virgin Mary: Plan to redeem mankind for Second Coming is complete

Thursday, December 22, 2011 09.30 hours

My child the world must prepare for my Son through prayer.

My precious Son's plan to redeem mankind for the Second Coming is complete.

Time has been given to allow faith to be spread through these and other Divine Messages.

Even a small group of devoted Christians, who pray for those who deny my Son, can save these souls.

You, my child, must ask as many followers as possible to pray for immunity for those poor souls in sin.

I urge all of my Son's followers never to give up hope for the whole of mankind.

Many poor souls do not understand what they are doing when they deny the existence of God the Heavenly Father.

Their minds are dictated by human logic where all things are based on how they are seen by the naked eye.

They fail to understand that earth is simply a planet, which was Created by God for His children. It is only a temporary place.

The New Paradise is their True Inheritance.

Pray, pray, pray for these children so that the Holy Spirit will touch their souls and spark love in their hearts for my Son.

Never forget that Christmas is a Holy Feast to celebrate the Saviour who was sent to give you, all my children eternal life.

Your Blessed Mother

Queen of the Heavens

God the Father: My Son is being sent to claim His Rightful Throne

Saturday, December 24, 2011 18.00 hours

My daughter, just as I sent a Saviour into the world the first time to save humanity I am now ready to send My Son, Jesus the Redeemer of mankind, once again to salvage those souls who could not be otherwise saved.

My children must understand the significance of the bittersweet Sacrifice I made for mankind when I sent My Son the first time.

When I realized that the only way to redeem mankind was to send a

Saviour I knew I could not expect any prophet or chosen soul to suffer such a Sacrifice. I decided through the Second Person of My Divinity that I would send a Son to save humanity. This was the only effective way to foil the plans of Satan such was My Love for My children.

To watch My Son grow up to become a man was both delightful and painful knowing what lay ahead of Him. Yet because of the deep tender Love I have for each of My children this was a Sacrifice endured willingly in order to save My family.

Now that The Warning approaches I am also preparing the World, through these Holy Messages, to welcome My Son for the Second Time.

The Second Coming of My beloved Son is close, children. He is being sent to claim His Rightful Throne when He will Reign as King of Mankind.

This Glorious Event will be spectacular and is the final part of the plan to save the human race from the evil that exists in your world. Satan will be cast away shortly. His followers and those wicked of heart will be shocked and dismayed. They will be expected to make a choice at that stage. Drop down and plead for Mercy and be saved. Or refuse the Great Gift, which will be presented to them.

My children unite all of you and do not fear ridicule. You are all being guided by The Holy Spirit and are being afforded the protection of the angels and saints in Heaven. It will be up to you, My followers, to proclaim the Word and Promise of My Son who wishes for these Messages to be spread around the world.

It will also be through your prayers that lost sinners can be plucked from the arms of the Evil One.

Children you are in the early stages of the final battle. Your second chance of eternal salvation is being given to you through the Mercy of My dearly beloved Son. Don't squander this opportunity. Join as one in union with your family in Heaven to save your brothers and sisters on earth. Rejoice this Christmas for it will be a special celebration as you must now help souls prepare for The Second Coming of My Son, after The Warning takes place.

I love you all children. Take my Love. Embrace Me, your Eternal Father who will do everything possible to take you all into the New Era of Peace.

God the Father

Honour the importance of the Family
Sunday, December 25, 2011 18.00 hours

Today My daughter is a celebration of My Birth. It is also a special day for families.

Remember the Holy Family was also born on this day. This Holy Family has a bearing on people all over the world today.

Just as all souls on earth are part of My Eternal Father's family then, so too, should people everywhere honour the importance of the family.

It is only through the family that true love is born. While many families in the world suffer from disruption, anger and separation it is important to understand this.

If there were no families on earth there could be no life. The family represents all that My Eternal Father wishes for His children on earth.

Families, when together, create an intimate love known only in the Heavens. Damage the family and you will damage the Pure Love that exists within each soul, which is part of that family.

Satan loves to divide families. Why? Because he knows that the kernel of love, essential to the spiritual growth of humanity, will die when the family is split.

Please pray children for families to unite. Pray for families to pray together. Pray to keep Satan from entering your family home.

Never forget that you are all part of My Father's family and you must emulate this unity on earth whenever possible. It is not always the case I know but strive always for family unity in order to retain love for one another.

If you do not have a family on earth then remember you are part of the family that My Father created. Strive to join My Father's family in the New Era of Peace.

Pray for the graces needed to enable you to find your rightful home in this New Paradise, which you will be invited to enter at My Second Coming.

Your beloved Jesus

Saviour of Mankind

I was accused of Heresy and Blasphemy when I walked the earth

Monday, December 26, 2011 15.50 hours

I am your Jesus who never leaves you no matter how much you suffer. I am the Alpha and the Omega, Son of God made man and born of the Immaculate Virgin Mary.

My dearly beloved Daughter, rise above this sudden burst of suffering and never forget the number of souls you are saving in the process.

My children must suffer purification in order that their souls be cleansed at this time. So they must get used to this. Many of My children are still being purified before The Warning takes place. They will understand why this is happening to them in time, My daughter.

The angels are with you all the time, like never before. For you, My daughter you will now attract the greatest number of attacks, so far, because of these Messages.

Every Word I utter will now be pulled asunder.

Every Lesson and Truth I try to impart to the world now will be questioned and deemed to be blasphemous.

My Holy Word, when taught to My followers when I walked the earth was also criticized.

I was accused of heresy, blasphemy and for condoning sinners when I walked among My people. My Word was not accepted then in many quarters and especially among the priests and Pharisees.

My daughter those people, whose boastful taunts because of their self-proclaimed Scriptural knowledge continue to attack these Messages, will be the worst offenders They will arrogantly argue that their flawed interpretation of the Holy Gospel is more important than the Truth.

Their pride prevents them from recognizing My Voice when it is being imparted to the world today.

Never engage with these poor souls My daughter for they are not of the Light. Sadly, they believe themselves to be. Remember those who look down and sneer at others in My Name do not represent Me.

They do not show love, understanding or humility.

These attacks are being mounted to stop you in this Work and to create new doubts in your mind. Pray for these people. Ignore them. Focus only on My Voice and do not allow this Sacred Work to be affected in this way.

Satan is working actively within these souls and will use every form of cunning argument to undermine these Messages from My Lips. By engaging or responding to these attacks you give Satan the power he seeks.

Go now in peace. Keep looking ahead and remain obedient to My wishes at all times. Remember you have given Me the gift of your free will. Allow Me, therefore, to guide you. Trust in Me completely.

I love you.

Your Jesus

Virgin Mary: Birth Pangs have commenced

Tuesday, December 27, 2011 14.00 hours

My child the birth pangs have commenced.

The time has come for the birth of a New World, a New Beginning.

Many changes will now take place on earth the likes of which have not been witnessed before.

My Heavenly Father is sending My beloved Son Jesus Christ to once again save mankind from his wickedness.

You, my child, will witness a series of events, which have already been revealed to you.

You must not be frightened for this cleansing is essential in order to wake up mankind if souls are to be saved.

The signs will commence as foretold. My children must accept these changes with a humble and contrite heart.

Pray, pray for souls to discard the sin of pride and seek forgiveness for their offences against God the Father.

Failure to redeem themselves will result in a severe chastisement.
My Son's Mercy is so great He will give time to my children to repent.

But you must pray now for all souls so that they may be worthy to enter into the New Era of Peace.

Your beloved Mother

Mary Queen of the Heavens

God the Father: Accept this last chance or face a terrible chastisement

Wednesday, December 28, 2011 15.15 hours

My daughter you now have a duty to inform My children everywhere of the urgent need to seek redemption.

Because of My Great Mercy I now send My Son to offer humanity a last chance to turn back to Me their Heavenly Father.

I can reveal that the Great Mercy to be shown to all of My children will take place only the once.

They, My children, must accept this last chance of salvation or accept that a terrible chastisement will fall upon the world.

Every single soul on earth will shortly witness the signs of the Illumination of Conscience.

Each of them will be brought to their knees in shame when they see, probably for the first time, how painful their sins appear in My Eyes.

For those with a kind and humble heart they will accept this Great Mercy with gratitude and relief.

For others they will find this a very difficult trial and many will reject My Hand of Love and Friendship.

Pray for these souls urgently, My daughter. for without prayers they cannot be given a second chance.

The world will finally accept the Power of their Heavenly Father when the miracle in the skies will be witnessed by everyone everywhere.

The birth of the New World is almost upon you. Grasp My Mercy now while you can. Do not leave it until the last minute.

Join as one in union with Me to embrace the New Era of Peace, which awaits all those gracious souls who love Me.

My Mercy is so great, however, that the Prayer that My Son has given to the world through you My daughter for immunity for these souls (see below extract from Crusade of Prayer number 13) will be so powerful that souls who are still in darkness can and will be saved.

"O Heavenly Father through the Love of your beloved Son Jesus Christ whose Passion on the Cross saved us from sin please save all those who still reject His Hand of Mercy. Flood their souls dear Father with your token of Love. I plead with You Heavenly Father, hear my prayer and save these souls from eternal damnation. Through Your Mercy allow them to be the first to enter the New Era of Peace on Earth. Amen."

Remember children the power of prayer and how it can mitigate the chastisement.
Pray, pray, pray that the world can and will be saved and that the Great Tribulation can be averted.

Your Heavenly Father

God the Most High

Virgin Mary: My Rosary can save nations
Thursday, December 29, 2011 14.15 hours

My child reciting my Holy Rosary can save nations.

My children must never forget the power of my Holy Rosary.

It is so powerful that it renders the deceiver useless. He can do nothing to you or your family when you recite this daily.

Please ask my children to begin to say my Holy Rosary from this day forth in order to protect, not only their families, but their communities also.

The Rosary is the most powerful weapon against the evil one's plans to destroy what he can in these, his last days, on earth.

Never underestimate the lies that he plants in people's minds in order to turn my children away from the Truth.

So many, under his influence, will kick and fight against the Truth of my Son's Great Mercy.

By saying my Holy Rosary you can protect these souls from lies

Their hearts can and will be opened if you set aside the time to say my Rosary.

Pray now for my children to open their hearts to the Truth. Pray too that all my children will find the strength to accept my Son's Mercy.

Your beloved Mother

Queen of the Angels

Every kind of Mercy will be shown to those who don't love My Father

Thursday, December 29, 2011 15.00 hours

My dearest beloved daughter My children everywhere will be awakened from a deep empty slumber shortly.

When they awaken to The Warning many will be terrified. To those who will be fearful I have this to say.

Be thankful you are being woken up from the darkness.

Be joyful that you are being shown My Light of Mercy. If you find this painful then I implore you to endure this cleansing with humility. For without this cleansing you will not have eternal life, which is your right.

Pray to Me to help you during these difficult moments and I will lift you up and give you the strength you need.

Reject My Hand of Mercy and you will be given only a very short period in which to repent.

There will be every kind of Mercy shown to those of you who do not love My Father. But know that His patience is running out.

There will be one great Act of My Mercy shown. It will be up to you to become humble and beg for Mercy. You cannot be forced to do this. Pray that if you cannot deal with this cleansing that others will then pray for your soul.

Never fear Me, never reject My Hand of Salvation. For without Me you are nothing. Don't wait to cry out for My love when it will be too late to help you.

Your Saviour

Jesus Christ

Without My Act of Mercy nations would destroy each other

Saturday, December 31, 2011 12.00 hours

Extract from private message revealed to Maria Divine Mercy, which includes the 16th Crusade of Prayer for people to accept the graces to be given to them by Jesus during The Warning and a pledge to proclaim His Most Holy Word to the world.

My daughter, The Warning will prove to all the authenticity of these My Holy Messages to the world. You must never doubt them. None of them have been contaminated in any way.

Prepare for The Warning and tell your family and children to say a little prayer seeking forgiveness for their sins.

I will give you a special Crusade Prayer now for the world to help souls. Stay strong during the Great Act of Mercy I now present to the world.

"O My Jesus keep me strong during this trial of Your Great Mercy. Give me the graces needed to become little in Your Eyes. Open My eyes to the

Truth of Your promise of Eternal Salvation. Forgive me my sins and show me Your love and hand of friendship. Embrace me into the arms of the Holy Family so that we can all become one again. I love you Jesus and promise from this day forth that I will proclaim Your Holy Word without fear in my heart and with purity of soul forever and ever Amen."

Never fear this Great Act of My Mercy, which must take place or nations would destroy each other.

Most of mankind will convert but the battle for souls will now intensify.

Your beloved Jesus

Redeemer of all Mankind

Virgin Mary: Temporary peace in the world if dark souls convert

Sunday, January 01, 2012 15.00 hours

My child time is close but my children must show patience. Everything is going to be according to the Holy Will of my Father.

Children you must realize that the forces of evil in your world threaten your faith in God the Father. These evil forces will not win for they have no power over my Heavenly Father. Yet they will torment their fellow brothers and sister through murder, war and control.

Pray that these dark souls see the Light of my Son soon. If they do see and convert during The Warning then there will be a temporary peace on earth.

My Son, Jesus Christ, for whom all souls need to rely on for salvation, is impatient to bring to mankind His Great Mercy.

Pray hard my children for the salvation of these dark souls who may not survive The Warning.

These poor souls will be terrorized not only when they witness their sins, but when they see the darkness which they are in. This darkness has clouded their souls so much that the Light of my Son's Mercy will make them feel weak and powerless.

Many will be too weak to grasp the Mercy my Son will offer them.

Pray for these souls I urge you. My Son is determined to save these souls first. He needs more prayer children. You must beg for Mercy for these darkened souls.

My child, ask my children to dedicate this Crusade of Prayer to me, The Mother of Salvation:

"O Immaculate Heart of Mary, Mother of Salvation and Mediatrix of all Graces, you who will participate in the salvation of humanity from the wickedness of Satan, pray for us. Mother of Salvation pray that all souls can be saved and will accept the Love and Mercy shown by your Son, Our Lord Jesus Christ who comes once again to save Humanity and to give us the chance of eternal salvation. Amen. "

Your beloved Mother

Mother of Salvation

There is only one Truth. One Light. Anything else is a lie.

Sunday, January 01, 2012 17.30 hours

My dearly beloved daughter know that no matter how difficult this Mission is I will not fail to direct you.

My Voice encourages you at all times. My Spirit moves your heart so that you are powerless against it. My Love is so enveloping that you are unable to turn your back on Me or deny Me. Yet you find that you stumble along the way.

When you try to analyze My Word you will find you are unable to do this successfully. No amount of analysis can change the Truth of what I say.

No one, including you My daughter, has the authority to twist the meaning of My Holy Word so that it becomes more acceptable in your eyes.

This applies to My Word contained in the Holy Bible and My Word contained within these Messages.

Trust in Me more My daughter. Ask My children and all of My beloved followers to trust in Me completely.

I will never let humanity down. I will never turn My back on the pleas of My cherished children. I will always respond to poor souls who plead for My Mercy.

What I will never do My daughter is to speak to My children in order to suit their needs and to give them what they want to hear.

The Truth must be told. My Holy Word must never be diluted or the Truth tampered with.

My Holy Word must never be changed, adjusted or twisted so that it becomes a lie.

Know that the time for My Justice is close. Understand that My Mercy is great but the wickedness I see in your world disgusts Me.

This wickedness is even justified by those who profess My Word and who claim to know Me.

They have twisted my Teachings for centuries to suit their avarice, lust, pride and greed.

How it breaks My Heart to see acts of depravity paraded before Me and witness how My children are fooled into believing that these acts are acceptable in My eyes.

Wake up to the Truth. My Great Mercy is available to every single soul during The Warning.

But beware. Those Christians who believe that the twisted truth of My Teachings will be acceptable in My eyes will be shocked during The Warning. They will resist the Truth when I reveal how their sins greatly offend Me.

I urge these people to accept that I am the Truth and the Light. There is only One Truth, One Light. Anything else is a lie.

Examine your conscience children honestly before The Warning takes place. Learn to identify the Truth before you come before Me. For then and only then will your suffering be less.

Your Teacher and Redeemer

Saviour of all Mankind

Jesus Christ

Virgin Mary: Time for the Triumph of my Immaculate Heart not far away
Monday, January 02, 2012 12.00 hours

My child the time for the Triumph of my Immaculate Heart is not far away.

As Satan's power diminishes he becomes more ruthless in his pursuit of souls.

Even strong souls will find this period difficult, as their faith will be tested to the limit.

My child, when the faith of my children is tested in this cruel way they must not falter but stay alert. They must remain pure of heart at all times.

They must also remain silent when they feel envy in their souls. Envy and jealousy leads to hatred. Envy of chosen souls is increasing even amongst those who love my Son.

Children you must never succumb to this temptation, which is placed in your hearts by the Evil One.

There will increase now a widespread jealousy of all visionaries and holy messengers in the world. This has been foretold for these are among the many saints of the end times.

Their lot is hard and they will suffer intensely because of the tasks accorded to them.

My child I call on all those who revere me, their Blessed Mother, to pray to me for the protection of visionaries and end time prophets.

They need your prayers. If you have doubts about these souls who have been chosen to impart the Truth to the world, then pray for them regardless.

You are all God's Creation. You must show love to each other. Proclaim the Holy Word of my Son but never at the expense of insulting another of God's children.

Insults do not spring from love. They come from the deceiver whose hatred for humanity knows no bounds.

If you love my Son and find fault with another soul then you must seal your lips.

Never slander another in the Name of my Son.

My Heart is pierced like with a sword when I see those souls who are dedicated to me, the Holy Mother of God, pour scorn on those visionaries chosen to help save souls.

Pray, pray, pray for the visionaries chosen by God the Father in the world today.

Be assured that it is those who suffer the biggest insults who speak in the Name of my Son.

Those, whose messages are challenged fiercely, frowned upon and torn asunder, are usually the chosen souls.

They are the primary targets of the evil one who, through others, will taunt believers into rejecting these seers.

Remember these messengers represent my Son and His Holy Word.

Reject the authentic seer and you reject the Word of my precious Son.

Always pray for discernment. However you must never publicly scorn those Divine Messages given to humanity in order to save souls from the fires of Hell.

Block the work of these visionaries and you block the salvation of souls.

Your beloved Mother

Queen of Heaven

Mother of Salvation

God the Father: Two billion souls will convert as a result of these messages

Tuesday, January 03, 2012 15.30 hours

My daughter the gift of today's vision where I revealed to you the Face of My Son and Me, your beloved Heavenly Father, is rare.

You are blessed to have been given this extraordinary gift from the Heavens. This was necessary to make you stronger. Your suffering will ease now and you will become much stronger than before.

Never fear this Work for you must know by now that all power on earth is in My Heavenly Hands. No one has power over The Father. Even the deceiver cannot tamper with or change My Heavenly Plan for humanity.

Heaven rejoices because of the conversion, which has evolved from these, My Messages for the world. Over two billion souls will now convert as a direct result of these Divine Messages.

No man will stop this Work. They may try but it will be useless.

My Divine Protection covers all souls who proclaim the Truth of eternal salvation.

Never give up children no matter how hard your suffering becomes. Suffering, never forget, brings you closer to My Heavenly Kingdom.

You, My children, will rejoice shortly when you feel the Graces being poured out upon you through My Son.

Stay alert. Keep praying for all souls and never doubt for one minute that it is I, your Eternal Father, who brings you peace of mind, body and soul through these messages.

Treat these Messages as Sacred. They are and will always be in accordance with My Word given to man since the beginning of time. They will ignite the flame of your soul in ways, which you will find difficult to ignore.

Allow My Spirit to reach you and relax. Only then can I touch your soul so that a spark of recognition will fire your heart.

I call you to run to Me so I can embrace you in the only way that a Father can.

Let Me offer you My Protection and Graces to make you strong enough to fight in My army against the evil in your world.

My army will bring about the peace you desire and the love you need to quench your thirst.

Go in Peace children in the knowledge that the Truth is contained in these Messages which I have sanctioned for the whole world.

You will, if pure and humble of heart, recognize My Love. Become little, as a child, in My Eyes. Only then will I lift you up like an angel in My Hierarchy when the time is right.
Go in peace. Rest your weary head upon My Shoulder and I will bring you the comfort and solace you desire.

I love you children, every single one of you.

I rejoice for when the day comes for Our Holy Family to reunite all the Heavens will sing in praise and glory for eternity.

God the Father

Note: Reference 2 billion souls - Maria Divine Mercy wishes it to be known that in an earlier private message received from God the Father to her, she was told that "Two billion more souls than would otherwise have been lost will be saved because of these Messages". Many people have interpreted the above message to mean that only two billion people in the world will be saved which is not correct. There will be much more than that. This two billion is in addition.

I will make Myself known very soon

Wednesday, January 04, 2012 18.15 hours

My daughter I will make Myself known very soon.

The preparations are complete but I need more prayer for those who will die a wretched death in a state of mortal sin during The Warning.

I urge My followers to pray, pray, pray for their poor souls.

I love you My beloved followers. How I rejoice at the love and purity of heart I witness amongst you. You bring Me so much comfort and ease My suffering. Your devotion is like a balm on My festering Wounds.

In the world, just as I am dismissed and rejected by so many it is the loyalty of you My beloved followers which brings Me great joy.

My suffering is dictated by the level of godlessness in the world. This world which honours ambition, self-glory and false idols.

My Name is not deemed important. My Voice is not heard above the din of the voices of the self-obsessed.

How loud they shout and boast of their worldly gains. But it is the whispers of My beloved followers, which allow Me to speak so that My Voice is heard.

You, My followers are now in union with Me in a way that will surprise you.

Go, My daughter and tell My beloved followers that I love them and that My Graces will make them strong enough to proclaim My Holy Word to a world that needs to hear the Truth so that souls can be saved.

Your beloved Jesus

Attempts at Nuclear War in the East

Wednesday, January 04, 2012 19.20 hours

Note: Extract from a message received, much of which was a personal message to Maria Divine Mercy.

My dearly beloved daughter head Me now while I inform the world that nations will attempt to begin to destroy each other in the East.

Much prayer is needed to ensure that this Nuclear War and other atrocities are averted. Never forget that prayer is powerful and can mitigate many evil events.

I must remind you of My desire to have prayers said to save souls.

I need more souls My daughter especially those who are destined to die during The Warning.

You must know by now that this is My greatest desire and it will be the prayers of My followers, which can bring about the salvation of these souls.

I urge prayer groups everywhere to pray hard now for such souls.

God My Eternal Father will respond accordingly to your requests and offer a lifeline to these poor souls.

You are tired now My daughter. Go in peace. Rest.

Your Jesus

Maria has been receiving daily messages since 8th November 2010 and they can be viewed online via **www.thewarningsecondcoming.com**